## DATE DUE

| Jan 3, 2014 | |
|---|---|
| | |
| | |
| | |
| | |
| | |
| | |
| | |
| | |
| | |
| | |
| | |
| | |
| | |
| | |
| | |
| | PRINTED IN U.S.A. |

# Introduction to U.S. Health Policy

## The Organization, Financing, and Delivery of Health Care in America

**THIRD EDITION**

## Donald A. Barr, M.D., Ph.D.

*Associate Professor, Department of Pediatrics*

*Stanford University*

*Stanford, California*

The Johns Hopkins University Press | *Baltimore*

© 2007, 2011 The Johns Hopkins University Press
All rights reserved. Published 2011
Printed in the United States of America on acid-free paper
First edition published in 2002 by Benjamin Cummings, Inc., California
Johns Hopkins edition published 2007, 2011

9  8  7  6  5  4  3  2  1

The Johns Hopkins University Press
2715 North Charles Street
Baltimore, Maryland 21218-4363
www.press.jhu.edu

*Library of Congress Cataloging-in-Publication Data*
Barr, Donald A.
Introduction to U.S. health policy : the organization, financing, and delivery of health care in America / Donald A. Barr. — 3rd ed.
    p. ; cm.
Introduction to United States health policy
Includes bibliographical references and index.
ISBN-13: 978-1-4214-0217-8 (hardcover : alk. paper)
ISBN-10: 1-4214-0217-3 (hardcover : alk. paper)
ISBN-13: 978-1-4214-0218-5 (pbk. : alk. paper)
ISBN-10: 1-4214-0218-1 (pbk. : alk. paper)
1. Medical policy—United States.  2. Health planning—United States.  3. Medicine—United States.  I.Title.  II. Title: Introduction to United States health policy.
[DNLM:  1. Delivery of Health Care—United States.  2. Economics, Medical—United States.  3. Financing, Government—United States.  4. Health Planning—United States.  5. Health Policy—United States.  6. Medicare—organization & administration. W 84 AA1]
RA393.B335 2011
362.10973—dc22          2011000983

A catalog record for this book is available from the British Library.

*Special discounts are available for bulk purchases of this book. For more information, please contact Special Sales at 410-516-6936 or specialsales@press.jhu.edu.*

The Johns Hopkins University Press uses environmentally friendly book materials, including recycled text paper that is composed of at least 30 percent post-consumer waste, whenever possible.

*For Debra*

# CONTENTS

# PREFACE

In teaching my class on American health policy, I often show the students two statements, and then ask which is correct. The first slide states:

The United States has the best medical care system in the world.

The second states:

The United States has one of the worst health care systems among the developed countries of the world.

We spend several minutes in a discussion and debate regarding which of the statements is more accurate. The irony of U.S. health care, and a principal message of this book, is that both statements are simultaneously true. From one perspective, we have the best health care available anywhere. From another, equally valid perspective, we are close to worst among developed countries in the way we structure our health care system. Which perspective one adopts depends on the measure of quality one selects.

This seeming paradox is illustrated by the way health care is provided in the communities adjoining the office in which this book was written. Approximately five hundred yards to the north is Stanford University Medical Center, a world leader in technological sophistication in medical care. Physicians there, who are among the best in the world, are able to perform remarkable feats, such as a life-saving organ transplantation or the reattachment of a severed hand. The physician-scientists at the Lucile Packard Children's Hospital are able to save amazingly tiny, premature babies weighing less than this book. Specialist physicians in the emergency room are able to reverse heart attacks and strokes after they have already happened. Nowhere in the world is a higher level of advanced medical care available.

Approximately two miles to the east of this office is the community of East Palo Alto. The population of East Palo Alto is predominantly low income, mainly nonwhite, and to a large extent without health insurance. Many of the people there have no regular source of medical care. When they or their children become ill, the only source of care available to them is often the emergency room at Stanford Hospital, where physicians-in-training will see and treat them between treating patients with heart attacks or major traumatic injuries. If patients from East Palo Alto need to be hospitalized, those without a life-threatening condition who have no insurance and no means of paying for care out of pocket are not allowed treatment in Stanford Hospital. Rather, they are referred to a county hospital, several miles away. East Palo Alto has a high rate of premature babies; violence is a major health problem; diseases such as diabetes and high blood pressure often go untreated; children can go without needed checkups and immunizations.

We are simultaneously the best and one of the worst. This is the dilemma of health care in the United States.

This book is about the U.S. health care system. It provides an introduction to the various organizations and institutions that make our system work (or not work, as the case may be). It identifies historical forces that have brought us to our current state of health care and examines the way in which the need of the American people for health care services is sometimes met and sometimes not.

As this book describes, the United States spends more on health care, both overall and per capita, than any other country in the world. Yet the health of our society, measured by indices such as infant mortality and life expectancy, and our access to care are worse than those of nearly all other industrialized countries.

Two broad forces contribute to the relatively poor state of health in the United States: (1) socioeconomic factors, such as education, poverty, and lifestyle, and (2) the quality of our health care system. It may be that socioeconomic factors have more to do with the overall health of our society than does our system of health care. This book, however, looks at only the latter—our health care system.

It has been health care, not health, which has focused national attention and stirred national discourse for the past several years. During the intense debate over the health reform proposals that resulted in the Patient Protection and Affordable Care Act (ACA) of 2010, we had a graphic illustration of how our health care system is made up of various organizations and groups that often can't agree on how the system should be structured. This was not the first time we tried to initiate broad reform of the health care system in this country. In the 1930s, a national health care plan was considered as part of Social Security. It was seen as too far-reaching and was dropped from Social Security to assure passage. In the years following World War II, President Harry Truman proposed a national system of health insurance but was defeated by the forces of organized medicine. In the 1960s, Congress adopted major policy reforms in the financing of health care for elderly or poor people but stopped short of comprehensive national reform. In the 1970s, facing for the first time the rapidly rising cost of health care that characterized the last part of the twentieth century, Congress came close to adopting comprehensive national reform, only to back away in the wake of the Watergate scandal. Again, in the 1990s, we came very close to enacting comprehensive health care reform, only to see the Clinton reform proposals defeated and abandoned following a midterm election that shifted the center of power within Congress.

As health care costs continued to rise and more and more people were left without health insurance, the beginning of the twenty-first century required that we deal with the same problems we confronted at the end of the twentieth century. Congress came close to inaction, but in the end did approve ACA and a companion reconciliation bill, the combination of which promises access to affordable health insurance to more than 30 million Americans who previously were uninsured. ACA did not solve all the problems inherent in our system of health care, however. While access to health insurance will expand substantially, the rise in health care costs is predicted to continue unabated. No doubt, Congress will at some point in the future again try to deal with the continuing problems of health care in America.

How much can we as a country afford to spend on health care? Can we both constrain the growth of health care expenditures and improve access to care? Whether as a health care professional who participates in the system, as an academician who studies the system, as a business manager who must arrange health coverage for your workers, or as a patient who turns to the system for care, you, the reader of this book, will doubtless confront these questions again. It is my hope that, by reading this book, you will be in a stronger position to help find an answer to them.

Who will be the leaders in finding the answers and making the difficult choices? Physicians, health care administrators, and those responsible for the public sector will all play an important role in this process. Many physicians and other health care professionals, however, do not receive adequate training in the knowledge and skills necessary to make informed choices about health care delivery. In 1995, Drs. Ira Nash and Richard Pasternak reported their experience in interviewing applicants for one of the most competitive and prestigious fellowship training programs in the country. They found that nearly all the applicants had consistently high clinical qualifications. They then asked these young physicians, the future leaders of the medical profession, what they thought about the issue of health care reform.

> We were shocked when we barely got a response. A few residents offered some brief insight into the scope of the challenge to reform. Fewer enunciated some broad goal of reform such as universal insurance coverage. *None* had any well-formed ideas about how to actually address these challenges or realize these goals, or could even render a reasoned opinion about *somebody else's* well-formed idea . . . How can it be that the apparent "best and brightest" of internal medicine are on the intellectual sidelines of the debate over health system reform?
>
> If, as is now the case, we find time in medical school and residency training to teach things that most physicians will never need to know, we should find the teachers and the time to teach what nearly every physician will soon need to know to help address the health care needs of the nation. (Nash and Pasternak 1995, p. 1534)

Medical science has been expanding steadily since the beginning of the twentieth century. Initially, physicians had a fairly small core of knowledge they needed to acquire. As scientists learned about bacteria and other micro-organisms, physicians needed to expand their base of knowledge to include microbiology. When X-ray technology began to expand, physicians needed also to learn the basics of radiology. In the 1960s and 1970s, as a phenomenal number of new drugs were discovered, physicians needed to learn more about pharmacology. Every time a new development has occurred in medical practice, physicians have needed to expand their base of knowledge to include the new area.

Another new area has developed, with at least as much significance for the practice of medicine as others that came before it. This development is the tremendous change we are seeing in the financing and organization of health care and the profound consequences this change is having on health care delivery. Just as physicians expanded the knowledge required for the practice of medicine in the face of technological advances, many now suggest that health care professionals of all types need to expand their knowledge to include a familiarity with the health care delivery system and the effects of alternative delivery and financing methods on the outcomes of care. Whether acquired as part of an undergraduate education or as part of the curriculum of health professions schools, an understanding of health policy will be an important part of professional knowledge in the twenty-first century.

The purpose of this book is to provide the reader with just such knowledge. Developed from a course I have taught at Stanford University for nearly two decades, it describes the historical, social, political, and economic forces that have shaped our health care system and created the policy dilemmas we face. The information offered in this book has proven to be of interest to undergraduates, medical students, and practicing professionals alike, all of whom have participated in the course.

## WHAT IS HEALTH POLICY?

This book provides an introduction to health policy in the United States. The growing problems that have surrounded health care over the past several decades have created the field of health policy. Forty years ago, few if any universities or professional schools had teaching or research programs in health policy. Today, nearly every major university includes active programs in health policy. Academic journals specializing in health policy are increasingly numerous and well respected. The advent of the Internet has made an extensive library of health policy data and information immediately available to all with basic computer access.

As with any new academic discipline, there is not universal agreement as to what precisely constitutes the field of health policy. Overlapping interests among those in fields such as public health, health economics, and health services research have made agreement on a precise definition of health policy difficult to attain. This book hopes to address this problem by approaching health policy as the study of the way health care is organized, financed, and delivered. It does this by drawing on theories from fields such as economics, sociology, and organizational behavior to offer a view of the broad social forces that coalesce to create the structure of our system of health care and the problems inherent to it.

In its broadest sense, health policy includes all those factors and forces that affect the health of the public. This book, however, focuses its study of health policy more on the structure of health care than on the health of a community or society.

Health policy overlaps with health economics but broadens its scope to include social and political processes affecting health care. Health policy and health services research have much in common; however, the latter tends to look more at specific clinical issues, such as the optimal way to treat coronary artery disease, whereas health policy looks at questions such as the optimal way to structure care overall.

## WHO MAKES HEALTH POLICY?

The organizing, financing, and delivery of health care in the United States is affected by a broad range of forces, public as well as private, national as well as local. Congress and the federal health agencies within the executive branch have major roles in developing health policy. Federal laws such as Medicare and Medicaid that affect the financing of care have reshaped health care organization and delivery in a number of ways. Rules established by the U.S. Department of Health and Human Services govern much of the health care that is provided in this country. As we experienced during the debate over ACA, the congressional system of committees and subcommittees plays a continuous role in monitoring the delivery of health care throughout the country and initiating reform when necessary.

States also play a major role in the organization and financing of health care. Most laws governing professional licensure and medical practice come from the states. Financing care for the poor has become largely the responsibility of the states.

Health policy, however, includes more than just the creation of governmental policies pertaining to health care. As discussed later in this book, private businesses play a major role, both as purchasers of health insurance and as providers of health insurance, in driving recent changes in the way health care is organized, financed, and delivered. The shift to a market-based system of managed care was largely the result of the need to control costs. The effect this shift has had on the delivery of care at every level is profound.

The providers of care also play a large role in developing health policy. The American Medical Association (AMA), the private organization representing physicians, has been one of the most powerful forces behind the creation of the private practice, fee-for-service model of delivering health care that came to dominate the health care system for much of the twentieth century. Other providers, competing with the AMA, formed cooperative associations of physicians and hospitals as an alternative to fee-for-service care. These alternative, prepaid systems created the model on which the concept of the health maintenance organization (HMO) was based.

Local communities also play a role in creating health policy. Community hospitals, community clinics, and local government health departments continue to play a major role in the organization and delivery of care at the local level.

So the creation of health policy is more than simply passing laws. It is the coalescence of forces on multiple levels, representing multiple interests and constituencies, to organize and finance a system to deliver health care to the American people.

## THE STRUCTURE OF THE BOOK

The fourteen chapters of this book present the dilemma of U.S. health care, describe its basic structure, and identify recent changes and trends in the system. For each chapter, I identify key concepts that summarize the way social, economic, and political factors have acted to shape the delivery of health care in this country, either historically or currently. By fully understanding these concepts, the reader will have a comprehensive grasp of our system of care.

Chapter 1 offers an introduction to ACA, how it was passed, and what it is intended to do. In noting the extreme social and political polarization that emerged as part of the debate over ACA, I also provide a historical perspective on other attempts to pass health care reform and the polarization of opinion they engendered.

Chapter 2 offers a brief historical background about some of the important policy decisions our country has made over time to create the system we now have. It provides data about the rising cost of health care in this country, and the burdens these costs place on both government and the private sector. It compares our country to other developed countries, in both the amount we spend on health care and the overall health of our population.

Chapter 3 describes how many of the institutional norms and expectations that are unique to the United States have created a health care system that is also unique. By means of comparison, it traces the history of the Canadian health care system and examines how fundamental cultural differences between U.S. and Canadian societies are reflected in our health care systems. It looks at institutional aspects specific to the U.S. system such as the "technologic imperative" and the approach we take to medical malpractice.

Chapter 4 looks at the professional structure of U.S. health care. It describes the history of the medical profession, examining such issues as the number of physicians in practice and their practice specialty. It covers the history of the nursing profession and the evolving role of advanced practice nurses. Finally, it examines the structure of hospitals and other types of specialized referral centers.

Chapter 5 addresses the various ways health insurance can be structured. It provides a close look at the health maintenance organization, or HMO. It looks at the evolution of the Kaiser Permanente system, for years the nation's largest HMO. It then describes the emergence over the last several years of newer types of HMOs and various other types of managed care organizations. It then moves on to a discussion of the managed care revolution and distinguishes between the concepts of managed care and managed competition.

Chapters 6 and 7 explore the two principal government health care programs: Medicare and Medicaid. Established in the 1960s, these programs had two important outcomes: (1) they simultaneously extended health insurance coverage to millions of Americans who were previously without insurance coverage, and (2) they set off the escalation in health care costs that continues to plague us today. Chapter 6 describes some of the policy questions confronting Medicare and identifies changes in the Medicare system involving HMOs and other types of managed care organizations. It looks at some of the weaknesses and problems that have developed with the system of Medicare HMOs, as well as steps Congress has taken to reform this program. Chapter 7 describes recent efforts by several states to restructure their Medicaid system to both constrain costs and broaden coverage. It also summarizes the State Children's Health Insurance Program (S-CHIP) enacted by the federal government to reduce the number of children without health insurance.

Chapter 8 asks how the rapid shift to for-profit health care seen in the 1990s has affected the delivery of care. It considers the effects of the increasing prevalence of for-profit hospitals and specialized for-profit treatment centers for conditions such as heart disease and kidney disease. It then considers the extent to which physicians have allowed the profit motive to affect their professional practice.

Chapter 9 explores the world of pharmaceuticals and pharmaceutical policy. It describes recent increases in the cost of pharmaceutical products and steps taken by managed care organizations and state Medicaid programs to control pharmaceutical costs. It goes on to describe the expansion of Medicare through the Medicare Modernization Act to include coverage of outpatient pharmaceuticals.

Chapter 10 explores the often hidden side of U.S. health care: our system of long-term health care. It covers a variety of long-term care options, including nursing homes and home health care. It documents the expected surge in frail elderly Americans who will soon need long-term care services, and it looks at alternative ways of providing and financing long-term care.

Chapter 11 brings up the issue of the uninsured: the more than 50 million Americans who are without any type of health insurance coverage and, as a result, lack access to many types of basic medical care. It finds that the majority of the uninsured are not people who are poor and unemployed, but rather are people in families with at least one adult who works on a regular basis. It looks at the success of two states' efforts to reduce the number of uninsured: Hawaii's employer mandate for the provision of health insurance to workers and Massachusetts's individual mandate for basic health insurance coverage.

Chapter 12 looks at social factors other than health insurance that affect the delivery of and access to health care. It asks, What are some of the other factors that impede people's access to health care even after financial constraints have been removed? It describes how forces such as culture, ethnicity, and social class can independently affect access to care.

Chapter 13 describes a unified model of our current health care dilemma. It suggests that forces of cost, quality, and access compete for pre-eminence in the health policy arena, and that the interjection of the for-profit motive has complicated the model and made a solution more difficult. It proposes an ethical heuristic that physicians and other health professionals can use to navigate the currents of for-profit health care. It explores the issue of health care rationing and the lessons that can be learned from the country's response to recent shortages of flu vaccine and from the Oregon Medicaid plan, the country's first attempt at the explicit rationing of health care services as a means to expand access.

In Chapter 14 I suggest that, despite the substantial improvements that will result from the enactment of ACA, we will continue to face unanswered questions that are central to eventually finding a means of stabilizing and securing our system of health care for the long term.

At the end of each of the above chapters, I describe the specific changes contained in ACA that affect the topics discussed in the chapters. At the end of the book I combine these descriptions into an outline of the major changes that will result from ACA. It would not be possible to include in this outline every change contained within the ACA legislation, given its length and level of detail. Instead, I also identify a series of websites that provide a nonpartisan summary of ACA and its specific policy effects.

I would like to offer the reader a brief note on how the bibliographic references used in preparing this book are organized. Much of the data I present come from the extensive archive of web-based resources available to those interested in health policy. At the end of the book, I have listed separately the sources I used that are available online, providing the Internet address from which I accessed them. Many of these sources will have more recent data available, and I encourage the reader to explore these sites to learn about recent policy initiatives.

I hope that, at the completion of this book, the reader will have gained an appreciation of how health care in the United States in all its complexity still presents a fundamental dilemma: How much health care can we afford and who will have access to that care? I will consider the book a success if, as a result of this appreciation, the reader will be in a better position to contribute to solving this dilemma.

# AUTHOR'S NOTE

As this book is going to press, a series of court challenges to the implementation of the Affordable Care Act (ACA) have been heard and decided at the federal District Court level. Filed in different parts of the country, the district court decisions have been contradictory, necessitating resolution by federal Courts of Appeal and eventually by the United States Supreme Court. Should the Supreme Court rule that ACA violates, either in whole or in part, the U.S. Constitution, the descriptions in this book of the impact of ACA will not be fully accurate.

In order to address this issue, and to provide the reader with information that is both current and accurate, I will provide a description and analysis of any court-mandated changes to ACA at the website www.press.jhu.edu/books/supplemental/barr_policy .html. In addition, I recommend Hall (2011) and Tribe (2011), two recently published analyses of the underlying constitutional issues and legal implications of the court challenges, each written by a nationally recognized legal scholar.

# The Affordable Care Act and the Politics of Health Care Reform

The headlines in March 2010 just about said it all. On March 22, a *New York Times* editorial declared, "Health Care Reform, at Last." Two days later, the *New England Journal of Medicine* announced, "Historic Passage—Reform at Last" (Iglehart 2010b). President Barack Obama had signed the Patient Protection and Affordable Care Act (ACA)—the most significant reform of our health care system since the 1965 enactment of Medicare and Medicaid under President Lyndon Johnson. After what Bruce Vladeck, administrator of the Health Care Financing Administration under President Bill Clinton, characterized as "the epochal, exhausting, and contentious task of enacting comprehensive health care reform" (Vladeck 2010, p. 1955), the tumultuous process that had begun more than a year before with the release of President Obama's first federal budget proposal had finally come to a conclusion.

The passage of reform legislation over the unanimous and strident opposition of congressional Republicans was assuredly a major step in the evolution of health care in America. Unless it somehow is repealed or substantially altered, ACA will extend publicly funded health insurance coverage to millions of formerly uninsured adults whose income falls near or below the federal poverty line (FPL). ACA will also make reasonably affordable health insurance available to millions more Americans who are not poor, yet who previously could not afford the cost of acquiring health insurance in the private marketplace.

As it moved through Congress, the proposed health care reform legislation exposed deep divisions among politicians and within the U.S. population over core issues of health policy. Do Americans have a right to health care? What should the role of government be in financing or regulating health care and health insurance? To what extent should we rely on the private marketplace as the source of health insurance? How much should government pay for health care? Perhaps even more important, how much can the government *afford to pay* for health care?

The passage of ACA did not provide definitive answers to these questions. We may well be discussing and debating them again in the not-too-distant future. In light of the likelihood of this ongoing discussion and debate, it is appropriate to look more closely at the process by which Congress and the president enacted the reforms included in ACA and then to place that reform process in the considerably broader context of the history of health care reform efforts in the United States.

## HEALTH CARE REFORM AND THE 2008 PRESIDENTIAL ELECTION

The presidential election scheduled for November 4, 2008, began in earnest with the primary elections in January and February of that year. Before the first vote was cast, health care reform was an important issue in the minds of most voters. A series of public opinion polls conducted between 1994 (the year the Clinton health reform proposals collapsed) and 2007 showed that "about 90% of Americans were fairly consistent in agreeing that the U.S. health care system should be completely rebuilt or required fundamental changes" (Jacobs 2008, p. 1881).

In January 2008, Robert Blendon and his colleagues published the results of a series of opinion surveys of likely primary voters from thirty-five states with early presidential primaries (Blendon et al. 2008b). They found widespread awareness of problems inherent to health care in the United States among both Republicans and Democrats. While Republicans and Democrats were in general agreement on the need to enact some type of health care reform, however, they were divided on what the reform should look like. Among Democrats, 65 percent favored providing health insurance to "all or nearly all of the uninsured" and were willing to accept substantially increased government spending to accomplish this goal. By contrast, 42 percent of Republicans supported extending coverage "to only some of the uninsured," with an additional 27 percent preferring "keeping things basically as they are now" (Blendon et al. 2008b, p. 420). Before the first vote was cast in the presidential primaries, our country was divided largely along political party lines as to how we should address health care reform.

In November 2008, Blendon and colleagues reported a second series of opinion polls, this time comparing those who had voted for John McCain in the primary with those who had voted for Barack Obama (Blendon et al. 2008a). Consistent with the earlier polls, most Obama voters wanted the government to take responsibility for extending health insurance to the uninsured, while McCain voters were of the view that responsibility for acquiring health insurance should rest with the individual consumer. Obama voters favored a larger, more comprehensive reform plan, while McCain voters favored a more limited, smaller-scale approach. Before President Obama was to take office, a substantial polarization of views between Democrats and Republicans was already in place.

Shortly after his inauguration, President Obama released his first budget proposal. In it he called on Congress to work collaboratively with the White House to design major reform of the health care system. It was clear, though, that Obama had learned the lesson of the failed Clinton reform proposals of 1993–94, which I describe in Chapter 5. Rather than defining the specifics of the reform proposals himself, President Obama wanted Congress to take the lead in developing reform legislation.

Within a few months of Obama's budget message, Congress had begun to work on reform legislation. The process of developing the actual legislation fell to five separate congressional committees: two in the Senate and three in the House of Representatives. A consensus began to emerge that the most promising approach to expanding health insurance coverage would be through requiring all U.S. residents to carry health insurance (individual mandate) while also requiring most U.S. employers to offer health insurance to their employees (employer mandate). This approach mirrored reforms that had been adopted in Massachusetts a few years earlier.

It did not take long in this process for the political divide evident in pre-election polls to resurface. Mandating health insurance coverage would require creating a place for individuals and employers to go to acquire coverage. As part of its mandate program, Massachusetts had created a central clearinghouse to connect insurance companies offering coverage options with individuals or employers seeking coverage. Fairly quickly, leaders of the Senate committees dealing with reform agreed to adopt a model similar to that in Massachusetts. They would establish health insurance "exchanges" through which those seeking insurance could select from among the insurance options various companies had available.

As chair of the Senate Finance Committee, Senator Max Baucus (D-Montana) initially proposed that among the insurance options available through these health insurance exchanges would be a "public option," an insurance plan analogous to Medicare, organized and administered by the federal government. Almost immediately, Senate Republicans condemned the public option approach. Senator John Cornyn (R-Texas) criticized the public option approach as "a Washington-directed unfair-competition plan" (quoted in Iglehart 2009a, p. 2386). Senator Charles Grassley (R-Iowa) argued that the Democrats' approach "would cause us to slide rapidly down the slope towards increasing government control of health care" (Grassley 2009, p. 2397).

President Obama countered these criticisms in a *New York Times* Op-Ed. He argued that the Democrats' plan "is not about putting the government in charge of your health insurance. I don't believe anyone should be in charge of your health care decisions but you and your doctor—not government, not bureaucrats, not insurance companies" (Obama 2009b).

With substantial majorities in both houses of Congress, Democratic leaders pushed for a comprehensive expansion of the existing health insurance system to include most of those who were without insurance. The federal government would take principal responsibility for organizing and financing this expansion. Republicans, on the other hand, with substantial support from the health insurance industry, argued for a more limited approach. As described by Karen Ignagni, CEO of America's Health Insurance Plans (a leading industry group), Congress should instead focus on "building on the strengths of the present public-private health care system rather than replacing it" (Ignagni 2009, p. 1134).

By the fall of 2009, the debate over health care reform had hit an impasse. There was a line drawn in the congressional sand separating Democrats from Republicans. It appeared there was no room for compromise—Democrats would not accept the approach supported by Republicans, and Republicans were equally unwilling to consider seriously the Democrats' proposals. It seemed to many that, once again, health care reform might end in failure.

At this point, President Obama chose to take decisive action, addressing a joint session of Congress in front of a prime-time viewing audience. Chiding both sides of the aisle for their impasse, Obama stated, "now is the season for action." He indicated that, from that point on, he was going to assert his leadership in the effort to enact health care reform. He identified three overarching goals for the reform effort: (1) expanding health insurance coverage to those who lacked it, (2) constraining the rising cost of health care, and (3) improving the security of coverage for those with chronic illness (Obama 2009a).

With a great deal of political maneuvering, carried out in the face of substantial public confusion, each house of Congress enacted health care reform legislation: the House of Representatives on November 7 and the Senate on December 24. While each bill had many things in common, each had unique features. Some form of compromise between the two versions would need to be agreed upon. Usually this process would involve the creation of a House-Senate Conference Committee, made up of members of both houses. The compromise struck by the Conference Committee would then be taken back for final approval in each house before being forwarded to the president for his signature.

This process turned out not to be an option, though. Senator Ted Kennedy of Massachusetts, a leader of Senate Democrats and for more than four decades a leading voice in the U.S. Senate for health care reform, died of cancer. A special election in Massachusetts to fill his seat resulted in a Republican being elected, thereby giving the Republicans the forty-one votes needed to mount and sustain a filibuster in the Senate. With unanimous Republican opposition to passage of any health reform bill approved by Democrats, there was no chance for compromise legislation coming out of a House-Senate Conference Committee to gain passage in the Senate. Nor was there any chance the Senate would simply approve the reform bill passed previously by the House. There was only one option open to the Democrats: for the House of Representatives to approve the bill passed by the Senate, even though the Senate bill had several provisions to which House Democrats were opposed. Following House passage of the Senate bill, however, the House and Senate could then agree on a series of modifications to the bill under a special provision referred to as "reconciliation."

Not being a scholar of the intricacies of the legislative process, I will leave it to others to describe in more detail the history, purpose, and intended use of the reconciliation process in Congress (Herszenhorn 2010; Iglehart 2010a). As I understand it, the reconciliation process was established by Congress in 1974 as a simplified means of changing federal programs or policies to align them more closely with previously established budget policy. If legislation is passed that is inconsistent with the budget guidelines set by Congress, or, similarly, if an existing program is inconsistent with those guidelines, Congress can change the programs or policies to align them with the budget. Making these changes under the reconciliation process requires a simple majority vote in both houses of Congress—and therefore is not subject to a filibuster in the Senate.

Congress had previously used the budget reconciliation process at various times and for various purposes. One of the best-known instances of reconciliation is the Consolidated Omnibus Budget Reconciliation Act, passed by Congress in 1986 and best known by its acronym, COBRA. COBRA gives employees who have lost their jobs the right to continue their previous group health coverage for a period of time. People frequently talk of their "COBRA benefits."

Sensing a potential procedural impasse, on February 25 President Obama convened an urgent summit meeting of leading Democrats and Republicans to discuss, and in front of a national television audience to debate, competing perspectives on health care reform. The political impasse that preceded Obama's summit was still there after it was over. All Republicans in Congress remained opposed to the bills that had been passed by the House and the Senate. President Obama and Democratic leaders had no choice but to invoke the budget reconciliation process. In an all-day session on Sunday, March 21, the House approved the health reform bill previously passed in December by the Senate, and on March 23 President Obama signed it into law. Then, on March 25, both the House and the Senate passed, by simple majority vote, the reconciliation bill that made a series of changes to the original bill that bridged the divisions between the original House and Senate bills. In essence, the reconciliation process replicated what the House-Senate Conference Committee process is intended to do: to find a middle ground between similar bills passed in the House and the Senate, and then to gain final approval of both houses of the compromise bill.

As Congress completed passage of ACA, the rhetoric on both sides made clear the continued deep divisions between Democrats and Republicans over how health care in the United States should be organized and financed, and the role government should play in the health care system. On the day he signed ACA, President Obama hailed the historic step that had been taken: "Today, after almost a century of trying . . . health insurance reform becomes law in the United States of America . . . We have now just enshrined the core principle that everybody should have some basic security when it comes to their health care" (Obama 2010).

Republicans were not so sanguine. Representative Marsha Blackburn (R-Tennessee), following the House vote in favor of the ACA legislation, remarked, "Freedom dies a little bit today" (quoted in Hulse 2010). Carl Hulse, reporting on the House's approval of ACA, reported that "Republicans were outraged, characterizing the legislation as a major step toward socialism and an aggressive government takeover of the health care system" (Hulse 2010). These comments echoed those made a few months earlier by Representative Michele Bachmann (R-Minnesota), that Democrats were pushing for "socialized medicine" and a "government takeover" of the American health care system (quoted in Herszenhorn 2009).

This continued polarization over what ACA represented for the United States—a new "core principle" assuring access to health care, or a "government takeover" and a step closer to "socialized medicine"—remained in the wake of the year-long health care reform process. It would be easy to point to President Obama and the political parties in Congress as the source of this polarization. It is fundamental to our understanding of U.S. health care reform, however, to consider, again, what President Obama said when he signed the ACA: "Today, after almost a century of trying . . . health insurance reform becomes law in the United States of America."

The health care reform process did not begin with the inauguration of President Obama. Nor did it begin with the presidential campaign leading up to his election. The United States had been arguing over health care reform for nearly a century before President Obama was elected. A review of the repeated efforts over that century for or against reform reveals a striking similarity between what was proposed in 2009–10 and what had been proposed previously, as well as a striking similarity between the rhetoric of health care reform in the past and the rhetoric of 2009–10.

## A CENTURY OF TRYING TO ACHIEVE HEALTH CARE REFORM IN THE UNITED STATES

Theodore Roosevelt first attempted to reform U.S. health care during his presidential campaign in 1912. As part of the Progressive Party's platform, Roosevelt proposed a system of national health insurance, modeled after the German system, to be administered by a new National Health Department. Those supporting national health insurance viewed health care as a right of all members of our society, analogous to the recently recognized right to a publicly financed education for children. Teddy Roosevelt lost the 1912 presidential election to Woodrow Wilson, however, and health care reform had to wait for another day.

In 1927, a group of physicians, public health professionals, and others concerned with national health care issues came together to form the Committee on the Costs of Medical Care (CCMC) (Ross 2002). CCMC was an independent group, and was supported by a number of foundations. Committee members set in motion a five-year project to study and report on the economics and organization of health care in America. On March 10, 1931, the *New York Times* carried an article entitled "Family Health Bill Put at $250 a Year" in which the CCMC was cited, stating that "the average family of five in an American city" spent $250 per year on medical care, a figure that raised serious concerns about the rising costs of medical care in a time of economic hardship. The committee's majority report, issued in 1932, recommended shifting the delivery of most medical care to a model that emphasized organized medical groups and prepayment of health costs through either insurance premiums or taxation. The American Medical Association (AMA), however, was stridently opposed to this approach, labeling such prepaid medical groups "medical soviets" and suggesting that "such plans will mean the destruction of private practice . . . they are, in a word, 'unethical'" (American Medical Association 1932, p. 1950). The AMA's House of Delegates unanimously approved a motion to oppose the majority report of the CCMC, and to mount "an intensive campaign . . . among the medical profession and the public" to prevent adoption of the CCMC's recommendations. A follow-up report to the House of Delegates reported that "all the facilities of the American Medical Association have been used to oppose this trend and the propaganda in support of it" (American Medical Association 1934b, p. 2200). The AMA prevailed in its efforts to block the recommendations of the CCMC's report, and the report was shelved.

Franklin Roosevelt took up the issue of health care reform in 1934 as part of his initial proposals for old age security and unemployment insurance for workers. In response to Roosevelt's early proposals to include national health insurance as part of Social Security, the AMA House of Delegates passed a resolution reiterating its position that "All features of medical service in any method of medical practice should be under the control of the medical profession. No other body or individual is legally or educationally equipped to exercise such control" (American Medical Association 1934b, p. 2200). When it appeared as though health insurance might be added to the pending legislation for creation of the Social Security system, the AMA House of Delegates met in special session to reiterate its "opposition to all forms of state medicine" and to "reaffirm its opposition to all forms of compulsory sickness insurance" (American Medical Association 1935, pp. 750–51). Once again AMA opposition to government involvement in health care was effective, and when Roosevelt signed the Social Security Act in 1935, health insurance was not part of it.

Roosevelt continued to support the creation of a system of national health insurance, and appointed an "Interdepartmental Committee to Coordinate Health and Welfare Activities," charging it with studying the issue of extending Social Security benefits to include health care. At a national conference held in July 1938, the committee proposed a series of changes to U.S. health care, including "a ten year program providing for the expansion of the nation's hospital facilities" and "a comprehensive program designed to increase and improve medical services for the entire population" (Interdepartmental Committee to Coordinate Health and Welfare Activities 1938, p. 433).

One month later, the AMA convened an emergency meeting of its House of Delegates to respond to the government's "campaign for some radical changes in medical practice" (American Medical Association 1938, p. 1192). The speaker of the House of Delegates reminded the delegates that the AMA had consistently "opposed legislation which would have the effect of vesting in some governmental agency power to enforce its decrees on patients and doctors" (p. 1192). The AMA president then addressed the delegates, stating that "the Association has constantly opposed the adoption of any form of state medicine by any definition of that term" (p. 1194).

It is interesting to note that at this special session, the leaders of the National Medical Association (NMA)—the national association of black physicians, most of whom were prevented from joining the AMA because of their race—were (after majority vote of the AMA delegates) invited to address the meeting. The past president of the NMA voiced his support for the position of the AMA, arguing that "if we have socialized medicine in America, I am very sure, as you must be sure, that the standards of medical practice will degenerate . . . and the patients again will suffer as they have suffered in Europe" (p. 1211).

Once again, fears that "governmental agency power" over the financing of health care would lead to "state medicine" and "socialized Medicine" were sufficient to derail Roosevelt's efforts. Health care reform would have to wait another decade before it was back on the table.

In January 1948, President Harry Truman asked Oscar Ewing, one of his senior administrators, to prepare a report on the status of health care in the United States. Released in September of that year, the Ewing Report outlined a series of steps the federal government should take to make health care more available. As Roosevelt's Interdepartmental Committee did in 1938, this report recommended extensive new hospital construction and a compulsory "system of Government prepayment health insurance" (Furman 1948) that over a period of three years would provide universal insurance for both hospital care and physician care, as well as coverage of certain prescription medicines.

The response of the AMA to the Ewing proposals is interesting. The AMA first went through a formal procedure to adopt the following definition: "*Socialized medicine*—Socialized medicine is a system of medical administration by which the government promises or attempts to provide for the medical needs of the entire population or a large part thereof" (American Medical Association 1948, p. 685). A few weeks later, Morris Fishbein, the longtime editor of the *Journal of the American Medical Association*, published a special editorial in which he warned physicians that the profession of medicine was "at a point of decision which may well determine the nature and the freedom of medical practice for many years in the future" (Fishbein 1948, p. 1254). Responding to politicians who denied that President Truman's proposals for national health insurance constituted "socialized medicine," Dr. Fishbein argued that "nations that embark on such programs move inevitably into a socialized state in which . . . practically all public services become nationalized, private responsibility and ownership disappear, individual initiative is destroyed and the result is a socialized state" (p. 1256). As reported by the *New York Times*, the AMA fought Truman's proposals "with all the vigor and manpower it [could] assemble" (Phillips 1949), with the result that, once again, the efforts at health care reform went down to defeat in Congress.

It would be seventeen years before Congress would take up health care reform again, this time under the leadership of President Johnson. With large majorities in both houses of Congress following the 1964 election, Johnson moved quickly to enact Medicare (health care for the elderly) and Medicaid (health care for the poor) as amendments to the Social Security system. Headlines in the *New York Times* announced, "A.M.A. Opens Bid to Kill Medicare" (Wehrwein 1965). Testifying before the Senate Finance Committee, Dr. Donovan Ward, president of the AMA, warned senators, "This may be your last chance to weigh the consequences of taking the first step toward establishment of socialized medicine in the United States" (American Medical Association 1965, p. 16).

In 1965, Congress was not swayed by claims that government financing of health care for the elderly and the poor constituted a government takeover of the health care system. It was swayed even less by claims that the proposed Medicare and Medicaid programs would be "the first step toward establishment of socialized medicine in the United States." By substantial margins, both houses of Congress passed the Social Security Act of 1965, establishing the Medicare and Medicaid programs. President Johnson flew to the Missouri home of Harry Truman to sign the legislation in the presence of the former president.

Of course, providing government payment for health care for the elderly and the poor was only a partial fulfillment of earlier proposals for universal health insurance.

As monumental an accomplishment as it represented, the passage of Medicare and Medicaid left substantial segments of the American population without the means to pay for health insurance. As we will see in later chapters, the aggregate cost of health care began to rise sharply in the years following the enactment of Medicare and Medicaid. By 1970, both President Richard Nixon and Senator Ted Kennedy were calling for expanded health insurance coverage to help individuals and families offset the rising costs of care. Nixon's plan called for private financing through what we today would call an employer mandate. Kennedy's plan called for direct government financing of care. Neither plan gained approval, and any further steps toward health care reform were lost in the wake of the Watergate scandal and President Nixon's resulting resignation.

Health care reform was again on the table in the early years of President Clinton's administration, as I discuss in Chapter 5. An effective national ad campaign by the health insurance industry, warning of a new, massive federal bureaucracy taking over American health care, coupled with a shift of congressional control from Democrat to Republican majorities, led to the defeat of the Clinton reform proposals. As many had warned, in the years following the defeat of the Clinton proposals health care costs continued their steep rise, and growing numbers of Americans became or remained uninsured against the cost of illness or injury—the situation confronting the candidates in the 2008 presidential election.

## PLACING THE OBAMA REFORMS IN THE HISTORICAL CONTEXT OF PREVIOUS REFORM EFFORTS

During the intensity of the yearlong debate over President Obama's proposals for health care reform, it was often difficult to gain a clear sense of what the core issues were. The heated rhetoric from all sides led to widespread confusion as to what the proposed reforms would or would not accomplish. A national poll (Kaiser Family Foundation 2010b) taken two weeks after President Obama signed ACA showed that 55 percent of respondents were confused about what was in the new law. Support for the law fell largely along party lines, with 79 percent of Republicans having an unfavorable view of the law and 77 percent of Democrats having a favorable view.

Which view was correct? Would the law assure most Americans access to needed health care, as many people seemed to believe? Or would it mean the potential destruction of our health care system through a government takeover, as many others appeared to believe?

Taking a step back from this debate, it is informative to compare ACA and the political response to it with various proposals for health care reform made over the last century. As illustrated in Table 1.1, there is a remarkable similarity between what ACA was intended to accomplish and what earlier proposals hoped to accomplish, and an

Table 1.1. A History of Arguments for and against Health Care Reform

| Year/President | Argument in Favor | Argument Opposed |
| --- | --- | --- |
| 1931 / Herbert Hoover | Modern medicine can be brought within reach of persons of average means.<br>—Committee on the Cost of Medical Care | Medical soviets . . . such plans will mean the destruction of private practice.<br>—American Medical Association |
| 1934–38 / Franklin Roosevelt | A comprehensive program designed to increase and improve medical services for the entire population.<br>—Committee to Coordinate Health and Welfare Activities | Opposition to all forms of state medicine.<br>—American Medical Association<br><br>If we have socialized medicine in America . . . standards of medical practice will degenerate . . . and patients will suffer.<br>—National Medical Association |
| 1948 / Harry Truman | A system of Government prepayment health insurance to provide universal access to hospital and physician care.<br>—Ewing Report | Nations that embark on such programs move inevitably into a socialized state in which . . . practically all public services become nationalized.<br>—American Medical Association |
| 1965 / Lyndon Johnson | To improve health care for the American people, [I propose] hospital insurance for the aged under social security.<br>—President Johnson, 1965 budget message to Congress | The President's proposal would be the first step toward establishment of socialized medicine in the United States.<br>—American Medical Association |
| 1993 / Bill Clinton | We must make this our most urgent priority: giving every American health security, health care that can never be taken away.<br>—President Clinton, special address to Congress, September 1993 | New government bureaucracies will cap how much the country can spend on all health care.<br>—"Harry and Louise" TV ads, sponsored by the Health Insurance Association of America |
| 2010 / Barack Obama | We have now just enshrined the core principle that everybody should have some basic security when it comes to their health care.<br>—President Obama, on signing the health reform law | A major step toward socialism and an aggressive government takeover of the health care system.<br>—Congressional Republicans |

equally striking similarity between the rhetorical opposition to ACA and the rhetoric in opposition to those earlier proposals.

In 1931, when the Committee on the Cost of Medical Care recommended programs to bring health care "within reach of persons of average means," the opposition predicted that the programs would "mean the destruction of private practice." When Franklin Roosevelt proposed "to increase and improve medical services for the entire population," the AMA labeled his proposals "socialized medicine" and predicted that, if Roosevelt's plan were implemented, "standards of medical practice will degenerate . . . and patients will suffer." Truman's proposal for "universal access to hospital and physician care" was predicted to lead to "a socialized state in which . . . practically all public services become nationalized." Johnson's proposal for Medicare and Medicaid would, the AMA predicted, "be the first step toward establishment of socialized medicine in the United States." President Obama's proposals were characterized by many Republicans as "a major step toward socialism and an aggressive government takeover of the health care system."

The history of health care reform in the United States is the history of our deep-seated divisions over core principles of health care delivery and of the role of government in the provision of health care. Is a basic level of health care a right of all Americans? If so, should the government enact and enforce the mechanism to ensure that right? Alternatively, is it inappropriate for government to interfere in the private provision of health services? Our society has struggled with these issues for a century. The kerfuffle surrounding the passage of ACA was simply the latest episode in our attempts as a society to address these divisions.

Despite the confusion surrounding it, it is clear that ACA will bring major change to our health care system. Among other things, it will:

- Extend Medicaid coverage to an estimated 16 million people living in or near poverty who are currently uninsured
- Provide health insurance to an additional 16 million uninsured people with low to moderate incomes through a combination of regulated insurance exchanges and tax subsidies for the cost of insurance
- Make a series of changes to regulations affecting companies that provide health insurance with the intent of making that insurance more affordable
- Make a series of changes in the Medicare program to reduce costs and improve benefits
- Create a series of new sources of tax revenues to support these programs

When Congress passed Medicare and Medicaid in 1965, our health care system was changed fundamentally. Yet those changes stopped short of solving many of the policy issues at the heart of our health care system. Nor did the passage of Medicare and Medicaid resolve our national ambivalence over what the role of government should be in our health care system.

When Congress passed ACA in 2010, our health care system was again changed fundamentally. Yet Congress again left unaddressed many continuing core questions. In future years and in future Congresses we will undoubtedly again be talking about health care reform. Rather than debating how to extend coverage to the uninsured, we likely will be debating how to rein in the incessantly rising cost of health care. When we have these discussions, the appropriate role of government will again be a topic of sharp debate.

Rather than trying to describe in one place what the ACA does and does not do, I instead address the changes contained in the 2,000-plus-page ACA legislation sequentially as we go through this book. In the following chapters I address issues of the cost, quality, and availability of health care; the cultural factors unique to the United States that surround health care; the professional organization of health care; the various private and public mechanisms for financing health care; and specific health care issues such as pharmaceutical policy and long-term care. In each chapter I describe how these aspects of health care have evolved to what they are now. I then address specifically how the new policies enacted by ACA will affect or change the topic under discussion. At the end of the book I address what ACA has left undone—the problems in the organization, financing, and delivery of American health care that have yet to be resolved. Finally, as an appendix to the book, I provide a comprehensive listing of the various components contained in ACA.

# 2

# Health, Health Care, and the Market Economy

## WHOSE RIGHT? (WHO'S RIGHT?)

After signing the Affordable Care Act (ACA) into law in March 2010, President Barack Obama declared that, in passing the act, "we have now just enshrined the core principle that everybody should have some basic security when it comes to their health care" (Obama 2010). As seen by President Obama (and by many of his supporters), Americans have a right to a basic level of health care, and ACA was the acknowledgment of that right.

Others, however, hold a very different view of the core principles of American health policy. In an opinion piece published in August 2009 in the *Wall Street Journal*, John Mackey, the co-founder and CEO of Whole Foods Markets, wrote, "How can we say that all people have more of an intrinsic right to health care than they have to food or shelter? Health care is a service that we all need, but just like food and shelter it is best provided through voluntary and mutually beneficial market exchanges . . . This 'right' has never existed in America" (Mackey 2009).

This debate over who in America has a right to health care and what level of care that right entails has been going on for nearly a century. In 1918, Dr. John Bowman, at the time director of the Board of Regents of the American College of Surgeons, wrote that "as a people we are accustomed to hospital service; we look upon that service no longer as a luxury which we may buy, but rather as an inherent right. The humblest patient is entitled to the best of medical service. In the last twenty years especially this idea has taken hold of us. We regard the right to health today much as we regard the right to life" (Bowman 1918, p. 1). Made by the leader of one of the most prestigious groups of physicians in the United States, this statement bespeaks a commitment on the part of the medical profession and the country to approach health care as a basic right for all individuals. This was the position President Obama was supporting in asserting that all Americans have a right to some "basic security when it comes to their health care."

Those opposed to President Obama's position would instead agree with the comments of Dr. R. M. Sade, published in the *New England Journal of Medicine*, one of the most prestigious medical journals in the country: "Medical care is neither a right nor a privilege: it is a service that is provided by doctors and others to people who wish to purchase it" (Sade 1971, p. 1289). In Dr. Sade's approach, medical care is no different from any other type of commodity that is bought and sold in the open market. If you want new sneakers, you buy a pair from the shoe store. If you do not have enough money to pay for the sneakers, then you are out of luck—you do not have a right to sneakers. Neither do you have a right to medical care, suggests Dr. Sade. If you do not have enough money to pay for care, then you are out of luck.

While Dr. Bowman's remarks from 1918 offer for many a laudable perspective on the issue of who by rights should have access to health care, they do not accurately describe the direction health care in America actually took in the decades following 1918. Instead, for much of the twentieth century, the structure of our health care system was more consistent with Dr. Sade's perspective and with that of John Mackey of Whole Foods.

## THE UNIQUE HISTORY OF HEALTH CARE IN THE UNITED STATES

When Dr. Bowman published his statement in 1918, the future direction and shape of the U.S. health care system was still in a formative state. By the time Dr. Sade published his remarks in 1971, the shape of our system had largely been decided through a series of political and economic choices. The history of U.S. health care during this period largely reflects the comments of Dr. Sade. With a few notable exceptions, which I address in subsequent chapters, before President Obama signed ACA, Americans did not have a right to medical care.

In 1948, as part of the founding of the United Nations, the UN General Assembly adopted a Universal Declaration of Human Rights, with "recognition of the inherent dignity and of the equal and inalienable rights of all members of the human family." Article 25 of the declaration states: "Everyone has the right to a standard of living adequate for the health and well-being of himself and of his family, including food, clothing, housing and medical care."

The United States, despite its role in founding the United Nations, did not adhere fully to the declaration, instead choosing a market approach to medical care. In approaching medical care as a market commodity that can be bought or sold, rather than as a social good that should be made available to all people, the United States adopted a policy position that was unique among developed countries. In the words of economist Uwe Reinhardt, "Americans . . . decided to treat health care as essentially a private consumer good of which the poor might be guaranteed a basic package, but which is otherwise to be distributed more and more on the basis of ability to pay" (Reinhardt and Relman 1986, p. 23).

The United States was alone among industrialized nations in approaching health care in this market-oriented way. By the end of the twentieth century, all other developed countries had adopted national health plans that assured citizens access to basic medical care. These plans ranged from fully socialized systems such as that in Great Britain to systems such as Canada's, in which all physicians are in private medical practice.*

The decision to approach medical care as a market commodity rather than a right was closely linked to a second national policy decision that was to have equally profound effects on the way health care would evolve in the United States. This was the decision made in the early part of the twentieth century to vest in the medical profession substantial authority over the organization and financing as well as the practice of medical care. At the beginning of the twentieth century, the U.S. medical profession was a complex array of practitioners from diverse educational backgrounds with a variety of knowledge and skills. There were no standards, either legal or ethical, to maintain a consistent level of quality in the way physicians practiced medicine.

In response to what was perceived as a national crisis, a prestigious commission was asked to conduct a national study of the issue of medical education and to make recommendations about a thorough restructuring of medical education, and as a result, medical practice. In 1910, the commission published its recommendations in its report, *Medical Education in the United States and Canada*, often referred to as the Flexner Report. Based on the views expounded in this report, state and local governments increasingly relied on the American Medical Association (AMA) (the principal professional association of physicians) and on the AMA's affiliated state and local medical associations to guide the restructuring of medical practice. (For a more comprehensive discussion of this period in the history of U.S. medicine, see Paul Starr's Pulitzer Prize–winning book, *The Social Transformation of American Medicine*.)

The rise in the sovereignty of the U.S. medical profession was based on a some-

---

* Until 1994, there was a second developed country that continued to approach medical care as a market commodity. In that country, those citizens without the ability to pay for it had little, if any, access to care. As a result of a major restructuring of the country's government in 1994, the country adopted the policy of health care for all as a basic right, leaving the United States alone in treating it as a market good. That other country is South Africa.

what idealized view of physicians. Consistent with the increasing legitimacy of science and technology common during that time, physicians were typically seen as altruistic agents who possessed valuable scientific knowledge and technical skills (Parsons 1951, 1975). Their role as social agents was guided by a code of medical ethics that placed the utmost importance on acting at all times in the best interest of the patient. They could be trusted to make decisions on behalf of the patient in a paternalistic manner, acting always as a disinterested agent on the patient's behalf. This view of the medical profession led state and local governments to vest considerable authority in physicians and their professional organizations over medical education and the practice of medicine.

In 1938, Dr. Irvin Abell, then president of the AMA, spoke to a special meeting of the AMA's House of Delegates, reminding physicians of this professional responsibility. "The medical profession by principle and tradition is committed to the idea that the prime object, the standard of value and the social reason for its existence are all one thing—the service it can render to humanity" (Abell 1938, p. 1192). Part of this obligation of service, Dr. Abell explained to the assembled physicians, was "the fundamental tenet of the American Medical Association that the poverty of a patient should demand the gratuitous service of a physician" (p. 1193). Beyond this obligation to treat the poor without charge, however, Dr. Abell stated the AMA's position that "the individual physician has a right to determine the conditions of his service" (p. 1193).

While this view of physicians as agents of reason, worthy of our trust to act autonomously on behalf of patients, exerted substantial influence over governmental policy toward medical care, a historical examination of the ways in which physicians' professional organizations actually exerted the authority delegated to them offers a very different picture (Freidson 1970). While physicians were granted this authority because of their specialized knowledge and skills, they often used this power to further their own ends. In this view of physicians as agents of power, the medical profession is seen as using its control over knowledge to limit entry into the profession and to maintain political sovereignty over the system of medical care. The power of the medical profession has been used to support and protect the role of the individual physician as self-interested entrepreneur. Those interests were best served by establishing and maintaining the policy principle that medical care was, as described by Dr. Sade, "a service that is provided by doctors and others to people who wish to purchase it" (Sade 1971. p. 1289) under "conditions of . . . service" determined solely by the physician, as Dr. Abell described (Abell 1938, p. 1193).

By creating and maintaining a system that approached medical care as a market commodity, physicians were able to establish their right to charge a separate fee for each service they provided, and to base that fee on whatever the market would bear. In 1934, the AMA established the explicit policy that once the fee for the medical service was set, "the immediate cost should be borne by the patient if able to pay at the time of service" (American Medical Association 1934a, p. 2200). Except for the poor, patients were purchasing medical care from their physician as a market commodity, and as is typical of market exchanges, were expected to pay for it at the time the service was rendered. Thus the name applied to the system of medical care that predominated throughout much of the twentieth century: fee-for-service.

In making medical decisions in a fee-for-service system, physicians were simultaneously looking out for the needs of the patient and for their own financial interests. As medical science and medical technology evolved and expanded, more care came to be perceived as better care. More care also generated higher fees. Both the perceived quality of care and the physician's income went up as the physician did more for the patient. This system of dual loyalties, while seemingly good for patients, can also place the physician in the role of an imperfect agent when making or recommending treatment decisions on the patient's behalf (Freidson 1970). In deciding whether a patient does or does not need additional care, the financial incentive might push the physician to provide care that otherwise might not be seen as medically necessary.

> **CONCEPT 2.1**
>
> Two policies established early in the twentieth century had major effects on our system of care and contributed to our current problems:
> 1. Approaching medical care as a market commodity
> 2. Granting sovereignty to the medical profession over the organization and financing of medical care

These alternative views of the medical profession, as agents of reason or as agents of power, are described in Table 2.1. As we proceed in our examination of health care in the United States, we will find that neither view offers a fully accurate description of the U.S. medical profession. Physicians act neither as agents of pure reason nor as agents of pure power. Medicine in this country has instead evolved as a blending of the two models.

For much of the twentieth century, our health care system and the medical profession's authority over it were stable and noncontroversial. Only in the last few decades, as the rising cost of health care and the growing number of uninsured Americans have commanded the public agenda, has there been a full examination of the effects of approaching medical care as a market commodity and sanctioning the use of medical

TABLE 2.1. Two Ways to Look at the Medical Profession in the United States

| Physicians as Agents of Reason (see Parsons 1951, 1975) | Physicians as Agents of Power (see Freidson 1970) |
|---|---|
| Authority of physicians based on:<br> Specialized knowledge<br> Technical skills<br> Professional ethics | Authority of physicians based on:<br> Control of knowledge<br> Limited entry into profession<br> Sovereignty over system |
| Physicians are seen as altruistic healers | Physicians act as self-interested entrepreneurs |
| Physicians adopt a paternalistic approach to patients | Physicians face conflicting loyalties in their dealings with patients |
| Physicians act as unbiased agents for their patients | Physicians act as imperfect agents for their patients |

knowledge as a source of political and economic power. Nonetheless, these two policies have had profound impacts on the development of our health care system and have differentiated our system from those of other industrialized countries.

## THE COST OF CARE—NOW AND IN THE FUTURE

In 1970, people in the United States spent a total of $73 billion, or an average of $341 per person per year, on all types of health care combined. The total national expenditure on health care in 1970 represented 7.1 percent of the gross domestic product (GDP). At that time, people talked about a national health care expenditure of 7 percent of GDP as representing a "crisis" that needed to be addressed urgently.

In 2009, people in the United States spent $2.5 trillion on health care, or about $8,200 per person (Sisko et al. 2010). This level of expenditure represented 17.3 percent of GDP, more than twice the amount of GDP apportioned to health care in 1970. The rate of increase in health care costs slowed somewhat in 2008, rising only 4.4 percent to 16.2 percent of GDP, the lowest rate of growth in health care costs since we began keeping track of costs in 1960 (Mitka 2010). The federal government estimated, however, that health care costs had risen 5.7 percent in 2009, to 17.3 percent of GDP. Based on the continuing increase in the cost of health care in the face of the falling GDP that characterizes a recession, this 1.1 percent increment in the percent of GDP going to health care represented the largest annual increase since we began keeping track in 1960. Without taking into account the effects of ACA, federal analysts also predicted continued future growth in national health care expenditures, with health care consuming 19.3 percent of GDP by 2019 (Truffer et al. 2010).

Economist Victor Fuchs has pointed out that, over the years, health care costs have risen an average of 2.8 percentage points faster than GDP. If this gap continues, Fuchs suggests, the percentage of GDP going to pay for health care can be expected to double every twenty-six years (Fuchs 2010). Fuchs argues that there are "distinctive institutional features of health care and their consequences" that "distinguish health care from other goods and services" (p. 1859) Fuchs suggests that market competition alone cannot change this long-term pattern. Instead, we will need to rely on a combination of "government regulation and self-regulation [of the medical profession] through professional ethics" (p. 1860).

Where does all this money for health care come from and where does it go? Figures 2.1 and 2.2 show the sources of the money that pays for health care and the principal categories of national health care expenditures. To gain a better sense of what these data mean, we can compare our country to other developed countries. The Organisation for Economic Co-operation and Development (OECD) compiles economic and other statistics from thirty-three of the world's leading developed countries. Table 2.2 shows national expenditures on health care for a selection of OECD countries. In 2008,

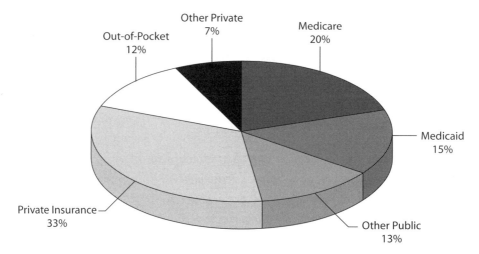

FIGURE 2.1. Health Care Expenditures in the United States, 2008: Where the Money Came From. *Source:* Data from U.S. Centers for Medicare and Medicaid Services

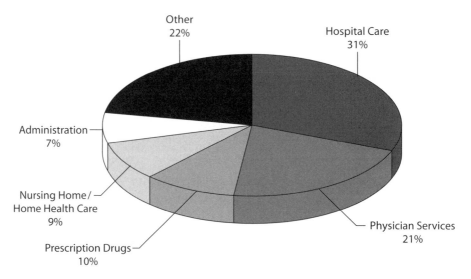

FIGURE 2.2. Health Care Expenditures in the United States, 2008: Where the Money Went. *Source:* Data from U.S. Centers for Medicare and Medicaid Services

the United States reported to the OECD that it spent 16 percent of GDP on health care. This was by far the highest expenditure in the world. The closest countries to the United States were France, with a total expenditure of 11.2 percent, and Switzerland, with an expenditure of 10.7 percent.

Every year, the U.S. government publishes predictions of where health care costs will go in the future. If current government projections through 2019 are accurate, by that time nearly $1 of every $5 in the entire national economy will be spent on health

TABLE 2.2. National Health Care Expenses as a
Percentage of GDP for Selected Countries, 2008

| Country | Percentage of GDP |
|---|---|
| Canada | 10.4 |
| France | 11.2 |
| Germany | 10.5 |
| Greece* | 9.7 |
| Japan* | 8.1 |
| Sweden | 9.4 |
| Switzerland | 10.7 |
| United Kingdom | 8.7 |
| United States | 16.0 |

*Source:* Data from OECD.
*Data are for 2007.

care. The difference between the share of our economy going to health care and what other developed countries spend will be even larger than it is today. This investment in health care will be at the expense of other sectors of the economy, such as education and national infrastructure. We will have less money available for schools, for roads and other forms of transportation, and for investing in the capital and technology necessary for continued expansion of the economy.

Beyond the effects on the U.S. economy in general, health care expenditures in the range of 20 percent of GDP will have severe consequences for government as well. Recall from Figure 2.1 that in 2008 governments at all levels—federal, state, and local— were responsible for a combined 48 percent of all health care expenditures (Medicare, Medicaid, and other public expenditures). Following the enactment of ACA, government expenditures will rise to more than half of all health expenditures. Governments rely on taxation to obtain revenue. Unless tax rates change, tax revenues generally rise at the same rate as GDP. As described above, however, historically the cost of care has risen more rapidly than GDP—especially during times of recession, when health care costs have continued to rise even in the face of a shrinking economy.

Consider the effect on governments of health care expenditures continuing to rise faster than GDP, and therefore faster than tax revenues. More than half of future increases in health care costs that are over and above the rise in GDP will have to come from government sources. *For every dollar that health care costs go up faster than GDP, government sources will pay more than half.* This is an important concept to understand.

How will government come up with the money to pay for this rise, given that *tax revenues increase only as fast as GDP increases?* There will be two options:

1. Increase tax rates to cover the increased cost of care.
2. Borrow the needed money, thus adding to government debt.

Neither option is palatable to politicians or the American public. Either would have a severe, long-term, destabilizing effect on the U.S. economy. Chernew and colleagues have written about "The Specter of Financial Armageddon" if nothing is done to change this pattern (Chernew, Baicker, and Hsu 2010). Governments will face a serious dilemma if a solution is not found to the rising cost of health care.

This dilemma will be especially difficult for state and local governments, which typically are forbidden by law from engaging in deficit spending. To maintain health care expenditures at this level, growing faster than GDP growth and thus faster than the growth in state and local tax revenues, state and local governments have to either raise taxes or divert funds away from other programs such as education. This is why many states, facing an increasing crisis in their attempts to keep up with health care spending, are instead considering reducing the amount of care they pay for. Because those who receive the care paid for by state and local governments are typically the least well-off members of our society, this means that any cuts in state and local spending on health care will be felt disproportionately by those who can least afford to pay for care on their own.

## What's Causing the Rising Cost of Health Care?

To fully appreciate the implications of the rising cost of health care in this country, we need to have a better grasp of its causes. Simple inflation is, of course, one reason—both prices in general and medical prices in particular tend to rise with time. Typically the price of medical care will rise faster than prices in general, contributing to the rising share of GDP devoted to care. Even when one adjusts for price inflation, however, the cost of health care measured in constant dollars continues to go up at a rapid rate.

Three general forces contribute to this increase in the cost of care:

1. The U.S. population increases over time.
2. The number of people receiving treatment for a specific illness may go up for reasons not associated with increases in the population. (This is referred to as the "treated prevalence.") Either the illness is becoming more common, or more people with the condition may seek treatment (for example, mental illness).
3. The cost of treating a specific illness may go up independently of the number of people who have that illness. This will typically be due to new, more advanced (and more high-tech) treatments becoming available, replacing older, less expensive (and more low-tech) treatments.

A study published by researchers at Emory University differentiated between these three causes of rising costs in health care (Thorpe, Florence, and Joski 2004). They looked at the increase in the cost of care for the non-institutionalized U.S. population between 1987 and 2000. Controlling for inflation, health care costs increased about 3 percent per year during this period. As a proportion of GDP, health care rose from 10.5 percent to 13.3 percent during this period.

The researchers found that ten specific illnesses accounted for nearly half of this rise in the cost of care; five of these conditions accounted for more than 30 percent of the rise. They then estimated how much of the rise in the cost of care attributable to these five conditions could be assigned to each of the three possible forces described above. They found that increases in the cost of treating a specific disease, caused by the increased costs of newer, more high-tech treatments, were the largest source of the rising cost of care.

## GROWING CONCERNS ABOUT THE QUALITY OF HEALTH CARE IN THE UNITED STATES

Beyond the rising cost of health care in the United States, it is also important to consider the quality of that care. To what extent can we be assured that the increasing amounts we spend on our system of health care provide us with care that is of the highest available quality? This question pertains both to the care provided by physicians and other health professionals, and to the care provided by hospitals and other health care institutions.

### The Quality of Care Provided by Physicians

Dr. John Wennberg, of Dartmouth Medical School, first started looking in the 1970s at differences in the way physicians treat specific diseases. He found that, for a variety of conditions, there were consistent differences across geographic regions in the rates at which certain surgical procedures and other treatments were applied. Physicians in community A, for example, might use a surgical approach to prostate cancer at a certain rate, while physicians in community B might use that procedure at a substantially lower rate, relying instead on nonsurgical treatments. Wennberg and his colleagues consistently found these differences in regional patterns, referred to as "small area variations," for a wide variety of medical conditions.

Which community of physicians uses the higher-quality approach to treatment—community A or community B? That depends on whom you ask. Physicians from community A might respond that they are being appropriately aggressive in using a surgical approach, while their colleagues in community B are being too cautious. Physicians from community B, of course, might respond in the opposite way. They are using surgery appropriately, while their community A colleagues are being too cavalier in using surgery. A principal benefit of the decades of research done by Dr. Wennberg, culminating in the publication in 1998 of the *Dartmouth Atlas of Health Care*, has been the need for physicians to confront this quality conundrum.

The answer as to which community of physicians—A or B—is using a higher-quality approach to treating their patients can be determined only by using scientific evidence from well-designed studies comparing alternative approaches to care. There is a growing consensus both among physicians and among health policy analysts that "evidence-based medicine"—that is, medical care determined by scientific research to provide optimal outcomes—should be the standard by which the quality of physician care is judged. Scientific research of this type has an especially important role to play when there are multiple alternatives available for treating a specific condition. Research that compares outcomes of alternative treatments is often referred to as "comparative effectiveness research" (CER). The federal government has charged its Agency for Healthcare Research and Quality (AHRQ) with supporting research to develop the evidence-based standards by which health care quality should be judged, and by which the effectiveness of treatment alternatives can be compared. The federal Medicare program, discussed in Chapter 6, is looking at ways to adjust its method of paying physicians to reward those who consistently practice higher-quality, evidence-based medicine.

## The Quality of Care Provided by Hospitals

The Institute of Medicine (IOM) of the National Academy of Sciences saw a need to study the issue of quality in the care provided to patients in hospitals and other large health care institutions. In the 1990s, it convened a Committee on Quality of Health Care in America. This committee of national experts, drawn from industry, health care organizations, professional organizations, and universities, studied the issue of quality and delivered its report in 1999 (Kohn, Corrigan, and Donaldson 1999). The report, titled *To Err Is Human: Building a Safer Health System*, came to some disturbing conclusions about the quality of the care provided in U.S. hospitals: "At least 44,000 people, and perhaps as many as 98,000 people, die in hospitals each year as a result of medical errors that could have been prevented . . . preventable medical errors in hospitals exceed attributable deaths to such feared threats as motor-vehicle wrecks, breast cancer, and AIDS" (p. 1).

The IOM report concluded that the problems with medical mistakes are not principally due to individual human error, but rather, "are caused by faulty systems, processes, and conditions that lead people to make mistakes or fail to prevent them" (p. 2). It recommended two principal mechanisms to improve hospital safety:

1. Creating a "nationwide public mandatory reporting system," as well as additional voluntary reporting systems
2. Relying on existing oversight organizations to focus added scrutiny on the issue of health care quality

Both mechanisms have been initiated, with some preliminary but positive results.

Hibbard, Stockard, and Tusler (2005) reported on a study done in Wisconsin comparing the change in quality over a two-year period for three groups of hospitals: (1) those who received an independent report on the quality of their care with that report made public; (2) those who received an independent report on the quality of their care with that report kept confidential; and (3) those who received no report on the quality of their care. The quality in hospitals confronting public disclosure of their report increased significantly more than in hospitals receiving a confidential report. The lowest improvement in quality was in those hospitals receiving no report. This and other studies (for example, Jha et al. 2005b) suggest that a system of publicly distributed "report cards" may encourage hospitals to take steps internally to improve the quality of the care they provide.

> **CONCEPT 2.3**
>
> Despite spending increasing amounts on health care in the United States, substantial problems remain in the quality of our care. Efforts to improve quality focus on evidence-based medicine, rewarding high-quality care, and monitoring the quality of care through "report cards" and accreditation standards.

The Joint Commission on Accreditation of Healthcare Organizations (JCAHO) is the principal body nationally that monitors hospital performance directly and sets standards for hospital accreditation. In 2002, JCAHO implemented a new program of quality improvement based on standardized performance measures. Williams et al. (2005) reported that these new standards were associated with significant improvement in the quality of care for diseases such as heart disease and pneumonia.

Following the publication in 1999 of *To Err Is Human*, Congress directed AHRQ to study the issue of health care quality and to issue an annual report of its findings. The National Healthcare Quality Report for 2009 (Agency for Healthcare Research and Quality 2009) identified three main themes that needed attention in order to attain the goal of higher-quality health care:

1. "Health care quality needs to be improved, particularly for uninsured individuals, who are less likely to get recommended care."
2. "Some areas merit urgent attention, including patient safety and health care-associated infections (HAIs)."
3. "Quality is improving, but the pace is slow, especially for preventive care and chronic disease management."

AHRQ will continue to monitor the issue of health care quality, and will issue reports on a regular basis regarding our progress toward meeting established quality goals.

## THE GROWING NUMBER OF UNINSURED AMERICANS

The two aspects of the U.S. health care system discussed above that make us unique in the developed world—approaching health care as a market commodity and the amount of GDP spent on health care—have led to a third characteristic of our system that is also unique: the large segments of our population living without health insurance. Health care has become so expensive that fewer and fewer people can afford basic health insurance. In 2009, 50.7 million people in this country were without health insurance for the entire year. Despite two national programs to provide health insurance to children from low-income families, this number included more than 7.3 million children (data from U.S. Census Bureau website). For those under the age of 65, more than one person in six was unable to afford insurance. California had one in five residents without health insurance; Texas had more than one in four residents without insurance. In families earning less than $25,000 per year, 24.5 percent of people were uninsured, even after taking into account government-financed insurance through the Medicaid program for poor families. In families earning between $25,000 and $50,000 per year, 21.4 percent of people were without health insurance.

During much of the twentieth century, little attention was paid to the issue of the uninsured. Most physicians would take care of some poor and uninsured patients for free. Physicians would often include a number of these "charity cases" in their practice, in a manner similar to lawyers taking certain cases "pro bono." As described above, the ethics of the medical profession expected physicians to provide this type of care. With the rising cost of medical care, and with the advent in the 1960s of government programs to pay for care for the poor and the elderly, the "charity patient" tradition has largely been abandoned by U.S. physicians.

Who are the uninsured? It is easy to think of them as chronically poor people who do not work and who rely on government welfare for their existence. This picture could not be further from the truth. Unemployed or homeless individuals make up only a small part of the uninsured. Seventy-two percent of adults between 18 and 64 without health insurance in 2008 worked either part-time or full-time during the year. They are the workers in low-wage jobs, often in small companies that do not offer health insurance to their workers.

A full-time worker can be uninsured for one of three reasons (Kaiser Family Foundation 2009):

1. The person works for a company that does not offer health insurance to any of its workers. (In 2009, only 60% of firms offered health insurance benefits to their workers.)

2. The company offers health insurance, at least to some workers, but the worker is not eligible for the company-sponsored plan. (In 2009, 19% of workers in companies that offered health insurance benefits were ineligible for those benefits.)

3. The company does offer health insurance and the employee is eligible; however, the worker chooses not to sign up for the plan, due to the share of the plan cost he or she must pay. (In 2009, 19% of workers eligible for health insurance benefits chose not to enroll in those benefits.)

For each of these categories, the lower the worker's wage, the more likely he or she is to be affected.

A factor that contributes to this disproportionate lack of insurance among lower-wage workers is the size of the firm employing the worker. The smaller the firm, the less likely it is to offer health insurance to its workers. Forty-six percent of firms with fewer than 10 employees offer health insurance to their workers, while 98 percent of firms with more than 200 workers do so. Accordingly, 31 percent of workers in firms with fewer than 25 workers were uninsured, while 10 percent of workers in firms with more than 500 workers were uninsured.

If one thinks of the jobs that involve low-wage workers and small firms, it should be clear that the service sector is a principal source of uninsured workers. Restaurants, small businesses, contractors, and similar types of firms often fail to provide health insurance for their workers. These types of firms play a crucial role in our economy, yet they have been hit especially hard by the rising cost of health care. Chapter 5 looks at the historical roots of our employment-based system of health insurance. We will see that the adoption of a system that relies on employers to bear most of the cost of health insurance was never fully thought out.

## THE HEALTH OF OUR SOCIETY: WHAT DO WE GET FOR OUR MONEY?

The United States pays more for health insurance than any other country, both per capita and as a percentage of GDP. What do we get for all the money we spend? One would hope that paying for so much health care would make our society one of the healthiest in the world. Nothing could be further from the truth. In comparing ourselves to other developed countries, we lag far behind in most of the broad indices that measure the overall state of a society's health.

Infant mortality is one of the most common indicators used to gauge the health of a

TABLE 2.3. Infant Mortality (infant deaths per 1,000 live births)
for Selected Countries, 2008

| Country | Percentage of GDP Spent on Health Care | Infant Mortality |
|---|---|---|
| Canada* | 10.4 | 5.1 |
| France | 11.2 | 3.8 |
| Germany | 10.5 | 3.5 |
| Greece | 9.7 | 2.7 |
| Japan | 8.1 | 2.6 |
| Sweden | 9.4 | 2.5 |
| Switzerland | 10.7 | 4.0 |
| United Kingdom | 8.7 | 4.7 |
| United States* | 16.0 | 6.7 |

*Source:* Data from OECD.
  *Data are for 2007.

nation. Infant mortality measures how many of 1,000 babies born alive will die before their first birthday. Infant mortality for selected OECD countries is shown in Table 2.3, along with the percentage of GDP each country spends on health care. In 2007, the United States reported an infant mortality rate of 6.7 deaths per 1,000 live births. This placed us in twenty-eighth position among OECD countries, worse off than countries such as Hungary, Poland, and the Slovak Republic. Only Mexico and Turkey reported worse infant mortality than the United States.

It should be apparent that there is little relation between how much a country spends on health care and the health of that society, as measured by infant mortality. Even though the United States spends nearly twice as much as Japan on health care, babies in the United States still die at more than twice the rate of babies in Japan.

Another common health index is life expectancy. Life expectancy can be measured in two ways:

1. Life expectancy at birth
2. Age-adjusted life expectancy (How long, on average, can a person who is a certain age today expect to live?)

Life expectancy, like infant mortality, is often used to measure the health of a society. It is usually reported separately for men and women, because biological differences between the sexes historically give women an advantage over men in longevity. How does the United States compare to other developed countries in this statistic? The answer is shown in Table 2.4.

In 2007, male babies born in the United States could expect to live, on average, 75.3 years, while females born the same year could expect to live 80.4 years. Of the thirty OECD countries, the United States ranked twenty-fourth for both male life expectancy and female life expectancy.

In addition to measuring life expectancy at birth, additional information about the health of a society can be obtained by looking at age-specific life expectancy: for adults who have attained a certain age, how many additional years can they expect to live on average? Table 2.5 compares the United States with the other developed countries shown in Tables 2.3 and 2.4. Using data from the OECD for 2006 (the last year complete data are available), it compares additional life expectancy in these nine countries for those who have reached age 40, age 65, and age 80.

The United States is ninth of these nine countries in life expectancy at birth. We also have the lowest additional life expectancy for both men and women at age 40. We are still in last place for men, and are eighth out of nine for women at age 65. The United States has risen to eighth place for both men and women at age 80.

It appears that a principal health benefit our society enjoys as a result of our heavy investment in health care, at least in terms of additional life expectancy, only starts to show up for our 80-year-olds. This is understandable, because the common causes of death for people in this age group—heart disease, cancer, and strokes—are often amenable to high-tech treatment. Because the United States has more health care technology available than any other country, it stands to reason that our oldest citizens should fare relatively well. At ages younger than 80, however, there seems to be little relationship between the amount we spend on health care and the health of our popu-

TABLE 2.4. Life Expectancy at Birth, in Years, for Selected Countries, 2008

| Country | Male | Female |
| --- | --- | --- |
| Canada* | 78.3 | 83.0 |
| France | 77.6 | 84.3 |
| Germany | 77.6 | 82.7 |
| Greece | 77.5 | 82.5 |
| Japan | 79.3 | 86.1 |
| Sweden | 79.1 | 83.2 |
| Switzerland | 79.8 | 84.6 |
| United Kingdom* | 77.6 | 81.8 |
| United States* | 75.3 | 80.4 |

Source: Data from OECD.
*Data are for 2007.

TABLE 2.5. Life Expectancy for Men and Women at Ages 40, 65, and 80 for Selected Countries

| Country | Men at Age 40 | Women at Age 40 | Men at Age 65 | Women at Age 65 | Men at Age 80 | Women at Age 80 |
| --- | --- | --- | --- | --- | --- | --- |
| Canada | 39.7 | 43.8 | 17.9 | 21.1 | 8.3 | 10.1 |
| France | 38.8 | 45.1 | 18.0 | 22.3 | 8.3 | 10.5 |
| Germany | 38.5 | 43.3 | 17.2 | 20.5 | 8.1 | 9.2 |
| Greece | 38.8 | 42.8 | 17.4 | 19.6 | 7.9 | 8.1 |
| Japan | 40.3 | 46.7 | 18.5 | 23.4 | 8.5 | 11.3 |
| Sweden | 39.9 | 43.7 | 17.6 | 20.8 | 7.6 | 9.4 |
| Switzerland | 40.7 | 45.2 | 18.5 | 22.1 | 8.3 | 10.3 |
| United Kingdom | 39.0 | 42.7 | 17.4 | 20.1 | 8.0 | 9.4 |
| United States | 37.6 | 41.7 | 17.0 | 19.7 | 7.8 | 9.3 |

Source: Data from OECD.
Notes: For a person who has attained the specified age, the table shows how many more years that person can be expected to live. Data are for 2006.

lation. (The reader should note that for all ages, and for both men and women, life expectancy is better in Canada than it is in the United States. This fact will be of particular relevance when we compare the U.S. and Canadian systems of health care in the following chapter.)

As we have seen so far, it is difficult to compare the quality of national health systems when different measures of quality give such disparate rankings. To reconcile some of these differences, the World Health Organization (WHO) combined eight different measures to create a single measure of the overall quality of a nation's health system. Using this combined measure, the United States ranked thirty-seventh in the world (World Health Organization 2000). Two more recent studies arrived at similar conclusions. Comparing the United States to five other developed countries in areas such as cost, access, and quality, Davis et al. (2007) found the United States last of the six. In a comprehensive review of studies comparing U.S. health care with that of other developed countries, Docteur and Berenson (2009) concluded, "on the basis of this review it is safe to say that the U.S. is not pre-eminent in quality."

> **CONCEPT 2.4**
>
> The United States spends more on health care than any other country in the world. Despite this high level of expenditure, we have one of the lowest levels of overall health of any developed country.

## WHAT DETERMINES THE OVERALL HEALTH OF A SOCIETY?

It should by now be clear that, at the level of the society, health and health care are not the same thing. Using the above indicators, we find little if any correlation between the amount spent on the health care system and the health of a society. As the country spending by far the most, the United States still has health indices close to the worst. The only exception is in the survival of our 80-year-olds, and this difference is relatively small.

Rather than the amount of money spent on health care, other factors largely determine the overall health of a society. Principal among these factors is overall standard of living, typically measured by per capita income and the average level of education in a society. Victor Fuchs, one of the founders of the study of health economics, has repeatedly emphasized this relationship: "The basic finding is the following: when the state of medical science and other health-determining variables are held constant, the marginal contribution of medical care to health is very small in modern nations . . . For most of man's history, [per capita] income has been the primary determinant of health and life expectancy—the major explanation for differences in health among nations and among groups within a nation" (Fuchs 1986, pp. 274–76).

An excellent example of the ways in which social class and standard of living affect health independently from health care is seen in Great Britain. The Whitehall study looked at the health of people working in the British Civil Service (Marmot and Theo-

rell 1988). Because Britain has had universal health coverage and a nationalized health system since World War II,
all members of the Civil Service have access to basically
the same level of health care. Thus, differences in health
care cannot explain differences in health.

The study found a clear correlation between occupational category (and therefore education) and health.
There was a threefold difference in mortality between the
highest and the lowest ranks of the Civil Service. Even at
the upper ranks, the higher on the scale a worker was, the
lower the mortality he or she faced. This was true even though all subjects of the study

> **CONCEPT 2.5**
>
> Among developed countries, there
> is little correlation between the
> amount a country spends on health
> care and the overall level of health
> of that country. The health of a
> society has more to do with the
> level of education and income than
> it does with health care.

- worked in office jobs
- were regularly employed
- came from a relatively uniform ethnic background
- lived and worked in greater London

These data should not be taken to mean that, in the face of the growing cost of
health care in this country, there has been no improvement in overall health. Quite
the contrary, data from the last forty years show dramatic increases in health. In 1960,
when the United States spent 5.2 percent of GDP on health care, infant mortality was at
the level of 26 deaths per 1,000 live births; now it is 6.7. Male life expectancy was 66.6
years in 1960, compared to 75.4 years now. Female life expectancy went from 73.1 to
80.7 years. It is simply that, despite these improvements in overall health, the United
States still lags far behind other developed countries.

There is substantial suggestion that improvements in the level of health in this
country may be due more to lifestyle changes than to improvements in health care.
Studies from 1991 (Burke et al.) and from 2010 (Wijeysundera et al.) confirmed that
the substantial decline in the death rate from heart disease was related as much to
improved diet, exercise, and other lifestyle factors as it was to improvements in drugs
or surgical treatments.

Victor Fuchs provides an example of the importance of lifestyle issues in his book
*Who Shall Live?* (1983). He cited data for Nevada and Utah, two states with roughly
comparable populations in terms of ethnic background, socioeconomic status, education, climate, and availability of medical care. In the 1960s, infant mortality in Nevada
was 40 percent higher than in Utah, while life expectancy in Nevada was 40 to 50 percent lower than in Utah. If income, education, and medical care cannot explain these
differences, what can?

Cigarette and alcohol consumption was markedly lower in Utah, due largely to the
influence of the Mormon Church. Correspondingly, death rates from lung cancer and

cirrhosis of the liver were two to three times higher in Nevada than in Utah. Lifestyle factors in Nevada and Utah, rather than medical care, seem to have explained the different levels of health in the two states.

It appears that further increasing expenditures for health care cannot be expected to result in substantial improvements in the overall health of American society. Nonetheless, there has been a strong social movement to provide increased access for the uninsured. Providing health insurance to the one-sixth of our society that is uninsured will of course add to the overall cost of health care.

There has also been an equally forceful movement to restrain the cost of medical care. Thus, for years we have faced two powerful, opposing forces: the need to expand access to health care and the need to restrain costs of care.

## SUMMARY

For several decades the United States has faced three major policy challenges in the area of health care:

1. The rapidly rising cost of providing care has resulted in an increasing share of our national economy going to support our health care system. We spend more of our GDP on health care than any other country in the world, even though we trail most developed countries in measures of population health such as infant mortality and life expectancy.
2. Researchers have raised serious and continuing questions about the quality of the care provided by our doctors and our hospitals.
3. We have been confronted by a rising number of Americans with no health insurance and, as a result, seriously impaired access to care.

The roots of our three-part dilemma are nearly one hundred years old. Early in the twentieth century, our society elected to approach health care as a market commodity, available to those with the resources to pay for it. Physicians, working through their professional organizations to influence political and legal aspects of health care delivery, were able to attain a position of substantial power. They used that power for much of the twentieth century to ensure that health care remained a market good, with government playing a relatively minor role. At the beginning of the twenty-first century, we are confronting the policy consequences—cost, quality, and access—that evolved as a result of those earlier policy choices. ACA, signed into law in March 2010, was an important step in addressing these policy issues.

## HOW THE AFFORDABLE CARE ACT ADDRESSES THE ISSUES OF HEALTH CARE COST, QUALITY, AND ACCESS

In an Op-Ed published in August 2009, President Obama laid out four broad policy goals for health reform: (1) expanding the availability of health insurance to those who are uninsured; (2) controlling the cost of health care; (3) making Medicare more efficient in order to reduce costs; and (4) providing consumer protections against discrimination by health insurance companies based on a pre-existing illness or condition. In his targeting the issues of health care costs and access to insurance, Obama was addressing two of the three principal policy issues facing U.S. health care. In his Op-Ed remarks he also addressed the issue of quality by promising the American people that "we will make sure that no insurance company or government bureaucrat gets between you and the care you need" (Obama 2009b)

Once it was signed into law, ACA, in combination with the accompanying reconciliation act, largely carries out President Obama's stated goals. Starting in 2014, health insurance will become available to an estimated 32 million people who previously were uninsured. This expansion of coverage will take place through a combination of reform of the private market for health insurance and a major expansion of the existing federal-state Medicaid program. I describe these changes in more detail in Chapters 5 and 7. These expansions will result in nearly 95 percent of all Americans having health insurance coverage. Those remaining uninsured will typically be those working for small companies not required under the new law to provide health insurance to their workers and those residents who are undocumented. I discuss these issues in Chapter 11.

ACA addresses the issue of cost containment in two main ways: changes to the Medicare program (discussed in Chapter 6) and new sources of tax revenues (described in Chapter 5). While there seems to be broad consensus that ACA will meet the goal of expanding health insurance coverage, there is substantially less agreement as to whether ACA will be able to meet the long-term goal of constraining health care costs. A report issued in September 2010 by the chief actuary for the federal Center for Medicare and Medicaid Services predicted that, as a consequence of ACA, national health expenditures for the period 2010–19 would increase more than if ACA had not been passed, with expenditures rising to 19.6 percent of GDP by 2019, rather than the previously predicted amount of 19.3 percent (Sisko et al. 2010). I discuss the long-term issue of health care costs in more detail in Chapter 14.

ACA addresses the issue of maintaining the quality of health care in two principal ways. The first is through an expansion of primary care services through a restructuring of the way primary care is delivered, described in Chapter 4. The second is through a major expansion of CER. CER will bring a major new focus to the issue of comparing the costs and clinical outcomes of alternative ways of approaching the diagnosis and treatment of illness. CER, if successful, will shift the definition of "quality" in medical care from one that focuses on whether a treatment is newer or more high-tech, to one focusing on how well the treatment actually works in the context of its comparative costs. In Chapter 13 I describe CER and the related issue of whether balancing costs with clinical outcomes constitutes health care "rationing."

# Health Care as a Reflection of Underlying Cultural Values and Institutions

## THE CULTURAL BASIS OF HEALTH CARE: COMPARING THE UNITED STATES AND CANADA

In 1932, Walton H. Hamilton wrote that "the organization of medicine is not a thing apart which can be subjected to study in isolation. It is an aspect of culture, whose arrangements are inseparable from the general organization of society" (Hamilton 1932, p. 190). Hamilton was responding to the Report of the Committee on the Costs of Medical Care, described in Chapter 1. This statement, made almost eighty years ago, still rings true in our examination of health care in the United States in the twenty-first century. To understand a nation's health care system, we must first understand the social and cultural norms and values around which that nation is organized.

To appreciate fully how the health care system in the United States reflects our unique American value system, we will first look to our neighbors to the north. Using Canada and its health care system as a mirror, we will see how differences in the organization of health care in our two countries reflect differences in the basic institutions around which our systems are organized.

It is important to recall that the American Revolution involved fourteen colonies, not just the thirteen that eventually became the United States. In some of the earliest fighting of the war, revolutionary armies captured Montreal and laid siege to Quebec. This revolutionary activity was short-lived, however, and what is now Canada remained under British rule. For many in the "fourteenth" colony of Canada, life after the Revolution seemed more attractive south of the border in the newly independent colonies. Many of those in Canada who supported the Revolution migrated south.

Similarly, loyalists living in the successful, now-independent thirteen colonies thought life would be better either north of the border in Canada or back in England. Thus, in the aftermath of the American Revolution, there was a cultural migration, with those supporting the British Crown moving north and those in Canada supporting "life, liberty, and the pursuit of happiness" moving south.

Lipset (1990, p. 2) summarizes the fundamental similarities and differences between U.S. and Canadian societies. Speaking of the cultural differences that arose from the time of the American Revolution, he reminds us that "the very organizing principles that frame these nations, the central cores around which institutions and events were to accommodate, were different. One was Whig and classically liberal or libertarian—doctrines that emphasize distrust of the state, egalitarianism, and populism . . . The other was Tory and conservative in the British and European sense—accepting of the need for a strong state, for respect for authority, for deference."

In the United States, school children study the Declaration of Independence and learn that our society continues to be organized around the principles of "life, liberty, and the pursuit of happiness." Canadian children also learn about the founding principles of their country. In the British North America Act, the act that created the Dominion of Canada, they find that the role of the Canadian government is to assure "peace, order, and good government." Lipset (1990, p. 3) describes the fundamental differences between these two founding documents: "The Canadian Charter of Rights and Freedoms is not the American Bill of Rights. It preserves the principle of parliamentary supremacy and places less emphasis on individual, as distinct from group, rights than does the American document."

Since the American Revolution, the United States has been a country that puts primacy on the rights of individuals. Social justice is most often defined in terms of the individual. In the United States, conflicts between individual needs and group needs tend to be resolved in favor of the individual. Canada, on the other hand, has a strong social democratic tradition, a tradition of redistribution so as to maximize the common good. Canadians have come to accept and expect social policies that embody this individual-group relationship. In Canada, conflicts between individual rights and group rights tend to be resolved in favor of the common good. Table 3.1 summarizes these differences between U.S. and Canadian societies. To see how these cultural differ-

TABLE 3.1. Cultural Differences between the United States and Canada

| United States | Canada |
|---|---|
| Distrust of central government | Accept the need for strong central government |
| "Life, liberty, and the pursuit of happiness" | "Peace, order, and good government" |
| Justice often defined in terms of what is good for the individual | Justice often defined to maximize the common good |

ences are reflected in our health care systems, we first examine the history of Canadian health care, followed by a parallel examination of the history of U.S. health care.

## THE HISTORY OF MEDICAL CARE IN CANADA

The British North America Act of 1867 created the Dominion of Canada. In it, responsibility for managing the delivery of health care was explicitly vested in the provinces rather than the central government. This separation of powers for health care issues remains in place today.

Canada took a serious look at establishing a national system of health care following World War I. At that time, several provinces granted statutory authority for municipalities to become directly involved in the provision of medical care. During the period of the Depression, these "municipal doctor" plans, in which local governments hired physicians to provide care to area residents, became an increasingly important source of medical care. This was especially true in the rural, agricultural provinces (Meilicke and Storch 1980).

In 1943, the report of a governmental Economic Advisory Committee recommended that a national program of medical insurance be established. It was to have been part of a larger social insurance program also covering unemployment insurance and old age security. Despite the support of both the Canadian Medical Association and the Canadian Hospital Council, the program did not become law, the result principally of the failure to achieve a financing mechanism that adequately preserved perceptions of provincial autonomy.

As a largely rural province with a widely scattered population especially hard hit by the Depression, Saskatchewan faced a particularly pressing need for governmental support of medical care. In 1944, Saskatchewan elected a populist government by giving a large legislative majority to the Cooperative Commonwealth Federation (CCF). In the face of the earlier defeat of the proposed national health care program, one of the first priorities for the CCF in Saskatchewan was to bring provincial government support to the financing of hospital care. The Saskatchewan Hospital Services Plan was passed in 1946, establishing a universal, compulsory hospital care insurance system. The program did not cover physicians' fees.

Despite increased rates of hospital use and costs in excess of initial estimates, the Saskatchewan plan maintained popular support. By 1950, three other provinces had established similar hospital insurance programs. It was only a matter of time before the others would follow. In 1957, the federal government of Canada adopted the Hospital Insurance and Diagnostic Services Act, establishing a national program of universal, compulsory hospital insurance, based on the Saskatchewan model. The program established three important principles:

1. Shared financing between the federal and the provincial governments that partially compensated for economic inequities between provinces
2. Provincial administration of the plan
3. Federally established minimum standards of participation

Saskatchewan, having previously financed hospital care solely from provincial funds, again took action that was to have national impact. The sudden addition of federal hospital funds enabled the CCF government to extend their medical insurance program to include physician care. In 1962, the province established the Saskatchewan Medical Care Insurance Plan, creating a universal, compulsory medical care system, with the provincial government maintaining a monopsony over the purchase of all medical care. (While a monopoly is an economic system with only one provider of a good, a monopsony is a system with a single payer for a good.) The plan was financed by a compulsory enrollment premium for all provincial residents. It maintained the fee-for-service method of paying physicians, but established the principle that physicians must accept payment from the plan as payment in full (that is, the physician was not allowed to bill the patient for any additional amount).

> **CONCEPT 3.1**
>
> A monopsony is an economic system that has a single payer for a set of goods or services. The Canadian health care system is an example of a government monopsony in health care, sometimes called a "single-payer" system.

The concept of government monopsony was stridently opposed by the Canadian Medical Association, its Saskatchewan division, and the American Medical Association (AMA) south of the border. (The role of the AMA in actively opposing national health insurance in Canada is seldom fully appreciated.) Nonetheless, the Saskatchewan plan was enacted over the objections of the medical profession.

On July 1, 1962, physicians in the Saskatchewan Medical Association went on strike, refusing to participate in the plan. Leaders of the association contended that "the preservation of the basic freedoms and democratic rights of the individual is necessary to insure medical services to the people of Saskatchewan" (Taylor 1987, p. 278). Saskatchewan physicians were seen as the shock troops of the medical profession, fighting the battle against governmentally imposed medical insurance on behalf of the entire Canadian medical profession. They received strong support from the AMA in the United States, which was adamantly opposed to the plan. The AMA attempted to convey a sense of crisis to the physicians and public in Saskatchewan.

While there was some support for the strike within Saskatchewan, it received little backing from the rest of Canada. To many people, the striking physicians were seen not as altruistic professionals but as lawbreakers. By July 23, a little more than three weeks after the strike had begun, the medical profession and the government reached a compromise, and the strike was called off. The Saskatchewan Agreement created a role for private insurance companies as fiscal intermediaries, allowing physicians to bill an insurance company for their services with the insurance company being reimbursed by the government. In return, physicians agreed to accept plan payment as payment in full. In addition, the Saskatchewan government promised not to establish a salaried government medical service.

In 1964, the Royal Commission on Health Services, established by the federal government to study the issue of national health insurance, recommended that Canada set up a national program of medical care similar to Saskatchewan's. The commission's goal was to make care "available to all our residents without hindrance of any kind" (Royal Commission on Health Services 1964, p. 10). It proposed federal financial assistance for provincially administered programs. Initial response to the report was mixed. Several provinces opposed further extension of government authority over health care, supporting instead a market-based program of insurance subsidies for low-income individuals and families, as had been proposed by the Canadian Medical Association.

The Liberal Party in Canada had first made a commitment to a program of national health insurance as early as 1919. In 1965, the Liberals came to power on a widely supported platform that included establishing a national system of medical care. Under the leadership of Lester Pearson, the party pushed for such a program. In contrast to the legislative system in the United States, in a parliamentary government such as Canada's the prime minister is able to exert considerable influence over the legislative process. Pearson pursued and, despite the opposition of several provinces, in December 1966 achieved passage of the national Medicare program. Provincial participation was to be voluntary; participation, if adopted by the provinces, would result in federal payment of approximately one-half of the cost of the program. For a provincial program to qualify, it had to be comprehensive, universal, publicly administered, and portable across provinces. (A fifth principle of accessibility was added later.)

The Canadian Medicare program went into effect in 1968. The lure of a 50 percent federal cost subsidy proved to be powerful. By 1971, all ten provinces had qualifying programs, creating on a national scale the same government monopsony over the purchase of medical care that had been established in Saskatchewan. Over a period of three years, and with widespread popular support, the private market for medical insurance in Canada was effectively eliminated.

The Canadian Medicare program did not adopt a specific model for the organization or delivery of care. It was solely a financing mechanism, leaving the delivery of care to physicians and the provinces. The federal government simply agreed to reimburse 50 percent of the cost of care to any province that created a plan meeting the guiding principles. In this regard, despite some who characterize the system incorrectly, Canada does not have a system of socialized medicine. Socialized medicine involves direct government involvement in the actual provision of care through policies such as the ownership of hospitals or the employment of physicians. Hospitals in Canada are mostly privately owned. Most physicians in Canada are private, independent practitioners.

When Canadian Medicare was passed by Parliament, physicians in the province of Quebec went on strike in opposition to the plan. In Quebec, there were two separate provincial medical associations: one for general practitioners and one for specialists. The association of specialists wanted their members to be able to opt out of the plan on a case-by-case basis, billing patients directly and allowing patients to seek reimbursement from Medicare. (Those familiar with the Medicare program in the United States, discussed in Chapter 6, will note that the payment mechanism sought by the specialists in Quebec was precisely the mechanism adopted by the U.S. program only a few years earlier. The influence of the AMA on Canadian physicians' opposition to Canadian Medicare is clear.)

The specialists in Quebec voted to strike rather than participate in Medicare. In early October 1970, they held a large rally in opposition to the plan. The leaders of the specialists spoke at that rally and criticized Medicare as a "threat to liberty, freedom, and quality of care" (Taylor 1987, p. 404). The executive vice president of the AMA traveled north to speak at this rally. He supported the strike and assured any specialists who chose to do so that they could move south and establish their practices in the United States. (One should note that the cultural values espoused by the physician leaders of the Quebec strike—"liberty, freedom, and quality of care"—are more consistent with the organizing principles of U.S. society than with the organizing principles of Canadian society. See Lipset's comments above.)

René Lévesque, at that time leader of Le Parti Québécois and later premier of Quebec, publicly criticized the physicians' strike. In doing so, he stated the following principle of Canadian society: "Organized medicine derives its power from the state, and the fact that the state has granted it a monopoly on such an indispensable service involves the responsibility to make that service available" (quoted in Taylor 1987, p. 404).

Despite government opposition, the specialists did go on strike on October 8. They refused to provide any care except for emergency cases. The Canadian press voiced a common criticism of the striking physicians, characterizing them as "operating in a social vacuum" (Taylor 1987, p. 408). Pierre Trudeau, then the prime minister of Canada, was explicit in his condemnation: "Those who would defy the law and ignore the opportunities available to them to right their wrongs, and satisfy their claims, will receive no hearing from this government. We shall ensure that the laws are respected" (quoted in Taylor 1987, p. 409).

On October 10, in an act unrelated to the Medicare controversy, Quebec's minister of labour was kidnapped and later murdered by radical separatists. Amid concerns of potential civil insurrection, the specialists called off their strike without gaining any of their demands. On November 1, Quebec Medicare began without incident, with full participation of the specialists.

Following an initial leveling of medical care costs in the period immediately following enactment of Medicare, rapid increases in the mid-1970s led to a growing concern that the costs of the program were unacceptably high, and rising. The share of Canadian gross domestic product (GDP) going to health care began to rise in ways similar to the rise seen in the United States. The federal government of Canada recognized that it needed to make future medical care costs more predictable, while the provinces wanted more direct control of financing. Accordingly, in 1977, a new arrangement was negotiated. In exchange for transferring a portion of its taxing authority to the provinces, the federal government's share of program costs was reduced from 50 percent to approximately 25 percent. In addition, future increases in the federal contribution would be limited to actual increases in GDP. Under the new formula, 100 percent of new costs exceeding the corresponding population/GDP increase would be borne by the provinces. The provinces went from being responsible for only fifty cents of every dollar spent on health care to facing responsibility for one hundred cents on the dollar for any increases in the cost of care that exceeded the growth in GDP. This limitation had a powerful effect, leading to more stringent efforts at cost control throughout Canada. For the following several years, medical care costs as a percentage of GDP were stable. As shown in Figure 3.1, it was largely in this period that the gap developed between Canada and the United States in percentage of GDP going to health care.

An important modification to the original Medicare program was passed in 1984. Even though Medicare created a government monopsony on the purchase of medical care, many physicians continued the practice of "balance billing," charging patients a fee over and above the established Medicare payment. In the eyes of the Canadian government, balance billing was contrary to the principles of universality and accessibility. Led by the Ontario Medical Association, many physicians clung tenaciously to this last vestige of individual entrepreneurship. In response, the government passed the Canada Health Act in 1984. While not outlawing balance billing, it mandated that, for every dollar of balance billing that occurred in a province, the federal allocation to that province would correspondingly be reduced by a dollar.

The Ontario Medical Association, adamantly opposed to the act, organized a physicians' strike to protest the new restrictions. Its president contended that "today's physicians believe we have a solemn duty to preserve the professional freedom that has been handed down from generation to generation for 5000 years. It is unthinkable to us that

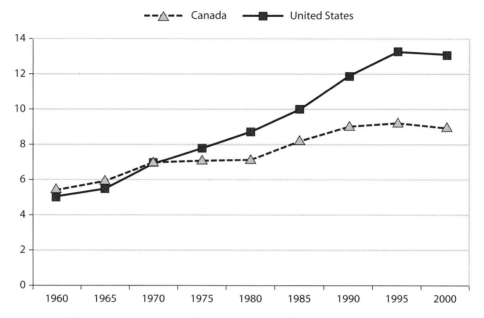

FIGURE 3.1. Changes in the Percentage of GDP Going to Health Care in Canada and the United States, 1960–2000. *Source:* Data from OECD

our profession's traditions, honored through the ages without the benefit of legislation, could be struck down in a modern society that has enacted a Charter of Rights and Freedoms" (quoted in Taylor 1987, p. 460).

Representatives of the Ontario government responded, "When the state grants a monopoly to an exclusive group to render an indispensable service it automatically becomes involved in whether those services are available and on what terms and conditions" (quoted in Taylor 1987, p. 460). With little support in the media, the strike was called off after twenty-eight days. As was the case in Saskatchewan twenty-two years earlier and Quebec fourteen years earlier, the Ontario physicians' strike achieved neither widespread public support nor its stated goals.

By now it should be clear that in Canada, the power of physicians and their professional associations is substantially limited, both by law and in the eyes of the public. Consistently, when physicians went on strike to protest the implementation of new health care initiatives, they were seen as violating their obligations to Canadian society. Those obligations resulted from the authority granted them over the clinical practice of medicine.

## The Organizing Principles of the Canadian Health Care System

From this examination of the Canadian health care system, it is possible to identify four principles around which it is organized.

*1. Health care is a basic right of all Canadians.*

Canada has made a social commitment to the concept that health care is a right of all citizens. Based on this right, the payment for health care is through taxes, with no direct connection between receiving care and paying for care.

*2. The power of the medical profession is limited by its social obligation.*

The medical profession derives its monopoly authority over the practice of medicine from the state, and has a responsibility, in return, to participate in and cooperate with programs established by the government.

*3. The government retains monopsony power over the payment for health care (that is, Canada's is a "single-payer" system).*

The success of the program depends on the monopsony power of the state. No other purchasers of health care (that is, private insurance companies) are allowed.

*4. There is one standard of health care for all Canadians.*

All people in Canada, regardless of income or social position, receive essentially the same level of care. (There is an important exception to this principle, discussed below.)

Based on these principles, Canada has maintained its level of national expenditure for health care at between 9 and 10 percent of GDP for more than two decades. During this same time, U.S. spending grew from less than 12 percent of GDP to more than 16 percent. How is it that Canada has been able to keep its expenditures so low relative to those in the United States? Most of the provinces have instituted a series of fiscal policies that ensure that rises in health care expenditures parallel rises in GDP. These policies include

- a yearly, global budget for physician fees, with fee levels negotiated between the government and physicians so as to stay within the budget
- fixed annual budgets for all hospitals
- government requirements that all capital expenditures for new hospital facilities and new technology (such as MRI machines) be separately approved and financed

> **CONCEPT 3.2**
>
> The Canadian health care system is based on the following principles of social policy:
>
> - Health care is a basic right of all Canadians.
> - The power of the medical profession is limited by its social obligation.
> - The government retains monopsony power over the payment for health care (that is, Canada has a "single-payer" system).
> - There is one standard of health care for all Canadians.

While these fiscal policies have been successful in holding down the cost of the system, they have had an important consequence for Canadians seeking care: queuing. Queuing refers to the need for many patients to go on a waiting list before receiving certain types of test or treatment. Once referred by their physician, people often have to wait many months before obtaining an MRI or other types of test that rely on expensive technology. The policy of holding down expenditures for these technologies has resulted in their short supply relative to demand. Similarly, patients referred for surgical procedures such as heart bypass, cataract removal, or hip replacement (all elective procedures that do not carry a major risk if delayed) may be scheduled for surgery months in the future. Generally, careful attention is paid to assure that patients in urgent need of these procedures are put in the front of the line, although budgetary problems that developed in the 1990s opened this principle to question.

Despite the spending controls that were part of their system, the cost of medical care in Canada continued to escalate throughout the 1980s. Faced with mounting economic problems at both the federal and provincial levels, many of the provincial plans began to experience severe shortages of both personnel and facilities in the mid-1990s. Newspaper and television reports documented increasing waits for services—often needed ones such as emergency room care or biopsies of possibly cancerous breast lumps. Public support for the health care system declined substantially; whereas 61 percent of the population rated the system as excellent in 1991, only 24 percent rated it as excellent in 1999 (Iglehart 2000).

The principle behind queuing for care in Canada is that, in allocating scarce health care resources, those resources will go first to those in the greatest need, measured in terms of the risk to their life or health. Those with lesser need must simply wait their turn. Here is where the Canadian system of providing one level of care for all people breaks down somewhat. Nearly 90 percent of all Canadians live within one hundred miles of the U.S. border. For those waiting in the queue for an elective test or procedure, the option is always there of simply traveling to the United States (where health care is available as a market commodity) and paying cash to obtain the test or procedure. Given the expense involved, this option is realistically available to only the wealthiest Canadians. Thus, to a certain extent, Canada operates a two-tiered system. One tier is available to every Canadian, although it frequently results in queuing for expensive tests and procedures. The second tier is available without queuing to those few who can afford to travel to the United States and pay out of pocket. A study of the extent to which wealthy Canadians seek medical care in the United States, however, determined that "the numbers found are so small as to be barely detectible" (Katz et al. 2002, p. 20).

The rising level of concern over queuing, shortages of facilities, and inadequate care led the Canadian government to undertake an exhaustive review of their system of health care. In 2001, the federal government established the Commission on the Future of Health Care in Canada. It gave the commission the charge "to recommend policies and measures . . . to ensure over the long term the sustainability of a universally accessible, publicly funded health system, that offers quality services to Canadians and strikes an appropriate balance between investments in prevention and health maintenance and those directed to care and treatment" (Romanow 2002, p. iii). While the commission was asked to make serious recommendations about reforming the Canadian system of care, it was clear from the outset that Canada intended to maintain a "universally accessible, publicly funded" system, and that the central principle of the system was to remain a balancing of the costs and benefits of care.

Led by Commissioner Roy Romanow, the commission held extensive meetings with health policy experts, medical care providers, and ordinary Canadians. In November 2002, it published its report, which included a series of recommendations that fell into two general categories.

1. The Canadian system was underfunded, leading to shortages and waits that were not consistent with the level of quality Canadians deserve in their health care. To remedy the situation, the federal government should work with the provincial governments to invest additional public resources in health care, and to monitor over time that the health care system is adequately funded.

2. Canadians did not want to change the core structure or values of their system of health care. In the words of Commissioner Romanow, "Canadians have been clear that they still strongly support the core values on which our health care system is premised—equity, fairness and solidarity. These values are tied to their understanding of citizenship. Canadians consider equal and timely access to medically necessary health care services on the basis of need as a right of citizenship, not a privilege of status or wealth" (Romanow 2002, p. xvi).

Thus, while Canadians want the assurance that funds will be adequate to pay for needed care in a timely manner, they want to maintain the concept of equal care for all within fiscal limits established through open and public discussion.

While the Romanow Report, as it has come to be called, addressed most criticisms of the Canadian system, some Canadians remain opposed to certain aspects of that system. One of the issues that remain contentious is the relatively low level of payment for physician services. Recall that, as part of the financing mechanism in most of the provincial systems in Canada, a yearly budget is adopted to cover all physician services. Based on that budget, a provincial fee schedule is established by which physicians are paid for the services they provide. (Recall that all payment comes from the Provincial Health Plan.)

As has also been the case historically in the United States, a fee-for-service system of paying physicians tends to make constraining aggregate costs for physician care difficult. Under a fee-for-service system, in which the physician is able to charge separately for each service provided, there is a clear economic incentive for the physician to provide more care. When one aggregates this incentive across all physicians, it makes it difficult to stay within a global budget intended to cover all physician services. The solution established by most provinces in Canada has been to establish a global budget for all physician services within the province, and then to monitor the extent to which physicians in aggregate stay within that budget.

For several years, provinces found that the aggregate charges of their physicians exceeded the budget established for physician care. The policy response was to reduce the fee schedule for the following year, so as to stay within the established budget. The problem with this model is in what one might consider a natural response to reductions in the payment for a given service. If a physician does not want to sustain a reduction of income, she or he will need to increase the number of services provided—either seeing more patients or providing more extensive services to each patient. While, at the level of the individual physician, this response to reduced fees might seem reasonable, if one aggregates this change in practice across all physicians, there is again a problem at the provincial level. Despite the reduction in fees enacted to account for the budget excess in the previous year, the increased level of services will again cause the province to go over budget for physicians' care.

This response of the medical profession as a whole—to react to reduced fees by providing more care—has come to be called "churning." For several years running, a reduction in physicians' fees was followed by churning among physicians, leading inevitably to further reductions in fees. As we will see later in this chapter, patients in Canada have about 40 percent more visits to the doctor per year than patients in the United States, while doctors in the United States charge more than twice as much for the care they provide. The result is that physicians' incomes in Canada tend to be substantially lower than those in the United States. While Canada has been dealing with the issue of physician churning in response to reduced fees, only in the last several years have physicians in the United States faced the issue of a global budget for their fees—with precisely the same response as their Canadian colleagues. I discuss the issue of the sustainable growth rate (SGR) further in Chapter 6 when we look into the current problems confronting the U.S. Medicare system.

## Growing Pressure for a Two-Tier System in Canada

With the passage of the Canada Health Act in 1984, the Canadian federal government added a fifth core principle to their national system of health care: accessibility. As described by the act, "the intent of the accessibility criterion is to ensure that insured persons in a province or territory have reasonable access to insured hospital, medical and surgical-dental services on uniform terms and conditions, unprecluded or unimpeded, either directly or indirectly, by charges (user charges or extra-billing) or other means (e.g., discrimination on the basis of age, health status or financial circumstances)" (Health Canada 2009, p. 4).

The issue of "extra-billing" or "balance billing" had been largely settled by the failure of the 1984 physician strike in Ontario, discussed above. A growing number of physicians, however, began to develop private clinics for services such as outpatient surgery or radiology. While the physicians in these clinics would accept payment from the provincial health plan as payment in full for their services, they would also charge the patient a "facility fee"—an extra charge for the use of the clinic facilities. A 1995 ruling by Canada's minister of health stated, "the facility fees charged by private clinics for medically necessary services are a major problem which must be dealt with firmly . . . such fees constitute user charges and, as such, contravene the principle of accessibility set out in the *Canada Health Act*" (Marleau 1995).

Canada's federal government left it to each province to regulate private clinics and to report to the federal government any extra charges to patients levied by private clinics for "medically necessary services" that should have been provided without charge under the provincial health plan. The federal government would then deduct that amount as a penalty from the federal reimbursement to the province under the national health plan. While some provinces simply prohibited any private clinics, others permitted private clinics under certain circumstances. For example, British Columbia, Alberta, and Ontario elected to permit private facilities under certain circumstances.

With the numbers of these private clinics expanding, the provincial governments were sometimes lax in monitoring them for compliance with the federal prohibition of extra charges to patients (Lett 2008). The federal Health Ministry's 2009 report on compliance with the Canada Health Act found that "in 2008–9, the most prominent concerns with respect to compliance under the *Canada Health Act* remained patient charges and queue jumping for medically necessary health services at private clinics" (Health Canada 2009, p. 1).

Reports in the Canadian press provided examples of both the success of these private clinics in attracting affluent patients and the consternation of the Canadian public with these clinics. A June 18, 2007, *Montreal Gazette* news story ("Munro M. Layton Accused of Hypocrisy for Visiting Private Clinic") criticized Jack Layton, leader of the New Democratic Party, for "jumping the queue" and undergoing hernia surgery at a private clinic. The same story reported that the president of the Canadian Autoworkers union had jumped the queue to get an MRI of his leg. During the H1N1 flu epidemic of 2009, public health agencies in Toronto and Vancouver were reported to have given several thousand doses of the H1N1 vaccine to private clinics that only treated patients who had paid an "annual membership fee," thus allowing those affluent patients to jump the queue to obtain their vaccines (Howlett, Paperny, and Walton 2009).

A 2005 ruling by the Canadian Supreme Court added to Canada's ongoing national debate about the future role of private clinics in the Canadian health care system. In the face of ongoing shortages of facilities and queues for important services, a number of physicians have argued that they should be permitted to provide these services on a private basis. Allowing such practices would, of course, create a two-tier health care system: one tier for those willing to pay for private services and one tier for those unable or unwilling to pay privately and thus relying on those physicians and hospitals who participate in the provincial plan.

The province of Quebec had enacted a law prohibiting private clinics from operating. A family physician in Montreal filed a lawsuit against the provincial government, claiming that, by creating long waits for care and prohibiting people from buying care privately, the health care system in Quebec was violating both his and his patients' constitutional protections of "liberty, safety and security" (Krauss 2005). After losing in two lower courts, the physician appealed to the Supreme Court of Canada, and in 2005 the court ruled by a 4–3 margin in the physician's favor. In the province of Quebec (the court ruling applied only to Quebec), physicians are now permitted to set up a private medical care system in parallel to the publicly financed provincial system—the beginnings of a two-tier system.

Reaction throughout Canada to the court ruling was vocal. One newspaper commentator wrote, "The sacred trust—or sacred cow—of public-only medicine is finished . . . Canada will have more private health-care delivery. The only questions are when, where, and how much" (Simpson 2005). Roy Romanow, author of the Romanow Report, responded to the court decision by stating, "The evidence is overwhelming and clear: The two-tiering of health care represents a march backward in time, to when good health care depended on the size of one's wallet" (Romanow 2005). The debate over shifting the Canadian system to a two-tiered system is likely to go on for a number of years.

Most Canadians want to maintain their current system but invest more resources in that system to make care more generally available. The Canadian Medical Association commissioned a national poll of public opinion regarding the issue, and found that only 15 percent of Canadians were in favor of allowing the development of private-sector alternatives to Medicare (Picard 2006). Most Canadians want to maintain Canada's single-payer system that assures the same level of care for all Canadians. They want a system that provides better access to care and enhanced quality of care, however. Canada continues to struggle with providing full access to the "medically necessary services" required under its Medicare law, while also constraining the cost of its national system. It remains to be seen whether a two-tier system of care will evolve as a response to these conflicting priorities.

## THE HISTORY OF MEDICAL CARE IN THE UNITED STATES

While the health care system in Canada has evolved over the period of nearly one hundred years to its current form, the system in the United States was undergoing a parallel evolution, with a very different outcome. Looking back to the period surrounding World War I, we see progressive groups in the United States proposing a system of government-financed health care. While the AMA considered the issue, its affiliated state medical associations were clear and determined in their opposition to a publicly administered system. Enjoying the new legal protections that followed the publication of the Flexner Report in 1910, the medical profession was intent on consolidating its authority over medical care. By the 1930s, that authority had been firmly established. While towns and provinces in Canada were reacting to the Great Depression through a system of municipal physicians and hospitals, the medical profession in the United States was taking steps to make the private employment of physicians illegal. Even systems of paying for physician care through lump-sum payments, rather than fee-for-service payments, was deemed unethical by the AMA. (See Chapter 5 for further discussion of the implications of fee-for-service versus prepayment systems of paying for care.)

The power of the medical profession, both through the AMA and through affiliated state medical associations, was substantial. As described in Chapter 1, it was clear to Franklin Roosevelt that any attempt to include medical care as part of Social Security would arouse such opposition from the medical profession that it would make passage of Social Security unlikely. Harry Truman also faced the power of the medical profession to derail his attempts at reform. Despite the fact that his proposals left largely intact the private delivery system, Truman's plan was branded as "socialized medicine" by physicians and their political allies, and it was decisively defeated.

By 1960, the power of the U.S. medical profession had reached its peak, and the system of private, market-based, fee-for-service medicine had been firmly established. While private health insurance was becoming more widespread, the medical profession maintained substantial authority over how those private plans were structured. The principle had been firmly established that there was little role for federal or state governments in the health care system. That role was largely limited to providing care for poor patients in local city or county hospitals. Only in 1965, when Lyndon Johnson was recently elected as president with large Democrat majorities in both houses of Congress, was the federal government able to take its first steps into the medical care system through the enactment of the Medicare and Medicaid systems, discussed in Chapters 6 and 7.

## The Organizing Principles of the U.S. Health Care System

The principles around which the U.S. health care system has come to be organized stand in sharp contrast to those of the Canadian system. They reflect our society's view of the importance of the rights of the individual and of our general distrust of government programs.

*1. Health care is a market commodity to be distributed according to ability to pay. Other than basic emergency services, there is no acknowledged right to health care for those under 65 years of age.*

I discussed this principle in Chapter 2. It reflects a decision made during the early part of the twentieth century and continues to guide the distribution of access to care.

*2. For much of the twentieth century, power over the organization and delivery of health care was concentrated in the medical profession.*

Both state and federal governments relied on the medical profession to establish standards of education and licensure, guide medical ethics, define financing mechanisms for care, and control the ways in which hospitals are used.

*3. Government has historically had relatively little role in guiding our system of health care.*

Although government's role has increased in recent years due to its growing role in paying for care, throughout most of the twentieth century there was little in the way of government policy or programs intended to establish a national system of either providing care or paying for care.

*4. There is no uniform standard of care. The quality of care received often reflects the ability to pay.*

Ours has evolved into a multi-tiered health care system, with differing levels of quality at different tiers. Differences in quality reflect both differences in the training and skills of the physician and differences in access to care.

> **CONCEPT 3.3**
>
> The U.S. health care system is based on the following principles of social policy:
>
> • Health care is a market commodity to be distributed according to ability to pay.
> • Power over the organization and delivery of health care has historically been concentrated in the medical profession.
> • Government has historically had a relatively minimal role in guiding our system of health care.
> • There is no uniform standard of care. The quality of care received often reflects the ability to pay.

It should by now be clear that the system of care in the United States is quite different from that in Canada, reflecting fundamental cultural and historical differences between our two countries. This conclusion reinforces what is one of the principal messages of this text: to understand our health care system, it is necessary to understand the institutional forces unique to the United States that shape that system.

## THE CULTURAL INSTITUTIONS THAT DRIVE HEALTH CARE IN THE UNITED STATES

The concept of an "institution" refers to the rules a society adopts that create its social, political, and economic structure. To appreciate more fully the way culturally derived institutions shape our lives, consider the following examples.

- When meeting someone in this country for the first time, one typically offers a handshake. There are no written rules that say we must; nevertheless, failure to do so might be considered rude.

- When eating in a restaurant while traveling away from home, we typically leave a tip. Even though we may never be at that restaurant again and may never again encounter our server (thus not having to worry about how good the service will be the next time we are here), we still feel obliged to leave a tip. To not do so would be insensitive to the server.

- People often discuss "the institution of marriage," its pros and cons, and the way it has changed. Here they are talking about both the formal laws that govern marriage and the social roles people fill when married.

- In most circles, Stanford University is seen as a well-respected academic institution. In both the written rules that govern the education it offers and the unwritten rules that govern relationships among individuals and groups, the very character of the university is created.

What links all these U.S. institutions? What do they all have in common? To understand the answer to this question is to understand one of the key driving forces behind the problems we face in health care today.

Each example above represents rules of social interaction that most people understand and take largely for granted. Douglass North, a Nobel Prize–winning economist, described how institutions shape our social as well as our economic lives: "[Institutions] are a guide to human interaction, so that when we wish to greet friends on the street, drive an automobile, buy oranges, borrow money, form a business, bury our dead, or whatever, we know (or can learn easily) how to perform those tasks . . . Institutions may be created, as was the United States Constitution; or they may simply evolve over time, as does the common law" (North 1986, pp. 3–4).

Institutions can be formal, as in written laws, codes of ethics, and prescribed procedures, or they can be informal, such as common courtesy and the strength of family ties. Many institutions have both formal and informal aspects. Consider, for example, the medical profession. As discussed above, in this country the medical profession is commonly viewed as exercising authority over the use of specialized knowledge in ways that contribute to the social good. This perception arose informally over time. The widely held view of the medical profession led to the creation of laws that formalized this role, granting the profession autonomous authority over medical education, licensure, and practice.

Institutions have four defining characteristics (Scott 1987):

1. They are rules that guide behavior in certain situations.
2. The rules can be formal or informal.

3. Over time, those rules come to be taken largely for granted.
4. Disobeying the rules will invoke some sort of sanction, either formal or informal.

In one way, institutions tend to be socially efficient. They allow us to enter into situations without having to figure out from scratch what to do every time. Not all institutions turn out to be quite so efficient, however. Again quoting Douglas North: "Institutions are not necessarily or even usually created to be socially efficient; rather they, or at least the formal rules, are created to serve the interests of those with the bargaining power to devise new rules" (North 1986, p. 16).

Where do institutions come from? The process through which institutions are created has been characterized as "profoundly political and reflect[ing] the relative power of organized interests and the actors who mobilize around them" (DiMaggio 1988, p. 13). Economists, political scientists, and sociologists seem to agree that institutions often reflect—at least initially—the needs of powerful, organized interests. While institutions may reflect organized economic and political interests at their outset, however, they do not change easily or quickly even in the face of a changing economic or political context. Once established, institutions limit the opportunity for further changes in social policy over the course of a nation's history. Institutions "may assume a life of their own, a life independent of the basic causal factors that led to their creation in the first place" (Krasner 1983, p. 357). This is not to say that institutions do not change; rather, they change gradually, reflecting only changes in economic forces and social perceptions that persist over time.

In comparing health care in the United States and Canada, we find fundamental differences in policy. I identified two key policies that differentiate health care in the United States from that of Canada and other developed countries: (1) approaching medical care as a market commodity and (2) granting sovereignty to the medical profession over the organization and financing of care. In addition, I discussed how health care in Canada is organized around improving the common good, while health care in the United States is organized around the rights of the individual. These three differences in policy represent institutional differences that have developed out of the social and political differences between the United States and Canada. In the United States, these institutions tend to push up the costs of health care, while other institutional forces (for example, the American aversion to paying taxes) hold down the funds available to pay for health care. As a result, one person in six has no health insurance coverage.

## Protein Deprivation, Prime Rib, and Declining Marginal Returns

To understand more fully how institutional forces affect the cost of care, let us consider a basic principle of economics: the law of declining marginal returns. To illustrate this law, I offer the following story from personal experience.

One summer I was on a backpacking trip with my son in the Wind River wilderness in Wyoming. After seven days of hiking at high altitude, during which we survived mostly on freeze-dried food, nuts, and raisins, we came out of the wilderness and went in search of a real meal. I usually don't eat much red meat, but when we walked into the restaurant in the small town near the trailhead, the aroma of prime rib of beef hit us. Having been protein deprived during our trip, my digestive system cried out for a plate of prime rib. I gave in. Never have I enjoyed a meal quite so much as I enjoyed that prime rib. I would gladly have paid $50.00 for it. Fortunately for me, at that time it cost only $11.95.

Now, while I actually stopped at one plate, for the sake of discussion let us assume a clever waiter. Seeing how much I enjoyed the first plate, he might then have encouraged me to order a second. "After all, you enjoyed the first one so much, think how much you'll enjoy the second." So, I give in and order a second plate. I find that I derive substantially less enjoyment from the second than the first. While I would have paid $50.00 for the first plate, I wouldn't pay a penny more than $11.95 for the second.

The waiter then encourages me to order a third plate. Again I give in. While I did derive some benefit from eating the third plate, it was only a small benefit—say, $1.00 worth of benefit. The waiter starts to get very pushy and brings me a fourth plate. Not wanting to hurt his feelings, I begin to eat it, but part way through I get up, go into the rest room, and throw up everything.

This story seems on the surface a bit silly. What rational person would pay $11.95 for a plate of prime rib from which he derived only $1.00 worth of benefit? Even more, who would ever willingly pay for food that he knows will probably make him sick? And besides, what does this have to do with health care? To understand, let us create a graph describing my folly in ordering prime rib, as shown in Figure 3.2.

It should be clear that, consistent with the law of declining marginal returns, for each successive meal I order, I derive less benefit than from the previous meal (measured here in enjoyment and willingness to pay). It should also be easy to see that a person who is acting rationally would never order more than two meals. He or she would stop at the point where the marginal benefit equals the marginal return—often referred to as the point of indifference. Because the marginal cost and the marginal benefit are exactly the same, a rational person could choose either to accept or not to accept one more meal. This point—the intersection of the line of marginal costs and that of marginal benefits—is one definition of economic efficiency.

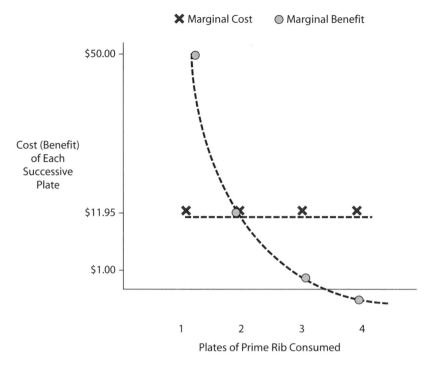

FIGURE 3.2. Relationship between Marginal Cost and Marginal Benefit When Eating Plates of Prime Rib

Let us stay with the law of declining marginal returns but move back to health care. While the issues are quite different, the principle is the same. Figure 3.3 illustrates the effect of declining marginal returns in health care. The graph can be used to represent decisions at the level of the individual patient or at the level of the health care system overall. For the individual patient, consider the example of a college student who falls down and twists her knee while playing recreational soccer. Her knee becomes somewhat sore and swollen. Her first decision is whether to go to the doctor for an exam, or simply wait to see what happens if she rests the knee and gives it a chance to heal. If she does go to the doctor, the first decision the doctor may face after performing an examination is whether to x-ray the knee to see if it is broken. (While it is unlikely an injury of this type will break a bone, it is possible.) Assuming the physical examination performed by the doctor shows no clear evidence of a torn ligament or torn cartilage and the X-ray is negative, should the doctor obtain an MRI just to be sure he is not missing anything? In the face of a negative MRI, should the doctor perform exploratory arthroscopic surgery, just to be absolutely sure nothing is wrong?

Here the physical exam represents Q1 on the graph, the X-ray represents Q2, the MRI is Q3, and arthroscopic surgery is Q4. The marginal benefit is measured as the increase in the probability the student's knee will be completely healed in six months. The one difference in this graph is that the cost of each successive test, rather than

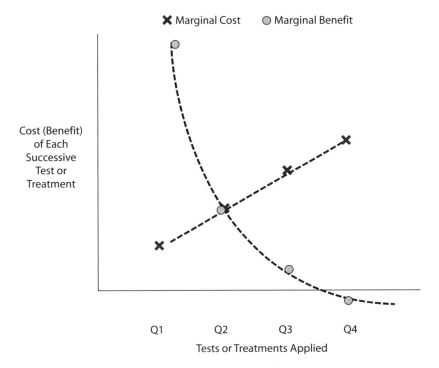

✕ Marginal Cost    ◯ Marginal Benefit

Cost (Benefit) of Each Successive Test or Treatment

Q1    Q2    Q3    Q4

Tests or Treatments Applied

FIGURE 3.3. Relationship between Marginal Cost and Marginal Benefit in Health Care

being constant, is increasing. How many tests should the patient obtain? In this example, the benefit derived from the physician's exam is more than the cost of the exam. The added benefit from the X-ray is approximately equal to its added cost. The chances of an MRI helping (given a negative exam and negative X-ray), while real and measurable, however, are less than its cost. Similarly, exploratory arthroscopic surgery not only may not help but also carries with it the chance of making the patient worse from a postoperative joint infection.

Where should a rational patient stop in obtaining tests or treatments? Where should a rational physician stop in ordering these procedures? These questions are answered differently in the United States and Canada, based on the different approaches to the tradeoff between the benefit to the individual and the benefit to society. In Canada, technology such as MRI is applied sparingly, because it is felt that the added benefit to society overall does not justify the added cost of making it more widely available. In the United States, we typically expect technology to be available to us, despite its position on the marginal cost/marginal benefit curves. It is not fair to the individual, we believe, to deprive her or him of the possible benefits of the test even though they are small compared to the cost.

As in the case of consuming prime rib, the point of intersection of the marginal cost/marginal benefit curves provides a measure of efficiency in the allocation of health care resources. In Canada, tests and procedures more closely approximate Q2 on the graph, where costs and benefits are about equal. In the United States, they typically are available all the way to Q3. (Some would say we sometimes reach Q4, providing some tests and procedures that are to the patient's detriment.) Our belief in the importance of making tests and procedures available to individuals even though the marginal costs substantially exceed the marginal benefits is uniquely American.

To illustrate, let me relate the story of a patient I took care of in my clinical practice. He was in his forties, a successful local attorney. He had twisted his knee playing sports and wanted my evaluation. After a thorough examination, I was able to determine that, in all likelihood, he had sprained a ligament in his knee without causing any permanent damage. I saw no evidence of a torn ligament or torn cartilage. Because he had simply twisted the knee and not fallen on it, the chance of a broken bone was remote. I chose not to get an X-ray, and I reassured him that he should soon have a full recovery.

"How can you be sure?" he asked. "Don't we need an MRI? Last time this happened, my doctor got the MRI right away, and even though it was negative, he went ahead and did arthroscopic surgery, *just to be sure* he hadn't missed anything. It was a good thing he did, too—during surgery he found a micro-tear in my cartilage and fixed it!"

Here was a well-educated, professional patient (an attorney, no less) whose previous doctor, in the face of a negative exam, negative X-ray, and negative MRI, had gone ahead and performed arthroscopic surgery. In doing so, he had subjected the patient to the risk of a serious joint infection with no reasonable benefit expected. I am convinced that the "micro-tear" the surgeon reported was simply a justification for having performed the surgery. I had not previously heard of "micro-tears" of the knee joint as a problem justifying surgery, but I was acutely aware that recent research reports had documented hundreds of thousands of unnecessary knee surgeries in the United States each year. Nevertheless, the patient considered my care—stopping at the exam to see if the knee healed—to be low-quality care and the care his previous surgeon had recommended to be high-quality care. To this patient, questions of marginal cost/marginal benefit had no relevance.

> **CONCEPT 3.4**
>
> In the United States, the value we as a society place on technology and technological advances encourages the development and use of high-tech medical treatments, even when the added benefit of these treatments is small compared to their cost.

In Canada, it is unlikely this patient ever would have seen an MRI machine.

## The "Technological Imperative" and Its Effect on Health Care

Why is the lure of an MRI or of high-tech surgery so powerful, for both the physician and the patient? As a society, we have come to put substantial faith in new technology, and we often measure the benefit of a test or treatment not only in its actual benefit (often measured in the cost of saving an additional year of life), but also in its perceived benefit. A large part of our resistance to reducing the use of expensive, new technologies is due to what Victor Fuchs (1983, p. 60) describes as "the 'technological imperative'—namely, the desire of the physician to do everything that he has been trained to do, regardless of the benefit-cost ratio." The technological imperative shapes what we define as "best medical practice." This perception, based to a large extent on the extensive use of technology so pervasive in academic medical centers, is "imprinted" on physicians during their medical school and residency training. Physicians learn to do all they feasibly can and tend to follow this institutional imperative throughout their career. Patients, in turn, tend to adopt the physician's perspective as the norm.

During the last several decades, most advances in medicine have been due to the technology we have been able to develop. New types of imaging devices such as MRI scanners, the use of fiber optics for both diagnosis and surgery, the use of lasers, and bioengineered medications all have had substantial impact on our ability to treat specific patients and specific illnesses. They have been so successful that we have come to equate technology with quality. We have a commonly held belief that the more technological a treatment is, the better it is. We also have come to believe that as patients we have not received complete treatment unless we receive the most advanced technology. Thus, physicians in the United States have a tendency to do everything that is possible, regardless of the cost/benefit ratio.

I would add to Fuchs's description a corollary institution that I refer to as the "technological benefit of the doubt." In comparing a new, high-tech approach to a problem with an older, low-tech alternative, we tend to expect the newer approach to be superior based on its use of advanced technology, even in the absence of empirical evidence to that effect. Take, for example, the prostate specific antigen (PSA) blood test, first introduced in 1987 as a screening test for prostate cancer. It was substantially more high-tech than the traditional method of screening for prostate cancer by digitally examining the prostate gland as part of a rectal examination. The PSA test was relatively expensive, and was shown early on to have a high risk of false-positive results. Early data suggested that widespread use of the test "may result in poorer health outcomes and will increase costs dramatically" (Krahn et al. 1994, p. 773). Nonetheless, the test became widely accepted and used before it was approved by the U.S. Food and Drug Administration and before data about its effectiveness became available. A poll reported in 1993 (Kolata 1993) found that 92 percent of physicians in one state used the test routinely on men over 50. By 2009, the PSA test had become a routine part of men's health care, with most men over the age of 50 getting the test despite a continuing lack of evidence that the test actually reduced prostate cancer death rates (Barry 2008).

In 2008, two large studies were published on the effect of PSA screening on death rates. One found no difference in death rates after 7 to 10 years of follow-up in men chosen randomly to be screened on a regular basis compared to men receiving their usual care (Andriole et al. 2009). Another found that after 9 years of follow-up, men screened with the PSA test had a reduction in the death rate of 0.71 deaths per 1,000 men screened (Schröder et al. 2009).

Both studies found that PSA screening identified the presence of prostate cancer more often than avoiding screening, typically leading to surgical removal of the prostate gland, a procedure that can have substantial side effects such as sexual impotence and urinary incontinence. By identifying and treating tumors in many men that would otherwise not have caused illness or death, the screening process led to substantially higher rates of these adverse outcomes, with resulting reduction in quality of life for the men affected. In the words of one commentator responding to the results of the studies, "I think that there is convincing evidence of harm . . . The two studies together show marginal to no benefit across several years of follow-up at the cost to so many men of overdiagnosis and overtreatment" (McNaughton-Collins 2009, p. 4).

Based on the available research results, the U.S. Preventive Services Task Force has recommended that "given the uncertainties and controversy surrounding prostate cancer screening in men younger than age 75 years, a clinician should not order the PSA test without first discussing with the patient the potential but uncertain benefits and the known harms of prostate cancer screening and treatment" (U.S. Preventive Services Task Force 2008, p. 186). For more than twenty years, physicians in the United States have routinely used a newer, more high-tech screening test on the faith it would reduce prostate cancer deaths, absent evidence that it actually did so. When the evidence finally came in, it showed little if any benefit of the test.

Physicians and patients seem to be willing to adopt newer, more expensive technologies on the faith that they will, in the future, prove to be superior to existing alternatives. Once they have been adopted, it is extremely difficult to go back and change established patterns of behavior that prove to have little scientific or economic justification.

As another example of the technologic benefit of the doubt, let us look at the way high blood pressure has been treated in the United States over the years. For a number of years, physicians had relatively few choices for the treatment of high blood pressure. The standard treatment was to give the patient a diuretic to reduce the salt and fluid balance in the body, thereby lowering blood pressure. In clinical trials involving comparisons to patients who received only dummy placebo pills, diuretics had been proven to be effective.

Calcium-channel blockers were a category of drug that became widely used in the 1980s. They too were shown to be effective in treating high blood pressure, when compared to treatment with a placebo. Then, in the 1990s, an even newer category of drug came into use—angiotensin-converting enzyme inhibitors, commonly referred to as ACE inhibitors. As with calcium-channel blockers, these were also proven to be effective, compared to treatment with a placebo.

Which medicine should a physician prescribe for the treatment of high blood pressure? When calcium-channel blockers became widely available, they largely supplanted diuretics as a first-line treatment. After all, they were newer, so they must be better. When ACE inhibitors became available, many physicians switched to using these. Again, as an entirely new class of drug, they were considered to be better than the older alternatives. The problem, of course, is that each successive new drug category is more expensive than the older alternatives. This is especially true when the newer drug is available only in its brand-name form. (See Chapter 9 on pharmaceutical policy for additional discussion of brand-name drugs, patent laws, and the cost of pharmaceutical products.) While treatment today with a diuretic pill might cost $10 to $15 per month, treatment with the newer ACE inhibitors or calcium-channel blockers can easily cost 5 to 10 times as much.

For more than two decades, physicians relied on the newer medicines to treat high blood pressure, without clinical evidence that they were better than the older diuretics. Each category had been proven effective when compared to treatment with a placebo, but no test had compared the efficacy of the three in a head-to-head trial. Then, in 2002, a large national team of researchers reported on just such a study. In what is called a "double-blind" trial—neither the patient nor the treating physician was told what was in the pill received—they studied patients with high blood pressure who were at high risk of complications. They compared the effectiveness of the three types of drugs in a number of ways. The main outcome of the study—whether the patient had a heart attack—was no different for any of the three medicines. In other measures of outcome, however, the diuretic proved to be most effective, leading the researchers to conclude that "diuretics are superior in preventing one or more major forms of [cardiovascular disease] and are less expensive. They should be preferred for first-step anti-hypertensive therapy" (ALLHAT Collaborative Research Group 2002, p. 2981).

In this case, physicians for years gave the technologic benefit of the doubt to the newer drugs. Only after a well-designed scientific study finally became available, directly comparing the clinical effectiveness of the available alternatives, did they learn that giving the newer alternatives the technologic benefit of the doubt had no added benefit in clinical outcomes but led to substantial increases in cost. Despite this evidence from the 2002 study, however, by 2008, only 40 percent of patients with hypertension were receiving a diuretic medication, compared to 30 to 35 percent of patients before the study was published (Pollack 2008). Once physicians give newer, high-tech treatments the technologic benefit of the doubt, it becomes extremely difficult to change their behavior.

## DIFFERING CULTURAL INSTITUTIONS AFFECT THE COST OF HEALTH CARE

We have seen that Canada spends about 10 percent of GDP on its health care system, while the United States spends more than 17 percent. It is not simply in limiting the availability of expensive care through long waiting lists, however, that Canada spends less than the United States. There are fundamental differences in the way physicians in the two countries practice medicine, with resulting differences in costs.

Victor Fuchs has done a number of studies comparing the patterns of care in comparable populations of patients in the United States and Canada (Fuchs 1993d). The results of these comparisons have a great deal to say about why health care costs so much more in this country than it does in Canada. Table 3.2 shows the pattern of care Fuchs found for physician services and hospital services. It shows the ratio of the United States to Canada in three areas: (1) expenditures on care, (2) prices of resources used in care, and (3) quantity of resources used.

Several patterns can be seen from these data. While people in the United States go to the doctor less often (28% less often than people in Canada) and are admitted to the hospital less often (9% less often than Canadians), we nonetheless spend a great deal more per patient per year (72% more for physicians' services and 26% more for hospital care). How is it that we use health care less frequently but spend a great deal more for the care? Part of the answer is the price of resources. Resources such as laboratory tests, medications, and supplies used in providing care in physicians' offices cost 30 percent more in the United States than comparable resources in Canada. The prices physicians charge for their services are nearly two-and-one-half times more than what Canadian physicians charge. Similarly, the resources used in providing hospital care cost somewhat more in the United States (4% more).

In addition to higher prices for resources in the United States, we find a clear pattern

TABLE 3.2. Comparison of the Use of Health Care Resources between the United States and Canada

| Services | Ratio of U.S. to Canadian |
| --- | --- |
| Physician services | |
| Health expenditures per capita | 1.72 |
| Physicians' fees | 2.39 |
| Prices of resources used in providing service | 1.30 |
| Number of services provided per capita | 0.72 |
| Quantity of resources used per service | 1.84 |
| Hospital services | |
| Hospital expenses per capita | 1.26 |
| Expenses per admission | 1.39 |
| Prices of resources | 1.04 |
| Hospital admissions per capita | 0.91 |
| Quantity of resources used per admission | 1.24 |

*Source:* Data from Fuchs 1993d.

of using more resources per service in the United States, for both physician care (84% more) and hospital care (24% more). This means that every time we go to the doctor or the hospital, we have more tests, X-rays, medications, and treatments than Canadians with similar conditions do.

## Differing Approaches to the Treatment of Heart Disease in the United States and Canada

For people with heart disease, especially those with clogged blood vessels due to coronary artery disease, there is always the risk that something will cause the normal heart rhythm to malfunction. When this happens, the result is often sudden death. Anyone who has watched a television show about hospitals or emergency rooms will know that the treatment is to try to shock the person back to life, using a defibrillator. Unfortunately, if a person is not in the immediate vicinity of a defibrillator and someone who knows how to use it, little can be done to prevent death due to a cardiac arrhythmia.

In the 1990s, physicians began using a new device to treat patients who might be at risk of sudden death from a cardiac arrhythmia. The device combined a small computer that can monitor the heart rhythm and determine if a life-threatening abnormality has begun and a stored electrical charge that, on command from the computer, will automatically deliver an electric shock to the heart. With advances in computer technology, these devices became small enough to implant surgically under the skin of a patient's chest.

The next question to be answered was whether these implantable cardiac defibrillators (ICDs) would be effective in saving patients' lives. In 2005, a major study appeared showing that, for patients with severe heart failure, having an ICD reduced the death rate after about four years from 29 percent of patients to 22 percent (Bardy et al. 2005). The results of this and other studies also carried with them some cautions. Some patients were found to have a difficult time with inappropriate, painful shocks being delivered by the devices, leading to a decrease in the quality of their lives. In addition, the cost of the devices was quite high—it might typically cost $50,000 to have one implanted.

Because many of the patients who might be helped by ICDs are 65 years old or older, the federal Medicare program is one of the principal payers for these devices. As we will see in Chapter 6, Medicare is facing rapidly increasing costs and concerns about the long-term fiscal viability of the program. To what extent should Medicare pay for the use of ICDs? Given that fewer than one in ten patients will actually be helped by them, should Medicare pay for ICDs only for the sickest patients, leaving some low-risk patients to suffer sudden cardiac death that might have been prevented by an implantable defibrillator? Alternatively, should ICDs be made more widely available to patients with heart disease, placing the lives of patients above economic concerns about the financial impact on the Medicare program?

These were the questions the health policy experts at the federal Centers for Medicare and Medicaid Services grappled with. In early 2005, they came down on the side of preventing as many deaths as possible, substantially widening the range of patients eligible for the devices (McClellan and Tunis 2005). As a result, the aggregate cost of using ICDs is expected to rise substantially. Based on the earlier research results, it will likely turn out that, while a relatively small number of patients are helped by them, for most patients the use of ICDs will make no difference in the course of their disease.

Despite the recent research studies, it simply is not possible to say with certainty which patients will be helped and which will not. To cover the few who will be helped, many who will not be helped will need to be treated, leading to substantially higher costs. This is the approach typically taken in the United States when a new device or treatment becomes available. It is the approach most compatible with our historic emphasis in the United States on the needs of the individual rather than on the needs of the social group.

How has Canada dealt with ICDs? In 1999, Canada convened a national Working Group on Cardiac Pacing to study the issue. This group issued a preliminary report in 2000. After the publication of further studies on the efficacy of ICDs, a national consortium of heart specialists published more detailed guidelines on the use of ICDs that recognized the usefulness of the devices and recommended a plan to make them more available to Canadians with heart disease. Recognizing that it is not possible to provide all care to all people in a health care system that must function under a fixed yearly budget, they outlined a careful approach based on the best available clinical evidence. Patients who were found by their primary care physician to be potential candidates for an ICD will be seen by two consulting specialists before a decision is made to use an ICD. They acknowledged that patient queues would develop in this process and recommended a careful monitoring program to assure that those queues do not become excessive. In addition, as is typically the case in Canada, they emphasized that the ordering of patients in the queues would be based on need—the sickest patients would always be in the front of the queue.

As a result of the more cautious approach Canada has taken compared to that of the United States, Canadian patients with heart disease receive far fewer ICDs than those in the United States. In 2003, 84 ICDs were used per 1 million people in Canada, while about 470 ICDs were used per 1 million people in the United States (*Canadian Journal of Cardiology* 2005).

The extent to which the disparity in the use of ICDs described above will affect death rates from heart disease in the two countries is yet to be determined. Recent

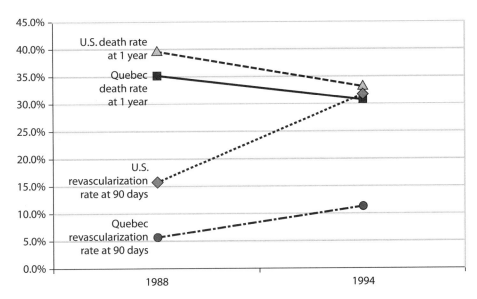

FIGURE 3.4. Comparing Treatment Rates and Death Rates in the United States and Quebec for Elderly People with Heart Attacks, 1988 and 1994. *Source:* Data from Pilote et al. 2003

comparisons of differences over time in the treatment of heart attacks in Canada and the United States, however, suggest that

- the overall reduction of death rates will be significant in both countries
- the reduction in death rates will be similar for both countries, despite the substantially greater use of ICDs in the United States

Pilote et al. (2003) were able to obtain the treatment records of all patients age 65 or older who were treated for a heart attack in either the United States or the Canadian province of Quebec. For these two patient populations, they compared the increase in the use of new, high-tech treatments for heart attacks and the death rate from heart attacks. They compared the percentage of patients with a heart attack who had a revascularization procedure (a procedure to open up the clogged blood vessels to the heart that had caused the heart attack) and the percentage of patients who died within one year of their heart attack. These data are shown in Figure 3.4. It can be seen that, between 1988 and 1994,

- the rate of revascularization approximately doubled in both countries
- revascularization was used approximately three times more often in the United States than in Canada at both points in time
- the death rate decreased for both countries by approximately the same amount
- the death rate was lower in Quebec than in the United States at both points in time

It appears that, while the substantially higher rates of revascularization in the United States undoubtedly helped some of the patients treated, the marginal benefit of the extra procedures was not large enough to show up in the overall death rate from heart attacks.

Despite these data showing little long-term benefit of revascularization procedures as measured by death rates, the frequency of diagnostic tests that often lead to revascularization has been growing in the United States. One reason is that these tests are being used increasingly in patients with a low likelihood of having clogged blood vessels in the heart (Patel et al. 2010). In response to this study, Brenner suggested that "it is appropriate to ask whether current coronary imaging techniques are being used optimally" (Brenner 2010, p. 943).

The editors of the journal *Health Affairs* suggested that there has been an "imaging boom" in U.S. health care, with the use of CT scanners, MRI scanners, PET scanners, and other similar devices proliferating over the past several years (*Health Affairs* 2008). Hillman and Goldsmith have argued that "an unknown but substantial fraction of imaging examinations are unnecessary and do not positively contribute to patient care . . . the evidence basis for using imaging is incomplete; much imaging practice is driven by habit or anecdote" (Hillman and Goldsmith 2010, p. 1).

In a commentary published in *JAMA*, Leff and Finucane refer to this explosion of high-tech imaging and other devices as "gizmo idolatry." They explain this concept as follows: "gizmo is used to refer to a mechanical device or procedure for which the clinical benefit in a specific clinical context is not clearly established, and gizmo idolatry refers to the general implicit conviction that a more technological approach is intrinsically better than one that is less technological unless, or perhaps even if, there is strong evidence to the contrary" (Leff and Finucane 2008, p. 1830). The explosion in the use of high-tech tests and treatments represents three common beliefs that are at the core of the U.S. health care system: (1) that high-tech is better than low-tech, (2) that newer is better than older, and (3) that patients deserve the most advanced treatment available regardless of considerations of marginal cost/marginal benefit.

## The Institutional Basis of Medical Malpractice

A final example of an institution with powerful effects on health care and its costs is our current malpractice system. Errors in medical care are dealt with under the broad category of personal injury law, often referred to as tort law. If a health care provider provides negligent care, and if a patient is injured as a result, that patient has a right to sue the provider and, if successful, to obtain economic compensation for the injury. The compensation is typically of two types:

1. Compensation for the actual costs that result from the injury for things such as required medical care and lost income, referred to as "economic damages"
2. Payment to compensate the patient for the added pain and suffering that result from the injury during the patient's lifetime, referred to as "noneconomic damages"

To be protected from the possibility of having to pay these costs, nearly all physicians and hospitals purchase an insurance policy—malpractice insurance—that protects them should they be named in a malpractice suit. Malpractice suits are governed by state, rather than federal, law.

For several years after the turn of the twenty-first century, a "malpractice crisis" was seen as sweeping our country. Responding to increasing jury awards and decreasing financial returns, companies that provide physicians with malpractice insurance had been raising the rates charged for coverage by substantial amounts. Newspapers regularly reported on physicians who had chosen to leave practice rather than pay the increased cost of malpractice insurance and on the communities that found themselves without enough physicians as a result. A review of the changing world of medical malpractice in the United States concluded that "physicians revile malpractice claims as random events that visit unwarranted expense and emotional pain on competent, hardworking practitioners . . . Within the health care industry, there is a nearly universal belief that malpractice litigation has long since surpassed sensible levels and that major tort reform is overdue" (Studdert, Mello, and Brennan 2004b, p. 283).

As a society, we have often adopted the implicit assumption that a poor outcome from medical care implies negligence on the part of the physician. Responding to the perception that malpractice awards are based on irrational responses of lay jurors, physicians have added billions of dollars to our health care budget by ordering extra tests and procedures that add little to care but present a stronger defense in the case of a malpractice suit. This practice of "defensive medicine" offers little added benefit to patients.

Negligence in medical care occurs when a physician provides care that is not consistent with the "community standard of care"—that is, with what an expert or panel of experts would expect a reasonably competent physician to do under similar circumstances. Thus, malpractice is derived from other physicians' assessments of the quality of the care provided.

As part of a large research project, a panel of expert physicians looked at more than 30,000 hospital records in 51 different hospitals. Based on their independent review of these records, they found that hospitalized patients experienced some sort of adverse outcome from their care about 4 percent of the time. They then looked to see how many of the patients who experienced a bad outcome did so because the physician or the hospital had provided substandard care (the legal basis for a finding of negligence). They found that 28 percent of bad outcomes could be traced to negligence (Brennan et al. 1991).

The researchers then asked, of those patients who had a bad outcome and who experienced substandard care, how many filed a malpractice lawsuit? Among the patients who received negligent care, only a tiny fraction (between 1 and 2%) filed a malpractice suit in response to their care.

The panel looked at the same data in a different way. They asked, of those patients who filed malpractice suits, how many had experienced negligent care? According to this expert panel, less than 20 percent of the malpractice suits represented instances of negligent care. Thus, when negligent care occurs, the patient usually does not sue, and when a patient does sue, it more often than not does not involve negligent care. As the researchers concluded, "the civil justice system only infrequently compensates injured patients and rarely holds healthcare providers accountable for substandard care" (Localio et al. 1991, p. 250).

The panel went on to look at the eventual judgment against the physician or hospital (if any) from the malpractice suits that were filed. They found no association between the amount of money received by the patient and whether the patient had received negligent care. The only factor that was associated with the level of judgment was the level of disability of the patient. The more disabled the patient as a result of treatment, the larger was the malpractice award, independent of negligence occurring (Brennan, Sox, and Burstin 1996).

Another series of studies looked at a small group of obstetricians who had a record of repeated malpractice suits against them. A panel of experts compared the quality of the care provided by these physicians to the quality of care provided by comparable physicians who had not been sued in the past. The panel found no difference in the quality of the care between the two groups (Entman et al. 1994).

The panel again looked at the obstetricians who had been sued and those who had not. This time they evaluated patients' satisfaction with the quality of their interpersonal interaction with these doctors. The doctors who had been sued were rated much lower on this scale of quality. From the perspective of their patients, these doctors did not communicate well, and the patients' interactions with the doctors felt more awkward (Hickson et al. 1994). It appears that the reason these obstetricians were being sued and their colleagues were not was not because the quality of their care was lower; it was because they had a

---

**CONCEPT 3.5**

In the United States, the institution of medical malpractice represents a combination of the following factors:

- A poor outcome for the patient
- A substantial level of disability as a result
- A poor interpersonal relationship between the patient and the physician
- Only in rare circumstances, actual physician negligence

weaker interpersonal relationship with their patients. An editorial that accompanied this research concluded, "The same communication skills that reduce malpractice risk lead to patient satisfaction and improved quality of care. Caring, concerned physicians who communicate well with their patients are likely to provide the best quality of care" (Levinson 1994, p. 1620).

How does malpractice in Canada differ from that in the United States? As with health care more generally, the answer lies in the differing historical and cultural traditions of the two countries. Canada's legal system is based on the British tort system. The standards by which suits are judged differ, and the rate at which lawsuits are filed is substantially lower than in the United States. Canadian physicians still have to be concerned about malpractice, but not nearly as much as their colleagues in the United States. This is because

- patients in the United States file three-and-one-half times as many malpractice suits as patients in Canada (measured as suits per one thousand population)
- plaintiffs are successful in obtaining either a judgment or a settlement at approximately the same rate in the two countries
- even though the average malpractice judgment or settlement is slightly higher in Canada than in the United States, the overall costs of the malpractice system account for $16 per capita in the United States and $4 per capita in Canada (Anderson et al. 2005)

## SUMMARY

In the United States, our fascination with technology, our orientation to the needs of the individual, our expectation that we will have expensive tests and procedures even if the added benefit is relatively small, and our propensity to sue physicians for malpractice all add up to care that is much more resource intensive and thus much more expensive than that in Canada. The marginal benefit of this extra care, measured in overall mortality rates, appears to be relatively small. The cost differences between the two countries take on even more significance, however, when we recall that, whereas all Canadians have health insurance as a right of residency, more than 50 million people in the United States have no health insurance.

The U.S. health care system has developed over time in response to our dominant cultural and political institutions. As a consequence, that system provides the most expensive care in the world while also excluding the largest number of people from care.

**CONCEPT 3.6**

Cultural and political institutions unique to the United States have helped create a health care system that is the most expensive in the world while also excluding more people from care than any other developed country. Any attempt to reform the system to address these problems must consider the institutions that led to the problems in the first place.

## PROVISIONS IN THE AFFORDABLE CARE ACT TO ADDRESS THE APPROPRIATE USE OF MEDICAL TECHNOLOGY AND OTHER HIGH-COST MEDICAL CARE

By 2014, the Affordable Care Act (ACA) will extend health insurance coverage to 32 million people who previously were uninsured. It has the goal of doing so without adding to the already high cost of our health care system. With the realization that one of the principal drivers of rising health care costs is the way we have come to use newer and high-tech approaches to diagnosis and treatment, ACA creates a mechanism intended to constrain the inappropriate use of these expensive care modalities. It does so by establishing a national program of comparative effectiveness research (CER).

From our discussion above of the evolution of treatment alternatives for high blood pressure, we saw how, as newer medications became available, they were tested only against dummy placebo pills to measure their clinical effectiveness. For a period of several decades, they were never tested against each other to compare their relative effectiveness. When this research was finally done, it was determined that, compared to the newer alternatives, the older diuretic medication provided the optimal clinical effectiveness.

Distinct from research that asks the question "Does this treatment work?" CER asks the question "Which of these alternative treatments works best?" Patrick Conway and Carolyn Clancy, both senior officials in the U.S. Department of Health and Human Services, have explained the purpose of CER: "We defined CER as the conduct and synthesis of research comparing the benefits and harms of various interventions and strategies for preventing, diagnosing, treating, and monitoring health conditions in real-world settings. The purpose of this research is to improve health outcomes by developing and disseminating evidence-based information to patients, clinicians, and other decision makers about which interventions are most effective for which patients under specific circumstances" (Conway and Clancy 2009, p. 328).

In order to expand the reach and impact of CER, ACA established a national Patient-Centered Outcomes Research Institute (PCORI). PCORI is structured as an independent, nonprofit organization. It will have a nationally representative board of governors, a series of national advisory panels, and a staff of experienced researchers. With funding provided by ACA, PCORI will either carry out or arrange to have carried out a series of research studies that compare existing alternatives for diagnosis or treatment. The Institute of Medicine of the National Academy of Sciences has recommended a list of one hundred topics that should receive priority in being addressed by PCORI-sponsored research (Iglehart 2009c). Perhaps the most important topic on this list is a study comparing alternative models for the organization of health care delivery so as to optimize health care access and quality. Second on the list is the broad topic of identifying optimal approaches to diagnosing and treating cardiovascular diseases.

ACA is explicit in requiring that CER provide recommendations for the optimal approach to care, but not create mandates as to how specific conditions should be approached. Similarly, CER results are not to be used to determine insurance coverage or payment for differing approaches to care. Thus CER, at least as carried out under ACA, is not intended to be cost-effectiveness research, in that it will not make recommendations as to which of the available alternatives provides the optimal balancing of costs and benefits.

In our above comparisons of the Canadian and the U.S. approach to balancing costs and benefits, we saw that Canada, under the constraint of a fixed, global budget for care, explicitly attempts to balance the cost of care and the effectiveness of care at the margins (that is, in deciding what treatments to provide and in prioritizing patients for access to resource-intensive care). The United States, on the other hand, has stridently resisted marginal cost/marginal effectiveness considerations, seeing such an approach to care as unwarranted rationing. Weinstein and Skinner have suggested that, in order to constrain the historical rise in health care costs, "at some point . . . we will have to confront the problem of cost-effectiveness at the level of the patient. The limitless pipeline of effective clinical strategies . . . offers improved outcomes, but the costs of development and production are often very high" (Weinstein and Skinner 2010, p. 463).

ACA leaves unanswered the question of when, if ever, it is appropriate to deny a patient care that has some small yet well documented marginal benefit, but an extremely high marginal cost. It also leaves unanswered the question of how the medical profession, for decades invested in the belief that more care is better care, will shift its institutional belief system to one that accepts health care resources as scarce, and not only supports but expects physicians and other providers to balance costs and effectiveness when making clinical recommendations for individual patients. As described by Alexander and Stafford, "Despite the allure, no amount of comparative effectiveness data alone, regardless of how rigorously assembled, will suffice to fundamentally transform clinical practice . . . The primary problem is not the absence of knowledge regarding comparative effectiveness, but the absence of the necessary mechanisms to put this knowledge to work" (Alexander and Stafford 2009, p. 2490).

# 4

# The Health Professions and the Organization of Health Care

The U.S. health care system is a complex combination of public and private mechanisms for providing care and paying for care. It is financed largely through health insurance, either public or private. Patients who have insurance generally pay only a small portion of the cost of care out of pocket, in the range of 25 percent of physicians' charges and 10 percent of hospital costs. The rest comes from insurance. Because patients rarely see the full bill for their care, they usually are shielded from knowing what that care costs. This is in sharp contrast to other market commodities.

In addition to a wide variety of private health insurance options, there are many different types of publicly financed health insurance. These include

- Medicare—the federal program for those 65 or older and for disabled people
- Medicaid—the combined federal-state program for poor people
- State Children's Health Insurance Program (S-CHIP)—a combined federal-state program for children in lower-income families who do not qualify for Medicaid
- Veterans Affairs health system—for certain categories of military veterans
- Defense Department health system—for those on active military duty
- Indian Health Service—for Native Americans both on reservations and in cities

We end up with a wide variety of payment mechanisms for health care. Each program has its own list of what is covered and what is not and how much the patient has to pay.

Regardless of what method is used for paying for care, health care decisions are still largely made by physicians. Even though physicians account for only about 20 percent of health care expenditures, they influence between 70 and 80 percent of all expenditures. Medications are prescribed by physicians, tests are ordered by physicians, and patients are admitted to a hospital or nursing home by physicians. Thus, physicians' decisions effectively determine how much health care costs.

In 2008, there were about 741,000 physicians in this country actively involved in providing patient care—about 1 for every 416 people. They are not distributed equally throughout the United States, however. States vary widely in how many physicians they have, from 1 for every 153 people in Delaware and for every 230 people in Massachusetts, to 1 per 628 people in Idaho and Oklahoma (Smart 2010).

Physicians continue to earn one of the highest average incomes of any professional. In 2008, the median income of physicians ranged from about $180,000 for family physicians and general pediatricians to about $450,000 for medical specialists such as gastroenterologists and $475,000 for orthopedic surgeons (Medical Group Management Association 2009). Being a physician in the United States, however, was not always such a rewarding profession.

## THE HISTORY OF MEDICAL EDUCATION AND THE MEDICAL PROFESSION IN THE UNITED STATES

In his prize-winning novel, *Arrowsmith*, Sinclair Lewis described Doc Vickerson in the 1890s: "A fat old man and dirty and unvirtuous was the Doc; his grammar was doubtful, his vocabulary alarming, and his references to his rival, good Dr. Needham, were scandalous" (Lewis 1924, p. 5). The novel describes a doctor living in a small midwestern town and struggling with inadequate training to cope with illness for which he has little to offer. As was the case with Doc Vickerson, being a doctor in the United States before 1900 was not necessarily a great distinction. While physicians were generally honored, they did not have nearly the power nor earn anywhere near the amount they do today. There were several reasons for their relative lack of occupational status.

### • Lack of consistency in training

Medical education at that time was based largely on older physicians sharing the knowledge they had accumulated through experience. These physicians represented a wide range of theories of practice, many of them conflicting in the ways they understood the nature of health and disease. These conflicting approaches to medical practice were referred to as "sects." The largest of the sects were the homeopaths, the osteopaths, and the allopaths. (Most modern physicians are descended from the allopathic sect.) The quality of the education within these sects varied with the quality of the instructor, often with little scientific basis for the training offered. Thus, one had little idea of what any particular physician knew and whether the chances of getting better were enhanced or impaired by seeking medical care. It was not until after the Flexner Report in 1910 that the concept of basing medical education and practice on scientific knowledge became widely accepted.

• *No licensure or certification, and thus no assurance of quality*

Because there was no firm scientific basis for most of medical practice, there was little on which to base laws pertaining to licensure or certification. Any person with some medical training could call himself a doctor, with no public or private body overseeing the quality of medical practice.

• *Large numbers of doctors*

In addition to the inconsistent quality of doctors, there were large numbers of doctors. Because it was relatively easy to operate a medical school (simply provide a space for senior physicians to lecture on what they knew and find enough students who were willing to pay for obtaining that knowledge), there were numerous medical schools. In the face of so many doctors representing a variety of theories of illness and treatment with little in the way of scientific basis for medical practice and no assurance of quality or consistency of care, physicians were not perceived as belonging to a high-status profession. The income they received from medical practice was accordingly much less than what is seen today.

The American Medical Association (AMA) started out as a group of young doctors who wanted to better the doctor's lot. Most of their members were drawn from the allopathic sect of practice. For about fifty years (1846–1900), the AMA had little effect in changing the nature of medical practice.

At the turn of the twentieth century, a new model of medical education was beginning to spread from Europe to the United States. It became established at places like Johns Hopkins and Harvard universities. Previously most medical schools were freestanding, without any association with universities. The new curriculum, supported by the Flexner Report (1910), required medical schools

- to be part of universities
- to have at least four years of training
- to have the first two years of that training concentrate on basic laboratory science

Most states adopted the recommendations contained in the Flexner Report and incorporated them into laws governing medical licensure. All new doctors, to be allowed to practice under these new licensure laws, had to graduate from a medical school that based its education on this model. The AMA and its state affiliates, representing allopathic physicians, in collaboration with the Association of American Medical Colleges, were given responsibility for certifying which schools met the standard. With the support of newly enacted state licensure laws, the AMA was able to effectively control the number of medical schools in the United States, and therefore the number of doctors, as well as to establish the criteria for licensure.

The overall quality and consistency of medical training and practice improved substantially—as did the income of doctors, due largely to their shrinking numbers. In addition, the new medical schools provided a place for medical research. Most medical advances in the twentieth century were developed in medical schools.

The AMA also worked to establish control over the manufacture of pharmaceuticals. Only the companies that pledged to follow the AMA's code of ethics were approved and allowed to advertise in the AMA's journals (Starr 1982). Physicians were discouraged from prescribing drugs that did not meet the AMA's approval. As a result, a mutually dependent relationship developed between the drug companies and the AMA, and the drug companies came to be very powerful. They formed their own association, the Pharmaceutical Research and Manufacturers of America (PhRMA) (formerly the Pharmaceutical Manufacturers' Association, or PMA). Over the years, the power of the PhRMA, both scientifically and politically, paralleled that of the AMA. Through its support of laws providing patent protection for new drugs and extensive marketing of new (often extremely expensive) drugs, the pharmaceutical industry has been able to maintain one of the highest profit margins of any American industry. Through their extensive program of medical research, pharmaceutical companies have provided many important advances in treatment, but they have also provided many expensive new drugs that offer relatively little benefit over older, less expensive drugs. As a result, the cost of drugs has been a major contributor to the rising cost of health care. (See Chapter 9 on pharmaceutical policy for a more in-depth examination of these issues.)

Building on the authority it was granted over medical school certification and medical licensure, the AMA also came to define the code of ethics that physicians must follow (Baker et al. 1999). This code of ethics covered not only issues of medical practice but also issues of medical economics. From rules governing the physician-patient relationship to methods of organizing and paying for medical practice, the AMA gained near total authority over physicians. This code of ethics was applied not just to physicians who were members of the AMA, but to all physicians. As we will see in Chapter 5 as part of our consideration of the origin of health maintenance organizations (HMOs), this extension of ethical standards to include the organization of medical practice led to significant splits within the profession. These splits were to have important ramifications for the efforts at health care reform in this country over the last fifty years.

Today, the AMA represents fewer than half of all physicians, but it is still the most powerful voice of the medical profession on matters of medical ethics, medical education, and the standards of medical practice. In addition, the AMA has for years been one of the biggest contributors

> **CONCEPT 4.1**
>
> The American Medical Association, acting as the representative of the medical profession, was able to exert considerable power during much of the twentieth century over the organization, financing, and delivery of medical care in the United States.

to politicians and has one of the most powerful lobbying organizations in Washington, D.C. During much of the twentieth century, the power of the AMA was such that it was repeatedly able to block efforts in Congress to establish a system of universal health insurance.

## RACIAL SEGREGATION AND THE MEDICAL PROFESSION

It is significant to point out that for much of its history, the AMA excluded African American physicians from membership. In addition, African American physicians were frequently blocked at the local level from joining the medical staff of predominantly white hospitals (Baker et al. 2008). As part of the unfortunate history of racial segregation in this country, we also maintained segregated systems of medical education and medical care, perpetuated for much of the twentieth century by the policies promulgated by the AMA (Smith 1999).

In the period following the Civil War, a small number of predominantly black medical schools gained substantial respect. Foremost among these were Howard University and Meharry Medical College. In the 1890s, the graduates of these schools, prevented from joining the AMA, formed a separate association—the National Medical Association (NMA)—to represent African American physicians. In the 1950s, the AMA and its affiliated state medical associations began to extend membership to African American physicians, although it was not until a period in the 1960s following the enactment of the Civil Rights Act that African American physicians became full members of the U.S. medical profession. In 2008, the AMA issued a formal apology for its historic role in maintaining racial segregation (Davis 2008).

Until the 1960s, there existed in many parts of this country a system of overt segregation of white and nonwhite hospitals. Black physicians were not allowed on the medical staffs of many white hospitals and black patients were not allowed treatment. Congress then passed both landmark civil rights legislation and the laws creating the Medicare and Medicaid programs. Together, these programs extended the availability of hospital care to the poor and the elderly and, as a result, became a major source of funding for most hospitals. Those responsible for enacting Medicare and Medicaid made it clear that any hospital that continued a policy of racial segregation would be in violation of the Civil Rights Act and would be ineligible for payment under either program. Few hospitals could continue to survive without any federal funding. As a result, there was a rapid dismantling of the segregated hospital system.

The NMA continues to exist as an independent association of physicians and continues to be active in efforts to increase the number of medical students and physicians from under-represented racial and ethnic minorities. The relatively low number of African Americans and other minorities in the U.S. medical profession continues to be a problem. For example, while African Americans currently make up about 13 percent of the overall U.S. population, only about 4 to 5 percent of physicians in the United States are African American. Coincident with the decreasing emphasis on affirmative action programs at many universities, the number of medical students from under-represented ethnic minorities fell 15 percent between 1994 and 2000 (Schemo 2000).

## GENDER SEGREGATION AND THE MEDICAL PROFESSION

For much of the early part of the twentieth century, women were not allowed member-ship in the AMA. This reflected a generally held view that women were inappropriate for practice as physicians. Many medical schools refused to admit women as students, and those that did admitted only a small number. Many women physicians in this country were educated in women-only medical schools. Following the success of the women's suffrage movement in the 1920s, the AMA and the rest of the medical profession began to open its ranks to women.

When, as a medical student in the 1970s, I served as a member of the admissions committee of a nationally prestigious medical school, women applicants were given extra scrutiny to assure that their interest in establishing a family did not conflict with their interest in becoming a physician. As a result, fewer than 10 percent of medical students at that school and nationwide were women. As women in this country have attained increasing status relative to men, their numbers in the medical profession have increased accordingly. Today, half of all medical students (more than half at some schools) are women. Over time, medicine will become a profession with as many women physicians as men.

## NURSING IN THE UNITED STATES

Another important profession in U.S. health care is nursing. Interestingly, the history of the nursing profession is also the history of war. Nursing was formed as a profession in the 1800s through the efforts of Florence Nightingale and others on the battlefields of the Crimean War. Following a growing public awareness of her work, schools of nursing began to be established in the United Kingdom and the United States.

Due to a shortage of nurses in World War I, a new category of subnurse was created, which eventually became the medical assistant. Today, medical assistants frequently work under the direction of registered nurses in both hospital and medical office settings. Another shortage of nursing personnel during World War II led to the creation of a third category of nurse, the licensed vocational nurse. Today, hospitals, clinics, and physicians' offices employ a combination of medical assistants, licensed vocational nurses, and registered nurses.

At the same time that the university-based medical school was spreading throughout this country, the model of the hospital-based nursing school was also expanding. Previously, nursing education had been as varied and haphazard as medical education.

In 1911, a group of alumnae from these hospital-based schools formed an association and argued that only graduates of these schools should be licensed to act as nurses. This was the birth of the American Nursing Association, or ANA. The ANA has never been as powerful as the AMA. To a large extent, it has acted in the role of a collective bargaining agent in nurses' struggle with hospitals to gain the professional status and level of pay that the profession deserved. In this effort, there were often rival labor unions for nurses, with a result that the profession had difficulty becoming unified.

For much of the twentieth century, the traditional training for nurses took place in hospital-based programs, typically two years in length. Beginning in the 1960s, a shift took place, with nursing education taking place increasingly at community colleges and other academic institutions, rather than being based in hospitals. These "associate degree" programs typically last three years.

Many nurses argue that all nurses should have four years of education, the equivalent of a college education. Those nurses who complete a full four years of education receive a baccalaureate degree and are referred to as baccalaureate nurses. Over time associate degree and baccalaureate programs have come to replace the traditional hospital-based diploma nursing programs. About two-thirds of recent nursing graduates received their training in associate degree programs, with about 30 percent having received a baccalaureate degree (Aiken, Cheung, and Olds 2009).

Many nurses have been able to upgrade their training through specialized programs to form highly skilled subgroups within the profession. For example, emergency room nurses, coronary care nurses, and neonatal care nurses have become indispensable members of the critical care team in hospitals and have considerable autonomy in the care of patients. In addition, several types of nurses have been able to obtain extra training to act as semi-independent practitioners, discussed below.

A major policy issue facing the nursing profession is a projected shortage of trained nurses. Current estimates predict a shortage of 285,000 nurses nationally by 2020, with the numbers projected to grow to 500,000 by 2025 (Buerhaus 2008). Several factors have contributed to a growing gap between the number of nurses working and the number of nurses needed. The first is an aging workforce, with nurses in their fifties comprising the largest age-group in the workforce. Once this baby boom generation of nurses begins to retire, shortages will begin to grow rapidly.

With a recent history of rising wages and opportunities for professional advancement, nursing has become increasingly attractive as a profession. With nearly all nursing education now taking place in colleges and universities, however, there is a growing shortage of nursing faculty to provide training to all those interested. As a result, many qualified applicants are turned away from nursing school or are placed on waiting lists. As described by Cleary et al. (2009, p. w636), "Today's shortage of nursing faculty is also shaped by the same demographics affecting the overall nursing shortage. The average age [in 2008] of a nursing faculty member is 53.5, and the average age of retirement is 62.5."

As fewer nurses enter the profession and more leave it, and as the shortage of trained nursing faculty grows, the problem will be felt most acutely in the hospitals. In 2001, about 13 percent of hospital positions for registered nurses were unfilled; 84 percent of hospitals reported staff shortages of nurses. Between 2001 and 2007, 63 percent of the growth in nursing employment took place in hospitals (Buerhaus 2008). A problem arises as more hospital nursing positions remain vacant, in that those nurses who remain must care for a greater number of patients. As the baby boom generation ages and the demand for hospital services increases, the problem is only going to become more acute. One study found a vicious circle, with nurses in hospitals with higher patient-to-nurse ratios experiencing greater rates of burnout and job dissatisfaction, making them even more likely to leave the profession. In addition, patients in hospitals with higher patient-to-nurse ratios experienced higher mortality rates than patients in hospitals with better staffing ratios (Aiken et al. 2002).

## LEVELS IN THE U.S. HEALTH CARE SYSTEM

In examining health care in the United States, we can divide our system into multiple levels:

- Primary care: care provided by physicians' offices and clinics
- Secondary care: care obtained from specialists and in hospitals
- Tertiary care: care obtained at regional referral centers
- Quaternary care: care obtained at national referral centers

We will look at each of these levels separately.

### Primary Care
#### PRIMARY CARE PHYSICIANS

There has been a great deal of discussion among physicians, among patients, and in the media about the role of primary care physicians. In these discussions, it is important to be specific in defining "primary care." There are at least two ways of approaching primary care and defining which physicians are primary care physicians.

*1. The disease-oriented approach: physicians who provide the first stage of treatment for a disease*

By this definition of primary care, nearly any type of doctor can be considered a primary care physician, depending on the nature of the illness. The following examples illustrate this approach to primary care:

- You see your family doctor for treatment of a sore throat
- You consult a dermatologist for treatment of acne
- You seek prenatal care from an obstetrician
- You consult a cardiologist regarding chest pains
- You are treated by an emergency physician for injuries sustained in an auto accident

*2. The person-oriented approach: a physician who provides continuing, comprehensive, coordinated medical care that is not differentiated by gender, disease, or organ system*

Under this definition, only those physicians who treat a comprehensive range of problems, getting to know a patient and his or her health status over time, are considered primary care physicians. From this approach, only physicians with training in one of three specialties are considered to be primary care physicians: family medicine, general internal medicine, and general pediatrics. Geriatrics, a field in which physicians focus on providing care to older patients, is also considered a primary care field. Geriatricians are typically trained in either family medicine or general internal medicine, and receive extra training in providing care to seniors.

> **CONCEPT 4.2**
>
> A primary care physician is a physician who provides continuing, comprehensive, coordinated medical care that is not differentiated by gender, disease, or organ system. Typically, primary care physicians are from one of three areas of training: family practice, general internal medicine, or general pediatrics.

For many, an obstetrician/gynecologist would not be considered a primary care physician because his or her practice is gender specific. Others point out that some women come to rely on their obstetrician to provide ongoing, comprehensive care for a range of problems. From this perspective, an obstetrician can be seen as a primary care physician.

A cardiologist or dermatologist would not be a primary care physician because each practice is limited to one organ system. An emergency physician, while treating a comprehensive range of problems, would not be a primary care physician because he or she does not develop a continuous relationship with a patient over time.

The recent debate over health care reform has focused a great deal of attention on the need for primary care physicians. For a period of time in the 1990s, it appeared that there was a crisis in the falling number of primary care physicians. Lured by the prestige of being a specialist, fewer and fewer medical students were choosing a career in primary care. In 1982, about one-third of all medical students indicated that they planned to enter primary care. In 1992, fewer than 20 percent of medical students opted for primary care. In the mid-1990s, there was somewhat of a turnaround in this area, with one-third of graduating medical students entering primary care residencies.

In 1998, that pattern was reversed, however, and every year since then fewer and fewer graduating medical students have selected residencies in a primary care specialty.

The decline has been the sharpest in family medicine (Whitcomb and Cohen 2004). Whereas in 1999 about 15 percent of graduating medical students entered residency training in family medicine, by 2009 only 7 percent of students entered family medicine training. In 1999, family medicine residency programs were able to fill about two-thirds of their positions with graduates of U.S. medical schools; in 2009, about 42 percent of training slots went to U.S. medical graduates (Steinbrook 2009a).

There are a number of reasons why medical students choose to be specialists rather than primary care physicians:

• *Prestige*

Specialists tend to deal with new technology; primary care physicians deal mainly with people. With our emphasis on technology as the basis of medical advances, physicians who use technology in their practice are frequently granted higher prestige, both by the profession and by society.

• *Money*

It is not uncommon for some specialists to earn two to three times as much as primary care physicians. Many medical students have to rely heavily on student loans to pay the cost of their education. A number of students come out of medical school owing $150,000 to $200,000, sometimes more. Many feel they need the higher salary available to specialists to be able to pay off their loans.

• *Frustration of primary care*

Some medical students view primary care as being boring and repetitive, dealing mostly with common problems and chronic illness for which there is no cure. As described in a report by a group of primary care physicians, the work of a primary care physicians includes many responsibilities that do not involve patients directly, such as reviewing laboratory and X-ray reports, refilling prescriptions, and responding to phone calls or e-mails (Baron 2010). Under traditional payment methods, physicians are not compensated for many of these types of duties. Specialists, on the other hand, are often perceived as dealing with challenging and interesting problems for which they might be able to offer a cure.

• *Lack of primary care role models*

Most physicians who teach in medical schools are specialists. Medical students come in contact with few practicing primary care physicians. Students are often counseled by their teachers to stay away from primary care—not to "waste" their career.

There are also reasons, though, why primary care is an attractive career option for many students:

• *Employability*

One factor that may be working in the favor of primary care physicians is their ability to find employment after their training. A study from the late 1990s showed that, for physicians just completing their residency, relatively few primary care physicians had difficulty finding employment, while as many as half of all physicians in certain subspecialties reported trouble finding employment (Miller et al. 1998). With the growing shortage of primary care physicians relative to specialists, this employment advantage is only going to increase.

One reason for this advantage in employment has been the increasing role of primary care physicians in managed care settings. (I discuss the origins of managed care systems in Chapter 5.) In traditional medical practice, a number of specialists did not have enough patients to fill their practice, so they would spend part of their time giving specialized care and part of their time giving primary care. In the managed care setting, most specialists provide only specialty care, with the result that they need fewer specialists. As a consequence, more primary care physicians are needed in these practice settings.

• *The nontangible benefits of primary care practice*

While it may be true that primary care physicians frequently deal with common problems and chronic illness, there is an aspect to this type of medical practice that many medical students are not aware of. In getting to know patients and their families over time and in dealing with the problems that most commonly confront patients, primary care physicians are able to develop a unique relationship with their patients. Patients tend both to trust and to admire the physician who is there for them day in and day out. It is difficult to put a dollar value on the strength of the interpersonal relationship many primary care physicians are able to establish with their patients. This can be the most rewarding aspect of primary care practice. Those physicians who value the quality of their relationship with their patients over professional prestige and income frequently feel at home in primary care practice, and they usually make the best primary care physicians.

An article in the *New York Times* illustrated how important an ongoing relationship of trust with a primary care physician is for many patients (Zuger 2003a). The article told the story of Robert:

> Robert is a middle-aged man with five chronic diseases and a doctor for each. He has the urologist for the prostate cancer, the rheumatologist for the arthritis, the cardiologist for the coronary artery disease, and so on. And then, like the extra candle on the cake for luck, he has yet another doctor, the one responsible for his primary care . . . But if you ask Robert about Doctors 1 to 5 he shrugs, barely remembering their names. Ask him about No. 6 and a soft smile crosses his face.

"I don't know what I would do without him," he says. "He's kept me alive all these years."

Abigail Zuger, a physician and the author of the article, goes on to conclude, "If complications and mortality were all there was to medical care, that might be the end of the story—and of primary care. But anyone who has ever emerged physically intact but emotionally battered, confused, furious or appalled from an encounter with the health care system knows otherwise."

While heavy debt loads and fascination with technological approaches to care may push many medical students toward a career as a specialist, there are some clearly identified factors that draw others to a primary care career. A study of the characteristics of students at the time they first entered medical school found that "those who planned to practice in underserved communities, espoused more altruistic beliefs about health care, and ascribed greater importance to social responsibility in their choice of medicine" were significantly more likely to select a primary care career. The study also found women medical students in general to be attracted to primary care more so than men (Jeffe, Whelan, and Andriole 2010, p. 947).

Currently about 30 percent of physicians in the United States are in primary care. Many people argue that we need to increase this number to closer to 50 percent of physicians, as is the case in Canada. Others respond that if we had 50 percent of physicians in primary care, there would be a shortage of specialists. Recall that Canada provides a great deal less specialized care than we do and thus needs fewer specialists. It may be that we could not keep up our current level of specialized care with 50 percent specialists. Policies adopted to influence the number of primary care physicians (and thus the number of specialists) will play an important role in determining the direction our health care system takes.

As a percentage of the medical profession, primary care has fallen steadily over time. In the period 1950–60, when there were about 145 physicians per 100,000 people, more than half of all physicians were in primary care. By 1970, there were about 160 physicians per 100,000 people, with about 37 percent of them being primary care physicians. The number of physicians rose to 278 per 100,000 in 2000 and to 293 per 100,000 in 2010. The physician supply is expected to remain at approximately this level for several years (Iglehart 2008).

In 1950, when more than half of physicians were in primary care, there were about 80 primary care physicians and about 65 specialists per 100,000 population. In 2010, with about 30 percent of physicians in primary care, there were about 88 primary care physicians and 206 specialists per 100,000 population. While the number of specialists more than tripled in these 60 years, the number of primary care physicians remained fairly constant. With fewer young physicians selecting primary care careers, however, there is growing concern as to whether there will be enough primary care physicians to provide primary care services once the expanded insurance coverage under the Affordable Care Act (ACA) becomes a reality. I discuss these issues at the end of this chapter.

### NURSE PRACTITIONERS AND OTHER ADVANCED PRACTICE NURSES

An alternative to training primary care physicians is training advanced practice nurses. Most common examples are the nurse practitioner and nurse midwife. Nurse practitioners take two to three years of training beyond registered nurse training, part of it a clinical internship. They can be trained in fields such as family medicine, adult medicine, pediatrics, or obstetrics. Following their training, nurse practitioners are eligible to see and treat patients for certain specified conditions under the supervision of a physician. The physician does not have to be present to provide supervision. The physician and the nurse practitioner do not even have to be in the same office. Nurse practitioners typically work from written treatment protocols worked out with their supervising physician and refer all things beyond their capabilities to the physician. In 2010, there were 135,000 nurse practitioners in the United States (American Academy of Nurse Practitioners n.d.). (Physician assistants differ from nurse practitioners in not being nurses, in having to work more directly under the supervision of a physician, and in being more limited in what they can do. In 2009, there were about 72,000 physician assistants in the United States [American Academy of Physician Assistants 2009].)

A problem for nurse practitioners historically has been that many physicians are not comfortable either supervising them or having their patients seen by them. Repeated studies (Salkever et al. 1982; U.S. Congress, Office of Technology Assessment 1986; Maule 1994) have shown, however, that nurse practitioners can give care that is the same quality as physician care for the specific conditions they are trained for. Also, patients accept nurse practitioners quite well. In many cases, patients are more satisfied with a nurse practitioner than with a physician, due largely to the extra time and personal attention nurse practitioners are able to give. Nurse practitioners seem especially well suited for those medical conditions in which a great deal of face-to-face contact is required (for example, well child care, arthritis, diabetes, high blood pressure).

> **CONCEPT 4.3**
>
> Nurse practitioners have been shown to be an effective alternative to physicians in a number of settings in terms of quality, cost, and patient satisfaction.

The question remains unanswered as to whether care provided by nurse practitioners costs less than care provided by physicians. Because nurse practitioners spend more time with patients, they see fewer patients. A study done in the 1980s by the Kaiser Permanente system of care in northern California found that overall care from nurse practitioners costs about the same as physician care, but patients liked them better than physicians in the clinic (Garfield et al. 1987).

Perhaps a more important issue than whether to train more primary care physicians or nurse practitioners is how primary care should be organized. With the spread of managed care plans, primary care is increasingly being provided by large groups of physicians. The solo physician, practicing alone in his or her own office, is rapidly become a thing of the past. Between 1996 and 2005, the number of physicians practicing in one or two physician practices declined from 40.7 percent of physicians to 32.5 percent (Liebhaber and Grossman 2007). Many people suggest that we need to look at new ways of organizing primary care practice to maintain the quality of the primary care process and to make it readily accessible to patients. This issue is especially relevant in light of the increasing load of chronic illness management that will come as the baby boom generation ages. As part of ACA signed by President Barack Obama, there will be substantial new emphasis on developing new models for the delivery of primary care. I discuss these at the end of this chapter.

## Secondary Care
### SPECIALIST PHYSICIANS

As discussed above, physicians are separated into two categories: primary care physicians and specialists. Specialists are those physicians who have received extra training in a specific field, and who treat only a certain type of patient. The point at which primary care physicians and specialists become identified and differentiated is during residency training. Nearly every medical student goes on after medical school to receive additional training in a residency. Residencies are usually based in a hospital and have faculty drawn from a specific field of medicine.

The concept of the "internship" no longer applies to medical training in the United States. During much of the twentieth century, medical students would initially complete a one-year, hospital-based training after medical school (the internship), and then go on to a separate residency training program. Over time it has become the standard that the first year of training after medical school is part of residency training, often referred to as the R1 year. It is possible to obtain a license to practice medicine in many states after the R1 year, but fewer and fewer students stop at this level of training. In the past, those physicians who stopped after one year of extra training were referred to as "general practitioners." General practitioners have largely been replaced by family practitioners and other types of primary care physician who take a full three years of residency training.

The length of residency training can vary significantly, depending on area of specialty. Emergency room specialists complete their residency training in three years, while certain types of surgeons (for example, cardiac surgeons or neurosurgeons) can take eight or more years before completing training. Some specialties may require two separate residencies, such as an initial period of residency in general surgery followed by a separate residency in orthopedic surgery.

A number of specialists in nonsurgical fields may begin their training in the same program as primary care physicians, but then go on to take extra training in a specialized field within their discipline. For example, students wishing to become cardiologists (heart specialists) or gastroenterologists (intestinal specialists) will often take the same three-year residency in general internal medicine as primary care physicians, but will then go on to take a "fellowship" in their specialized area of interest. Similarly, a physician completing a residency in general pediatrics may then go on to a fellowship in neonatology (the care of premature babies and other newborns). A fellowship is distinguished from a residency in that it is available only to those who have completed more general training in a specific field, and it provides training in only one segment of that field. Fellowships are typically between two and four years long.

Most specialists have an income that is considerably higher than that of primary care physicians. By spending a few extra years in training, physicians can more than double their expected earning power. The higher income a specialist can expect to earn continues to play a major role in drawing students into specialty areas. In addition, many young physicians want to use the latest technology in their practice or to have the challenge of performing surgery with its attendant risks for the patient. As described above, a substantial majority of medical students continues to choose careers in medical specialties.

> **CONCEPT 4.4**
>
> A number of forces, including the higher level of income available, have encouraged the majority of young physicians to become specialists. Fewer than one-third of physicians become primary care physicians.

Since the changes in medical practice that accompanied the shift to managed care in this country, the way a specialist practices medicine has also changed. Previously, any patient who wanted to consult a specialist about a problem simply called the specialist's office and made an appointment. Because specialty care tends to be more expensive than primary care, some insurance companies and managed care companies have placed limits on the patients' ability to be seen by the specialist of their choice. Now many patients often must first seek care from their primary care physician, and they may have the care of a specialist covered under their medical insurance only if it is first approved by the primary care physician. In addition, certain types of specialists use expensive tests and procedures as part of their practice. In an effort to control costs, many insurance companies require these specialists to obtain permission from the insurance company before providing expensive care.

The rising number of specialists in the United States, both in absolute numbers and as a percentage of the medical profession, raises serious concerns about the effect on the rising cost of care. As in many areas of medical care, changes in the number of specialist physicians do not necessarily lead to changes in the price of specialty care. If your community had a sudden increase in the number of house painters, you could reasonably expect the cost of having your house painted to go down. With most market commodities, as the supply of a commodity (such as house painters) goes up, the price should come down. Despite the market approach to medical care prevalent in this country for most of the twentieth century, the number of physicians did not seem to obey the laws of supply and demand. Instead, physicians were able to avoid becoming a surplus commodity by increasing the amount of care they provided. In the case of medical care, the demand for the commodity (that is, medical care) is determined not by the consumer but by the provider. Patients do not typically tell physicians how much and what type of care they need; physicians tell patients. Medical care in this case becomes a "market failure," in that it does not obey the classic laws of the market economy such as supply and demand (Arrow 1963).

> **CONCEPT 4.5**
>
> Historically, the supply of physicians in a community has not obeyed the economic law of supply and demand. The greater the number of physicians, the greater has been the amount of care and the number of procedures. Instead of reducing the price of care, the rising number of specialist physicians has contributed to the increasing cost of care.

A fundamental reality of contemporary U.S. medical care has been demonstrated again and again: the more specialists practicing in a given community, the more specialty care will be recommended to patients and the higher the cost of care. If more surgeons move into a community (all else being equal), there will be more operations. For a variety of medical conditions and geographic locations, John Wennberg and colleagues have demonstrated tremendous variation among communities in the rate that certain types of specialized therapy are applied. Whether it is rates of prostate surgery or rates of heart surgery, Wennberg concluded that a major factor driving the different rates of these procedures is the number of physicians practicing in the community: the more physicians, the higher the rate of surgery (Wennberg and Gittelsohn 1973; Wennberg, Barnes, and Zubkoff 1982; Wennberg 1993).

In 2009, physician/author Atul Gawande published an article in *The New Yorker* describing his visit to McAllen, Texas. Based on Medicare data, physicians in McAllen provide some of the most expensive medical care of any community in the country—second only to Miami. The question Dr. Gawande explored in his article was why care cost so much more in McAllen than in other parts of the country. He concluded: "there's no evidence that the treatments and technologies available at McAllen are better than those found elsewhere in the country . . . Health-care costs ultimately arise from the accumulation of individual decisions doctors make about which services and treatments to write an order for. The most expensive piece of medical equipment, as the saying goes, is a doctor's pen" (Gawande 2009). It seems that doctors in McAllen simply use their pen more often than doctors elsewhere in the country. They order more tests and do more procedures (and in doing so collect more fees from Medicare) than physicians elsewhere in the country. Yet as described by Dr. Gawande, patients in McAllen seem no better off for all this extra treatment.

### INTERNATIONAL MEDICAL GRADUATES AND THEIR EFFECT ON THE MEDICAL PROFESSION

Two policy decisions have combined to encourage young physicians completing medical school in other countries to come to the United States to live and practice medicine. The first decision was to create flexibility in immigration laws to allow hospitals in the United States that are unable to fill all their residency training slots with graduates of U.S. medical schools to fill those slots with graduates of medical schools outside of the United States or Canada. These international medical graduates (IMGs) must first pass two standardized examinations: one documenting that they have received a medical education equivalent to that in the United States, and one documenting facility in written and spoken English. Those who pass these examinations must then successfully complete an in-person assessment of their clinical skills. They are required to interact with ten standardized patients, and to demonstrate their ability to take a history from a patient, conduct a physical exam, and communicate orally with the patient. Those IMGs who successfully complete these exams are allowed to apply to U.S. hospitals for residency training. Once an IMG obtains a residency training slot, he or she is then eligible to receive a visa to enter the United States for the duration of the residency. The original intent of the immigration laws was to allow the doctor to return to the country of origin after completion of training. In recent years, however, most IMGs completing their training—typically 75 percent—have been able to obtain permanent resident status and remain in this country.

The second policy that facilitated the employment of IMGs by hospitals in the United States was the decision by the federal Medicare program to reimburse hospitals for the cost of residency training, without limits on either numbers or types of residencies. The history of this policy is an unusual one. A relatively minor policy decision in the 1960s, unrelated to the issue of international graduates or medical education, has had the unintended long-term consequence of encouraging the immigration of large numbers of international physicians.

When the Medicare program was first approved by Congress in the 1960s, the federal government used a complex formula to calculate how much to pay hospitals for treating Medicare patients. The formula allowed the hospital to obtain reimbursement for a share of the costs of running the hospital. A somewhat lengthy list was established detailing which expenses the hospital could include in calculating the federal government's share. One item that appeared on this list was the cost of any residency training programs the hospitals might have. When Medicare switched to its prospective payment system for reimbursing hospitals (discussed below), hospitals that previously had included the costs of residency training in their payment formula were allowed to continue to bill Medicare for these costs *in addition* to the payment they received under prospective payment. While this policy was originally intended to allow hospitals with existing residency training programs to continue their previous level of reimbursement, it soon became apparent that newly established residency programs were also eligible for federal reimbursement. Unintentionally, the Medicare program had written a blank check to hospitals to expand residency training programs. Hospitals were quick to respond. Adding a residency program (or expanding an existing one) not only adds to the prestige of the hospital, but also provides a source of inexpensive labor. In many hospitals, especially inner-city hospitals providing care to large number of poor patients, residents provide the bulk of direct patient care.

As a result of the expansion in residency training programs, paid for by the federal government, the number of entry-level training slots has become substantially larger than the number of medical students graduating each year from U.S. medical schools. U.S. medical graduates tend not to choose many of the inner-city hospitals for their training, leaving numerous unfilled training slots at these hospitals. To have sufficient personnel to take care of patients, these hospitals turn to international graduates to fill the residency programs. Hospitals in cities such as New York, Chicago, and Los Angeles that once had no problem filling their residencies with U.S. graduates now train mostly international graduates. In 2009, there were 29,488 (27.3%) IMGs out of a total of 108,176 physicians in residency training in the United States (Brotherton and Etzel 2009).

A consequence of the expansion of training that followed the federal government's decision to subsidize residency training has been increasingly rapid growth in the number of physicians in the United States. In addition, because IMGs are more likely than U.S. graduates to become specialists rather than primary care physicians, the policy has been a major factor contributing to the growing number of specialists in the country.

As a consequence of the declining interest in primary care residency training, especially in the case of family medicine, however, IMGs are increasingly filling the primary care training slots left empty by graduates of U.S. medical schools. In addition, IMGs who train in primary care and then locate their practice in a federally designated man-

> **CONCEPT 4.6**
>
> As a consequence of the decision by Medicare to pay for the residency training of physicians, the number of training positions has increased dramatically. One of every four physicians entering residency training is a graduate of a medical school outside the United States or Canada. The influx of international medical graduates has contributed to the oversupply of specialists and thus to the rising cost of care.

power shortage area can become eligible for permanent residency status and eventually U.S. citizenship.

## HOSPITALS

Throughout much of history, hospitals were not places of healing; they were places to die, mostly for poor people. It was during the Napoleonic Wars that doctors first started treating all of the wounded and sick soldiers in one place. Hospitals gradually became places for the scientific study of medicine instead of places for poor people to go to die. As part of the shift to medicine as a science-based discipline seen in the early twentieth century, hospitals increasingly became important for treating ill patients in an effort to prevent death. Following the Flexner Report on medical education and the affiliation of medical schools with universities, hospitals—especially university-based hospitals—became the principal locations for medical research. Thus, the hospital as we know it is a relatively young institution.

During the Great Depression of the 1930s, patients often could not pay their hospital bills, with the result that many hospitals had a hard time staying open. Hospitals decided to group together to offer, for the first time, insurance to cover the cost of hospital care. The hope was that people who could not afford to pay a large hospital bill once they got sick could afford monthly insurance premiums to protect themselves if they ever did get sick. These hospital-sponsored insurance plans, operated on a non-profit basis, were the origin of the nationwide Blue Cross program. Every state had its own program of Blue Cross hospital insurance. Some states added an option for insuring against the cost of physicians' services. These were the Blue Shield plans. The AMA and its local affiliates supported the establishment of the Blue Cross/Blue Shield program so long as physicians maintained control over all medical decisions within the hospital.

In much of Europe, specialist physicians typically work only in the hospital, with primary care physicians working only in the community. When a community physician has a patient who needs to be hospitalized, the patient will often be referred to the hospital-based specialist. In the United States, community physicians admit their patients to the hospital and supervise their care while they are in the hospital. This arrangement gives community physicians in the United States substantially more authority over hospital policies and practices than their counterparts in Europe. For a period of several years, however, a new type of physician has begun to develop in many areas of the country—the hospitalist.

A hospitalist is a physician who, similar to specialists in Europe, treats patients only in a hospital setting. Primary care physicians, especially those in large medical groups, may refer their patients in need of hospitalization to the hospitalist, who will then manage the care in the hospital. Upon discharge, the patient will return to the primary care physician for ongoing care. The hospitalist has reduced the workload for primary care physicians, who no longer must take the one to two hours per day required to see patients in the hospital as well as seeing patients in the office.

The initial expectation was that the growing number of hospitalists would increase the efficiency of the care process, thereby reducing costs, while maintaining (or perhaps improving) the quality of hospital care (Wachter and Goldman 1996). As hospitalists have grown in popularity, a number of analysts have questioned their role, suggesting that they weaken the underlying physician-patient relationship and make coordination of care more difficult (Pham et al. 2008). A study comparing hospital care provided by hospitalists with that provided by family physicians and general internists found that patients treated by hospitalists had a slightly shorter length of stay in the hospital, without any adverse effect on clinical outcomes. The costs of care provided by hospitalists were less than that provided by internists, but no different from hospital care provided by family physicians (Lindenauer et al. 2007). It remains to be seen how the role of hospitalists will change as the reforms triggered by ACA evolve.

Hospitals in the United States generally have a dual system of administration. The physicians who treat patients in the hospital are members of the medical staff. No physician may treat a patient in the hospital unless he or she has first been accepted to membership in the medical staff. The medical staff governs all aspects of hospital care relating to physician care, such as quality review. A nonphysician hospital administrator governs all other nonphysician aspects of hospital activities, such as the nursing, managerial/administrative, and facilities staffs. Most hospitals have an executive committee where the leaders of the medical staff and hospital administrators can jointly discuss hospital management issues.

Hospitals in the United States are more expensive both per day and per stay than hospitals in European countries and Canada. Part of the reason for this is that up until 1983 hospitals had no incentives to limit the amount of care they offered. In fact, the payment system encouraged the acquisition of new facilities and technology, even if they duplicated facilities and services readily available elsewhere in the community.

Since the 1940s, there had been a government program (the Hill-Burton program) to finance the construction of new hospitals throughout the country, many of them in rural communities. In addition, the federal Medicare program included a payment formula that reimbursed hospitals for a large part of the cost of new technology. The result was considerable expansion of the number of hospital beds and the level of hospital technology throughout the country. For most patients, hospitals simply submitted bills to insurance companies (or the federal government, in the case of Medicare) and were fully reimbursed. There was little questioning of whether the care or the cost of care was appropriate.

Because the federal government typically paid about 40 percent of hospital bills throughout the country, primarily through the Medicare and Medicaid programs, it was beginning to cost the federal government a huge amount to continue simply reimbursing hospitals for whatever they spent taking care of patients. The federal government came up with a series of plans to reduce that cost. The first, in the 1970s, was the system of professional standards review organizations, or PSROs. PSROs were groups of local physicians who would review the care provided to Medicare and Medicaid patients to assure that it was appropriate. While this effort was well intentioned, it had little effect, and hospital costs continued to rise.

In an effort to reduce rapidly rising costs, the federal government established a new program. Under this program, rather than simply reimbursing a hospital for the costs of care after the fact, the Medicare program began to pay a fixed amount each time a patient was admitted to the hospital. This plan has two names: the diagnosis-related group (DRG) system and the prospective payment system (PPS); both names mean the same thing. Under the PPS, instead of paying the hospital for each individual service, the government pays hospitals a fixed amount based on how much, on average, it should cost to take care of a patient of a particular type. (The PPS currently only covers hospital costs. Physicians' charges for taking care of patients in the hospital are paid under a completely different system.) The amount of payment is based on what is wrong with the patient. For example, if a patient comes to the hospital with a heart attack that does not have any complications, the government pays the hospital the calculated average cost of taking care of this patient, regardless of what the hospital does to treat the patient. If the patient has a heart attack with complications, the payment is more, based again on the average cost of taking care of such a patient. The same goes for treating pneumonia, appendicitis, or breast cancer. For each type of illness, or DRG, the government pays a fixed amount. If the hospital is able to provide care for the patient at a lower cost than what the government pays, then the hospital keeps the difference. If the hospital's care costs more than what the government pays, then the hospital has to absorb the difference.

Under the previous payment system, with few controls on what the hospital could charge, the incentive was to keep a patient in the hospital as long as possible. Clearly, the incentive under the PPS is to get patients out of the hospital as quickly as possible. This situation led to many hospitals sending patients home (or to less expensive nursing homes) before they were fully recovered. The claim was made that hospitals were discharging patients "quicker and sicker." To counteract this tendency and to assure that patients admitted to the hospital had a legitimate need for hospital care, the federal government replaced the PSRO system with peer review organizations, or PROs. A PRO is a local corporation that contracts with the government to provide oversight of the quality and necessity of the hospital care provided to Medicare patients. While many PROs have considerable participation by local medical associations, they give physicians substantially less control over the review of hospital care than under the previous PSRO system.

What the PPS did was to completely reverse the financial incentives given to hospitals that provide care to Medicare patients. The result was that between 1983 and 1993, there was a substantial decrease in the average length of hospital stay. Because patients were staying in the hospital fewer days, it meant that fewer hospital beds had patients in them at any one time. Fewer patients in the hospital meant less money for the hospital. The reduction in the use of hospitals following the initiation of the PPS resulted in substantially decreased revenues for hospitals.

An additional factor placed a financial squeeze on hospitals: both the federal PPS program and many private health insurers began to encourage outpatient treatment of many conditions that formerly were treated in the hospital. In 1981, only about one of six operations was performed on an outpatient basis, with the rest performed in the hospital. By 1991, about half of all operations were performed on an outpatient basis. Operations such as gall bladder surgery and knee surgery that previously had kept the patient in the hospital for several days were now being done in outpatient "surgicenters," with the patient going home the same day. There has been tremendous growth in the number of these centers dedicated to outpatient surgery. Many patients now being treated in surgicenters as outpatients used to be treated in hospitals. Again, the result was that hospital revenues went down substantially.

The net result of these changes was a decrease in the number of patients in the hospital on any given day (that is, a decrease in the hospital occupancy rate). For several years, a typical hospital may have had 50 percent of its beds empty on any given day. This low occupancy presented a serious problem because of hospital expenses, which break down to 54 percent for labor costs, 37 percent for nonlabor costs, and 9 percent for capital (Iglehart 1993a).

Of the labor and nonlabor costs, some are fixed and some are variable. An example of fixed costs is the need for a hospital administrator. A hospital must have an administrator no matter how many patients are in the hospital. An example of variable costs is the number of nurses working on any given day. It is possible to adjust the number of nurses working based on the number of patients in the hospital. If a hospital is only 1 percent full, almost all the costs are fixed costs. If a hospital is 100 percent full, most of the costs are variable costs. The lower the occupancy rate, the fewer patients there are to share the fixed costs. The larger the share of the fixed costs that must be paid out of each patient's bill, the more expensive the care.

Hospitals that function at low occupancy are inefficient. Hospitals that function at high occupancy are much more efficient. Having large numbers of hospitals that function at low occupancy makes for an inefficient system of health care and adds substantially to the overall cost of care.

In many cities, there were several hospitals, each with 50 percent occupancy or less, when one medium-sized hospital functioning at near capacity could have provided all the hospital care for the entire city. One of the biggest problems facing the hospital industry was what to do about the oversupply of hospital beds. Few people were willing to close local hospitals, especially in rural areas. Dealing with the problem of an over-supply of hospital beds and resultant inefficiency in hospital care was a major policy challenge.

As we will see when we discuss managed care and the growth of the for-profit sector in health care, the effects of declining hospital occupancy were felt throughout the country in a number of ways. Many hospitals incurred large financial losses and faced the possibility of closing down. Hospitals began to merge so they could operate more efficiently. Many smaller hospitals had to close down completely. Hardest hit by these changes were many of the one thousand or so small rural hospitals that are the only health care facilities available in many parts of the country, and many of the inner-city hospitals that take care of the poorest patients, most of whom rely on public support for their medical care.

> **CONCEPT 4.7**
>
> The prospective payment system coupled with the movement to out-patient surgery led to a substantial decline in hospital occupancy rates. Lower occupancy rates mean less hospital income *and* a less efficient hospital. As a result, many hospitals faced serious financial problems in the 1990s, leading to a restructuring of the hospital sector.

An additional change in the organization and structure of medical care has begun to affect how hospital care is provided. In many areas of the country, private investors have developed specialized facilities for treating specific types of medical or surgical problems. Typical examples are specialized cardiac care hospitals, orthopedic hospitals, and surgical hospitals. These are licensed hospitals to which patients are admitted, as is the case for general hospitals. In treating only specific diseases, such as heart disease, however, the specialty hospital can focus on providing care that typically pays well, assuring the financial success of the hospital. In contrast, general hospitals provide both care that pays well, such as cardiac or orthopedic care, and care that does not pay well, such as emergency care. For the general hospital, care that pays well balances care that does not pay as well. If the specialty hospital siphons off only those cases that pay well, however, the general hospital will be left with a higher proportion of cases that do not pay as well, threatening its financial viability. This issue becomes even more complicated when the investors who operate the specialty hospital include the physicians who provide the care in the hospital. This issue will be addressed in more depth in the Chapter 8 on for-profit care.

## Tertiary Care, Quaternary Care, and the Academic Medical Center

If primary care is provided in the physician's office and secondary care is provided in either the specialist's office or the hospital, tertiary care—the third level of care—is provided in specialized regional facilities that serve the needs of many hospitals and communities. Examples of tertiary care centers are neonatal intensive care units, burn centers, and transplant surgery centers. In many cities, each hospital will have facilities for taking care of newborn babies. But when a baby is born prematurely, weighing just a fraction of what a normal baby weighs, that baby is often transferred to a hospital in the region that has developed the hugely expensive facilities and personnel necessary to provide intensive care for these neonates. Similarly, patients with severe burns will typically be transferred to a facility specializing in the treatment of burns. It is at these highly specialized, tertiary referral centers that much of the training of future physicians takes place. Numerous studies have shown that when highly technical care is provided in tertiary referral centers, with a staff that frequently treats patients with those specialized needs, the outcomes for the patient are significantly better. There appears to be a strong, direct relationship between the frequency with which a physician or facility performs a specialized medical procedure and the quality of the outcome for the patient. This growing awareness of the improved quality available at many tertiary referral centers has strengthened the role of these types of facilities in the era of managed care.

For some types of new, often-experimental procedures, a fourth level of care has developed—quaternary care. Some facilities function as national referral centers for certain diseases and procedures. Examples might be combined heart and lung transplantation or experimental cancer treatment.

Most tertiary care centers, and nearly all quaternary care centers, are within hospitals affiliated with a university medical school. These academic medical centers fulfill a dual role. They provide most of the medical research that leads to new types of treatments, and they train the future physicians who will be applying those treatments. Academic medical centers play a crucial role in maintaining and advancing the quality of medical care in this country. Yet, in the current environment of reduced hospital occupancy and reduced payments for hospital services, even academic medical centers have been facing serious financial problems. Academic hospitals have responded to these pressures in a variety of ways, including merger, closure, and conversion to for-profit status. These changes are indicative of the magnitude of the transformation that has been taking place in the structure of academic medical centers in the United States.

> **CONCEPT 4.8**
>
> There appears to be a strong, direct relationship between the frequency with which a physician or facility performs a specialized medical procedure and the quality of the outcome for the patient.

## SUMMARY

The structure of our medical and nursing professions has evolved substantially over the past one hundred years. From a profession that limited entry to women and racial minorities, our medical profession has become one in which half of all new medical students are women. While the need to expand racial and ethnic diversity persists, the explicit barriers confronting nonwhite physicians were largely removed by the 1970s.

Even as the number of primary care physicians has risen slightly over time, the number of specialists within the profession has increased substantially. Economic forces tend to pull physicians toward specialized training. The attraction of primary care is less tangible, drawn principally from the quality of the relationship that develops over time between physician and patient. Establishing and maintaining policies that result in the optimal number and distribution of physicians will remain an important policy issue for years to come.

Though not enjoying the political power of organized medicine, the nursing profession has also evolved to one with high standards of education and training. Nursing has expanded the roles and responsibilities for those nurses with advanced training in areas such as critical care. There are growing concerns, however, as to whether nursing schools will be able to train enough nurses to meet future needs for nursing services.

In light of the increased specialization within these professions, the hospital as an institution of care has also become more specialized. Many of the most technologically advanced procedures and facilities are available only at tertiary centers that serve wide geographic regions.

## PROVISIONS IN THE AFFORDABLE CARE ACT TO EXPAND PRIMARY CARE DELIVERY

By 2014, ACA will expand the availability of health insurance to more than 32 million people who are currently uninsured. Those who drafted ACA were acutely aware that expanding access to health insurance is not the same thing as expanding access to health care, especially to primary care. If there are not enough primary care physicians, those with newly acquired health insurance may have no place to go for their care.

ACA addresses this issue in three important ways. First, it shifts the policy focus of federal funding for graduate medical education (GME), described above, to expanding training in primary care. It does this by shifting a portion of GME funding away from programs that train specialists and redirecting it to programs that train primary care physicians. It also provides for new types of primary care training programs that are based in community settings rather than the traditional hospital setting. These "teaching health centers" will represent collaborations between academic training centers and nonprofit, federally certified community clinics.

A second important policy shift in support of primary care are the provisions in ACA that provide for increased payment for primary care services. Beginning in 2011, the federal Medicare program (discussed in Chapter 6) will provide a 10 percent bonus payment to primary care physicians who treat Medicare beneficiaries. Beginning in 2013, primary care physicians who treat Medicaid patients (discussed in Chapter 7) will see their payment rates, historically substantially lower than Medicare rates, raised to the same rates as those paid by Medicare. In addition, increased federal funding will go to the National Health Service Corps and other programs that provide repayment of educational loans for primary care physicians who practice in areas of the country, typically rural areas and inner cities, which have documented medical manpower shortages.

The third important policy shift ACA makes in support of expanding primary care delivery is substantially increased support for a new model of organizing primary care: the patient-centered medical home. Larson and Reid have described the history of "The Patient-Centered Medical Home (PCMH) Movement" (Larson and Reid 2010). A joint statement issued by a consortium of primary care professional organizations defines the PCMH as "an approach to providing comprehensive primary care for children, youth and adults [in] a health care setting that facilitates partnerships between individual patients, and their personal physicians, and when appropriate, the patient's family" (American Academy of Family Physicians, American Academy of Pediatrics, American College of Physicians, and American Osteopathic Association 2007).

Stange et al. (2010, p. 601) have identified four core components of a PCMH:

1. the fundamental tenets of primary care: first contact access, comprehensiveness, integration/coordination, and relationships involving sustained partnership
2. new ways of organizing practice
3. development of practices' internal capabilities
4. related health care system and reimbursement changes

Rather than a traditional physician's office, the PCMH will involve a team of providers, including physicians, allied professionals such as nurse practitioners or physician's assistants, as well as support personnel with a range of professional skills. While individual patients or families may identify with one particular member of the team as their principal provider, it will be the responsibility of the team as a whole to assure quality and accessible care. This team approach will be supported by an electronic health record system that will be able to track a patient's care, enable providers access to the records of a patient's care, and facilitate ongoing quality assessments of the care provided to patients.

ACA provides targeted funding to develop, expand, and evaluate PCMH models of care in a range of geographic locations. Over time, as evidence is developed evaluating the optimal arrangements of PCMHs, reimbursement for care will be enhanced for those centers meeting established guidelines. The expectation is that by expanding the training of primary care physicians, increasing the payment for primary care services, and supporting high-quality PCMHs, ACA will expand access to quality primary care not only for those expected to obtain new health insurance coverage, but for patients throughout the country.

# 5

# Health Insurance, HMOs, and the Managed Care Revolution

In looking at alternative ways to pay for health care, we must appreciate that health care does not fit well into the traditional insurance model. Insurance is based on the concept of the random hazard: houses will burn down somewhat at random, people will get into car accidents somewhat at random. It is possible to separate people into risk categories, but within a risk category, hazards are assumed to occur somewhat randomly. One can predict the average rate at which hazards will occur within a certain risk group, estimate the aggregate cost of these hazards, add on a certain percentage for profit and administrative costs, and divide the total by the number of people to be insured. This gives the insurance premium to be charged.

Two aspects of health care make it particularly inappropriate for this insurance model:

1. Rather than being a truly random occurrence, the need for health care is to a large extent defined by physicians. The pattern of treatment and the associated costs of an illness or injury can vary substantially from physician to physician.
2. Health insurance is particularly subject to the problem of "moral hazard": once a person is insured, that person is more likely to define a problem as an illness and is more likely to seek care.

These factors make it difficult to predict health care expenditures for a population group. As a result, many traditional insurance companies shied away from insuring for health care. Before the 1930s, few options were available for purchasing insurance to cover the cost of medical care. Those plans that did exist usually provided services directly to members of certain employee or other work-based groups and were not available to the general public.

This all changed during the Great Depression of the 1930s. As discussed in Chapter 4, the inability of many individuals and families to pay the cost of medical care led to the creation of the Blue Cross and Blue Shield programs. Both the American Medical Association (AMA) and the American Hospital Association (AHA) supported these new plans, as long as doctors maintained control over medical decisions. By 1939, the majority of states had developed insurance programs of this type.

Before World War II, these insurance plans covered a relatively small number of people. An important decision was made in the 1940s, however, that was to have far-reaching effects on health insurance and health care. During World War II, in order

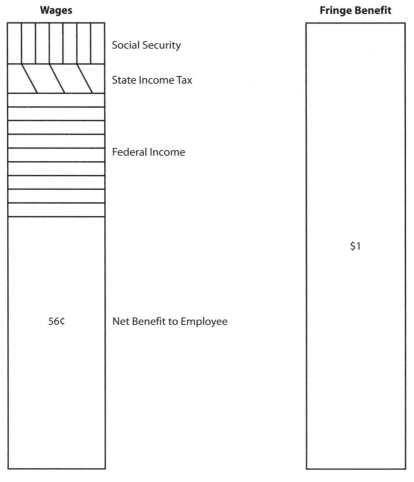

FIGURE 5.1. Net Benefit to the Employee of $1 Taken Either as Added Wages or as Added Fringe Benefits

to prevent inflation, the federal government placed price controls on most consumer goods. This included a freeze on all wages. The government ruled, however, that any fringe benefits from work were exempt from price controls. Thus, employees and their labor unions could not bargain for increased wages, but they could bargain for better health insurance as a fringe benefit. These policies carried over into the period after World War II, leading to greater and greater emphasis on increasing fringe benefits from work as well as wages. The main fringe benefit workers sought was health insurance.

A second government decision was to have equally powerful effects. In 1954, the government ruled that fringe benefits did not count as taxable income and thus were not subject to income tax. The combination of these two policies has had profound effects on the way we pay for health care as a society and what we have come to expect from health care as individuals. Consider the following example, as illustrated in Figure 5.1.

If an employer wanted to raise an employee's pay by $1, the employer would have two choices: give the $1 as additional cash wages, or use the $1 to purchase additional fringe benefits. To the employer, the two options are roughly equivalent, because either can be considered a tax-deductible business expense. (The employer would have to pay certain payroll taxes on the cash contribution that are not required to be paid for the added fringe benefits.) From the perspective of the worker, however, the two options look very different. Under tax law, the added $1 of wages would be subject to a combination of federal, state, and Social Security taxes that would, for a typical middle-income worker, eat up as much as 44¢, leaving the worker with a net gain of 56¢. On the other hand, by taking the added $1 as fringe benefits such as health insurance, the worker would gain a full $1 worth of benefit, because no taxes would apply. To the worker, it is often preferable to take a wage increase as added fringe benefit rather than as cash wages. To the employer, it makes less difference. Workers have thus come to expect to receive their health insurance as a fringe benefit of their employment.

In essence, this policy provides a federal tax subsidy for the purchase of health insurance as a fringe benefit. It is not a direct subsidy, but rather an indirect subsidy, in that less money comes into the federal treasury. This federal subsidy costs the treasury tens of billions of dollars in lost tax revenues every year and constitutes the third largest federal health care program after Medicare and Medicaid. The laws that created this subsidy were passed to address problems very different from health insurance, yet their

> **CONCEPT 5.1**
>
> Largely as a result of two decisions by the federal government in the 1940s and 1950s, neither of which dealt specifically with health care, the United States has adopted an employment-based system of financing health care. Most people now obtain their health insurance as a nontaxable fringe benefit from work.

cumulative effect over time has been to create a de facto national policy of employment-based health insurance. As is often the case, policy decisions at the federal level have long-range effects that were never envisioned at the time of their original passage.

A consequence of these tax policies is that people who receive health insurance as a fringe benefit tend to want more health insurance than they would if they were paying for it themselves.

Consider the following example. Assume for the moment that you are a patient with a health insurance policy with a $500 yearly deductible. (That is, you pay the first $500 for medical care each year, and the insurance policy pays 100 percent of everything over $500.) Assume also that you have a medical condition such as asthma, and you expect to incur at least $500 in yearly medical expenses. Finally, assume that you have $1,000 in a savings account.

A friendly insurance agent offers you the following option.

Option 1: The agent offers to sell you an additional health insurance policy to cover the first $500 of medical expenses each year. The cost of this policy is $600 ($500 to cover your expected medical costs, $50 to cover the administrative costs of the policy, and $50 to cover profit for the agent and the insurance company).

Do you want to buy the policy? Would any reasonable person in your situation choose to buy this policy?

It does not make much sense to purchase a policy to cover $500 in medical expenses when that policy costs $600. It makes more sense to politely refuse the insurance agent's offer and to pay the expenses directly, thus saving the $100 you would otherwise have to pay to cover overhead and profit for the insurance company. For people without a known medical condition, it makes even less sense to buy the additional policy.

Your employer, it turns out, has had a very good year, and decides to give you a salary raise of $600 per year. Now consider option 2.

Option 2: The agent has heard of your good fortune and again offers to sell you the additional health insurance policy to cover the first $500 of medical expenses each year. The cost of the policy is again $600, but the agent reasons that because you have received a raise of $600 you will now be more interested in the policy.

As illustrated in Figure 5.1, however, you pay 44 percent of any additional salary in taxes. Thus, despite your employer's generosity, you receive only $336 more per year in take-home pay after the raise ($600 × 56%). For the same reasons cited in option 1, it still makes no sense to buy the additional policy.

Option 3: Your employer, instead of giving you a raise in salary, offers to buy you the same supplemental health insurance policy to cover the first $500 in medical expenses each year. The cost of the policy to the employer is still $600.

Now do you want to buy the policy? What is the cost of the policy to you, in terms of income you have to forgo?

If you take the raise in pay as wages, you will receive $336 in net benefit per year. If you take the raise as added health insurance, you will receive $500 in benefit (the $500 you would otherwise have paid out of pocket for the care for your asthma). In this case, it makes sense to ask your employer to give you the raise in the form of added health insurance, even though you would never buy the same level of insurance if you were paying with your own money.

If you went out to purchase a car and you were guaranteed a government subsidy for 44 percent of the car's price, you would buy a very different car from what you would buy if you had to pay the full price yourself. The same is true of health insurance. This federal policy has led to people choosing, wanting, and expecting health insurance policies that are more comprehensive than they would select if they were paying with their own money.

Based on these federal policies, employer-provided, government-subsidized private health insurance came to be the predominant model of health insurance in this country. Until the 1980s, this employer-based health insurance provided in nearly all cases what has been referred to as indemnity insurance. The company indemnifies the patient for the cost of health care. The patient seeks medical care, pays for it directly to the provider, and in turn is reimbursed by the insurance company.

> **CONCEPT 5.2**
>
> The tax exclusion of health insurance obtained as a fringe benefit from work encourages employees to obtain more insurance than they would if they were paying for it themselves, often involving more comprehensive benefits and lower out-of-pocket expenditures.

Most of these employer-provided health plans used what is called "experience rating" in determining how much to charge the employer for the cost of care. Premiums were set according to a combination of factors: the projected cost of providing care for employees, administrative costs and profit for the insurance company, and the carryover of any losses from the previous year. So long as insurance companies were able to predict accurately how much it would cost to provide medical care for all the employees each year, premiums paid by employers would rise at a gradual, predictable rate. If medical care costs were to rise rapidly and unpredictably, however, yearly increases in indemnity insurance premiums could be quite large, as illustrated in Figure 5.2.

For a period of time in the 1980s, this was precisely the situation confronting both employers and insurers. Due largely to the explosion in medical technology, health care costs began to rise more rapidly than anyone expected. The result was that many indemnity insurance carriers found that the health care costs for which they were responsible were considerably more than they had predicted, resulting in a loss for the year. This "underwriting loss" would then be added to the premiums charged to an employer for the coming year. The employer was hit with a double increase, paying both for the projected increase in the cost of care for the current year and for the underwriting loss for the previous year. Employers faced increasing costs for their

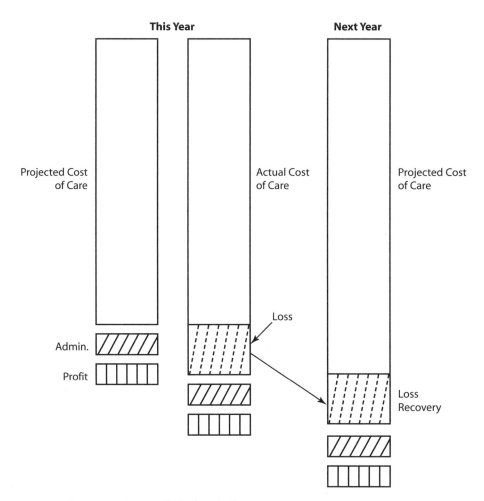

FIGURE 5.2. Setting Premiums under Indemnity Insurance

employees' health insurance based on the experience of their employees during the previous year (thus the term "experience rating"). In essence, the insurance company passed on to employers the risk involved in insuring their employees for the cost of health care.

Many of the indemnity insurance companies acted mainly as pass-through agents, taking a share of all premiums to pay overhead and profit while assuming relatively little risk. A number of large companies concluded that it would be cheaper to pay for their own employees' health care directly than to pay an insurance company to do it for them. They established self-insurance plans that lowered administrative costs, and they kept the part of the premium paid to cover insurance company profit. The money that they would have paid for health insurance premiums was put aside in a special health care fund. When employees got sick, they simply gave the bill to their employer, with no insurance intermediary. Many companies hired consulting firms to handle only the administration of the plan. At one point in the early 1990s, just before the explosion in managed care, nearly half of all employers and more than 80 percent of companies with more than five thousand employees provided health insurance through these self-insured plans. As discussed in Chapter 2, however, the cost of medical care continued to rise sharply. Paying for the cost of health insurance was an increasingly large part of the cost of doing business. Insuring employees based on the indemnity model, in which most physicians and hospitals could still count on a fee for every service they performed with little oversight or constraint on the use of services, was proving to be unworkable. Thus, in 1993, when President Bill Clinton proposed a national system of care based on managed care and managed competition, many employers were initially supportive. They saw health maintenance organizations (HMOs) and other managed care plans that had developed in the previous twenty years as attractive options to traditional fee-for-service, indemnity insurance.

## INSURANCE PLANS, SERVICE PLANS, AND CAPITATION

Before discussing the origins of HMOs, I will first distinguish two alternative means of providing payment for health care services and define capitation as a method of paying for health care. The traditional means of paying for health care was with indemnity insurance plans under which patients sought their own source of care and were reimbursed for the cost of that care. Under these insurance plans, doctors were typically paid on a fee-for-service basis, with each separate service generating a professional fee.

As an alternative to fee-for-service medicine, a number of organizations in the early part of the twentieth century wanted to provide health care directly to a defined population of patients rather than reimbursing patients for the cost of care. These included organizations such as farm cooperatives, factories, and mining towns. Under these arrangements, a certain amount of money would be contributed each month, either by the workers or by their employer. This money would be pooled and would be used to hire physicians to take care of the people and to pay for hospital care for the people. Each patient covered under this type of service plan was assured the opportunity to receive all necessary medical care with no fees other than the previously established monthly contribution. Physicians working under service plans were typically paid a salary rather than on a fee-for-service basis.

> **CONCEPT 5.3**
>
> Under an *indemnity insurance plan,* patients arrange care on their own and are reimbursed for the cost of the care. Reimbursement for care is financed by insurance premiums. Under a *service plan,* patients come to an identified source of care and receive whatever service they need. Payment for these services comes from the pooling of monthly contributions.

> **CONCEPT 5.4**
>
> *Capitation* is a method of paying for health care under which a service provider receives a fixed amount of money per person (the capitation rate) and in return agrees to provide all necessary care to enrolled members. Capitation rates are usually per month or per year.

Both insurance plans and service plans work on a prepaid basis. The insurance plan depends on insurance premiums, paid by either the employer or the individual employee. The service plan depends on a fixed amount of money contributed (again, by either the employer or the individual employee) to a central pool of funds. From this pool of funds, the costs of providing service to patients enrolled in the plan must be drawn. Thus, for the service plan, a fixed amount of money is available for care each year. Any losses incurred cannot simply be added to the costs of next year's care. Service plans use what has come to be called the "capitation" method of paying for health care.

Throughout the early part of the twentieth century, as it was gaining increasing power over the practice of medicine, the AMA opposed the creation of service plans. The AMA objected to two aspects of service plans: (1) doctors being paid a salary instead of fee-for-service, and (2) doctors being employed by an organization rather than being independent practitioners. Even though many patients and doctors liked these types of arrangements, the AMA declared both practices to be unethical. Any doctor who violated the ethical rules established by the AMA was barred from using local community hospitals. Because these doctors could not use a hospital, they could not take care of their patients. In the face of this opposition from the AMA, by the 1930s most of these service plans had gone out of business.

A few service plans, however, were able not only to survive but also to prosper as an alternative to the traditional fee-for-service insurance model. These included the Group Health Cooperative of Puget Sound in Seattle, the Health Insurance Plan of New York, and the Kaiser Permanente Health Care System on the West Coast. I will examine the origins of Kaiser Permanente, the most successful of these service plans, to understand more about why these plans not only survived but also eventually provided the model around which the entire movement to managed care was centered.

## KAISER PERMANENTE AND THE DEVELOPMENT OF HEALTH MAINTENANCE ORGANIZATIONS

In 1932, the city of Los Angeles began work on what was then a mammoth construction project: a 242-mile-long aqueduct across the Southern California desert to bring water from the Colorado River to the growing metropolis of Los Angeles. A number of industrialists collaborated on the project, among them Henry J. Kaiser. With more than five thousand workers in the field, and with on-the-job injuries all too frequent, there was a pressing need to provide medical care for workers close to the construction site.

Dr. Sidney Garfield was a young physician who had just completed training as a surgeon at Los Angeles County Hospital. With meager prospects for employment during the depth of the Depression, he saw an opportunity for an independent medical practice in the desert, close to the construction sites. He borrowed $50,000, built a small hospital, and set up a traditional fee-for-service practice in the desert. Unfortunately, he soon found the income from such a practice to be much less than he expected, and his hospital was near bankruptcy (Smillie 1991).

Dr. Garfield met with a representative of Mr. Kaiser's construction company. The construction company did not want the hospital to close, as it was the only source of care close to the construction site. The two of them worked out a plan under which the company would pay Dr. Garfield $1.50 per worker per month, and in return Dr. Garfield would provide all necessary medical care for on-the-job injuries. In addition, workers were offered the opportunity of having an additional $1.50 taken out of their paychecks each month, in return for which they could go to Dr. Garfield for treatment of medical problems not related to their work. Mr. Kaiser enthusiastically approved, and the plan was put in place.

This capitation arrangement offered workers a service plan rather than a traditional insurance plan and turned out to be very successful. In a short time, the hospital was on firm financial ground, and Dr. Garfield was receiving a good income.

In 1938, Mr. Kaiser received the contract to build the Grand Coulee Dam on the Columbia River in eastern Washington. Because this construction project was far away from cities, many workers brought their families with them. Dr. Garfield and Mr. Kaiser agreed to establish a service plan for medical care for the workers as well as their families, based on the successful model in the California desert. For a fixed fee per person per month, paid partially by Kaiser and partially by the workers, workers and their families could receive all necessary care at the hospital and medical offices organized by Dr. Garfield. Again, the plan was successful, with Dr. Garfield hiring a number of young physicians to work for his new medical plan. The labor unions representing the construction workers were especially pleased, as previous attempts at providing medical care had been of questionable quality.

Recall, however, that the AMA had declared prepaid service plans based on capitation for workers and salaries for doctors to be unethical. An editorial published in *JAMA* in 1932 labeled these prepaid group practice plans "medical soviets" and went on to say that "such plans will mean the destruction of private practice . . . they are, in a word, 'unethical'" (American Medical Association 1932, p. 1950). Because both the Los Angeles aqueduct project and the Grand Coulee project were in rural areas, however, the AMA and their local affiliates paid little attention to them. Also, because Dr. Garfield operated his own hospital close to the work sites, he did not need to have the medical society's approval to use a hospital. World War II, however, was to change all of this. In Dr. Garfield's own words, "It is interesting to note that those ten years of basic development of our health plan took place in remote isolated areas of the country—areas that required us to innovate to survive, and also where we had no opposition. Nobody cared what we did. I don't think it could have ever happened in any other fashion" (Garfield 1974, p. 2).

When World War II came, Mr. Kaiser quickly began producing liberty ships at shipyards in Portland, Oregon, and Richmond, California. Much of the steel for these ships came from the Kaiser steel mill in Southern California. Again, Mr. Kaiser turned to Dr. Garfield to organize the medical care for shipyard workers and their families. This time the AMA and their state affiliates opposed the plan and would not permit Dr. Garfield or his team of more than ninety doctors to use local hospitals. Despite a personal visit by Mr. Kaiser to its Chicago headquarters, the AMA would not relent. Faced with no alternative, Mr. Kaiser either built or bought a hospital in each of the three locales where the new Kaiser health plan was in operation.

After World War II, many employee groups beyond the shipyard workers wanted to join Kaiser's health plan. It provided a guarantee of all necessary care for a fixed fee per month. People liked both the price and the guaranteed availability of care. The AMA, however, continued to oppose Kaiser and other prepaid group practices. Through a series of legal actions in the 1940s and 1950s, the organized medical profession aggressively tried to put these plans out of business. Based largely on antitrust laws, the health plans were able to gain court protections, and in the late 1950s, a truce of sorts was achieved. The AMA ended its efforts to close Kaiser's health plan.

The Kaiser plan grew and flourished due largely to its success with labor unions and other large employee groups. Unfortunately, this growth and success contributed to tension between Mr. Kaiser and Dr. Garfield. Each wanted to control the growing organization. After lengthy negotiations, they agreed to maintain three separate organizations: a health plan, a hospital corporation, and a doctors' group. Kaiser would be in charge of the hospital and health plan organizations. Garfield would be in charge of the doctors' organization. Mr. Kaiser agreed that he would use only Dr. Garfield's doctors' organization for the patients covered by his health plan. Dr. Garfield agreed that his doctors would treat only patients in Kaiser's health plan. Thus, they were each dependent on the other.

The resulting Kaiser Permanente Health Plan grew and prospered throughout the 1950s and 1960s. It consistently cost less than comparable care under fee-for-service insurance. From its original three hospitals, it grew to become the largest HMO in the United States, providing care in several regions of the country. It depended on the continued cooperation and interdependence of the physicians, the hospitals, and the health plan. The health plan was set up as a nonprofit foundation, allowing it to remain tax-exempt. Likewise, the hospitals were owned and operated by a nonprofit corporation. Only the doctors operated on a for-profit basis. The structure of the Kaiser Permanente Health Plan is illustrated in Figure 5.3.

The model represented by Kaiser Permanente and other similar plans was initially called "prepaid group practice." For a fixed monthly fee (the capitation rate) paid to the Kaiser Foundation Health Plan by either patients or their employer, the health

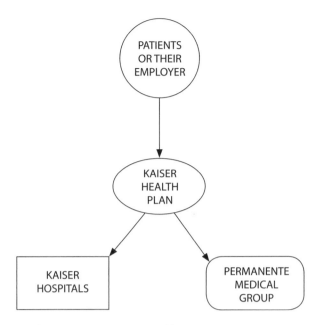

FIGURE 5.3. Structure of the Kaiser Permanente Health Care System

plan would provide its members with all necessary health care. They would do this by contracting with the Kaiser Hospital Corporation for hospital care and with the Permanente Medical Group for physician care and other outpatient services.

The service plans represented by prepaid group practices such as Kaiser Permanente were consistently able to provide comprehensive care at a substantially lower cost than the insurance plans using the traditional fee-for-service method of paying for care. Repeated research studies documented this fact. Critics of these service plans, however, suggested that their lower cost of care was because they tended to attract younger, healthier patients who needed less care. If they took care of patient populations comparable to those covered by fee-for-service insurance plans, it was suggested that the service plan's cost advantage would disappear.

This issue was settled convincingly by an experiment done by the RAND Corporation in the 1980s (Manning et al. 1984). This experiment enrolled a group of 1,580 patients in Seattle and paid for their health insurance for a period of between three and five years. To be sure that patients in one type of system were not sicker on average than in the other, the experiment randomly assigned patients to receive all care either from the Group Health Cooperative of Puget Sound (a large, prepaid group practice similar in many ways to Kaiser Permanente) or from traditional fee-for-service physician offices. The results of the experiment, shown in Table 5.1, demonstrated that, given comparable patient populations, prepaid group practice service plans could be as much as one-third less expensive than fee-for-service insurance plans for comparable care.

Table 5.1. Comparison of the Cost of Care (per year) under Prepaid Group Practice and Fee-for-Service Systems

| System | Total Cost per Patient | Hospital Admissions per 1,000 Patients | Office Visits per Patient |
|---|---|---|---|
| Prepaid group practice | $439 | 8.4 | 4.3 |
| Fee-for-service | $609 | 13.8 | 4.2 |

*Source:* Data from Manning et al. 1984.

Table 5.2. Comparison of Patient Satisfaction with Prepaid Group Practice (PPGP) and Fee-for-Service (FFS) Systems

| | Differences in Mean Satisfaction ($p < 0.05$) with | |
|---|---|---|
| | PPGP | FFS |
| Access to care | − | + |
| Waiting time in the office | + | − |
| Technical quality of care | No difference | |
| Interpersonal nature of care | − | + |
| Overall satisfaction with care | − | + |

*Source:* Data from Davies et al. 1986.

The researchers also studied whether patients' health was any better in one type of plan or the other. Poor people in the prepaid group practice tended to have problems in two areas: control of blood pressure and control of glaucoma. Otherwise, the health of the two groups of patients was substantially the same (Sloss et al. 1987).

---

**CONCEPT 5.5**

Certain types of prepaid group practice service plans are able to provide care that is substantially less expensive than traditional fee-for-service care. Health outcomes under the two systems are approximately the same. The experience of obtaining care from a prepaid group practice, however, is often less satisfactory from the patient's perspective.

---

It is important to point out that the difference between prepaid group practice and fee-for service systems in this study was in the use of hospitals, and not in the use of outpatient physician services. There was no evidence that the use of primary care services and other outpatient services was different in prepaid group practices compared to fee-for-service. Patients found the experience of obtaining care from the prepaid group practices to be significantly less satisfactory than from the fee-for-service system, however (Davies et al. 1986). As shown in Table 5.2, there was lower patient satisfaction in a number of aspects of the primary care process.

## THE HEALTH MAINTENANCE ORGANIZATION ACT OF 1973 AND THE EXPANSION OF HMO MODELS

Even before the RAND health insurance experiment, a number of individuals and groups, both within government and in the private sector, had taken note of the cost savings available through prepaid group practice service plans. Several leaders of organized labor, led by Walter Reuther of the United Auto Workers Union, called for national health care reform based on expansion of the prepaid group practice model. In 1970, Senator Ted Kennedy introduced legislation to this end, setting off a national debate about health care reform. Even at that time, there remained laws in many states making prepaid group practice illegal. These laws were left over from the period when the AMA was fighting against the growth of prepaid group practice.

A number of groups introduced proposals for reform. While members of Congress were not able to agree on comprehensive reform, they did pass the Health Maintenance Organizations Act of 1973 (P.L. 93-222). Following the enactment of this law, prepaid group practices came to be known instead as health maintenance organizations, or simply HMOs. The HMO Act did five main things:

1. It removed pre-existing state laws prohibiting HMOs.
2. It offered federal subsidies for the establishment of new HMOs.
3. It defined minimum standards to be certified as a "federally qualified HMO." A key element of these standards was the requirement that the HMO be organized on a nonprofit basis.
4. Where HMOs were available, it required all employers who offered health insurance to their employees also to offer an HMO as an option.
5. In a compromise with the AMA, it broadened the definition of an HMO to include a range of organizational and payment structures

Figure 5.4 illustrates the basic structure of an HMO after enactment of the HMO Act. The HMO itself, as defined by the HMO Act, was intended to be a nonprofit corporation that contracted with employers or with individual patients to provide necessary medical care. To pay for the care, employers or individual subscribers would make a monthly capitation payment to the HMO. The HMO would then enter into contractual agreements with a range of physicians or physician groups, and with a range of hospitals. Patients who join the HMO (often referred to as subscribers) are eligible to obtain care from any physician or hospital that has contracted with the HMO. If a subscriber seeks medical care from a physician or a hospital that has not contracted with the HMO, however, there would be no payment from the HMO for that care. By joining an HMO, a subscriber agrees to obtain care only from doctors and hospitals who have joined the HMO.

There are a variety of ways in which the arrangements among the HMO, the doctors, and the hospitals can be structured. Under the most common arrangement, the HMO operates a health plan that does not provide care directly. It does not own hospitals and does not hire physicians. Instead, it contracts with groups of physicians to provide care for its members, and with either a chain of hospitals or a series of individual hospitals to provide hospital care for its members. The physician groups in turn are paid a "subcapitation" rate from the HMO. Through a contract with the HMO,

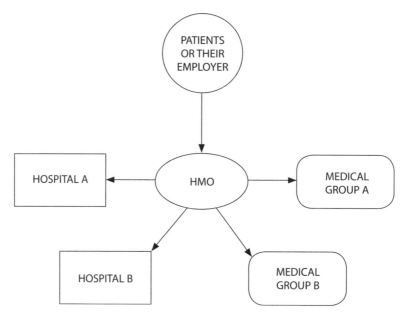

FIGURE 5.4. Model of an HMO Following Enactment of the HMO Act of 1973

the medical group is paid a share of the capitation rate received by the HMO, and in return, the group agrees to provide all necessary physician services for the members of the HMO who select that medical group for their care. Within each medical group, physicians can be paid by salary, by a fixed annual fee for each patient cared for, or by fee-for-service, depending on how the group is organized internally. Hospitals can be paid either a fixed amount per year or separately for each hospital admission. This type of arrangement is often referred to as a "group-model HMO."

A variation on the group-model arrangement is the independent practice association, or IPA HMO. An IPA HMO is a corporation usually formed and managed by physicians in smaller offices who are not part of large medical groups. The HMO accepts capitation payments for enrolled members and in turn contracts with individual physicians who have signed a contract with the IPA. Under the contract, the physician agrees to treat HMO patients either on a discounted fee-for-service basis or for a fixed amount per patient per year. Hospitals are paid in essentially the same manner as in a group-model HMO.

As a third option, the HMO might actually own the hospitals it uses and hire doctors as employees. This arrangement is often referred to as a "staff-model HMO." The Group Health Cooperative of Puget Sound in the state of Washington, one of the nation's oldest HMOs, was for many years structured as a staff-model HMO. In the years since passage of the HMO Act, staff-model and IPA HMOs have become much less common.

While there are similarities between the way the Kaiser Permanente system is structured, as shown in Figure 5.3, and the structure illustrated in Figure 5.4, there are key differences that set the two apart. Under the Kaiser system, there is only one group of doctors and only one group of hospitals. Each agrees to work only with the other. This sets up a mutual dependency in managing resources to assure success. Under the structure illustrated in Figure 5.4, the medical groups contracting with the HMO may actually be competitors of the other medical groups, and the hospitals may be competitors. Additionally, the doctors have no personal stake in the success of the hospitals. While the Kaiser Permanente system has been able to maintain a culture of cooperation and collaboration among its doctors and hospitals, the same cannot be said for many of the newer types of HMOs that developed following the HMO Act.

Whatever the structure of the HMO, it operates as a service plan in that patients receive service from an established list of physicians. Patients may be responsible for a limited, partial payment for care they receive, but after having made this co-payment, they have no further financial responsibility for their care. Recall that under traditional fee-for-service plans, there is no limit on how much can be spent on care each year. For all types of HMOs, a fixed amount of money is available each year, based on the capitation rate and the number of members enrolled. An HMO is obligated to provide all necessary care to all enrolled members for that amount of money, and must take steps to provide care to its members while staying within its budget.

In a fee-for-service insurance system, there is no incentive to hold down costs. Costs are not minimized

- by the patient, who pays only a small amount of the bill
- by the hospitals, which are paid for each patient regardless of how necessary the care is
- by physicians, whose incentive is to provide more care, because the more care they provide, the more money they get

In an HMO, on the other hand, there is a strong incentive to hold down costs. An excessive use of services early in the year can lead to a budget shortfall later in the year, leaving inadequate funds to cover salaries and other costs. Physicians in an HMO must be careful to provide only the care that is absolutely necessary. As we saw from the RAND health insurance experiment, the incentives in an HMO to hold down costs have been associated with cost savings of more than 30 percent relative to the fee-for-service alternative. These savings were mainly in the use of the hospital and of expensive, high-tech treatments and not in the use of primary care and other outpatient services.

> **CONCEPT 5.6**
>
> In a traditional fee-for-service insurance system, there are few incentives to constrain the cost of care. In an HMO system, there are powerful incentives to constrain the cost of care.

## OTHER TYPES OF MANAGED CARE PLANS

In the period following the enactment of the HMO Act, another new type of managed care plan was developed to compete both with HMOs and with traditional fee-for-service systems. Referred to as a "preferred provider organization" (PPO), this new plan uses many of the same mechanisms to reduce utilization and costs, but is more loosely structured than HMOs and does not technically qualify as an HMO.

As illustrated in Figure 5.5, a PPO is usually organized by an insurance company as an alternative to traditional indemnity insurance. The insurance company contracts with physicians and hospitals that agree to give a discount to patients with this insurance. These providers, called "preferred providers," continue to be paid on a fee-for-service basis, only at a reduced rate for PPO patients. A patient with this type of insurance can go anywhere for care, but if the patient chooses a physician or a hospital not on the list of preferred providers, the patient has to pay substantially more for care. For example, the PPO might pay 100 percent of the cost of care from a preferred provider (after the patient makes a predefined co-payment) and only 80 percent of the cost of care from other providers. There is usually some form of control over the use of hospital treatment in PPOs, but it is not as stringent as in an HMO. PPOs will typically negotiate reduced rates with a specific group of hospitals. Again, members are free to obtain care at any hospital, but will have a lower level of coverage for care received from hospitals that have not signed an agreement with the PPO. It should be noted that

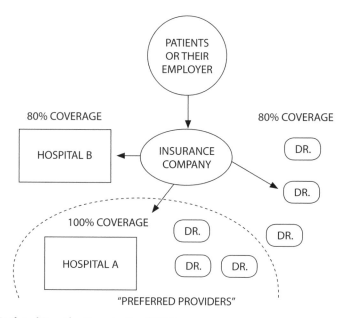

FIGURE 5.5. Preferred Provider Organization (PPO)

neither the physicians in a PPO nor the hospitals have any financial stake in the success of the company.

Some companies have offered hybrid plans that include elements of both an HMO and a PPO, often referred to as point-of-service plans (POSs). Patients in a POS plan have three choices for receiving care, each with a different level of coverage.

1. If the patient receives care from physicians in the HMO, the patient pays little for care (usually on the level of $20 to $30 co-payment per visit).

2. If the patient receives care from physicians on the list of preferred providers associated with the POS, the patient pays a larger portion of the cost of care (typically 20 to 30% of the cost of care).

3. If the patient receives care from a physician or hospital not associated with the POS, the patient pays a substantial portion of the cost of care (typically 40 to 50%).

Thus, in a POS, patients have three options for obtaining care. The more patients are willing to limit their choice of physicians to those contracting with the POS, the less they have to pay. Based on this ability to choose the level of coverage, POS plans are sometimes referred to as "triple option plans."

## COMPARING THE COST AND QUALITY OF NEW DELIVERY MODELS: THE MEDICAL OUTCOMES STUDY

The cost savings of HMOs documented by the RAND health insurance experiment pertained to large, centralized HMOs such as Kaiser Permanente and the Group Health Cooperative of Puget Sound. The structure of many of the newer HMOs was quite different from that of the traditional model with salaried physicians and centralized facilities. It was not known if many of the newer types of HMOs were able to achieve the same cost savings compared to fee-for-service systems. To answer this question, another large study was undertaken: the Medical Outcomes Study (Safran, Tarlov, and Rogers 1994). This study involved 1,208 patients with chronic diseases and followed them for four years. The patients were enrolled in one of three types of plan: a large group-model HMO, an IPA HMO, and a traditional fee-for-service indemnity plan. The study followed two main outcomes: primary care quality and the change in patients' health status over the four years of the study. Results of the study, comparing the three alternative systems, are shown in Table 5.3.

Compared to the IPA HMO and the fee-for-service option, the group HMO had a lower cost of care and better coordination among specialists and primary care physicians. But it had lower ratings than either of the two alternatives for access to care, continuity of care, and comprehensiveness of care. There were no significant differences in how patients viewed either the interpersonal or the technical skills of their

Table 5.3. Results of the Medical Outcomes Study Comparing
the Quality of Primary Care in a Group HMO, IPA HMO,
and Traditional Fee-for-Service (FFS) Delivery System

|  | HMO | IPA | FFS |
|---|---|---|---|
| Cost of care | ++ | + | – |
| Coordination | + | – | – |
| Access to care | – | + | + |
| Comprehensiveness | – | + | + |
| Continuity | – | + | ++ |
| Doctor |  |  |  |
|    Interpersonal skills | NS | NS | NS |
|    Technical skills | NS | NS | NS |

*Source:* Data from Safran, Tarlov, and Rogers 1994.
   *Notes:* Results show comparative levels of quality p < 0.05.
NS = no significant difference.

physicians. Overall, there were no significant differences in health outcomes for the patients studied, although low-income patients did show worse health outcomes in the group HMO.

These findings are similar to the findings of the RAND experiment: while HMOs save money, they have problems in the quality of the primary care process. These problems frequently lead to lower overall levels of patient satisfaction in HMOs versus traditional fee-for-service practitioners. IPA HMOs, which rely on fee-for-service payment to physicians under an overall capitation framework, seem to fall somewhere in between group HMOs and traditional fee-for-service. In addition, these studies consistently identify worse health outcomes for low-income patients enrolled in HMOs. The causes of these lower health outcomes are not fully understood, although they may have to do with low-income patients having problems navigating the complex organizational systems inherent in many large HMOs.

## THE SPREAD OF THE HMO

The development and expansion of the HMO and other types of managed care delivery systems brought a fundamental change to health care in the United States. Driven largely by concerns over rising costs, the HMO Act firmly established the role of the HMO in U.S. health care. The federal government took a series of steps to promote the spread of HMOs, including financial incentives and regulatory support. Under the original HMO Act, to be eligible for federal support, HMOs had to meet three basic requirements:

1. The HMO had to offer a specified list of benefits to all members.
2. The HMO had to charge all members the same monthly premium, regardless of their health status (referred to as "community rating").
3. The HMO had to be structured as a nonprofit organization.

Ironically, at first the HMO Act brought the creation of new HMOs in the United States to a halt. The list of covered services required by the act was substantially more

eting fee-for-service insur-
by the government and to
regardless of health status
y did *not* do), new HMOs
a consequence of these re-
following enactment of the

MOs must meet to receive
HMOs began as intended.
fifty new HMOs had quali-
rolled in HMOs nationwide.
century, the AMA opposed
itation method of payment.
at once HMOs were out of
1989, enrollment in HMOs
olled. The growth of HMOs
ver a period of thirty years,
nized almost exclusively on
nd other forms of capitated,

By the early 1990s, the accumulated evidence had demonstrated that HMOs and other types of managed care plans offered a way to reduce the cost of care without adverse effects on the health of most patients. The federal government, state governments, and employers began to look at HMOs as policy alternatives to traditional fee-for-service care. The growing popularity of these plans set the stage for the national debate on health care reform that followed the election of President Bill Clinton in 1992. At the center of this debate was a new concept: managed competition.

## MANAGED COMPETITION: AN IDEA WHOSE TIME (SEEMINGLY) HAD COME

At certain times in a nation's political history, windows of opportunity open, allowing for the possibility of major social and political change. As described by Kingdon (1984), three conditions must coexist for major policy changes to take place:

1. A policy issue must rise to the top of the national agenda, with broad public awareness and support.

2. The political circumstances prevailing at the time must be amenable to significant change in policy.
3. A plan for change must be available that offers realistic solutions to the problems that are present.

In the period 1992–94, many people thought a window of opportunity had opened for major reform of our national health care system. The election of President Bill Clinton put the need for health care reform close to the top of the national policy agenda. Members of Congress appeared broadly to support the need for change. A plan was immediately available that offered a compelling theoretical model of the new form health care in the United States could take: managed competition.

In 1980, in the midst of the changes to the health care industry described above, Professor Alain Enthoven of Stanford University published a book entitled *Health Plan: The Only Practical Solution to the Soaring Cost of Medical Care*. This book proposed a national system of health care centered on the concept of groups of health care purchasers banding together to obtain health insurance from competing health insurers.

Under general economic theory, markets will function efficiently only when well-informed consumers are able to choose among competing products. Both the producer and the consumer of a good or service should approach a potential market transaction on an equal basis. A purely market approach to providing health insurance or health care, however, involves a number of inherent problems regarding this classic economic theory. (See Arrow 1963 for a more complete discussion of these issues.) Potential problems include inequality in the information available to physician and patient, the likelihood that merely having health insurance will increase the rate at which people access health care services (the "moral hazard" described above), and the uncertainty involved in predicting the rate at which health services will be provided in the future.

Addressing these problems, Enthoven developed a proposal to reform the market for health insurance and health care to make it more efficient. He predicted that if the market were modified through regulation to counteract the forces that create market failure, "the health care system would be transformed, gradually and voluntarily, from today's system with built-in cost-increasing incentives to a system with built-in incentives for consumer satisfaction and cost control." He proposed "a system of fair economic competition in which consumers and providers of care, making decisions in an appropriately structured private market, would do the work of reorganization" (Enthoven 1980, pp. xxi–xxii). Building on this original work, in 1989 Enthoven collaborated with Richard Kronick to propose a modification of this original plan, called the "Consumer Choice Health Plan" (Enthoven and Kronick 1989). The ideas contained in these plans form the core of proposals for national health care reform based on the concept of managed competition.

A major tenet of Enthoven's proposals for managed competition is that through a reliance on market forces the country would be able to address problems of rising costs through improved efficiency. By removing many of the constraints that have led to past market failures, managed competition would encourage the spread of health care organizations and delivery systems that are able to reduce unnecessary expenditures while also maintaining quality.

Managed competition relies on four basic principles for the organization of the health care system.

1. Rather than selecting and purchasing health insurance directly through their employer, employees from a variety of companies would join together to form a "health insurance purchasing cooperative" (HIPC).

2. These HIPCs would in turn shop among HMOs and other managed health care plans to select the best options for their members. The HIPCs would be large enough to have professional staff able to evaluate the quality of the care offered by the various plans available. Based on this quality assessment, the HIPCs would select several plans to offer to members, thus assuring a range of choice. The HIPCs would offer only plans that, in the opinion of HIPC managers, offered high quality at competitive prices.

3. All managed care plans that wanted to compete for the business of the HIPC would be required to offer a basic benefit package, covering a specified range of health care services. Historically, it has been difficult for consumers (in this case, members of the HIPC) to compare the price of competing health insurance plans, because each plan would have its own unique set of covered services. By assuring that the benefit package was the same for all plans offered, consumers could make a direct price comparison of plans.

4. HMOs and other health plans that were competing for the business of the HIPCs would be free to offer coverage options that were more comprehensive than the basic benefit package. If a consumer selected a more comprehensive (and thus more expensive) option, however, the consumer would have to pay the added cost (that is, the difference between the plan selected and the basic plan) out of his or her own pocket. This added cost of the comprehensive plan would not be tax deductible, thus requiring the consumer to pay the full additional amount. (Recall that current tax laws encourage consumers to buy more health insurance than they would buy if they were paying for it themselves. This aspect of managed competition would require the federal government to change the tax laws.)

Under managed competition, all privately purchased health insurance would be obtained through HIPCs. HIPCs would be organized on a regional basis, with one HIPC per region. The exception to this would be that employers with more than one thou-

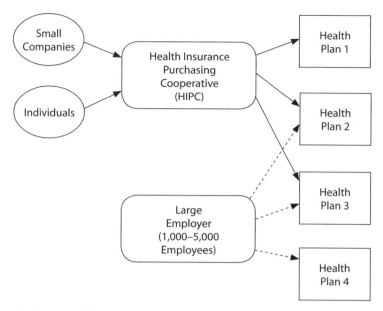

FIGURE 5.6. The Structure of "Managed Competition"

sand employees would be allowed to act as their own HIPC. Any type of health plan, from a staff-model HMO through a purely fee-for-service PPO, would be permitted to offer coverage through the HIPC. A health plan that did not meet the standard of quality established by the HIPC, however, would not be offered as an option to HIPC members. An exclusion of this type could mean the demise of noncompetitive plans. The theory of managed competition is illustrated in Figure 5.6.

At this point, it is important to be sure that the reader understands the difference between two fundamental concepts: *managed care* and *managed competition*.

*Managed care* is a means of organizing, paying for, and providing health care directly to consumers. It is paid for through a capitation arrangement, under which a particular group or organization is responsible for assuring that all necessary care is provided to a given population of patients, and that the cost of that care does not exceed budgeted funds. (The budget would be equal to the capitation rate times the number of members.) The responsible group then "manages" the care process to assure that the budget is not exceeded. The responsible group may be

- an insurance company
- a nonprofit corporation
- a for-profit corporation
- physicians and hospitals in combination

*Managed competition*, on the other hand, is a system for providing health care on a regional basis, in which patients choose between competing systems of managed care.

Managed care is a way of providing care directly to consumers. Managed competition is a theory of health care reform that relies on managed care as the basis of organizing, financing, and delivering health care.

Initially, critics of managed competition pointed out that the model was only a theoretical one that had never been tested. Even Enthoven and Kronick acknowledged that "the only proved method for bringing the growth in total expenditures into line with the gross national product

> ### CONCEPT 5.7
>
> *Managed care* is a way of organizing and financing the direct delivery of care. *Managed competition* is a way of restructuring the entire health care system. It relies on managed care as the basic model for the delivery of care.

is for government to take over most of health care financing and place it under firm global budgets." They concluded, however, that "in view of our historic preferences for limited government and decentralization," it would be more effective in the case of the United States to create a private, market-based system of managed competition that is based on "generally accepted economic theory" (Enthoven and Kronick 1989, pp. 100–101).

According to Enthoven's view of economic theory, a properly organized market would lead over time to the efficient provision of health care. Efficient in this sense refers to providing cost-effective care. As discussed in Chapter 3, a common measure of economic efficiency compares the relationship between marginal benefits and marginal costs. If the marginal benefits of an activity equal or exceed the marginal costs of acquiring those added benefits, it makes economic sense to take on those added costs. If marginal benefits turn out to be less than their marginal costs, it makes little sense to make those added investments. Efficiency is achieved at that point at which marginal benefits and marginal costs are approximately equal.

Applying this concept to health care, efficiency is achieved when, either for a specific health plan or for the system as a whole, the marginal benefits of additional care approximate the marginal costs. That is to say, the marginal resources that we apply to health care result in tangible benefits that justify the expenditure of those resources. Enthoven and Kronick predicted that, if adopted on a national scale, managed competition would lead to "a restructured market system in which the efficient prosper and the inefficient must improve or fail" (Enthoven and Kronick 1991, p. 2535). Such a state of equilibrium in the market for health care would, they argue, place reasonable limits on the cost of our health care system.

Historically, our health care system has embodied a number of political and social institutions that have resulted in substantial inefficiency in our system of care. These institutions include the tax treatment of health insurance premiums and the system of paying physicians a separate fee for each service provided regardless of the added benefits of that service. These incentives lead to patients expecting and physicians providing a great deal of expensive care with relatively little marginal benefit.

Enthoven proposed that, given the opportunity to operate without these and other perverse incentives previously embodied in tax laws and laws regulating medical practice, the market itself would tend to weed out inefficient providers of care. Whether they provide care that is of high cost or low quality, or whether they simply provide poor service to their patients, health care organizations that are not able to operate efficiently will not be able to survive in a system based on managed competition. By creating a system of competing organizations—large purchasers on the demand side and managed care organizations on the supply side—Enthoven predicted that the market would select for those organizations and organizational forms that operate efficiently, and in so doing would assure the provision of cost-effective, high-quality care. This belief in market efficiency forms the theoretical core of managed competition proposals. The theory behind managed competition predicts that if a properly structured market were created, "the health care system would be transformed, gradually and voluntarily, from today's system with built-in cost-increasing incentives to a system with built-in incentives for consumer satisfaction and cost control" (Enthoven 1980, p. xxii).

As we will see in the sections that follow, managed competition proved to be only partially successful in creating a more efficient health care system. The numerous social, economic, and political institutions that over time have created the structure of our health care system have continued to impede our ability to shift to an efficient system in the allocation of scarce health care resources. As Douglass North described (see Chapter 3), and as proved to be the case with managed competition, markets alone are often unable to change broad institutional structure.

## PUTTING MANAGED COMPETITION INTO ACTION: THE CLINTON HEALTH REFORM PROPOSAL

During the presidential election campaign in 1992, Bill Clinton promised that, if elected, he would move rapidly to reform the U.S. system of health care. Shortly after assuming office, he took steps to put this plan in action. In doing so, he made a policy decision that a number of authors suggest was fundamentally flawed (Johnson and Broder 1996; Skocpol 1997). Rather than relying on the process of congressional hearings to arrive at a final plan for reform, he chose to create a task force of experts within the executive branch, under the supervision of First Lady Hillary Clinton. He charged this task force with developing a comprehensive, detailed plan for national health care reform.

The plan developed by the task force and presented to Congress had at its core Enthoven's theory of managed competition. The Clinton plan differed from the plan proposed by Enthoven in a number of important ways.

- The Clinton plan proposed that states establish a single, statewide, publicly financed HIPC, and that all residents of the state obtain their health coverage through the HIPC. Enthoven saw HIPCs as much smaller, with one for each region within a state.
- The Clinton plan allowed employers with five thousand employees to act as their own HIPC. The Enthoven plan would have allowed employers with one thousand employees this option.
- The Clinton plan relied on a national health board to establish the benefits that must be included in the basic benefit plan. The Enthoven plan left this decision up to the HIPCs and the market.
- The Clinton plan gave the national health board the authority to regulate the rates that managed care plans could charge HIPCs for the basic benefit package. The Enthoven plan left the setting of rates up to the market and to competition among managed care providers.

Several other plans were proposed in Congress as alternatives to the Clinton plan. Many of these alternatives also relied on the theory of managed competition, only with less government authority to regulate care. It appeared that, after more than ten years of discussion and debate, the time had finally come for managed competition to be adopted as our national policy of care. Kingdon's "window of opportunity" for major national health care reform seemed to be open.

History, however, would prove otherwise. While President Clinton was taking more than a year to formulate the specifics of his plan, the political tide in the United States shifted dramatically. The Republican Party in Congress, under the leadership of Newt Gingrich, sensed that President Clinton and the Democrats had exposed their Achilles' heel—"big government." The plan offered by the Clinton administration sounded a lot like another "big government" solution to a social problem, typical of many of the failed solutions of the 1960s "War on Poverty." Through a series of parliamentary procedures, the Republicans were able to stall consideration of health care reform. During this time, the health insurance industry, feeling threatened by proposals to transfer the purchasing of health insurance from them to HIPCs, ran an amazingly effective series of TV ads attacking the Clinton proposal. These "Harry and Louise" ads portrayed a typical, white, middle-class couple who were afraid that they were going to lose their health insurance to coverage provided by an immense government bureaucracy. Even though the claims of these ads were of tenuous accuracy, they hit home with American consumers. The combination of the Republican stalling tactics and the fear of government bureaucracy in health care engendered by Harry and Louise shifted the political landscape almost overnight. The political circumstances were no longer amenable to change. The three conditions identified by Kingdon no longer existed. The window of opportunity for national health care reform slammed shut. The Clinton plan was defeated, and the new Republican congressional leaders made it abundantly clear there was little if any chance for health care reform in the foreseeable future.

## THE SHIFT TO MANAGED CARE: THE MARKET DOES WHAT THE GOVERNMENT WOULD NOT

Even though Congress failed to enact national health care reform, a fundamental shift took place nonetheless in the 1990s in our health care system. This shift had many, but not all, of the characteristics of managed competition as proposed by Enthoven. The rapidly rising cost of care, coupled with the growing awareness of the concept of managed care engendered by the debate over the Clinton plan, led many employers to turn to managed care to control the cost of providing care to their employees. In addition, employers banded together in some parts of the country to establish private purchasing cooperatives for health care, as envisioned by the original theory of managed competition. A number of these HIPCs were quite successful for a period of several years in holding down the price of health coverage by getting the various available health plans to compete among themselves to offer the lowest price.

An example of such a private, employer-sponsored HIPC was the Pacific Business Group on Health (PBGH), established in California. PBGH involved many of the biggest employers in California. All these employers chose to offer their employees only those health insurance plans approved by PBGH, at capitation rates negotiated by PBGH. Representing hundreds of thousands of potential health plan members, PBGH was effective in negotiating low rates for health plan coverage. Few managed care providers were willing to forgo the opportunity of enrolling PBGH members. To do so would mean the potential loss of thousands of health plan members. In contrast to the 10 to 15 percent yearly increases in health plan rates seen in the early 1990s, PBGH was able in many cases to negotiate reductions in rates from many managed care providers. For several years in a row, the cost of providing care to employees leveled out for the employers composing PBGH. Managed competition seemed to work, at least in some contexts.

> **CONCEPT 5.8**
>
> Despite the failure of the U.S. Congress to enact national health care reform during the 1990s, market forces acted to fundamentally restructure our system of health insurance. Most people in the United States with health insurance are now covered by some form of managed care plan.

Other groups had similar success in holding down the cost of care by adopting the model of managed competition. Notable among these were large, governmentally supported organizations that provided health coverage for public-sector employees such as the California Public Employees Retirement System and the Federal Employees Health Benefits Plan. In the mid-1990s, they too experienced a dramatic leveling in the cost of providing coverage to their members.

The economics of the entire health care system in the United States changed during the 1990s. Many of the large purchasing cooperatives organized on the model of HIPCs were having substantial success. Employers and managed care plans not involved in formally structured HIPCS were able to reduce the rate at which the cost of care was increasing. Even Medicare and Medicaid began to look to managed care and managed competition as a potential solution to the rising costs of these programs.

Over the period of only a few years, our national health care system changed to one based largely on managed care. An overwhelming majority of Americans covered by health insurance today are covered under one form of managed care or another. By the year 2000—only six years after the failure of the Clinton health reform proposal—more than one thousand PPOs and more than six hundred HMOs were operating in the United States. Even though there was no national legislation mandating a shift to managed care and managed competition, the private marketplace for health insurance brought about many aspects of this model. (See Oliver 2004 for an excellent discussion of the rise of managed care.)

## DID MANAGED COMPETITION AND MANAGED CARE DECREASE HEALTH CARE COSTS IN THE LONG TERM?

The economic theory behind the shift to managed competition and managed care relies on market forces to achieve a higher level of efficiency in our health care system, and in doing so, to control health care costs. A number of scholars in fields such as economics, political science, and sociology have questioned the ultimate ability of market forces alone to achieve the efficient provision of socially important goods such as health care. Their concern has been that broad social institutions inhibit the market's ability to attain efficiency.

As described in Chapter 3, institutions provide the rules, both formal and informal, that govern action within a society. Douglass North was awarded the Nobel Prize in Economics for his work showing how market efficiency is constrained by the institutional context in which the market exists. North predicted that problems may arise when the set of institutional forces that drive economic markets overlaps with institutions reflecting broader social and political phenomena. This interaction of social and economic institutions may impair efficient economic activity. "If political and economic markets were efficient . . . then the choices made would always be efficient . . . [However], institutions . . . are always a mixed bag of those that increase and those that decrease productivity" (North 1986, p. 8).

There have been numerous instances of inefficient institutions coming to predominate in American business even in the face of market forces. Take, for example, the standard computer keyboard, which begins with the letters QWERTY. This has been the standard keyboard configuration of typewriters and computers for decades, yet it is a relatively inefficient way to arrange the keys (David 1985). This inefficient institution has come to exist despite the effects of market forces.

Many types of institutional force inhibit the ability of markets to achieve efficiency. These countervailing forces frequently have to do with social belief systems and generally accepted rules of behavior that are not necessarily rationally or scientifically derived. These institutional constraints on market efficiency can be formalized, as in laws and regulations, or can exert their influence informally, as with social norms and professional ethics. They derive from a number of sources, both within the market itself and from the social context in which the market exists.

Chapter 3 describes the technological imperative and other institutions affecting health care in the United States. The effects of these institutions distinguish our system of health care from those in Canada and other developed countries. They also make it difficult to constrain the growth of medical technology and the inevitable increase in costs inherent in such growth.

Institutions such as these all too often are not economically efficient, at least not in the way economists approach the concept. The market's ability to improve efficiency—the basis of the economic theory behind managed competition—is constrained by the institutions that surround it.

Even under a fully capitated, competitive system it was unlikely that managed care plans would be able to overcome many of the inefficient institutions that add so much to the cost of care. To attain a meaningful, long-term stabilization in the cost of care, they must reduce the number of services they provide, especially expensive inpatient services and other types of specialized care. To do this, they must attempt to alter the behavior of the physicians practicing within their system and the expectations of patients. Public perceptions of what constitutes appropriate care, however, exist in response to the institutions that predominate in the broader social context.

There is little doubt that care provided under capitation systems costs less than comparable care under fee-for-service. The effects of capitation on the cost of care, however, may be limited. Managed care systems are able to eliminate certain types of inefficiencies within a given institutional context, but they may be powerless to change the surrounding context itself. Constraining the rapid escalation of technology, minimizing local variations in patterns of care, and coping with defensive medicine were no less a problem for successful managed care plans than they were for their fee-for-service competitors. Managed care and managed competition, while achieving improvements through altered financial incentives, proved not to be able to overcome the broad inertia of inefficient institutions. In the words of Victor Fuchs (1993b, p. 1679), "The market is a powerful and flexible instrument for allocating most goods and services, but it cannot create an equitable, universal system of insurance, cannot harness technologic change in medicine, and cannot cope with the potentially unlimited demand for health care by the elderly."

Figure 5.7 represents the long-term relationship between the cost of health care in the traditional fee-for-service system and in managed care organizations such as HMOs. While there is a clear cost advantage for the managed care organization, this advantage remains relatively constant over time. Both fee-for-service and managed care delivery systems must contend with broad social forces that seem inexorably to drive up the cost of care.

The theory of managed competition predicts that, by shifting from fee-for-service to a system of competing managed care organizations, it will be possible to arrest the increasing cost of care. This goal would be obtained by weeding out the inefficiencies inherent in fee-for-service.

Looking at the cost of care in the United States measured as a percentage of gross domestic product (GDP) spent on health care, we see at first that this prediction was accurate. Between 1993 and 1998, the period when managed care became the norm in the United States, health care expenditures remained relatively constant, averaging 13.6 percent of GDP.

What, though, would happen when the transition to managed care was complete? Would the cost of care remain level, as predicted by the theory of managed competition, or would the rise in the cost of care resume? Figure 5.8 illustrates this question.

The theory of managed competition predicted that the cost of care would remain level, illustrated by the line labeled A in Figure 5.8. If, however, managed care orga-

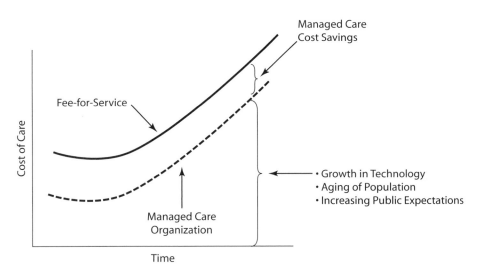

FIGURE 5.7. Managed Care and the Rising Cost of Health Care

nizations face the same institutional forces driving up the cost of care that affected the fee-for-service system, the cost savings of a national shift to managed care will be a one-time phenomenon. Once the cost of care bumps up against the managed care curve in Figure 5.8, it would resume its yearly increase at the same rate as before. This outcome is illustrated by the line labeled B.

Figure 5.9 shows the rise in the cost of our health care system between 1987, when managed care began its spread, and 2003, by which time most health insurance plans

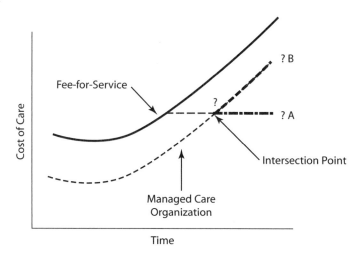

FIGURE 5.8. Can Managed Care Stop the Rising Cost of Health Care?

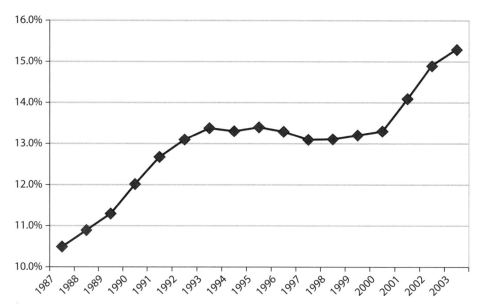

FIGURE 5.9. Health Care Expenditures in the United States as a Percentage of GDP, 1987–2003.
*Source:* Data from U.S. Centers for Medicare and Medicaid Services

nationally had shifted to a managed care model. It should be clear that option B was what actually occurred. During the several years in the mid-1990s when the shift took place, as we moved from the fee-for-service curve to the managed care curve, there was a flattening in the cost curve. Once the majority of the population had shifted from traditional, fee-for-service, indemnity insurance to managed care alternatives, however, the cost of care measured as a percentage of GDP began to rise again at approximately the same rate as before the shift. That rise continued throughout the first decade of the new century. Our health care system shifted from the fee-for-service curve to the managed care curve without changing the slope of either curve. The economic theory behind the shift to managed care appears to have failed the test of time.

> **CONCEPT 5.9**
>
> The move to managed care that took place in the United States in the 1980s and 1990s appears to have realized a one-time savings in the amount we spend on health care yet failed to arrest the long-term growth in the overall cost of health care.

## WHY DIDN'T MANAGED COMPETITION WORK?

To work successfully, managed competition relies on employees and others who have health insurance to obtain their insurance from a HIPC. It is expected that those with health insurance will act as "informed consumers," choosing from the plans offered by the HIPC the one that provides the best value to them. One reason that managed competition did not work is that this goal—having consumers select from a variety of health plans—has become available only in certain areas of the country and to certain types of employees. In 2009, only 13 percent of firms with fewer than two hundred employees offered their employees a choice of health plans; for firms with between two hundred and one thousand workers, 39 percent of firms offered their employees a choice of health plans. Only large firms—those with more than one thousand employees—were likely to give their employees a selection of plans from which to choose. As a result, 47 percent of employees receiving health insurance from their employer had only one plan available to them, while an additional 33 percent had only two plans (Kaiser Family Foundation and Health Research and Educational Trust 2009). Without a requirement that all health insurance be obtained from HIPCs and that employees be offered a choice of plans (such as was contained in the failed Clinton health plan), a fully competitive situation was never attained.

Even in places such as California, where fully functional HIPCs were established (for example, Pacific Business Group on Health, California Public Employees Retirement System), the reductions in the cost of health insurance were only temporary. For several years in the 1990s, these HIPCs were able to get HMOs and other managed care companies to hold down the cost of care. To do this, however, these managed care plans needed, in return, to hold down the cost of care for the patients they covered.

They did this through a combination of methods intended to reduce the use of care, and through a reduction in the amount they would pay physicians and hospitals for care. As described in Chapter 8, these methods came up against what is referred to as the "managed care backlash." In the long run, the managed care companies made it clear to the HIPCs that, to provide the type of care expected by patients, they would have to raise their rates. The HIPCs had little choice but to accept the renewed reality of increasing health care costs.

Another aspect of the managed care backlash was a growing tendency for employers to offer PPOs rather than HMOs to their employees, because of the broader choice of providers and fewer restrictions on care inherent in PPOs. In those companies offering both HMO and PPO options, employees began to favor the PPO. By 2009, PPOs had taken over the largest share of the market for employer-sponsored health insurance, with 60 percent of covered workers enrolled in PPOs. By comparison, 20 percent of workers were covered by an HMO with an additional 10 percent covered by a POS plan. An additional 8 percent of workers were enrolled in a high-deductible health plan (described in Chapter 12), with only 1 percent of employees nationally covered by traditional indemnity health insurance (Kaiser Family Foundation and Health Research and Educational Trust 2009).

The theory of managed competition ran aground on the rocks of the institutions and resulting expectations that have driven our system of care for decades. Because the fundamental institutions underlying health care were not changed, market forces alone proved powerless in altering the long-term rise in the cost of health care.

It appears that managed care as a means of controlling health care costs (the main reason our system of care turned to it in the first place) has a fundamental inconsistency. Unless the institutions and belief systems inherent in our society change regarding what constitutes high-quality care, any success managed care achieves in holding down the cost of care is at risk of being seen as a decrease in the quality of care.

## SUMMARY

Health insurance in the United States first became widely available following World War II. Decisions made as part of wartime economic policy were to have long-range effects on our approach to providing health insurance. Today, most people covered by private health insurance obtain their insurance as a tax-free fringe benefit from their employer. As a consequence, people have come to expect a level of coverage that is substantially more generous than the coverage they might otherwise select if they were paying for it themselves. This employment-based system with its incentives for increased coverage has been a principal factor contributing to the rising cost of care.

As an alternative to the fee-for-service model of insurance that predominated throughout most of the twentieth century, Kaiser Permanente and other nonprofit groups were able to develop systems of care financed prospectively, based on monthly capitation payments. Despite initial (and often strident) opposition from the medical profession, these prepaid systems were able to offer care of comparable quality for about one-third less than traditional fee-for-service insurance.

Building on the success of these prepaid systems (now referred to as HMOs), in 1973 the federal government passed legislation encouraging their growth and expansion. In an effort to both expand coverage to the uninsured and constrain rising costs, HMOs and other forms of managed care were at the center of efforts to enact fundamental health care reform. While reform efforts in Congress were unsuccessful, the market adopted managed care as its predominant form of health insurance coverage. This shift to managed care was associated with a leveling of health care costs during the mid-1990s. By the beginning of the new century, however, it became clear that the savings associated with the shift to managed care were only short term. Despite the extensive use of managed care systems, the United States once again faces steep and continuous increases in the cost of health care.

## THE AFFORDABLE CARE ACT AND THE MARKET FOR HEALTH INSURANCE

One of the ironies of the passage of the Affordable Care Act (ACA) is that the act resurrects one of the core elements of managed care delivery and managed competition that was at the heart of the failed Clinton reform proposal. In order to expand health insurance coverage to those currently uninsured, ACA requires that every employer with more than fifty employees must either offer health insurance coverage to their workers or else pay a tax to the federal government. ACA also mandates that all U.S. citizens and permanent residents obtain health insurance coverage. If workers are unable to obtain that coverage through their employer, they will be guaranteed the option of obtaining coverage through a newly created entity: the Health Benefit Exchange (HBE). The HBE largely replicates the HIPC that was at the heart of the Clinton reform proposal.

The HBE is an organization that is to be created by each state with the purpose of making competing health insurance plans available to those individuals and families who do not obtain coverage through their work. States have the option of collaborating among themselves to create multistate, regional exchanges. Large states can create multiple exchanges within the state, so long as each one serves an identified geographic area. In states that are unable or unwilling to create an exchange by 2014, the federal government will be authorized to establish and operate an exchange on behalf of the state.

The purpose of the HBE is to match those seeking health insurance coverage with companies offering coverage. In order to have their plans made available through the HBE, health insurance companies will have to obtain certification from the operator of the exchange. The plan will have to meet certain requirements having to do with level of benefits, and the company offering the plan will have to comply with licensure and regulatory requirements. Each exchange must arrange for at least two qualifying plans to be available, one of which must be offered by a nonprofit organization. Qualified plans will offer one of four predefined level of benefits, referred to as bronze, silver, gold, and platinum. Other than variations in price based on the subscriber's age, family composition, tobacco use, and geographic area of residence, each plan must be available at the same price to all subscribers without regard to the subscriber's past medical history.

Beginning in 2014, individuals who do not receive coverage through their work will be eligible to contact the HBE, get information about competing plans and their comparative prices for a given level of coverage, and select a plan for themselves and their families. In addition, small businesses with up to one hundred employees will be eligible to obtain coverage for their employees through the HBE, with employees selecting from among the competing plans.

For individuals and families earning between 133 and 400 percent of the federal poverty level (FPL), there will be a cap on the premium paid by the subscriber, with the balance paid through a federal subsidy. The cap ranges from 2 percent of income for those earning 133 percent of the FPL to 9.5 percent of income for those earning 400 percent of the FPL. (Those earning less than 133% of the FPL will be eligible for free coverage through Medicaid [discussed in Chapter 7].)

The concept behind the HBE is essentially that of the HIPC, described above as a central component of Enthoven's original theory of managed competition. As a HIPC was intended to do, an HBE is a publicly organized, nonprofit entity that evaluates competing health plans, and then makes qualifying plans available to individuals on a competitive basis. Individuals and small employers are able to select freely from among competing plans based on price, level of benefits, and quality. The concept of the HIPC, once portrayed by the Harry and Louise ads of 1993–94 as unreasonable bureaucratic encroachment on a family's access to health insurance, has, under another name, become one of the central components of expanded health insurance coverage through ACA.

6

# Medicare

A student who works part-time in a college or university dining hall is likely to be paid biweekly. A facsimile of a typical pay stub, shown in Figure 6.1, offers a statement of the extent to which workers and employers are currently paying for government programs in health care. Of the five categories of taxes withheld from the student's pay, three go, at least in part, to pay for such programs.

The federal Medicare program, which is our system of universal health insurance for everyone 65 years old or older, is paid for from both the Medicare withholding tax and the general federal withholding tax (shown on the pay stub as Fed tax). The Medicaid program (discussed in Chapter 7), which is a federal-state partnership to provide medical insurance to poor and disabled people, is paid for from a combination of federal taxes and state taxes (shown as State tax).

Even though every worker contributes to paying the cost of these programs, only a minority of people in this country are covered by them. In contrast to most other countries, which have adopted universal health insurance for all their citizens, the United States has historically pursued a policy of incrementalism: establishing government-funded programs for specific populations felt to be most vulnerable. The two largest groups benefiting from this incremental approach to national health care are elderly people and poor people. Both programs were established in 1965 after decades of debate about the proper role of government in paying for health care.

As described in Chapter 1, as part of the social programs enacted under Franklin Roosevelt's New Deal, proposals for comprehensive medical insurance were considered but ultimately abandoned in the face of overriding opposition from the American Medical Association (AMA) and other groups within the medical profession. Fol-

| Statement of Earnings and Taxes<br>University Office of Dining Services | | | | |
|---|---|---|---|---|
| **Employee:** xxxxx xxxxx | | **Social Security No.** 999-99-999 | | |
| **Hours:** | | | **Amount** | |
| Overtime | 10.70 | | 89.88 | |
| Regular | 78.60 | | 440.16 | |
| Total gross | | | 530.04 | |
| **Gross pay:** 530.04 | | **Taxes:** 115.19 | **Net pay:** 414.85 | |
| **Taxes deducted:** | | | | |
| FICA/OAS | 32.86 | | | |
| Medicare | 7.69 | | | |
| Fed tax | 63.26 | | | |
| State Tax | 6.61 | | | |
| VDI | 4.77 | | | |
| Total tax: | 115.19 | | | |

FIGURE 6.1. Sample Statement of Earnings and Taxes

lowing World War II, President Harry Truman again proposed a program of national health insurance, but again the opposition of the medical profession blocked the proposal. Only under the unique circumstances in the mid-1960s of a Democratic president, a strongly Democratic Congress, and a national momentum for social reform was the federal government able finally to overcome the opposition and enact the Medicare and Medicaid programs.

## MEDICARE: UNIVERSAL HEALTH INSURANCE FOR ELDERLY PEOPLE

Medicare is the federal program that helps to pay for health care for elderly people in this country. All people 65 years of age or older who qualify for Social Security benefits are automatically eligible for Medicare. Rather than being a separate law, Medicare was enacted as an amendment to the existing Social Security Act. It is thus often referred to as "Title XVIII."

When Medicare was passed in 1965, only 56 percent of elderly people had hospital insurance. The costs of treating a serious illness were seen as a threat to the financial security of seniors. There was a strong national consensus that none of the elderly people in our country should face financial ruin due to illness. Medicare was the way to ensure this outcome.

As discussed in Chapter 5, there are two general types of health plan: a service plan, in which all participants are provided with a given level of service, and an insurance plan, in which participants receive reimbursement for the cost of services. The initial

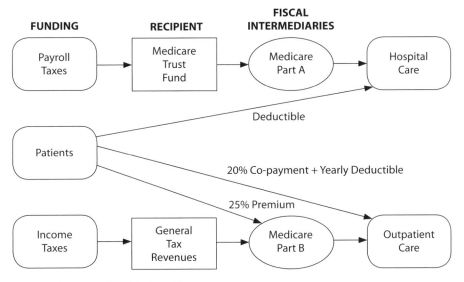

**FIGURE 6.2.** Structure of the Medicare Program

proposal was to create a service plan covering hospital care. Under this type of plan, elderly people would simply go to the hospital as needed, and the hospital would be paid directly by the government.

The AMA was opposed to the service plan concept. If Medicare was to be passed at all, they wanted to establish an insurance plan covering both hospital care and the care provided by doctors, with patients paying for care directly and being reimbursed from the government insurance program. The AMA also wanted to keep the government out of running the program; they preferred that it be run by private insurance companies.

A last-minute compromise was struck that incorporated both proposals (Ball 1995). Under the compromise, Medicare became a combined service and insurance program. The structure of the original Medicare program is illustrated in Figure 6.2.

> **CONCEPT 6.1**
>
> As a result of a last-minute political compromise, the federal Medicare program was designed as a combined service plan (Part A) and insurance plan (Part B).

## Medicare Part A

Medicare Part A is a service plan for hospital care. All eligible patients receive any necessary hospital care, paid for by the government. The patient is responsible for a deductible payment equal roughly to the cost of the first day of hospitalization. (In 2010, this amount was $1,100.) After this deductible amount, all the costs of hospitalization are paid by Medicare for up to 60 days in the hospital per illness. If the patient needs to stay longer in the hospital, the patient is responsible for $275 per day for additional days up to a maximum of 90 days per illness. If more time in the hospital is necessary, the patient must pay $550 per day, up to a total of 150 days. After these 150 days in the hospital, there is no further Medicare coverage for that illness.

Part A also pays for up to 20 days in a skilled nursing facility (SNF) following hospitalization, so long as the care is necessary to continue the healing or rehabilitation process. After 20 days of care in an SNF, patients must pay $137.50 per day, with Medicare paying the balance for up to 100 days. After 100 days in an SNF, there is no further Medicare coverage.

For those patients who need to spend time in a nursing home simply because they cannot care for themselves but are not undergoing an active treatment program, Medicare provides no payment whatsoever. These patients are referred to as receiving "custodial care" in contrast to "skilled nursing care." The problems associated with custodial care and other types of long-term care are discussed in Chapter 10.

Until 1997, Part A also paid for home health care. This is medically necessary care provided in the patient's home, involving such services as nursing care, physical therapy, or occupational therapy. These services are provided by Medicare-certified home health agencies by prescription of the treating physician. Because of the rising cost of the home health care benefit and the growing realization that it was not particularly effective in its intended purpose of keeping patients out of the hospital, in 1997 the costs of home health care were transferred to the Medicare Part B budget.

Finally, Part A pays for hospice care for terminally ill people. Enacted in the 1980s as an amendment to the original Medicare legislation, the Medicare hospice program pays for extra services during the last six months of a patient's life as long as the patient is certified by a physician as terminally ill (that is, not likely to survive more than six months), and the patient agrees to forgo aggressive treatment measures such as surgery or intensive care.

All the money to pay for Part A comes from a roughly 1.5 percent payroll tax levied on all workers. (On the pay stub in Figure 6.1, the tax labeled "Medicare" goes purely to finance Part A.) For every dollar in tax paid by employees, the employer is required to pay an additional dollar. The money from this tax is deposited into a Medicare trust fund, essentially a savings account established by the federal government to pay hospital bills when they come in.

The government does not actually pay bills submitted by hospitals. Instead, the government contracts with private companies to accept the bills from the hospitals and write the checks to them. These companies, referred to as "fiscal intermediaries," are then reimbursed from the Medicare trust fund. The creation of the fiscal intermediary was part of the compromise struck with the AMA at the time of the original passage of the Medicare legislation.

It is important to note that the money paid in payroll taxes into the Medicare trust fund is not put aside to pay for the care of current workers when they retire. Instead, it is used to pay for the care of people already retired. The financing of the Medicare program is based on the concept that current workers pay the medical care costs of current retirees. When today's workers are retired, their care will be paid for by those who are working at that time. Medical care during the retirement of the baby boom generation will therefore be financed by the substantially smaller number of people born after the baby boom.

About 90 percent of all Medicare funds come from people currently working. For the system to work, there have to be enough workers paying enough taxes to pay for the care needed by elderly people. In 2003, there were about 3.9 workers for each Medicare beneficiary. In 2009, this number had fallen to 3.5 workers per beneficiary. In 2030, as the last baby boomer turns 65, there will be only about 2.4 workers per beneficiary. The ratio will continue to decline until there are only 2.0 workers per beneficiary by 2080 (data from Medicare Payment Advisory Commission website). If the cost of care per beneficiary remains relatively constant, the tax burden on each worker will increase by nearly 70 percent in the next

> **CONCEPT 6.2**
>
> The Medicare program looks to today's workers to pay the costs of today's retirees. The number of active workers per beneficiary is projected to decline from 3.5 in 2009 to 2.4 in 2030.

thirty years. If the cost per beneficiary goes up (as it is almost certain to do), the tax burden will increase even more. This policy dilemma inherent in the current Medicare program is one of the most pressing aspects of the forces that threaten the long-term financial viability of Medicare.

## Medicare Part B

Medicare Part B pays for doctor bills and other medical care costs that are incurred on an outpatient basis (that is, for care provided outside the hospital). Under Part B, patients going to physicians, laboratories, X-ray offices, and other outpatient providers of care receive a bill for each service provided. As with Part A, private companies acting as fiscal intermediaries handle all paperwork and pay out all the funds. The government acts to hold the money collected, and to transfer it to the fiscal intermediaries as needed.

As an insurance plan, Part B involves an insurance premium paid by the beneficiaries. This premium is withheld from the Social Security checks of all those participating in the plan, so there is no need to bill patients for the cost of the premium. In addition, Part B is voluntary; only those seniors electing to have the premium deducted from their check are covered. (This is in contrast to Part A, which is universal for all seniors receiving Social Security.) Nearly all seniors select Part B coverage.

The original intent for Part B was to have the premiums collected from the patients cover about half the cost of the program, with the other half of the cost coming from general tax revenues. It rapidly became apparent that this 50/50 cost sharing was going to be too expensive for seniors to bear, so over time the premium was reduced substantially. Currently, the premium charged to beneficiaries for Part B coverage is set so that beneficiaries pay 25 percent of the cost. Thus, 75 cents of every $1 spent on Part B comes from general tax revenues. In 2010, the Part B premium was $110.50 per month for beneficiaries with incomes less than $85,000 for a single person or $170,000 for a married couple. For higher-income beneficiaries the premium is increased, up to a maximum of $353.60 for individuals earning more than $214,000 or couples earning more than $428,000.

> **CONCEPT 6.3**
>
> Medicare beneficiaries pay for 25 percent of the cost of Part B coverage. Thus, 75 cents of every dollar spent on Medicare Part B comes from general tax revenues.

Part B has two mechanisms to pay for the care seniors receive from physicians and other outpatient providers. They are referred to as the provider "accepting assignment" and "not accepting assignment." The choice is up to the provider (not the patient) and will affect the amount and the manner of payment for services. For both options, the patient is responsible for paying a yearly deductible of $155.

Under the first option, illustrated in Figure 6.3, the physician (or other provider) agrees to accept an amount set by Medicare as payment in full for the service provided. (See the section below on the resource-based relative value system for an indication of how these amounts are set.) In return for the physician's willingness to set the fee at this level, Medicare will pay the physician directly an amount equal to 80 percent of that fee. The patient then is responsible for paying the physician only the remaining 20 percent of the fee. Physicians and other providers who agree to accept assignment are referred to as "participating providers."

The fee allowed by Medicare, however, is generally much lower than the fee a physician usually charges other patients for the same service. Medicare fees typically are about two-thirds of the fees the physician usually charges. About half of all physicians have elected not to accept assignment, so they can charge Medicare patients a higher fee. In this case, illustrated in Figure 6.4, the patient is responsible for paying the physi-

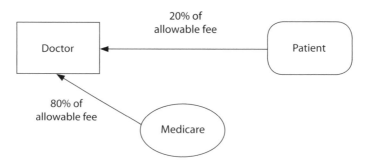

FIGURE 6.3. Medicare Part B Payment: Doctor Does Accept Assignment

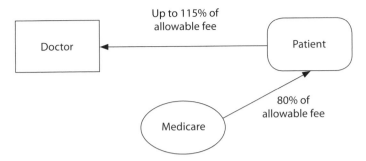

FIGURE 6.4. Medicare Part B Payment: Doctor Does Not Accept Assignment

cian directly for the full amount billed. The patient may then send a form into Medicare and be reimbursed for 80 percent of Medicare's allowable fee.

To protect Medicare beneficiaries from having to pay extremely high physicians' fees, a law was enacted that limits the amount any physician can charge a Medicare beneficiary to 115 percent of Medicare's allowable fee. Thus, if the allowable Medicare fee for a service is $100, the most a physician may charge a Medicare patient is $115.

Even with this limitation, the fees paid by Medicare patients to physicians and other providers can be quite high. The patient is responsible for 20 percent of the fee to begin with; going to a physician who does not accept assignment will add another 15 percent. Thus, even though they are covered by Part B insurance, patients can be required to pay 35 percent of all doctor bills out of pocket. (This is in addition to the $155 yearly deductible.) Considering that in 2009 nearly half of all people on Medicare (47%) had incomes less than 200 percent of the federal poverty line (FPL) ($21,660 for individuals and $29,140 for couples) (Kaiser Family Foundation 2010e), it is easy to see that out-of-pocket expenses for medical care can be a substantial burden on Medicare beneficiaries. For these families and individuals, one-third of their household income might go for health care.

A number of people in the country and in Congress want to eliminate any limit on the amount that physicians can charge Medicare patients. Legislation has been proposed that would allow "private contracting" between the doctor and the patient, whereby the doctor and the patient could agree to any fee schedule they want. Such a change would essentially allow physicians to charge Medicare patients whatever they wish. (Note that these proposals are closely tied to the "balance billing" issue that was so hotly debated as part of the Canadian health care plan.)

## MEDIGAP INSURANCE

As discussed above, patients covered by Medicare are still responsible for paying a number of different costs. These include

- the Part A hospital deductible for each time they are in the hospital
- the yearly Part B $155 deductible
- 20 percent of all charges covered by Part B
- the extra charges (up to 15% of allowable charges) of physicians who do not accept assignment

To gain coverage for these items, about 90 percent of Medicare beneficiaries obtain some form of supplemental medical insurance policy, often referred to as a "Medigap" policy. As the name suggests, a Medigap policy is a medical insurance policy that pays for these gaps in Medicare coverage. There are four principal ways for beneficiaries to obtain Medigap coverage.

1. The beneficiary can purchase the policy from a private insurance company (about 19% of beneficiaries).
2. The beneficiary can obtain the policy from her or his former employer as a retirement benefit (about 29% of beneficiaries).
3. The beneficiary can receive Medigap coverage from the Medicaid program or other publicly financed programs, if his or her income is below the FPL (about 19% of beneficiaries).
4. The beneficiary can join a Medicare managed care plan, described below, which includes coverage for these out-of-pocket costs (about 23% of beneficiaries).

---

**CONCEPT 6.4**

Only 10 percent of Medicare beneficiaries have coverage limited to Medicare. The other 90 percent of beneficiaries obtain a supplemental Medigap policy or other supplementary policy to cover costs not paid by Medicare.

---

Each Medigap supplemental insurance plan will have its own set of covered benefits. Most will pay for the Part A hospital deductible, the Part B yearly deductible, and the 20 percent share of providers' bills not covered by Medicare.

The cost of these Medigap policies has been increasing substantially in recent years. After several years of yearly premium increases in the range of 3 to 6 percent, Medigap policies began in the late 1990s to go up by as much as 10 to 20 percent per year. In addition, the rapid escalation in the cost of prescription drugs made Medigap coverage an unaffordable option for many beneficiaries before the enactment of Medicare's pharmaceutical coverage, described below.

## THE EXTENSION OF MEDICARE TO DISABLED PEOPLE AND PEOPLE WITH KIDNEY FAILURE

Within a few years of the enactment of Medicare, Congress made some additions to the program that were to have significant effects on long-term policy. The first was to extend eligibility for the program to disabled people under 65. People who are determined to be permanently disabled are eligible to receive Social Security benefits before they turn 65. As part of this benefit, in 1972 they were also included in Medicare.

Another category of patient eligible for Medicare coverage before age 65 is patients with kidney failure (referred to as end-stage renal disease, or ESRD). Before the 1960s, there was no effective treatment for people who developed ESRD—those who got it usually died. During the 1960s, the technology of kidney dialysis was developed. As with most new technologies, dialysis was very expensive and was in short supply. It became apparent that this life-saving alternative was available selectively to those with either the money or the insurance coverage to pay for it. People with ESRD who could not pay for it had no access to it and were left to die. This allocation of life-saving technology according to the ability to pay was viewed as unacceptable by many in Congress. Such a policy was simply not consistent with American norms and values. Accordingly, Congress acted to include all people with ESRD in the Medicare program, regardless of age. The costs of dialysis would be paid by the government.

The decision to include ESRD under Medicare coverage was to have long-range effects that could not have been fully envisioned in 1972. The technology of surgical kidney transplantation was improving rapidly at that time. These costs were also paid by Medicare. The technology of dialysis has improved over the years, keeping more and more people alive, but also adding more and more to the cost of care for ESRD. In the era of genetic engineering, new types of treatments were developed to improve the quality of life for people with ESRD. These newer treatments often cost as much as dialysis itself. Finally, in the era of the for-profit health care provider, the guaranteed availability of Medicare financing for all ESRD-related care led to the development of a growing number of for-profit, investor-owned corporations providing kidney dialysis. A number of analysts have questioned the quality of the care provided by these for-profit dialysis centers, and the appropriateness of the federal government being the principal source of payment (and thus profit) for them. (See Chapter 8 for further discussion of these issues.)

Perhaps not surprisingly, it is quite costly to pay for the care of patients with ESRD. For example, in 2002, Medicare spent on average $6,002 per elderly beneficiary. The figure for each beneficiary eligible for Medicare due to ESRD was $41,696 (data from Kaiser Family Foundation website). The unexpected costs involved in fulfilling the federal commitment to equal access to life-saving treatments for all people with ESRD regardless of income have made Congress hesitant to invoke such egalitarian values again. With expensive, life-saving treatments available for diseases such as AIDS, and with a growing number of poor individuals and families going without access to basic medical care, Congress has been unwilling to extend the values implied by the ESRD coverage to other diseases or groups.

## THE RISING COST OF MEDICARE

It did not take long after the enactment of Medicare in 1965 for the cost of the program to become much larger than expected. Within a few years, the cost of the program more than doubled, from $4.2 billion in 1967 to $9.3 billion in 1973. It doubled again between 1973 and 1977. As more and more people received Medicare coverage and as the increasing availability of technology led to a rapidly rising cost of care, the cost of the program continued to balloon.

Figure 6.5 shows the yearly cost of Parts A and B of the Medicare program between 1967 and 2009. It shows the cost of Part B added to the cost of Part A to give the total cost for these two programs each year. (These figures do not include the cost of Medicare + Choice, discussed below.) It can be seen that Part B, covering physicians' services and other nonhospital care, has become an increasingly large part of overall expenditures. In 1967, the year Medicare first provided coverage, Part B expenditures were about 30 percent of the Part A + Part B total. By 1990, Part B made up 39 percent of that total; in 2009, when Medicare expenditures for Part A + Part B totaled $448 billion, it was 46 percent of the total.

> **CONCEPT 6.5**
>
> The costs of Medicare Part B have grown as a proportion of combined Part A and Part B expenditures, from 39 percent in 1990 to 46 percent in 2009.

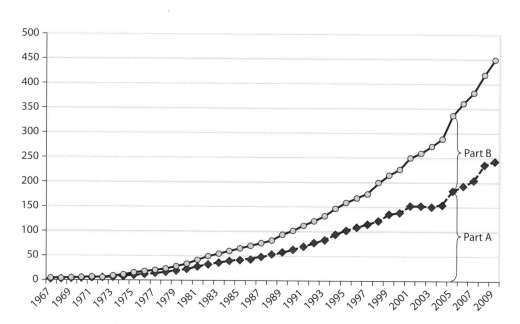

FIGURE 6.5. Medicare Expenditures, in Billions of Dollars, for Part A and Part B, 1967–2009 (does not include Medicare + Choice). *Sources*: Data from U.S. Centers for Medicare and Medicaid Services; Medicare Trustees Report

By 2010, the cost of all Medicare programs combined was $504 billion. This amount is bigger than the national health budget of most other countries and represents a 75 percent increase in just six years. (Part of the reason for this increase was the addition of a new prescription drug benefit to Medicare, discussed in Chapter 9.) With more and more of the cost of Medicare coming from Part B and 75 percent of the cost of Part B coming out of general tax revenues, the rising cost of Medicare is placing an increasing burden on the federal budget. As discussed below, the rising cost of Part A is also placing a severe strain on the Part A trust fund.

The political reality of Medicare's rapidly rising costs led Congress to make a number of changes over the years to the original Medicare program in an effort to constrain those costs. The first of these changes came in 1972 with enactment of the system of professional standards review organizations, or PSROs. These were independent review bodies, often created as an offshoot of local medical societies, charged with reviewing the appropriateness of the hospital care provided to Medicare and Medicaid patients. It was thought that groups of community physicians could advise their peers on avoiding unnecessary hospital costs and thus reduce the cost of hospitalization. While well-intended, the PSROs had little effect on stemming the rise in hospital costs.

The next major step intended to reduce hospital costs was the prospective payment system (PPS), discussed in Chapter 4. Enacted in 1983, the PPS reversed the incentives faced by hospitals, encouraging the rapid discharge of Medicare patients. The PPS was widely viewed as a success, with the increases in the cost of hospital care moderating substantially in the years following its enactment.

By the late 1990s, however, government reports began to indicate that the Medicare trust fund (the fund that holds the money to pay for Part A services) was spending money faster than it was bringing money in, and if nothing changed, the trust fund would go broke in 2001. These predictions started to come true. In 1997, for the first time, the trust fund spent more than it took in, by about $4 billion. As a result, Congress passed a series of changes to Medicare as part of the Balanced Budget Act of 1997, discussed below. These changes led to a short-term stabilization of the Part A trust fund. The continuing rise in Medicare hospital costs and the impending retirement of the baby boom generation, however, have led the Medicare trustees to predict that the trust fund will soon start once more to spend more than it takes in from payroll taxes. Actuarial projections from the Trustees' Report from 2009, before the enactment of ACA, predicted that funds in the Part A trust would be exhausted in 2017 (Boards of Trustees of the Federal Hospital Insurance and Federal Supplementary Medical Insurance Trust Funds 2009).

## CHANGES IN THE WAY MEDICARE PAYS PHYSICIANS

Largely as a result of the rising costs of Part B, Congress began to look closely at the fees it was paying physicians. The original schedule of acceptable fees for physician services was based on a weighted average of what other physicians in the same community charged for the same service, referred to as the usual, customary, and reasonable (UCR) charge. The original Part B payment schedule would pay physicians 80 percent of UCR. Analysts in the federal Health Care Financing Administration and Congress began to question the level of the physicians' fees. Under directions from Congress, the government commissioned a detailed study of physicians' fees and, based on the results of these studies, created the resource-based relative value scale (RBRVS).

The RBRVS created a system of measuring the resources that go into the provision of a medical service and assigning a value reflecting those resources, using a new scale based on the relative value unit (RVU). Every possible procedure was assigned a specific number of RVUs according to the resources required to perform the procedure. If one procedure involved twice as many RVUs as another, it was seen as requiring twice as many resources. Medicare simply established a standard payment rate per RVU and used this figure to calculate the eligible charge for all procedures.

The Centers for Medicare and Medicaid Services (CMS) is the federal agency that manages the Medicare program. (CMS was formerly called the Health Care Financing Administration, or HCFA.) Initially, CMS distinguished between an RVU involved in doing a procedure (for example, surgery or repairing a broken bone) and an RVU involved in the ongoing evaluation and management of a patient (for example, an office visit to treat high blood pressure). Physicians whose practice included procedures were paid more per RVU than those involved mainly in evaluation and management services. For a number of years, there was a debate as to whether procedural services and the services of evaluation and management should receive different levels of payment. CMS ultimately took steps to equalize payment for the two services.

The shift to the RBRVS system of physician payment achieved two principal results:

> **CONCEPT 6.6**
>
> The resource-based relative value scale (RBRVS) established a simplified method for paying physicians treating Medicare patients. Instituting the scale improved the equity in the way primary care physicians and procedural specialists are paid, and it provided a mechanism for controlling overall payments to physicians.

1. The historical income gap between surgeons and other procedure-oriented physicians on the one hand and primary care and other evaluation and management physicians on the other was initially narrowed, due to increased payment for evaluation and management services and reduced payment for procedures.

2. By creating a simplified fee schedule based on the concept of the RVU, it became fairly straightforward for Congress and CMS to control the amount paid to physicians. When the cost of physician care is seen as increasing too rapidly, CMS can simply reduce the reimbursement per RVU, thus reducing payment to physicians overall.

## TAKING CARE OF THE FEW: THE SKEWED NATURE OF THE MEDICARE POPULATION

Increases in life expectancy for all Americans and changes in demographic patterns are having a substantial impact on the cost of Medicare. When Medicare was established in the 1960s, approximately 9.5 percent of the country's population was 65 years or older. A man who was 65 years old at that time could expect to live an additional 13 years on average, and a woman, 17 years. By 1990, 12.3 percent of the population was 65 or older, and additional life expectancy at age 65 had increased to 15.1 years for men and 18.9 years for women. In 2010, 13.0 percent of the population was 65 or older. Current projections predict that the proportion of the population 65 or over will rise to 16.1 percent by 2020 and 19.3 percent by 2030.

In 2006, Medicare spent an average of $8,344 per elderly beneficiary (not including the cost of prescription drug coverage). This amount varies widely, however, depending on the health of the beneficiary. For beneficiaries enrolled in traditional, fee-for-service Medicare, the sickest 10 percent of beneficiaries had an average annual per capita cost of $48,210, and accounted for nearly 60 percent of all spending. By contrast, the healthiest 22 percent of beneficiaries that year had per capita costs less than $1,000, and accounted for 1 percent of expenditures. Twelve percent of beneficiaries incurred no expenditures at all that year (Kaiser Family Foundation 2010e).

> **CONCEPT 6.7**
>
> Medicare spends most of its money taking care of a very few people; the care of 10 percent of the elderly population uses 60 percent of Medicare funds.

## MEDICARE AND MANAGED CARE

As discussed in Chapter 5, the 1980s and 1990s were periods of rapid change in U.S. health care. As the cost of care began to skyrocket, employers and other large purchasers of health insurance turned to health maintenance organizations (HMOs) and other types of managed care delivery system. The number of Americans receiving their care from managed care organizations increased by several orders of magnitude.

During this time, the federal government experienced the same cost pressures as businesses. As the cost of the Medicare program began to increase rapidly, administrators in the federal government began to look to HMOs as potential solutions to the problem of rising costs. As early as 1976, Congress took steps to allow Medicare beneficiaries to enroll in HMOs as an alternative to traditional Medicare coverage. As the costs of Medicare continued to increase despite previous efforts to contain them, the federal government took several steps to reform the program. A number of these steps have been quite controversial. Not all have worked as intended.

Starting in the 1970s, the federal government began to pay HMOs enrolling Medicare beneficiaries based on cost reimbursement. The HMO would keep track of the cost of providing care to the beneficiary, and Medicare would reimburse a portion of that cost. This policy of cost reimbursement provided little incentive for the HMO to constrain the use of services for beneficiaries and did little to reduce Medicare costs. Accordingly, in the early 1980s, the federal government switched from enrolling Medicare beneficiaries in HMOs on a cost basis to enrolling them on a risk basis.

Medicare needed a way to take advantage of the potential cost savings that appeared to be inherent in HMOs. It created a new way of paying HMOs that shifted most of the risk for cost overruns to the HMO, yet provided the HMO with an incentive to control costs. The government estimated that, on average, an HMO should be able to take care of a Medicare beneficiary for about 95 percent of what it costs to take care of beneficiaries in traditional, fee-for-service Medicare. A well-run HMO might even be able to provide care for less than 95 percent.

In 1985, Medicare created a policy under which any HMO that enrolled a Medicare beneficiary would be paid a yearly capitation fee that was equal to 95 percent of the average cost of providing care to the other beneficiaries. Because the average cost of caring for a Medicare beneficiary varies substantially across different communities and different regions of the country, the 95 percent rate was based on the average cost of care locally. The HMO was required to provide the same range of services that were available to beneficiaries under the traditional plan. If the HMO could provide care for less than 95 percent of the average local cost, however, it was free to keep the difference so long as it used the remaining funds either to expand services to beneficiaries or to reduce the out-of-pocket expenses required of them.

Recall that Medicare beneficiaries enrolled in both Part A and Part B still face substantial out-of-pocket expenses. These include the Part A hospital deductible for each time they are in the hospital, the yearly Part B deductible, 20 percent of all charges covered by Part B, and the extra Part B charges (up to 15% of allowable charges) of physicians who do not accept assignment. In addition, there are a variety of things that traditional Medicare simply did not cover, including prescription drugs, dental care, eyeglasses, hearing aids, and foot care. To provide insurance coverage for these added expenses, most Medicare beneficiaries obtain supplemental insurance coverage (Medigap policies).

HMOs initially reacted favorably to the risk-contracting option. By 1987, 161 HMOs had signed risk contracts with HCFA allowing them to enroll Medicare beneficiaries. Following this initial enthusiasm, there was a period of several years of confusion and uncertainty, with the number of contracting HMOs falling to 93 in 1991.

The early 1990s saw the rapid expansion of HMOs in many areas of the country. As the number of HMOs increased, the number of HMOs willing to enter risk contracts also increased. States like California, Florida, Pennsylvania, New York, and Texas saw increases in HMOs operating in the market and HMOs contracting with HCFA. By 1997, 307 HMOs nationwide had signed Medicare risk contracts.

Most of the HMOs enrolling Medicare patients found that the cost of providing care for their members was below the 95 percent capitation rate. Accordingly, they began to expand the types of services they provided to these members. By 1995, 48 percent of all plans offered Medicare beneficiaries supplemental coverage for prescription drugs, 86 percent provided routine eye exams, 65 percent provided hearing exams, and 33 percent provided foot care. Most of the time, these added services were at no extra charge to the beneficiary. In fact, the cost to the beneficiary was often less than traditional Medicare, even before taking into account the cost of Medigap coverage.

In traditional Medicare, beneficiaries must obtain their own Medigap policies to cover many of the items not covered by Medicare. Those who enrolled in a Medicare HMO that offered the supplemental coverage for these costs and services, however, did not need their Medigap coverage. Thus, for many beneficiaries, enrolling in a Medicare HMO resulted in substantial savings. For less money than traditional Medicare, beneficiaries in HMOs were provided with substantially increased benefits. For many, this was an option that proved hard to pass up.

> **CONCEPT 6.8**
>
> In an attempt to reduce program costs, Medicare created the option for beneficiaries to enroll in certain approved HMOs. Because most of these Medicare HMOs offered benefits not provided by traditional Medicare, they proved to be successful in enrolling large numbers of beneficiaries.

By 1997, the number of Medicare beneficiaries enrolling in HMOs had increased to more than 5 million, representing nearly 15 percent of all beneficiaries. In states like California, Arizona, and Oregon, where HMOs had gained a wide share of the overall health care market, more than one-third of Medicare beneficiaries had enrolled in HMOs.

Enrolling in an HMO did have certain drawbacks for Medicare beneficiaries, mostly with the choice of physician or hospital. Under traditional Medicare, each beneficiary is able to obtain care from any physician who has registered with Medicare. Because nearly all practicing physicians in the country are registered, traditional Medicare essentially gives beneficiaries their choice of physician anywhere in the country. Similarly, beneficiaries are able to obtain hospital care at any hospital that is certified by Medicare. Thus, if a beneficiary in California chooses to fly to the Mayo Clinic in Minnesota for consultation with a physician and to undergo surgery, traditional Medicare will provide the same coverage as if the beneficiary had obtained the care in his or her hometown. Finally, under traditional Medicare, beneficiaries are free to consult a specialist without a referral. Under many HMOs, a beneficiary must first obtain a referral from a primary care physician before consulting a specialist. Once the referral has been obtained, the beneficiary is limited to those specialists who are on the HMO's list of eligible providers. Thus, even though enrolling in an HMO held a substantial cost advantage for beneficiaries, it also meant giving up a certain amount of choice in the selection of a physician or a hospital. For those beneficiaries who already had a doctor they felt comfortable with, however, there was little disadvantage in enrolling in an HMO in which their doctor participated.

## PROBLEMS IN HMO RISK CONTRACTING: FAVORABLE SELECTION AND THE AVERAGE COST OF CARE

Officials in the federal government closely followed the growth of Medicare HMO enrollment throughout the early and mid-1990s. As part of the risk contract, Medicare kept track of the care provided to beneficiaries enrolled in HMOs to determine if any cost savings realized by the HMOs were returned to beneficiaries in the form of added benefits. A pattern began to emerge: it appeared that HMOs were more attractive to younger, healthier Medicare beneficiaries. Beneficiaries with more serious medical problems seemed to be more likely to stay with traditional coverage.

> **CONCEPT 6.9**
>
> If a managed care health plan is able to enroll members who, on average, are healthier than the general population, it has benefited from *favorable selection*. If a plan finds that it has enrolled members who, on average, are sicker than the general population, it has experienced *adverse selection*.

Favorable selection refers to a situation that can exist when two or more competing health care plans are available to potential members. If the plans are equally attractive to all members, then the average health status of those enrolling in one plan should be approximately the same as the health status of those enrolling in the alternative plan. If one plan is more attractive to healthier members and the second plan is more attractive to members who, on average, are sicker, however, there will be favorable consequences for the first plan and adverse consequences for the second. Having a higher percentage of its members being sicker means the second plan will have higher costs than the first.

In the case of Medicare, it appears that favorable selection did occur. Those selecting the HMO option were healthier, on average, than those remaining in traditional Medicare. This pattern raised serious questions about the entire financing structure of Medicare HMO enrollment.

Figure 6.6 illustrates the tremendous potential impact that favorable selection and adverse selection can have, as applied to Medicare HMOs and traditional Medicare.

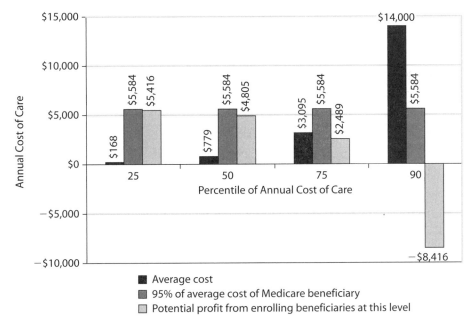

**FIGURE 6.6.** Comparing the Average Cost of Care for Medicare Beneficiaries at the 25th, 50th, 75th, and 90th Percentiles of Yearly Costs with 95 Percent of the Average Cost of All Beneficiaries, 1997. *Source:* Data from U.S. Centers for Medicare and Medicaid Services

Using CMS data for 1997, the graph looks at the cost of providing care to beneficiaries at the 25th, 50th, 75th, and 90th percentiles of yearly cost. For each level it shows

- the average cost per beneficiary at this level
- 95 percent of the average cost of all beneficiaries
- the difference between 95 percent of the average cost of care and what it actually costs to provide care to a beneficiary at this level

The third point above is, in essence, the profit (or loss) that a Medicare HMO will realize if it enrolls a Medicare beneficiary whose cost of care is at the specified level.

Take, for example, a beneficiary at the 50th percentile of annual cost. In 1997, it cost an average of $779 to provide care for this beneficiary. Ninety-five percent of the average cost of taking care of other beneficiaries was $5,584, which was the amount an HMO received from Medicare to care for the beneficiary. The HMO received $4,805 more than it actually cost to provide care for the beneficiary.

Now look at a beneficiary at the 90th percentile of annual cost. It took $14,000, on average, to provide care for this beneficiary which was $8,416 *more* than the HMO was paid. For approximately 80 percent of beneficiaries, the annual cost of care was less than the amount paid by Medicare for HMO care. For the remaining 20 percent, the cost of care was more than the Medicare capitation rate. If an HMO could attract more of the younger, healthier beneficiaries and fewer of the older, sicker beneficiaries, it could keep its annual cost of care substantially below the amount it received from Medicare.

One additional point is worth mentioning. Recall that the 95 percent capitation rate was calculated based on what it cost to provide care to beneficiaries remaining with traditional Medicare. (Recall also that this figure was calculated regionally.) If, as appears to have been the case, those remaining with traditional Medicare were drawn disproportionately from the population of older and sicker beneficiaries, the cost of providing care for these remaining beneficiaries would be even higher than the overall average cost of providing care for all beneficiaries. This situation only magnified the potential benefit of favorable selection for those HMOs who enrolled younger, healthier beneficiaries.

Under the regulations established by Medicare, any surplus funds obtained through enrolling Medicare beneficiaries had to be returned to the beneficiaries in the form of either lower costs or higher benefits. The HMOs that benefited from the lower costs associated with healthier beneficiaries added the benefits described above. Even with these added benefits, it still cost many HMOs less to care for their beneficiaries than the capitation payment they received for providing care. These HMOs were able to increase their profits through enrolling Medicare beneficiaries. The end result was that the Medicare HMO program increased overall spending, rather than decreasing spending as was intended when the program was established.

> **CONCEPT 6.10**
>
> Data gathered by the federal government demonstrated that, in the 1990s, most Medicare HMOs benefited from substantial favorable selection in the enrollment of beneficiaries.

Analysts within the federal government were able to build a strong case for adjusting downward the capitation rate paid to HMOs. They estimated that, as a consequence of disproportionately enrolling younger, healthier beneficiaries, HMOs were facing actual costs that were 5 percent lower than the costs initially estimated. At a time in the 1990s when there was a major national effort to reduce the overall federal budget deficit and control the rising cost of Medicare, the identification of *overpayments* to HMOs was of concern to both federal analysts and members of Congress. In response to these calculations, Congress took action that would prove to have a profound effect on the entire Medicare HMO program.

## THE BALANCED BUDGET ACT OF 1997 AND ITS EFFECT ON MEDICARE

The Balanced Budget Act of 1997, approved by Congress and signed by President Bill Clinton, was a complex set of changes in the financing and organization of a broad range of federal policies. Medicare was only one of the topics covered in this attempt to shift the federal government from chronically spending more on programs than it received in taxes. Years of deficit spending had led to what was then perceived as a huge federal debt. The Balanced Budget Act attempted to ensure that the federal government would balance its budget on an ongoing basis.

One of the first things the Balanced Budget Act did was to change the way that Medicare paid HMOs to enroll beneficiaries. As discussed above, for years Medicare had paid HMOs 95 percent of the average cost of caring for fee-for-service Medicare patients, adjusted for regional differences. The 95 percent payment rate was thought to be too generous, so the act cut this yearly capitation rate to approximately 90 percent of the average cost of providing care to fee-for-service Medicare beneficiaries. Medicare contended that the pattern of favorable selection that had gone on previously made the 90 percent figure more appropriate.

At the same time that Medicare was raising concerns about the financing structure of the Medicare HMO program, members of Congress were looking to reform Medicare in a number of additional ways. Leaders of the Republican Party in Congress, in a position of control of both houses for the first time since Medicare was established, wanted to shift certain portions of Medicare to reflect a more market-based approach. The concept was to allow Medicare beneficiaries a wide range of choices for obtaining care in addition to traditional Medicare and Medicare HMOs. Two principal options were put forward: the medical savings account and Medicare + Choice.

## Medical Savings Account

The RAND health insurance experiment, discussed in more detail in Chapter 12, showed that when patients are required to pay for a substantial portion of their care out of pocket, they will use less care. The concept of the medical savings account (MSA) builds on this finding. It is based on the assumption that if a Medicare beneficiary is personally responsible for the first several thousand dollars of medical care costs per year, that beneficiary will use less care and the overall cost of care will be less. The MSA would provide a modified, high-deductible plan for those beneficiaries who selected it. This plan, based on the traditional fee-for-service payment method, would take effect only after the patient had met the required annual deductible of several thousand dollars per year. It can reasonably be expected that the cost of such private, high-deductible plans would be substantially less than the cost of providing care under traditional Medicare. Under the MSA, an amount equal to the difference between the cost of the high-deductible plan and the cost to Medicare to enroll the beneficiary in a Medicare HMO would be placed in a savings account in the beneficiary's name. For example (using figures for 1998, the year after Medicare MSAs were first approved), if the annual premium for the high-deductible plan were $3,000 and the amount available for HMO enrollment were $5,800, Medicare would deposit $2,800 into a savings account for use by the beneficiary. If the beneficiary did not use the full $2,800 during the year, the remaining balance would be rolled over to the following year. Medicare would deposit an additional $2,800 into the account for that next year.

Recall from Figure 6.6 that, for 75 percent of Medicare beneficiaries, the cost of providing their medical care in 1997 was $3,095 or less. For the majority of these beneficiaries, there was a good chance that money would be left over in the MSA at the end of the year for several years in a row. The amount in the MSA could easily build up. So long as the beneficiary maintained at all times an amount in the MSA equal to 60 percent of the yearly deductible, the beneficiary would be allowed to withdraw additional funds and use the money for any purpose the beneficiary chose. Funds used in this manner would be subject to income tax.

There was a great deal of uncertainty surrounding the MSA proposals, so the Balanced Budget Act of 1997 created the option for up to 390,000 beneficiaries to enroll in MSAs on a trial basis for 4 years, ending in 2002. CMS was then to evaluate the plans to see if they did provide a viable alternative to the traditional fee-for-service program and the Medicare HMO option. Unfortunately, few insurance companies and few Medicare beneficiaries found this option to be attractive. During the trial period, MSA enrollment was less than 20 percent of what had been hoped for. While Medicare MSAs are still technically an option, the Internal Revenue Service reported that, as of 2004, no private, high-deductible policies had been approved by Medicare, so it was not possible for beneficiaries to establish an MSA (IRS Publication 969 website). The MSA model was adopted on a much broader basis, however, as part of the Medicare Modernization Act passed in 2003. Renamed health savings accounts (HSAs), they are now available to the general public. HSAs are discussed in more detail in Chapter 12.

## Medicare + Choice

Several members of Congress wanted the Medicare HMO program to be amended to allow a wider range of managed care options for beneficiaries. While the shift to managed care in the broader health care system had begun with HMOs, the 1990s had seen the proliferation of other managed care financing and delivery systems that were not strictly HMOs. (See Chapter 5 for a discussion of some of these other options.)

To many in Congress, HMOs represented a form of health care that was overly bureaucratic and that unnecessarily limited the options open to patients. The widely held belief in the ability of market forces to improve the efficiency of health care delivery led to proposals to open Medicare to a wide variety of options that were less closely regulated by the government. The proposal was to assure Medicare beneficiaries the range of services covered by Medicare, but to allow them a wide choice of market-based options beyond HMOs as an alternative. Thus the name for this new program: Medicare + Choice (renamed Medicare Advantage in 2004).

Medicare + Choice allowed Medicare beneficiaries to select from any of the following options for their Medicare coverage:

- A Medicare HMO
- A Medicare HMO that in addition provides a point-of-service (POS) option
- A preferred provider organization (PPO) that allows a wide range of choice of physician and hospital and pays for care on a discounted fee-for-service basis
- A physician-hospital organization set up by a coalition of physicians and hospitals willing to accept risk contracting for Medicare beneficiaries
- An MSA
- A traditional fee-for-service insurance plan operated by a private insurance company
- The traditional Medicare program

All Medicare + Choice options would be required to provide the same level of benefits as the traditional program. Like Medicare HMOs, other Medicare + Choice plans would be required to return any cost savings to beneficiaries in the form of increased benefits or lower premiums. Beneficiaries would continue to have the premium for Part B withheld from their Social Security check. For the managed care plans under Medicare + Choice, the total out-of-pocket expenditures for beneficiaries could not exceed the average out-of-pocket expenses under the traditional plan. (Beneficiaries enrolling in the private, fee-for-service option under Medicare + Choice would be subject to somewhat higher out-of-pocket expenses.)

Medicare would pay a yearly premium to any of the plans eligible under Medicare + Choice, calculated in the same manner as the yearly capitation payment for Medicare HMOs. It would be based on a percentage of the average cost of care for beneficiaries in traditional Medicare. Beneficiaries would be eligible to change plans under Medicare + Choice, but after an initial transitional period, they would have the option of changing plans only once a year. The issue of favorable selection would be monitored by CMS, and yearly premiums or capitation rates adjusted accordingly.

> **CONCEPT 6.11**
>
> The Balanced Budget Act of 1997 added several new alternatives for Medicare beneficiaries to obtain care, referred to collectively as "Medicare + Choice." The intent was to reduce the long-term costs of Medicare by introducing a larger role for market forces.

### Other Changes Included in the Balanced Budget Act of 1997

To ensure that the cost of Medicare did not drag the federal government back into deficit spending, the Balanced Budget Act included a number of other changes in the way Medicare was financed. Some of the key provisions are described below.

The reader will recall that the Part A trust fund is financed through the payroll tax contributions of employers and employees. In contrast to Part B financing, which can draw on the general federal treasury if costs increase, there is no mechanism to increase funding for Part A if tax revenues are not sufficient to meet Part A expenses. The two principal categories of Part A expenses before 1997 were hospital care and home health care.

The Medicare home health care benefit had initially been designed to provide a means of getting patients who were being treated in the hospital back home as soon as possible. Medicare would pay for a range of services provided to patients in their home, including skilled nursing care, physical therapy, occupational therapy, and assistance with activities of daily living from a home health aide (see Chapter 10 for a description of "activities of daily living"). Because home health care was seen as a way of getting patients out of the hospital sooner, it seemed appropriate to place the budget for home health services under the Part A trust fund.

The experience with home health care proved to be different from the predictions. Home health care was successful in its goal of improving the quality of life of homebound, elderly individuals. Rather than providing care to recently hospitalized patients, however, the program ended up offering services mainly to patients who had not been in the hospital. Rather than being a substitute for hospital care, it turned out to provide services that were in addition to hospital care. While serving millions of elderly patients, it did not appear to cut down substantially on the cost of hospital care. Allocating the cost of home health care to the Part A trust fund appeared to be less appropriate than initially intended.

As discussed in Chapter 10, the cost of the home health care program increased dramatically between 1989 and 1996, from $3.2 billion to nearly $18 billion. Both the number of beneficiaries receiving care and the average number of visits per beneficiary increased. These changes were a major reason why the Part A trust fund was threatened with insolvency. In the Balanced Budget Act, the solution to this problem was quite simple: reallocate the cost of home health services that are not associated with an episode of hospital care from Part A to Part B. This switch did nothing to change the cost of home health care. It simply changed the fund from which the cost of these services would come. In doing so, it removed a major drain on the trust fund.

The Balanced Budget Act made other changes to home health care policy that were intended to cut down on the costs of the program. It cracked down on fraud and abuse in the way agencies that provide home health care bill for their services, thus saving millions of dollars per year. It also initiated a plan to create a method of paying for home health care per episode of illness rather than per visit. This prospective payment system (PPS) for home health care was intended to have many of the same effects as the PPS for hospital care.

### DECREASING PAYMENTS TO HOSPITALS

The need to maintain the solvency of the Part A trust fund led Congress also to reduce the amount Medicare would pay for hospital care. Recall that most hospital care is paid through the PPS. Historically, as the cost of providing hospital care rose, Medicare increased the PPS payment for that care. Based on a political decision to reduce payments to providers as a principal means of stabilizing Medicare's financing, the Balanced Budget Act mandated that Medicare reduce payments to hospitals in a variety of ways.

The first was to keep payments under the PPS the same in 1998 as they were in 1997, even though the actual costs faced by hospitals had gone up. For the years 1999–2002, PPS payments would rise, but at a rate that was less than the actual increase in the cost of care.

A second step was to further reduce payments to hospitals that treat large numbers of poor patients. Medicare keeps track of the percentage of poor patients treated in every hospital. Those hospitals that treated a disproportionate number of poor patients had received extra payment over and above the usual PPS payment, on the assumption that caring for poor patients can be more expensive than caring for comparable patients who are not poor. These "disproportionate-share" hospitals were thus hit twice by the Balanced Budget Act: their payments were reduced under the standard PPS reductions and also under the specific disproportionate-share reductions. The Balanced Budget Act also reduced the amount paid to teaching hospitals for training residents and fellows, capped the number of residents who can be trained, and provided financial incentives for hospitals to decrease the number of residents in their programs.

### "RISK-ADJUSTING" CAPITATION PREMIUMS TO MEDICARE MANAGED CARE PLANS

Analysts within Medicare, the academic community, and the business community agreed on the need to make the capitation payments made to Medicare managed care plans more in line with the need for services for the covered beneficiaries. As discussed above, the cost of providing care for a beneficiary can vary substantially. It may be possible to predict how much it will cost to provide care for an individual beneficiary or for a group of beneficiaries based on the health status of those beneficiaries. For example, a 70-year-old beneficiary with diabetes and heart disease will incur substantially more costs than a 70-year-old beneficiary with no chronic medical problems. Given adequate information about the health status of beneficiaries, it may be possible to adjust the capitation payment made to a managed care plan based on the previous health status of the beneficiary. Plans enrolling beneficiaries with better health status would receive lower capitation payments, while plans enrolling beneficiaries with worse health status would receive higher capitation payments. Altering the capitation payment according to the health status of the beneficiary is referred to as "risk-adjusting." Congress mandated in the Balanced Budget Act that Medicare develop a method of risk-adjusting capitation payments for its managed care options. Using its extensive database about the problems each beneficiary is treated for each year, CMS worked to develop a more equitable method of paying managed care plans for providing care to Medicare beneficiaries. In this way, the cost of the Medicare + Choice options should be more comparable to the cost of providing care under traditional Medicare, even if the traditional option is subject to adverse selection based on beneficiaries' health status. In 2004, the Department of Health and Human Services reported on its "hierarchical conditions categories" method of risk-adjusting payments to health plans enrolling beneficiaries under Medicare + Choice (Pope et al. 2004).

### INCREASING PREMIUMS PAID BY BENEFICIARIES FOR MEDICARE PART B COVERAGE

As discussed above, Part B of Medicare is optional for eligible seniors, with those who elect to sign up for Part B paying a monthly premium that is deducted from their Social Security check. When Medicare was first established in the 1960s, the funds received from the Part B premiums were intended to pay for 50 percent of the cost of providing Part B services. In the face of rapidly rising costs, Congress quickly backtracked on this initial policy goal and allowed the share of the cost covered by premiums to fall well below this level. By the 1990s, Part B premiums accounted for substantially less than 25 percent of the cost of services. The Balanced Budget Act mandated that Part B premiums be set at a level that would pay 25 percent of Part B costs.

## The Best-Laid Plans: Unintended Consequences of Policy Changes in the Balanced Budget Act

The Balanced Budget Act of 1997 was intended to stabilize the financing of the Medicare program while maintaining the quality and accessibility of care to beneficiaries. As is often the case with complex policy changes, the act failed to achieve many of its intended outcomes. In some cases, the results of the policy changes were the opposite of what was intended, as described below.

### FINANCIAL HARDSHIP FOR HOSPITALS

The payment reductions to hospitals included in the Balanced Budget Act were intended primarily to stabilize the Part A trust fund. Congress had no desire to cause financial hardship for hospitals. Nevertheless, the reductions created substantial financial hardship for a number of hospitals. Already hit by decreasing payment rates from HMOs and other managed care plans in the general health care market, many hospitals relied on Medicare payments to maintain financial stability. The reductions in Medicare payments were more than many hospitals could withstand. Hospitals in numerous cities faced either closing to prevent insolvency or selling out to larger hospital corporations. Teaching hospitals and disproportionate-share hospitals faced additional losses, leading many of them to the brink of insolvency. Perhaps hardest hit were those hospitals with the dual role of caring for the poor and training physicians. Many of these hospitals are in the inner city and are supported by local public funds. These hospitals lost out three ways: (1) through reduced PPS payments, (2) through reduced teaching payments, and (3) through reduced disproportionate-share payments. A number of hospitals in this situation had to close down, leaving many of the most vulnerable segments of the population with even greater difficulty in obtaining care.

Fortunately, Congress and CMS quickly became aware of the unintended consequences the Balanced Budget Act had on hospitals. They acted quickly to increase payments to hospitals (though not back to the level before the act) to maintain their financial stability.

### DECREASING AVAILABILITY AND INCREASING COST FOR MEDICARE HMOS

The government had data to show that many Medicare HMOs were being paid more than was intended, due to favorable selection of enrolled beneficiaries. The reduction in capitation rate included as part of the Balanced Budget Act was intended to rectify this imbalance. The intent was that HMOs and other managed care plans made available through Medicare + Choice would at least maintain their coverage, if not expand it.

Instead, many HMOs reacted to the decrease in capitation payment by simply canceling their risk contract with Medicare, and in doing so canceling the HMO coverage of beneficiaries previously covered in their plan. HMOs have the option of canceling contracts on a county-by-county basis. Because the capitation rates were set on a countywide basis, the rates in one county could be quite different from the rates in nearby counties. Thus, HMOs were allowed to "disenroll" covered beneficiaries in one county while maintaining coverage in others. In 1999 and 2000, the 2 years following enactment of the Balanced Budget Act, HMOs pulled out of more than 400 counties in 33 states, leading to the involuntary disenrollment of more than 700,000 Medicare beneficiaries. Between 1999 and 2003, 2.4 million Medicare beneficiaries were disenrolled in this way. The reason given by most HMOs for canceling their Medicare contracts was low payment rates.

In attempting to adjust the capitation rate to a more equitable level, the Balanced Budget Act led to a mass exodus of HMOs from Medicare, affecting more than 25 percent of those beneficiaries enrolled in HMOs. Some beneficiaries who lost their coverage were able to switch into other HMOs. Many did not have this option and were required to revert to traditional Medicare coverage. For those seniors with chronic medical problems who had to revert to traditional coverage, finding a private Medigap insurer to supplement Medicare coverage often proved difficult. Those seniors who were able to maintain HMO coverage faced substantial increases in premiums. In addition, they found that many of the extra benefits previously offered by HMOs were substantially reduced. Especially vulnerable to reductions in coverage were prescription drugs. Many seniors who joined HMOs principally to obtain prescription drug coverage found this coverage markedly reduced.

> **CONCEPT 6.12**
>
> The Balanced Budget Act of 1997 had a number of adverse consequences that Congress had not intended. Among these were a large-scale exodus of many HMOs from the Medicare program and severe financial hardship for many hospitals.

The exodus of HMOs from the Medicare market and the distrust this change created among Medicare beneficiaries dealt a severe blow to the concept of Medicare + Choice. Nonetheless, many still contend that private, market-based plans are a better long-term alternative than the traditional Medicare plan. As part of the Medicare Modernization Act passed in 2003, discussed below, Congress instructed CMS to increase capitation payments to private plans under Medicare + Choice (renamed by the act as "Medicare Advantage").

## WHY DID MEDICARE HMOs HAVE SO LITTLE SUCCESS IN HOLDING DOWN COSTS?

The rising cost of health care seen generally in this country over the thirty years leading up to the Balanced Budget Act contributed to rising costs for Medicare as well. The federal government took a number of steps that were successful in constraining that rise. Examples of these successful policy changes include the PPS and the RBRVS method of paying physicians.

Medicare's move to managed care as an alternative to fee-for-service was substantially less successful, however. Initially, enrollment in Medicare HMOs grew rapidly. When it was discovered that Medicare HMOs were benefiting substantially from favorable selection of enrollees, however, Congress acted to reduce payments to HMOs to a more equitable level. As a cost-saving device, Medicare + Choice turned out largely to be a failure. Rather than reducing costs, it increased costs.

Why did it turn out that Medicare HMOs and other Medicare managed care plans did not save money compared to the fee-for-service alternative? Recall that the original RAND health insurance experiment carried out in the 1980s demonstrated that HMOs saved money over their fee-for-service competitors largely in the way they used the hospital. HMO patients were hospitalized less often and for shorter periods of time. Now recall that the Medicare PPS, also enacted in the 1980s, was quite successful in reducing hospital costs for Medicare beneficiaries. It appears that the PPS had achieved roughly the same savings in hospital costs for Medicare beneficiaries that HMOs had achieved for the general public. There may not have been any further savings to be realized by switching Medicare from a fee-for-service to a capitated system of payment. While HMOs in the 1980s worked as less costly alternatives to fee-for-service plans, the basis of these cost savings (reduced use of hospitals) did not exist for Medicare in the 1990s. There was little reason to believe, and little scientific data to suggest, that market-based managed care plans would be any more successful in constraining the inexorable rise in Medicare costs than the traditional plan that is based on fee-for-service payment for physicians and prospective payment for hospitals.

## "MEDICARE ADVANTAGE" AS THE NEW MEDICARE MARKET OPTION

When President George W. Bush was elected in 2000, one of his principal campaign pledges had been to initiate fundamental reforms to Medicare. He was successful in this effort, securing passage of the Medicare Prescription Drug, Improvement, and Modernization Act (MMA) of 2003. The principal component of MMA was the creation of a prescription drug benefit for Medicare beneficiaries, discussed in Chapter 9. A second major outcome of MMA was to replace Medicare + Choice with a new plan referred to as Medicare Advantage (MA). MA fundamentally altered the method of funding the private plans available to Medicare beneficiaries. Instead of paying the private plans 90 percent of the average cost of beneficiaries in the traditional Medicare system, MA guaranteed these plans 100 percent of that average cost. In addition, private plans were guaranteed annual increases in their payment rates. With these changes, coupled with a complex formula for calculating plan reimbursement on a county-by-county basis, it rapidly became apparent that the cost of MA plans was substantially greater than that of traditional Medicare. Much of this added cost went to expanded benefits and lower premiums for those Medicare beneficiaries enrolling in them.

Not surprisingly, with this added funding and increased level of benefits, MA plans grew substantially in popularity. From a low of 5.3 million enrolled beneficiaries in 2004, the year MA first came into effect, enrollment grew to 11.1 million beneficiaries in 2010, representing 24 percent of all beneficiaries. Of those enrolled in MA in 2010, 65 percent were in an HMO, 19 percent in a PPO, 13 percent in a private fee-for-service option, and 3 percent in high-deductible plans supplemented by health savings accounts (Gold et al. 2010).

This expansion, however, came at a substantial cost to the Medicare program. In 2009, the average cost of a MA plan was 114 percent that of traditional Medicare, with some plans such as PPOs and private fee-for-service plans costing 118 percent of traditional Medicare (Medicare Pay-

> **CONCEPT 6.13**
>
> The Medicare Modernization Act of 2003 provided additional funding to managed care plans enrolling Medicare beneficiaries. Care provided in these plans costs an average of 114 percent of the cost of care under the traditional Medicare system.

ment Advisory Commission 2009). The added cost of these plans contributed to higher Part B premiums paid by all Medicare beneficiaries, and were seen as contributing to the long-term financial instability of the Medicare program. In the words of officials working with the Medicare Payment Advisory Commission, "The higher MA payment rates have financed what is essentially a Medicare benefit expansion for MA enrollees, without producing any overall savings for the Medicare program, and with increased costs borne by all beneficiaries and taxpayers" (Zarabozo and Harrison 2009, p. w66).

## PAYING PHYSICIANS UNDER MEDICARE—THE SUSTAINABLE GROWTH RATE

Starting in 1992, the RBRVS system created a mechanism to constrain the rising cost of physicians' services under Part B of Medicare. By establishing a single payment rate based on the relative value unit, or RVU, Congress could act to change the payment per RVU, and in so doing adjust the entire physician payment structure under Medicare either up or down. As part of the Balanced Budget Act of 1997 Congress took just such action, creating what it called the sustainable growth rate (SGR) for physician services.

Recall from our discussion in Chapter 3 the method various Canadian provinces used to control the cost of physician services. Each year the province would set a budgeted amount to spend on all physician services in aggregate. As physicians in Canada billed largely on a fee-for-service basis, only by setting and enforcing budget caps could the provincial health plans control the cost of physicians' services. As it turned out, in many of the provinces the aggregate cost of physicians' services exceeded the budgeted amount, leading the provincial health plans to reduce the amount they paid physicians for the following year.

Faced with these reduced fees, physicians tended to see patients more frequently and to perform more services each time they saw a patient. These increased costs, triggered in response to a reduced payment rate, once again exceeded the budget for that year, leading to a further round of fee reductions. This process of serial fee reductions and utilization increases, referred to as "churning," resulted in a downward spiral in physician incomes in Canada. The spiral was finally arrested when provincial medical associations, in collaboration with government agencies, were able to alter the pattern of physicians' care.

SGR, as established by the Balanced Budget Act, adopted essentially the same approach to constraining the cost of physicians' services as that used in Canada. Rather than setting a fixed yearly budget for physician care under Part B of Medicare, it set an expenditure "target" based on current year expenditures. To establish the target, the CMS adjusts expenditures from one year to the next based on the following factors (Congressional Budget Office 2006):

1. adjustment for inflation that accounts for changes in the prices of goods and services used by physicians' practices
2. changes in the number of people enrolled in Medicare's fee-for-service program
3. the average annual growth rate of real gross domestic product (GDP) per capita
4. changes in the benefit structure of Part B that result from new legislation or regulations

The SGR worked reasonably well in the first few years following its enactment in 1997. In 2000 and 2001, for example, physicians' fees under Part B went up 5.3 percent and 4.8 percent, respectively (Iglehart 2002). By 2002, however, physicians' charges had begun to exceed the SGR formula, and Medicare reduced physicians' fees by 4.8 percent. By 2003, charges had gone up even more, and payments were scheduled to go down an additional 4.4 percent. In testimony before Congress, Donald B. Marron, acting director of the Congressional Budget Office, reported that "considerable evidence exists that a reduction in [Medicare] payment rates leads physicians to increase the volume and intensity of the services they perform" (2006, p. 4). Physicians were treating Medicare beneficiaries more often (volume) and using more resources for each treatment (intensity). Physicians in the United States were, perhaps not surprisingly, responding to relative reductions in the fees Medicare paid as compared to their usual fees by increasing the volume and intensity of their services—that is, they were engaging in churning.

CMS, the federal agency that oversees the Medicare program, initially responded to the pattern of expenditures rising faster than the target rate by scheduling a 4.8 percent cut in the amount it paid per RVU, with an additional 4.4 percent cut scheduled for 2003. In 2003, however, Congress responded to intense lobbying on the part of physicians' professional organizations by postponing the scheduled fee reductions, instead granting physicians a 1.6 percent increase for that year. With SGR-mandated fee reductions then scheduled to take effect in 2004 and 2005, Congress acted again, giving physicians a 1.5 percent increase in fees for each year. Congress has acted every year since then to postpone scheduled payment cuts.

Each time Congress acts to postpone the scheduled SGR rate reduction and instead grants physicians a rate increase, the cumulative amount by which physician expenditures has exceeded the SGR target increases. This increased gap between targeted and actual expenditures leads to an even bigger reduction in physician fees. By December 2010, the SGR formula had mandated a 25 percent cut in physician fees. As the size of the cut grew bigger, the intensity of the physician lobbying increased accordingly.

> **CONCEPT 6.14**
>
> The Balanced Budget Act of 1997 established a capped target for annual aggregate expenditures for physician care under Medicare Part B, referred to as the sustainable growth rate (SGR). For several years, the SGR formula has called for substantial reductions in payments to physicians. However, Congress has repeatedly postponed these reductions.

Dire predictions were heard of large numbers of physicians exiting the Medicare program altogether in response to the scheduled cuts, leaving their Medicare patients to find another source of care. In December 2010, Congress acted once again, this time postponing the scheduled cuts for twelve months.

The SGR was modeled largely on the historically successful efforts in Canada to constrain the costs of physicians' services. The difference, of course, is in the political will to permit the mechanism to work. In Canada, provincial governments had the political will to enforce their budgets for physician care. In the United States, that will simply has not been there.

If Congress is not going to enforce SGR, why not just scrap it and come up with something else? That approach has been proposed by a number of analysts. The problem lies in how Congress approaches the budgeting process. Each year, Congress budgets the funds for Medicare's Part B expenditures, splitting the cost between the premiums charged beneficiaries and general income tax revenues. For several years Congress has set these budgets based on the assumption that physician fees will be 21 percent lower than they actually are—not just for the current year, but for every year in the future. If Congress were simply to scrap SGR and permanently cancel any scheduled cuts, it would have to refigure its Medicare budget for current and future years. It would have to find a way to pay for the increase in that budget that would result from abandoning the SGR formula. Since tax rates are not expected to go up any time soon, Congress would have to borrow those funds every year, thus adding to the federal deficit. For many in Congress, that idea is even less palatable than reducing physicians' fees. As a result, we have had a series of postponements—postponements in confronting the cuts mandated by SGR, and postponements in finally accepting that SGR does not work and needs to be replaced with some other mechanism for constraining the aggregate cost of physicians' services under Medicare.

## ADDITIONAL POINTS ABOUT THE MEDICARE PROGRAM

Two additional points should be made about the Medicare program. As discussed above, the cost of providing medical care to elderly people has become increasingly expensive over time. The result has been that most current beneficiaries receive substantially more in benefits—in the range of 5 to 10 times more—than they contributed to the system during their working years. Medicare is a system based on shifting financial resources from current workers to current elderly people.

The second point has to do with the administrative efficiency of the Medicare system. During the debate over national health care reform in 1993–94, opponents made much of the added federal bureaucracy that would be developed if the Clinton reform proposals were adopted. The implication was that giving the government greater responsibility in administering health care resources would lead to massive inefficiency.

The Medicare system, despite being one of the largest government programs in history, has proven to be one of the most efficient administrative systems for providing health care to a defined population of patients. A common measure of efficiency in health care is the percentage of all costs that go to administration rather than patient care. Employer-based insurance typically spends 10 to 30 percent of costs on administration and other expenses not related to patient care (for example, corporate profit). For nonprofit HMOs such as Kaiser Permanente, this figure is in the range of 3 to 7 percent. Part A spent 1 to 2 percent of all funds on administrative costs; the figure for Part B is typically 2 to 2.5 percent. Using this measure of administrative efficiency, Medicare is the most efficient medical payment system in the country.

> **CONCEPT 6.15**
>
> The administrative structure of Medicare, managed by the federal Centers for Medicare and Medicaid Services, is the most efficient medical payment system in the country.

## STRANGE BEDFELLOWS: MEDICARE AND PAYING FOR GRADUATE MEDICAL EDUCATION

Before ending this chapter, we should also consider Medicare's current policies of paying for graduate medical education (GME). GME refers to the training physicians receive after they graduate from medical school. It includes training offered in residency programs and specialty fellowship programs. Since 1983, the federal government has taken principal responsibility for paying the costs of GME, essentially reimbursing most of the training costs to hospitals that offer GME. The cost of GME is paid from the Part A trust fund.

It may seem odd that the program intended to pay for hospital care for seniors has taken on responsibility for paying the costs of GME. Such a perception is accurate and represents a strange and unintended twist in the history of Medicare. As described in Chapter 4, Medicare was not initially intended to be the principal source of funding for GME. As a result of a political compromise enacted at the time the PPS was initiated in 1983, however, Medicare became responsible for paying most of the costs of GME.

For decades, no limits were placed on the number of GME positions that could be funded, resulting in a powerful financial incentive for hospitals to increase the size of their GME programs. It became readily apparent to hospitals that by increasing the number of GME slots, they would receive a larger subsidy from the federal government. For many hospitals, particularly inner-city hospitals that provide care to low-income patients, resident physicians provide the bulk of the care (albeit under the supervision of fully trained physicians on the hospital staff). The Medicare payments for GME provided a source of inexpensive physicians for inner-city hospitals.

The effect on the system overall was a growing surplus of GME training slots compared to the number of medical students graduating from U.S. medical schools. It became necessary for hospitals to look to international medical graduates (IMGs) to fill their training programs, with a resulting influx of international physicians into the country. A substantial majority of IMGs trained in the United States under this program remain in the country after their training is completed.

## SUMMARY

In 1965, after decades of debate—and resistance from the medical profession—Congress enacted Medicare, providing tax-financed, universal health insurance for Americans age 65 or older. Following Medicare's initial success and popularity, Congress extended its coverage to include those with permanent disability and those with end-stage kidney disease.

As a result of a political compromise at the time of its initial passage, Medicare was divided into two parts, each part using a different method of financing and payment to providers. Medicare Part A pays for hospital care and is financed principally from payroll taxes. Medicare Part B pays for physician care and other types of outpatient care and is financed jointly from general income taxes (75%) and premiums paid by beneficiaries (25%).

Shortly after its enactment, it became clear that the system would cost substantially more than initial projections. Congress has made repeated efforts to constrain Medicare costs, including fundamental changes to the way it pays hospitals and physicians. While costs have been constrained somewhat as a result of these changes, Medicare nonetheless faces steep and continuing cost increases. Especially as the baby boom generation becomes eligible for Medicare, the long-term financial viability of the program is being increasingly questioned.

A principal factor contributing to the increase in Medicare costs is the highly skewed nature of Medicare expenditures, with most Medicare funds going to pay for a small segment of the covered population. Providing care to the sickest 10 percent of covered seniors accounts for nearly half of all expenditures.

One way the federal government has attempted to address this issue is to encourage seniors to enroll in HMOs and other forms of managed care. Unfortunately, more than a decade of experience has shown that managed care is not able to attain the same cost savings for Medicare beneficiaries that it has been able to for younger age groups covered through the private market for health insurance.

## CHANGES IN MEDICARE UNDER THE AFFORDABLE CARE ACT

Those responsible for the passage of the Affordable Care Act (ACA) knew that unless ACA addressed the growing issue of the cost of the Medicare program in the context of the entry into it of the baby boom generation, any attempt at system-wide reform would likely fail in the long run. Accordingly, ACA contains several major changes to Medicare, which I describe below. For a more detailed discussion of these changes I suggest that you consult the material developed on the topic by the Kaiser Family Foundation (2010h).

## Changes to Medicare Advantage

Acknowledging that there was little continuing support for providing a tax-financed subsidy to private health plans, ACA revised the formula under which these plans will be paid. Beginning in 2011, the rates paid to plans participating in MA will be gradually reduced, with the expectation that by 2014 they will be more nearly equivalent to the average cost of providing care for a beneficiary under traditional Medicare. Payments will also be risk-adjusted based on an enrollee's current and previous health status, so as to avoid favorable selection among MA enrollees. ACA also sets explicit quality targets for the care provided by plans under MA, paying a bonus to those plans that meet or exceed the target.

## Changes to Medicare Part D—the Prescription Drug Benefit

ACA makes changes to its prescription drug benefit, described in more detail in Chapter 9.

## Improved Coverage of Preventive Health Services

ACA changes the coverage for certain types of health services that have been recommended by the U.S. Preventive Services Task Force. Examples of these services are mammography screening for breast cancer in women and screening for colorectal cancer. Beginning in 2011, Medicare beneficiaries will have no co-payment or deductible charged for these services. In addition, beneficiaries may receive a yearly general preventive examination and consultation without charge.

## Creation of a New National Advisory Board

Reflecting the continuing conundrum of the SGR for physician services under Medicare, ACA does not address the issue of the SGR directly, but does establish a new mechanism for addressing the broader issue of the rising cost of Medicare over time. This issue will now be the responsibility of a newly established Independent Payment Advisory Board (IPAB) made up of fifteen members appointed by the president and confirmed by the Senate. Its explicit responsibility will be to monitor the rate at which Medicare's per beneficiary spending increases over time.

ACA sets a target rate of growth for Medicare spending, tied initially to the growth in the consumer price index (a general measure of overall price inflation) and subsequently to the overall growth in GDP. Beginning in 2014, if it turns out that projected per beneficiary spending will exceed the target amount, IPAB is charged with the responsibility of coming up with a plan to rein in spending to meet the target amount. The secretary of health and human services must then carry out the IPAB's plan to control spending, unless Congress overrides the plan with one of its own.

In creating the IPAB, Congress has done two important things:

1. It has created under law a strict limit on spending growth under Medicare.
2. It ceded authority to an independent body to enforce the limit.

In granting IPAB responsibility for enforcing the limits on Medicare spending growth, however, Congress has tied one of IPAB's hands behind its back. Section 3403.d.2.A.ii of ACA specifically states that any proposal from IPAB "shall not include any recommendation to ration health care, raise revenues [that is, taxes] or Medicare beneficiary premiums . . . or increase Medicare beneficiary cost sharing (including deductibles, coinsurance, and copayments), or otherwise restrict benefits or modify eligibility criteria."

As discussed in Chapter 13, the concept of "rationing" health care in the United States has come to have unusually negative connotations. For many, it simply is un-American to even consider rationing something as important as health care. Although ACA does not define what is meant by "rationing" care under Medicare, IPAB can be expected to avoid recommendations that might be construed by the public or by Congress as "rationing." This means that cost control mechanisms that weigh the costs versus the effectiveness of the services to be paid for by Medicare will be difficult, if not impossible, for IPAB to invoke. If IPAB is also prohibited from raising taxes or premiums, increasing cost sharing, or restricting benefits, it may be as difficult for IPAB as it has been for Congress and the federal Centers for Medicare and Medicaid Services to control the incessant rise in the cost of the Medicare program.

### Demonstration Projects Intended to Reduce Costs

ACA provides substantial funding for demonstration projects intended to identify new ways to reduce costs while maintaining quality. ACA creates a new Center for Medicare and Medicaid Innovations (CMMI) to study these new arrangements for care. One focus is on encouraging groups of physicians and hospitals to come together to form accountable care organizations (ACOs). An ACO would take full responsibility for planning, coordinating, and providing the care of a group of Medicare beneficiaries. If the ACO is able to reduce the cost of caring for its patients as compared to Medicare's average per beneficiary cost, the ACO would receive a share of the cost savings as an incentive payment.

A second type of demonstration project extends the PPS described in Chapter 4 to encompass physician care, hospital care, outpatient services such as laboratory or X-ray, and rehabilitative services. A single "bundled payment" would be made to cover a thirty-day period of care triggered by admission to a hospital. In theory, a prospective payment of this type, covering outpatient as well as inpatient services, would encourage physicians and hospitals to be more efficient in the allocation of care.

## Revenue Enhancements and Payment Reductions

ACA changes the formula by which the Part A Medicare payroll tax is calculated, increasing the tax rate from 1.45 to 2.35 percent for high-income taxpayers. It also creates some new taxes to be imposed on pharmaceutical companies, medical device companies, and certain health insurance companies. It also increases somewhat the Medicare Part B premiums on high-income beneficiaries. ACA also reduces certain payments to hospitals. Among these are payments previously made to hospitals that provide a disproportionate amount of care to the poor and the uninsured.

Perhaps the most significant payment reduction resulting from ACA is a change in the way yearly updates in payment rates to providers will be calculated. ACA assumes that, over time, providers of services under Medicare will be able to improve their efficiency and productivity, and thus their cost of providing service. Based on these assumed efficiency enhancements, Medicare's increases in payment to providers will be about 1.1 percent less each year than they would have been without the expected changes in provider efficiency.

In their Annual Report for 2010, the Medicare Boards of Trustees (2010) estimated that the combination of revenue enhancements and payment reductions called for in ACA will have a substantial, beneficial effect on the financial outlook for Medicare. The trustees estimate that, as a result of ACA, the predicted exhaustion of the Part A trust fund will be postponed, from 2017 (before ACA) to 2029. Annual increases in the cost of Part B are expected to fall from historical growth rates that were 4.2 percent greater than the growth in GDP to rates approximately equal to the growth in GDP.

The Medicare Boards of Trustees, however, include a pointed cautionary note in their report. They point out repeatedly that, as required by law, their financial projections assume that the cut in physicians' fees called for by the sustainable growth rate (described above) will be made as scheduled. In addition, the report assumes that physicians, hospitals, and other providers will be able to improve their efficiency and productivity by about 1 percent per year, thus balancing out the 1.1 percent reductions in reimbursement called for by ACA. The trustees' report questions both of these assumptions: "As a result of (i) the very improbable reductions in physician payments required under the current-law SGR formula, and (ii) the strong possibility that the productivity adjustments lead to payment rates for other health care providers that are inadequate in the long range, actual future Medicare expenditures are likely to exceed the intermediate projections shown in this report, possibly by quite large amounts" (p. 17).

# 7

# Medicaid and the State Children's Health Insurance Program

In 1965, the U.S. Congress made sweeping changes to the way health care was financed and provided. Medicare, the program to provide health care to elderly people, was discussed in the previous chapter. At the same time, Congress also enacted Medicaid, a program to provide health care to poor people. Like Medicare, Medicaid was created as an amendment to the existing Social Security Act, and thus is often referred to as "Title XIX."

Unlike Medicare, which covers all elderly people in the country who qualify for Social Security, Medicaid was not intended as a program for all people who fall below the federal poverty line (FPL). It pays for care only for certain subgroups of poor people. Also in contrast to Medicare, Medicaid was originally structured purely on an insurance model, with no direct service component. Finally, while Medicare is financed and administered purely by the federal government, Medicaid is administered by the states, with the federal government reimbursing each state for a portion of program costs.

As with Medicare, the design and structure of the Medicaid program reflects historical and political factors that existed at the time of its passage. Before 1965, a federal program (the Kerr-Mills program) distributed federal funds to each of the states to assist in paying for medical care for elderly poor people. This program had four principal characteristics:

1. It had a combination of federal and state funding.
2. It was administered by the states under broad federal guidelines.
3. Eligibility for the program was tied to eligibility for cash welfare grants.

4. As long as the basic benefits required by the federal government were provided, each state was free to set its own level of additional benefits.

When Congress enacted Medicaid, rather than going through the process of designing a new program, it simply replicated the characteristics of the Kerr-Mills program. These four principles continue to define the structure of Medicaid today.

Under Medicaid, each state designs its own program for paying for medical care for poor people, using existing hospitals and physicians and initially paying for care on a fee-for-service basis. Relying on the existing system was seen as a way to bring poor people into the "mainstream" of U.S. medical care. As discussed below, the rising costs of the program have made this goal very difficult to achieve.

> **CONCEPT 7.1**
>
> Medicaid differs from Medicare in three important ways:
>
> 1. Rather than being universally available to all poor people, it covers only certain subgroups.
> 2. Rather than combining a service plan and an insurance plan, it originally was strictly an insurance plan.
> 3. Rather than being administered by the federal government, it is administered by the states under broad federal guidelines.

Medicaid was established as a voluntary program for the states, with each state free to choose whether to participate. As a strong incentive, the federal government agreed to reimburse each participating state for a large part of the program's cost. The share of the program that the federal government pays depends on the economic condition of the state. States with lower per capita incomes have a higher share of the program costs paid by the federal government, while states with higher per capita incomes are reimbursed a lower percentage of program costs.

In 2008, the federal government reimbursed higher-income states, such as New York, Connecticut, and California, for 50 percent of expenditures. By contrast, the federal share of the Medicaid program was 74 percent in West Virginia and 76 percent in Mississippi. In 2008, the federal government paid 57 percent of the overall $338 billion cost of the Medicaid program.

As part of the American Recovery and Reinvestment Act (AARA), the federal government's response in 2009 to the impending national financial crisis, federal reimbursement rates were raised for all states. In 2010, federal reimbursement increased to a rate of about 62 percent in states like New York, Connecticut, and California to as high as 83 percent in West Virginia and 85 percent in Mississippi. For 2010, the federal government paid 66 percent of the overall cost of the Medicaid program. The increased reimbursement rates called for by AARA were originally scheduled to expire as of December 31, 2010. With many states continuing to experience severe budget deficits, a number of governors argued for an extension of the higher rates past the December 31 deadline. In August 2010, Congress responded, extending the increased reimbursement rates through June 2011.

As shown in Figure 7.1, funding for the Medicaid program, whether state or federal,

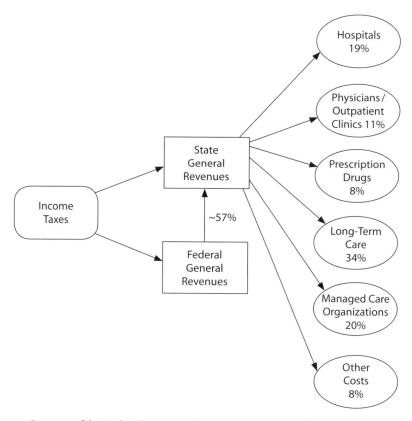

FIGURE 7.1. Structure of the Medicaid Program, 2008. *Source:* Data from Kaiser Family Foundation. *Medicaid—A Primer,* 2010

comes straight out of general tax revenues. Thus, on the pay stub shown at the beginning of Chapter 6, the employee is helping to pay for the program both through federal withholding tax and state withholding tax. As with Part B of Medicare, this reliance on general tax revenues means that at times of rapidly rising health care costs or of shrinking tax revenues a severe strain can be placed on both federal and state budgets. During times of recession, with more people out of work and thus qualifying for Medicaid coverage at the same time that tax revenues drop off sharply, the strain Medicaid places on both federal and state budgets can be a substantial problem for lawmakers.

## SERVICE PROVIDED UNDER THE MEDICAID PROGRAM

For a state Medicaid program to be eligible for reimbursement from the federal government, it must provide certain basic services to all beneficiaries. These basic services include

- hospital care (inpatient and outpatient)
- nursing home care

- physician services
- laboratory and X-ray services
- immunizations and other preventive medicine services for children
- family planning services
- services provided at federally approved community health centers
- nurse midwife and nurse practitioner services

States also have the option of providing certain additional services for which they receive federal matching funds. These additional services include

- prescription drugs
- institutional care for individuals with mental retardation
- home- and community-based care for the frail elderly
- personal care and other community-based services for individuals with disabilities
- dental care and vision care

Since 1977 and the passage of a federal law referred to as the Hyde Amendment, no federal funds may be spent to provide abortion services except for cases of rape, incest, or when the mother's life is in danger. This restriction also applies to the Medicaid program, although states are permitted to provide abortion services that are "medically necessary" to Medicaid recipients, as long as they do so using only state funds. Seventeen states provide abortion services under their Medicaid plans.

Figure 7.1 shows how the money in the Medicaid program was spent in 2008. About 20 percent of Medicaid funds were paid to managed care organizations, reflecting the increased role of Medicaid managed care, described below. About 19 percent paid for acute hospital care, with an additional 10.5 percent going to physicians and outpatient clinics. The cost of prescription drugs took 4.5 percent of all funds. An important thing to note is that 34 percent of all Medicaid funds go to pay for long-term care.

## ELIGIBILITY FOR MEDICAID

To be eligible for Medicaid, an individual must be within one of the following three groups:

### 1. Members of low-income families with children

Historically, Medicaid eligibility for this group was tied to eligibility for cash welfare grants under the Aid to Families with Dependent Children program. The changes included in the welfare reform that was enacted in 1996, however, broke this link. Currently, all children in families with incomes that fall below the FPL are eligible to receive Medicaid coverage. In addition, children under the age of 6 who are in families that earn up to 133 percent of the FPL are eligible for Medicaid. The parents of low-income children are eligible only if the family income is extremely low, typically 40 to 50 percent of the FPL. Pregnant women in families that earn up to 133 percent of the FPL, however, are eligible for Medicaid coverage for medical care during pregnancy and immediately after giving birth. In 2007, Medicaid covered 29 million low-income children and 15 million low-income adults.

### 2. Elderly people who meet certain income requirements

People over 65 whose income is below a level established by the federal government (typically about 75% of the poverty level) qualify for supplemental cash payments under the Supplemental Security Income (SSI) program. People eligible for SSI are also eligible for Medicaid. Some elderly people have incomes that are higher than the allowable Medicaid limit but they face larger medical expenses than they can pay. Before these people become eligible for Medicaid, they must first use most of their personal savings to pay for their medical care. After they "spend down" their savings to a certain level (usually a few thousand dollars), they then become eligible for Medicaid. Most people eligible for Medicaid in this manner are confined to a nursing home. In 2007, more than 8 million people covered by Medicare were also enrolled in Medicaid.

As discussed in Chapter 10, Medicare provides little in the way of coverage for nursing home care. Nonetheless, a growing number of elderly people are facing the prospect of nursing home care without the means to pay for it. They turn to the Medicaid program as the payer of last resort to pay for their care.

### 3. Disabled people

People under the age of 65 with long-term disabilities qualify for Medicaid in the same manner as elderly people. Nonelderly, disabled people who receive cash payments from SSI are also eligible for Medicaid. In addition, disabled people not covered by SSI but incurring large medical expenses are eligible for Medicaid after they meet the "spend down" requirements. In 2007, Medicaid covered approximately 9 million individuals with disabilities. As with elderly people, many of these individuals are confined to hospitals, nursing homes, or other institutional care facilities on a long-term basis.

All Medicaid beneficiaries must meet certain other general requirements, including in most cases being a U.S. citizen. Certain legal immigrants are eligible, depending on their date of entry into the country. Those immigrants who enter the country illegally are ineligible for Medicaid, except for emergency care. In certain cases, a woman who has entered the country illegally will have a baby at a hospital in the United States. The baby will automatically be a U.S. citizen and thus will be eligible for Medicaid (assuming the family meets the income requirements), while the mother will remain ineligible.

For a state to qualify for federal reimbursement, all members of these three groups within the state must be eligible for Medicaid. In addition, states have the option of covering other groups and receiving federal reimbursement. The additional groups include

- pregnant women and infants under the age of 1 whose family earns up to 185 percent of the FPL
- elderly, blind, or disabled people who are not eligible for SSI payments but still have an income below the FPL
- children up to the age of 21 in certain low-income families

Finally, each state has the option of covering individuals who are not in one of the above groups but whose income falls below a level set by the state. These people are the "medically needy," and most of them are low-income single adults or families without children. Because each state establishes its own cut off level for eligibility, and because general economic conditions vary substantially from state to state, there is a wide range of eligibility levels among the states. Few states cover all poor people.

In 2007, Medicaid spent an average of $5,163 per beneficiary. Because the states administer the program and can offer a wide range of options in eligibility and coverage, the average level of Medicaid spending per eligible beneficiary varies widely among states. In 2007, spending per beneficiary ranged from $3,168 in California and $3,892 in Georgia to $8,450 in New York and $8,796 in Rhode Island (Kaiser Family Foundation n.d.-a)

> **CONCEPT 7.2**
>
> Under the Medicaid program, eligibility for benefits, the level of benefits, and the average cost of care vary widely among states.

Poor people who are eligible for care in one state will often be ineligible in another. Treatments covered in one state may not be covered in another. The wide latitude left to states in creating their Medicaid programs and the resulting wide range of eligibility and coverage among the states has created a system of medical care for poor people that is distinctly different from our system of care for elderly people. Medicare is essentially government-sponsored, taxpayer-supported, universal care for elderly people. Medicaid is a program intended to cover certain segments of the low-income population while leaving other segments without the means to pay for medical care. As John Iglehart stated, "The nature of the Medicaid program underscores the ambivalence of a society that has never decided which of its citizens deserves access to publicly financed medical care or whether the problem of poverty should be addressed primarily at the national, state, or local level . . . This situation constitutes what has been characterized as 'the greatest inequity of the American health care system . . . not between the non poor and the poor, but between the insured poor and the uninsured poor'" (1993b, p. 896).

## THE RISING COST OF THE MEDICAID PROGRAM

Between 1975 and 1989, the cost of the Medicaid program increased by an average of 11.9 percent per year before adjusting for inflation. Reflecting both the rising cost of care nationwide and the increasing eligibility for program coverage, in 1989 program costs began to explode. Between 1989 and 1993, the yearly increase in overall Medicaid costs averaged 21.2 percent. As a result of these increases, both the federal government (which was already facing huge budget deficits as a result of changes in the tax laws enacted in the 1980s) and state governments (many of which were prevented by their state constitutions from engaging in deficit spending) were facing financial crises. If nothing was done to change the program, Medicaid threatened to bankrupt many of the states and the federal government. As discussed below, the federal government responded by initiating a number of changes on a state-by-state basis. Medicaid rapidly began to change from a purely fee-for-service payment system to a capitation system, shifting much of the financial risk of providing care to poor people from governments to health maintenance organizations (HMOs) and other types of managed care insurers and providers.

A common misperception is that, because Medicaid is primarily a program for low-income families and children, the rapid increase in program costs is due to increases in the number of poor people and to problems with fraud and abuse within the system.

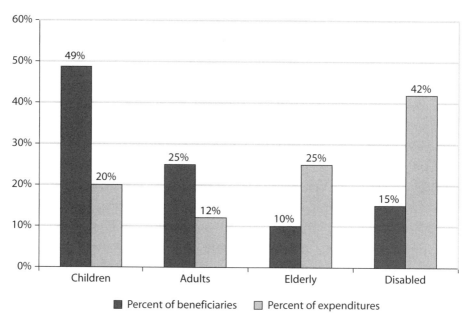

FIGURE 7.2. Distribution of Medicaid Beneficiaries and Costs among Eligibility Groups, 2007. *Source:* Data from Kaiser Family Foundation, *Medicaid—A Primer,* 2010

This picture is not at all accurate and constitutes one of the major public misperceptions regarding our health care system.

It is true that low-income children and adults make up 74 percent of Medicaid beneficiaries. As shown in Figure 7.2, however, children and adults account for only 32 percent of overall Medicaid spending. The bulk of Medicaid expenditures (67% in 2007) pay for care for low-income elderly and disabled individuals.

If one looks at the average cost of providing care for beneficiaries in each class of eligibility, shown in Table 7.1, it is easy to see how this situation arises. In 2007, average expenditures per beneficiary per year ranged from $2,135 for a child to $12,499 for an elderly beneficiary and $14,481 for a disabled individual. Medicaid has come to be our society's safety net to assure that no elderly or disabled individual who needs medical care or care in a nursing home or other long-term care institution will be left without care due to their inability to pay. The vast majority of Medicaid expenditures go to support that commitment.

There is also a common misperception that Medicaid beneficiaries abuse the medical care system and overuse medical services. Critics frequently cite data about the high rate at which Medicaid patients use hospital emergency rooms to obtain routine medical care. It is very expensive to take care of common, non-emergency conditions in the emergency room. In many areas, Medicaid beneficiaries may be more likely than the general public to use the emergency room rather than doctors' offices for the treatment of relatively minor ailments. A study by Tang and colleagues (2010) confirmed this finding. Using a nationally representative database, the authors found that, between 1997 and 2007, the rate of emergency room visits for "ambulatory care-sensitive conditions" (that is, those more appropriate for treatment in a physician's office than in the emergency room) went up at a substantially higher rate for adults on Medicaid than for adults with other types of insurance. The authors attributed this increased utilization of the emergency room to the increase in the number of people on Medicaid, coupled with "limited access to primary care services for Medicaid enrollees" (p. 669). Consistent with previous studies, the reason Medicaid patients visit the emergency room more often than insured patients does not appear to be abusive behavior on the part of Medicaid patients, but rather the poor availability of primary care services for many patients on Medicaid.

Soon after Medicaid's creation in 1965, most states began to restrict the amount they would pay physicians for treating Medicaid patients. As Medicaid costs skyrocketed in

---

**CONCEPT 7.3**

Sixty-seven percent of Medicaid costs go to provide care for 25 percent of beneficiaries: low-income elderly and disabled people, many of whom are in nursing homes. Low-income families and children account for 32 percent of Medicaid costs.

---

Table 7.1. Medicaid Expenditures per Beneficiary, by Type of Beneficiary, 2007

| Beneficiary | Expenditure |
|---|---|
| Elderly | $12,499 |
| Disabled | $14,481 |
| Adults | $2,541 |
| Children | $2,135 |

*Source:* Data from Kaiser Family Foundation.

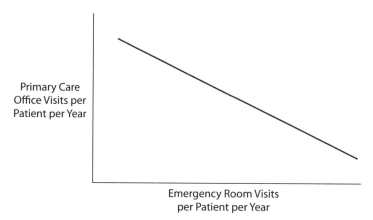

FIGURE 7.3. General Relationship between the Availability of Primary Care and the Rate of Emergency Room Visits for Medicaid Patients. *Source:* Data from de Alteriis and Fanning 1991

the 1980s and 1990s, states cut back even farther on what they were willing to pay. As a result, physicians in many areas of the country receive only 30 to 40 percent of their usual charge for taking care of a Medicaid patient. As a result of these payment policies, in 2006 only 52 percent of physicians were willing to accept new patients on Medicaid. The remaining 48 percent of physicians were about evenly split between those who accepted no Medicaid patients at all and those who had current Medicaid patients but were unwilling to accept new patients (Cunningham and May 2006).

This poor availability of physicians is largely responsible for the general relationship, illustrated in Figure 7.3, between the availability of primary care services in a community and the rate at which Medicaid patients in that community visit the emergency room. The more office-based or clinic-based primary care services are available to Medicaid patients, the less those patients visit the emergency room. Making primary care more available to Medicaid recipients will help to decrease the use of emergency rooms and will lower the overall cost of care somewhat.

## THE MOVE TO MANAGED CARE

In the face of rapidly rising costs, both state and federal governments began to look for ways to limit the budgetary drain of Medicaid. By the early 1990s, HMOs and the other types of managed care plans discussed in Chapter 5 became increasingly common in many areas of the country. It was apparent to federal and state officials that delivery systems based on the capitation method of payment had the potential of realizing the same cost savings for Medicaid patients as they did for patients in general. With the support of the federal government, many states established programs to try and enroll as many Medicaid beneficiaries as possible in HMOs. (In most states, elderly or disabled Medicaid beneficiaries were not included in the shift to HMOs.) In doing so, the state would pay a fixed premium per patient per year, and it would be up to the HMO to constrain costs.

Figure 7.4 shows Medicaid's rapid movement beginning in 1993 from a system based predominantly on fee-for-service payment to physicians and hospitals to one that relied extensively on managed care plans for providing care. By 2008, 71 percent of all Medicaid beneficiaries were enrolled in a managed care plan.

As with Medicare in the previous chapter, the question comes up regarding the shift of Medicaid beneficiaries from fee-for-service to capitated managed care: is managed care less expensive than fee-for-service care in programs such as Medicare and Medicaid that have already adopted policies to control the use of hospital services? For Medicare the answer was no. This question has not been addressed as explicitly for Medicaid as it has been for Medicare. Adopting a managed care approach for the majority of Medicaid beneficiaries, however, has had another policy effect that is perhaps even more important than the question of cost effectiveness of alternative delivery models. A capitated system of managed care allows a state government to limit its fiscal liability for Medicaid by setting a fixed yearly payment for the care of each beneficiary. Once that payment has been made, the

> **CONCEPT 7.4**
>
> Over the period 1991–99, Medicaid shifted from a predominantly fee-for-service system to a system based predominantly on capitation and the use of health maintenance organizations (HMOs).

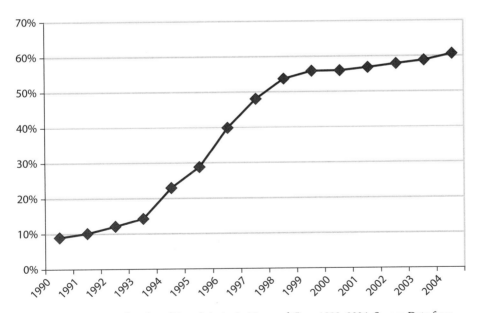

**FIGURE 7.4.** Percentage of Medicaid Beneficiaries in Managed Care, 1990–2004. *Source:* Data from Kaiser Family Foundation

risk for cost overruns shifts from the state to the managed care provider. Thus, managed care has become one means for states to limit the cost of their Medicaid program, irrespective of whether managed care is more cost effective.

## THE CREATION OF MEDICAID WAIVERS

For states to move their Medicaid beneficiaries from the fee-for-service system into HMOs and other managed care plans, a mechanism had to be developed to relax some of the federal guidelines that states must meet to qualify for federal reimbursement. The original guidelines required states to provide all necessary services in the categories described above. As discussed in Chapter 5, HMOs and other managed care plans save money by putting certain constraints on the use of hospitals and other expensive technologies. To reconcile the guidelines with the need to shift patients into HMOs, Congress amended the Social Security Act to allow the Secretary of the Department of Health and Human Services to waive certain guidelines on a state-by-state basis. States could apply for a "Section 1115 waiver" or a closely related "Section 1915 waiver" to create capitated systems of care for certain of their Medicaid beneficiaries. These waivers are typically granted for periods of five years at a time and are renewable for additional periods of five years.

By 2004, all fifty states either had been granted or had applied for a Section 1115 waiver or a Section 1915 waiver, accounting for the increase in managed care enrollment shown in Figure 7.4. Some of these waiver programs worked quite well, while others had serious problems. Some were quite controversial. Some waivers permitted states to restrict benefits and place new financial obligations on beneficiaries (Mann and Artiga 2006). States such as West Virginia, Idaho, and Kentucky were granted a waiver that permitted them to establish different "tiers" of benefits. The tier a beneficiary is eligible to receive will depend on his or her prior health status, as well as his or her adherence to medical treatment plans. Those who do not follow recommended treatment may be dropped to a lower tier, thus losing some benefits, until they have demonstrated that they are able and willing to follow recommended treatments. West Virginia's plan relies heavily on reducing benefits in response to unhealthy behaviors.

Not surprisingly, attempts such as these to lower Medicaid costs by reducing benefits have met with substantial criticism. These issues bring up again the recurring question first mentioned in Chapter 2: how much health care should every American be able to expect as a right of citizenship or residency?

While some states have used Medicaid waivers to reduce benefits, others have used waivers to expand benefits—though not always with full success. Typically efforts to expand benefits rely heavily on providing care through managed care organizations. The following sections look at the experiences of three states with these types of waivers.

## OREGON: EXPLICIT RATIONING OF MEDICAID HEALTH CARE

In the late 1980s, Oregon was facing the same high Medicaid costs that other states were confronting. The cost of the Medicaid program had put such a strain on the state budget that Oregon was able to pay for care for only a fraction of its poor adult population. Previously, while covering all children below the federal poverty line (FPL), Medicaid had been available only to adults younger than 65 with an income that was less than about 60 percent of the FPL, leaving those with incomes between 60 and 100 percent of the FPL without any coverage at all. Oregon wanted to find a way to provide care for all adults below the FPL, and to extend coverage to pregnant women and children with family income up to 133 percent of the FPL. They wanted to do this, however, without increasing the overall amount they spent on Medicaid.

To accomplish these seemingly irreconcilable goals, the Oregon legislature, under the leadership of one of its members who was also a physician, created an entirely new way of allocating Medicaid resources. This new program, referred to as the Oregon Health Plan (OHP), took an entirely new approach to the allocation of Medicaid funds. A broadly representative commission called the Oregon Health Services Commission undertook a lengthy process of studying all the services previously covered by Medicaid and dividing them into 712 treatment categories. The commission then ranked these treatments based on factors such as medical effectiveness, ability to avert death or disability, prevention of future costs, and public health risk. Treatments that ranked highest on these criteria (for example, treatment of severe head injuries or insulin-dependent diabetes) were given a low number, and those that ranked lowest (for example, treatment of viral colds and simple strains of the muscles of the back) were given a high number. The commission spent three years establishing this list. They had many public meetings and discussions about the plan, and they modified earlier versions of the plan based on this input.

Figure 7.5 illustrates the situation that existed before the OHP was established. The horizontal axis shows seven hundred treatment categories (for simplicity), ranked from most important (low numbers) to least important (high numbers). The vertical axis shows the poor adult population of Oregon, ranked according to the percentage of the FPL represented by their family income. It can be seen that, before the OHP, there was a sharp divide at about 60 percent of the FPL, with those below the line receiving full Medicaid coverage for all seven hundred treatment categories and those above the line receiving no coverage at all.

In establishing the OHP, the Oregon legislature decided to remove some of the least effective treatments from coverage (the high numbers). It used the money saved by limiting care in this way to provide coverage for the most effective treatments for

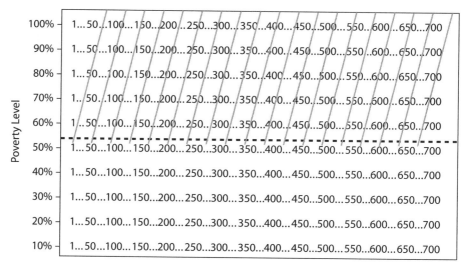

FIGURE 7.5. Medicaid Coverage in Oregon before the Oregon Health Plan

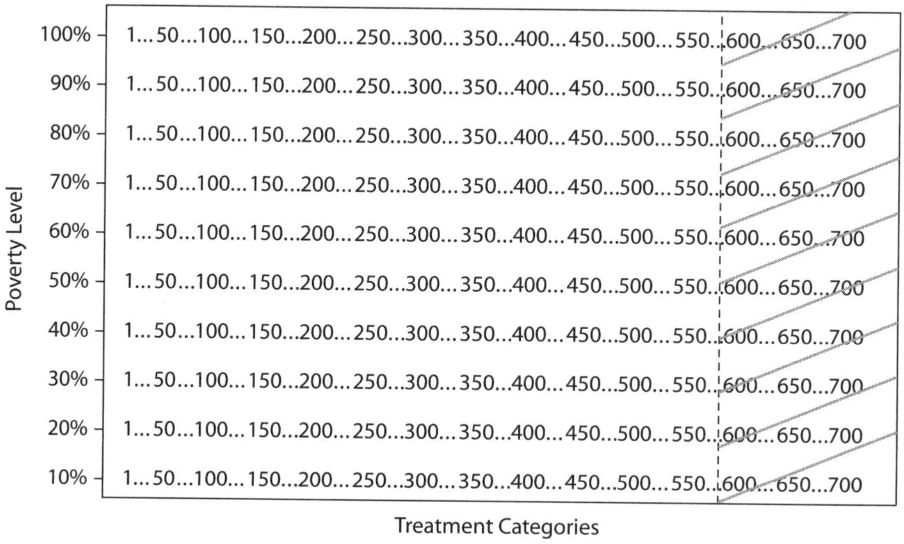

100% – 1...50...100...150...200...250...300...350...400...450...500...550...600...650...700
90% – 1...50...100...150...200...250...300...350...400...450...500...550...600...650...700
80% – 1...50...100...150...200...250...300...350...400...450...500...550...600...650...700
70% – 1...50...100...150...200...250...300...350...400...450...500...550...600...650...700
60% – 1...50...100...150...200...250...300...350...400...450...500...550...600...650...700
50% – 1...50...100...150...200...250...300...350...400...450...500...550...600...650...700
40% – 1...50...100...150...200...250...300...350...400...450...500...550...600...650...700
30% – 1...50...100...150...200...250...300...350...400...450...500...550...600...650...700
20% – 1...50...100...150...200...250...300...350...400...450...500...550...600...650...700
10% – 1...50...100...150...200...250...300...350...400...450...500...550...600...650...700

Poverty Level

Treatment Categories

FIGURE 7.6. Medicaid Coverage under the Oregon Health Plan

everyone below the FPL, and for pregnant women and children up to 133 percent of the FPL. These changes are represented in Figure 7.6.

As shown in Figure 7.6, the OHP initially provided coverage for only 565 of the 700 available treatments, but it provided this limited coverage to all those below the FPL. To reallocate its Medicaid funds in this way, Oregon first had to get a Section 1115 waiver from the federal government. This waiver application was quite controversial. After several years of discussion and debate, however, the federal government approved the waiver, and in 1994 the OHP took effect. Initially, it was largely successful in achieving its goal of increased coverage. In its first year of operation it extended coverage to approximately 100,000 new poor people in addition to the 188,000 originally covered.

While the plan has had a number of problems along the way, for several years it was able to offer coverage to those in Oregon whose income was below the FPL. The initial success of the OHP depended on broad public acceptance of the policy of limiting care to some so that others may be covered. Accusations of unethical health care rationing were leveled at the plan. This aspect of the plan, and its implication for overall U.S. health care policy, are discussed in Chapter 13.

One of the ways the OHP saved money was to enroll as many of its members as possible in HMOs or other managed care plans and to pay for their care under capitated risk contracts. It was quite successful in this effort, and by 1997 nearly 90 percent of beneficiaries were covered by a managed care plan. In 2004, 80 percent of Oregon's Medicaid beneficiaries were still enrolled in managed care plans.

Despite its initial success in expanding the number of beneficiaries by limiting treatment coverage and relying on managed care plans, Oregon continued to have fiscal problems at the state level. Once again, the costs of Medicaid were seen as a major contributor. To reduce the cost of its Medicaid program, Oregon went back to the federal government with a request for a new waiver. While expanding eligibility somewhat for children and pregnant women, the new waiver also included a number of steps intended to reduce enrollment and costs. These steps included

- reductions in covered benefits
- premiums and co-payments for some adult beneficiaries
- explicit caps on enrollment

These new policies were initiated in 2003, and in one year resulted in a reduction in adult enrollment of about 50,000 beneficiaries. Many of the beneficiaries losing coverage had chronic medical conditions; 72 percent of them ended up back in the ranks of the uninsured (Mann and Artiga 2004). While the OHP achieved many of its initial goals of expanding coverage to poor people, it was not successful in substantially slowing the continuing rise in health care costs related to Medicaid in Oregon.

## TENNESSEE: AN OVERNIGHT SHIFT TO MEDICAID MANAGED CARE

Tennessee faced a situation similar to that in Oregon: in the early 1990s, costs were rising substantially and coverage was limited to a fraction of Tennessee's poor population. Tennessee's previous Medicaid system was based almost exclusively on the traditional fee-for-service model. Planners felt that if a substantial number of Medicaid beneficiaries were shifted from fee-for-service to capitated managed care, the money saved could be used to extend coverage not only to the entire poor population in Tennessee, but also to those people whose income was above the poverty line but who lacked health insurance. The problem in Tennessee was getting existing commercial HMOs and managed care plans to accept large numbers of Medicaid patients at capitation rates that were lower than prevailing market rates. Tennessee decided to use the power of the purse to accomplish this task. The legislature passed a law that HMOs could only enroll public school teachers and state employees if they also agreed to accept Medicaid patients. Not wanting to lose access to the two largest groups of employees in the state, most managed care plans in Tennessee agreed to accept Medicaid patients.

Tennessee applied to the federal government for a Section 1115 waiver to allow them to make the shift from fee-for-service to managed care essentially overnight. On December 31, 1993, nearly all state Medicaid beneficiaries were in the traditional fee-for-service system. On January 1, 1994, the new Tenncare program started, and virtually all Medicaid patients became members of a managed care plan.

The rapidity of the shift to managed care created an initial period of confusion and frustration for many patients and providers. Typical of most managed care plans, Medicaid patients were limited to receiving care from the specific plan in which they were enrolled. The problem was that many patients did not understand the way managed care was intended to work. Medicaid beneficiaries had been given a short period of time in which to select a managed care provider. Those who did not select a plan from the dozen or so plans on the list were assigned at random to one. In many cases, patients were assigned to plans that did not include their regular provider of care. Other patients who did select a plan did so without a complete list of providers or a full understanding of the limits of managed care. For months, patients would show up at their usual provider, only to be told that they were ineligible for care. Often the provider they had been assigned to was a substantial distance away. Many providers were also frustrated, being unable to continue providing care to patients they had known for years.

Over time, the initial confusion subsided, and Tenncare achieved many of its objectives. In 1994, its first year of operation, Tenncare extended eligibility to 350,000 people in addition to the 770,000 people previously in Medicaid. Over time, though, it has developed a number of serious problems. Extending coverage to people with an income over the FPL who lacked health insurance turned out to be far more costly than expected. Many of these people lacked coverage for the very reason that they had chronic medical problems and were thus "uninsurable."

The experience in Tennessee paralleled that in Oregon. Despite the changes initiated under the original waiver, program costs continued to rise and to put a severe strain on the state budget. As was the case in Oregon, Tennessee requested and was granted a change in the conditions of its waiver. To reduce program costs, Tennessee

- reduced its capitation payments to managed care organizations
- initiated premiums and co-payments for some adults
- substantially reduced eligibility for low-income adults
- reduced the benefits provided to all Medicaid beneficiaries

It reduced covered benefits by redefining the term "medically necessary." As a condition of federal support, states must provide its Medicaid beneficiaries all services that are "medically necessary," but it is largely up to the states to define this concept. While most states have adopted a broad definition of medical necessity, Tennessee, by an act of its legislature, redefined it as including only services that are "the least costly alternative course of diagnosis and treatment that is adequate for the medical condition of the enrollee" (Schneider 2004, p. 3). Many common and previously available services are no longer covered, as they are not the "least costly alternative." As did Oregon, Tennessee adopted a public policy of rationing medical care to poor adults, making available only those services that meet the "least costly" test.

## CALIFORNIA: AN INCREMENTAL SHIFT TO MEDICAID MANAGED CARE

The Medicaid program in California, referred to as MediCal, is the nation's largest, with more than 6 million beneficiaries. In the 1980s, California also experienced rapidly rising costs. Having previously extended program eligibility to many children in families with income above the FPL, California shifted its policy focus to containing the cost of the MediCal program. To do this, California obtained permission from the federal government to begin a statewide shift to managed care for most beneficiaries. As early as the 1970s, California had enrolled certain MediCal patients in HMOs. These early experiences had not been fully successful, so California adopted a somewhat cautious approach. Starting in the early 1990s, California began to create managed care plans for MediCal patients on a county-by-county basis. Each participating county had substantial flexibility in designing its plan. Three general types of plan were used:

1. A county-organized health system (COHS) to provide coverage on a capitated basis to all MediCal beneficiaries within the county
2. A two-plan model, in which a COHS competed directly with a single commercial managed care plan
3. A market-based model, in which MediCal beneficiaries within the county were free to choose from a list of competing, private managed care plans

The two-plan model was by far the most common, with ten counties choosing this approach. By early 1999, 2.3 million MediCal beneficiaries, or 46 percent of the total enrollment, were enrolled in managed care plans statewide. By 2004, slightly more than 50 percent of beneficiaries were enrolled in managed care plans.

While the overall effectiveness of California's Medicaid reform, measured in terms of transferring beneficiaries to managed care plans, has been quite good, it has not been without its problems. Relying as it has on a county-by-county approach, the plan has proven to be quite complex from an administrative perspective. In addition, budgetary constraints in California have kept capitation payments to managed care providers quite low. Coupled with what are perceived to be overly stringent program requirements, the plan has raised continuing questions about the quality of the care available to Medicaid recipients. The shift to managed care, however, has made care more accessible. Patients who were having difficulty under the previous fee-for-service system due to low payment rates are now guaranteed access to a provider through their selected managed care plan.

California, however, has faced even more severe budget problems than many other states, first in the early 2000s and subsequently as part of the 2008–9 recession. Continued increases in the cost of medical care and a growing MediCal enrollment have contributed substantially to California's chronic budget deficits. A successful recall election in 2003 replaced Governor Gray Davis with Arnold Schwarzenegger. After coming to office Governor Schwarzenegger proposed substantial cuts in MediCal, including benefit cuts, enrollment limitations, and new cost-sharing requirements for beneficiaries. Despite enrolling more than half its beneficiaries in HMOs and other managed care plans, California has been no more successful than Oregon or Tennessee in solving its long-term problems with the cost of Medicaid.

## WHY WASN'T THE SHIFT TO MANAGED CARE MORE SUCCESSFUL IN HOLDING DOWN MEDICAID COSTS?

By 2008, 71 percent of all Medicaid beneficiaries nationwide had been enrolled in managed care plans. Nonetheless, states continue to experience severe difficulties in financing program costs. Why wasn't this shift to capitated systems of care more successful? There are two principal answers to this question: (1) the effect of shifting to managed care and (2) the dual nature of Medicaid.

Recall from Chapter 6 that a principal reason why managed care was not successful in reducing Medicare costs was the previous reductions in the use of hospitals that had resulted from the prospective payment system (PPS) of paying for hospital care. While state Medicaid programs continued to pay for hospital care largely on a fee-for-service basis before the shift to managed care, in many states there had been previous efforts to control hospital costs in other ways. Nevertheless, there were continuing inefficiencies in the use of hospitals. A comprehensive national study of the change in Medicaid costs between 1987 and 1997 was able to identify reductions in hospital use and costs as a result of the shift to managed care, although those reductions were modest (Kirby, Machine, and Cohen 2003).

It is also important to recall from Chapter 5 the overall lesson of the effect of shifting from a predominantly fee-for-service system to a system based on managed care. During the period of transition, cost savings will be realized. These are, however, one-time savings—managed care plans face the same pressure as fee-for-service plans in terms of newer and more costly forms of treatment.

During the mid-1990s, as the shift to Medicaid managed care was taking place, the yearly increases in the national cost of Medicaid had moderated substantially and were in the range of 3 to 5 percent. Between 2000 and 2003, however, costs again began going up an average of more than 10 percent annually. Therefore, there does appear to have been a modest reduction in the rate at which Medicaid costs increased, but the reduction was due to one-time savings. The cost of the Medicaid program seems to have resumed its steep upward trajectory.

Recall also from the discussion above that 67 percent of all Medicaid costs go to provide care for 25 percent of beneficiaries: low-income elderly and disabled people, many of whom are in nursing homes. Caring for elderly and disabled individuals accounts for by far the largest share of Medicaid costs. Of the more than 25 million Medicaid beneficiaries enrolled in managed care plans in 2004, however, less than 10 percent were elderly or disabled. Nearly all the movement to managed care was among children and nonelderly adults. Children and nonelderly adults, however, account for less than one-third of Medicaid spending. While the main driver of rising Medicaid costs is caring for elderly and disabled people, the major impact of cuts in Medicaid benefits and eligibility has been on children and nonelderly adults. Despite a significant shift to managed care, the Medicaid system will continue to place a major strain on both state budgets and the federal budget for years to come.

> **CONCEPT 7.5**
>
> The shift to Medicaid managed care involved mainly children and nonelderly adults and realized modest, one-time cost savings. With most expenditures going to care for elderly and disabled people, Medicaid costs will continue to place a severe strain on state and federal budgets for years to come. Attempts to reduce Medicaid costs through program reductions will disproportionately affect children and nonelderly adults.

## S-CHIP TO REDUCE THE NUMBER OF UNINSURED CHILDREN

As part of the national debate that arose surrounding the Clinton health reform proposals of 1993–94, the number of uninsured children became a major national concern. Few had been aware that nearly 10 million children were without health insurance and, as a result, without access to basic medical care. A strong national consensus developed around this issue. Republicans and Democrats alike felt that even if as a country we could not find an overall solution to the problem of the uninsured, we could at least find a way to extend basic coverage to children. Children, after all, are the least expensive age group to insure and can benefit the most from basic services such as immunizations and preventive care.

In 1997, a bipartisan coalition developed in Congress around this issue, and in August of that year, Congress enacted the State Children's Health Insurance Program (P.L. 105-33), often called S-CHIP, as Title XXI of the Social Security Act. Under S-CHIP, a federal-state partnership was established with the goal of significantly reducing the number of uninsured children. The target population was uninsured children in families that were not previously eligible for Medicaid and that earned less than 200 percent of the FPL.

Each state was given a financial incentive to create a new, statewide program for extending health insurance coverage to uninsured children. The states were given the option of three ways in which to do this. States could

1. expand the existing Medicaid program to include more children
2. establish a program separate and distinct from Medicaid to extend coverage to those children not eligible for Medicaid
3. use a combination of both Medicaid expansion and new program creation

S-CHIP appropriated between $3 billion and $5 billion per year for ten years, with the explicit goal of cutting in half the number of uninsured children nationwide. States would design a program and apply to the federal government to have the majority of the costs of the program paid by federal funds. The first S-CHIP funds became available to the states on October 1, 1997. Once allocated funds, a state had three years in which to spend the funds to provide health insurance for eligible children. After the three-year period, any funds not used for this purpose had to be returned to the federal government.

States responded enthusiastically to S-CHIP. Of the fifty-six states and territories eligible to participate, fifty-one had established plans by April 1999. The four states with the largest number of uninsured children—California, Florida, New York, and Texas—were allocated nearly half of the available funding. States were almost evenly divided between those that used expansion of Medicaid and those that created a new program, either stand-alone or in combination with Medicaid.

The first two years of S-CHIP showed considerable success in meeting its stated goal of cutting the number of uninsured children in half. In December 1998, a year after the program was enacted, 833,303 children were covered. By December 1999, 2 million previously uninsured children had obtained coverage.

S-CHIP began to run into trouble, however, in several states. Reports from state governments as well as children's advocacy groups began to suggest that the enroll-ment of eligible children was lagging far behind projections in a number of areas. Some states were reluctant to invest state funds in the program, often leading to delays of up to a year in the opening of enrollment. Other states established such complex applica-tion procedures that many eligible families simply failed to apply. Other states failed to establish adequate outreach programs and were unable to find the eligible children they had hoped to enroll.

The three-year period in which states were required to spend their initial allocation of funds ended on September 30, 2000, and remaining funds had to be returned to the federal government. Nearly half of the previously allocated money—$1.9 billion of $4.2 billion—remained unspent by the states on September 30 (Pear 2000). California had to return $590 million, or 69 percent of its original allocation. Texas had to return $446 million. New Mexico, with 30,000 uninsured children, could enroll only 1,000 of them in its S-CHIP program and had to return 92 percent of its original allotment. Only ten states were able to spend the full amount given to them by the federal government to enroll uninsured children in S-CHIP. Of these, New York was perhaps the most suc-cessful, with 550,000 new children enrolled, one-fourth of the national total.

Unfortunately, New York's success in enrolling children was soon cast in another light. Shortly after the federal government reported the failure of the S-CHIP program to meet its initial enrollment goals despite the success of New York's program, news-papers reported that as many as half of the children enrolled in New York may not have been eligible for S-CHIP (Steinhauer 2000). Federal law requires that uninsured chil-dren who are eligible for Medicaid be enrolled in their existing state Medicaid program and not in S-CHIP. The states pay a larger share of the cost of Medicaid, and Congress did not want them to shift Medicaid-eligible children into S-CHIP to gain a higher level of federal subsidy. It appears that this is precisely what New York did. As a result, New York was also required to return part of the funding it had received.

Figure 7.7 shows the number of children covered under S-CHIP from its inception in 1997 through 2009. Despite problems in some states, the number of children covered increased substantially during the first four years of the program. From 2003 through 2006, however, enrollment was mostly flat. In 2007, enrollment began to rise again, with nearly 5 million children enrolled by 2009 (Kaiser Family Foundation 2010a).

In 2010, the U.S. Census Bureau reported that 7.5 million children in the United States were uninsured—a number only somewhat smaller than the 10 million children who were uninsured at the time S-CHIP was passed by Congress (data from U.S. Cen-sus Bureau website). If S-CHIP enrolled nearly 5 million children between 1998 and 2009, yet the number of uninsured children decreased by less than 3 million children during this time period, where did the other 2 million children covered by the program come from? Some of them reflect the approximately 2.5 percent increase in the number

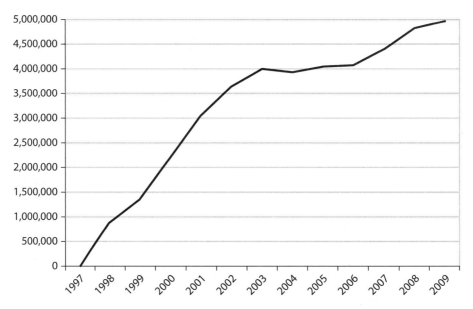

FIGURE 7.7. The Number of Children Enrolled in the State Children's Health Insurance Program (S-CHIP), 1997–2009. *Source:* Data from Kaiser Commission on Medicaid and the Uninsured

of children in the United States during that time period. It appears, however, that some of the children covered under S-CHIP in 2009 were previously covered under their parents' employment-based health insurance. The children lost private coverage either because the parents lost their health insurance at work, or because the parents chose to drop the children from their own insurance plan due to the increasing share of the coverage cost paid by employees. One study suggested that 38 percent of the enrollment in S-CHIP during its early years was for children who were previously covered under their parents' private health insurance (Cunningham, Hadley, and Reschovsky 2002). Thus, the enrollment totals for SCHIP may overstate the number of previously uninsured children who gained new coverage under the program.

By 2007, when S-CHIP's initial ten-year program authorization was set to expire, S-CHIP had covered several million children who previously were uninsured and a number of other children who had lost private coverage. It had not come close to achieving its initial goal of reducing the number of uninsured children by half, however. Furthermore, of the nearly 8 million children who remained uninsured, about two-thirds were eligible either for Medicaid or for S-CHIP but were not enrolled, due to either state caps on enrollment or barriers encountered in the enrollment process (Kaiser Family Foundation 2009).

Congress acted in the summer of 2007 to extend S-CHIP for an additional five years, and to permit states to expand eligibility to children in families with incomes above 200 percent of the FPL (the original income limit when S-CHIP was first enacted). The legislation approved by both the House and the Senate would also have nearly doubled the funding available to S-CHIP. President George W. Bush, however, saw such an expansion as an unwarranted extension of the role of government in the health care system. Accordingly, he vetoed the legislation, and his veto was upheld in Congress. In his veto message, President Bush argued that there was a "philosophical divide over the best approach to health care," and that "Democratic leaders in Congress want to put more power in the hands of government by expanding federal health care programs. Their S-CHIP is an incremental step towards the goal of government-run health care for every American" (quoted in Iglehart 2007, p. 2105). After a series of stop-gap funding extensions, in January 2008 Congress passed and President Bush signed a bill extending S-CHIP funding through March 31, 2009, without a significant expansion of either coverage or funding.

When President Barack Obama entered office in January 2009, one of the first things he asked Congress to do was to reauthorize and expand S-CHIP. Congress acted quickly. About two weeks after entering office, President Obama signed into law the Children's Health Insurance Program Reauthorization Act (CHIRPA) of 2009. The act extended S-CHIP for an additional five years, expanded eligibility to children in families up to 300 percent of the FPL, and more than doubled the funding available for the program (Iglehart 2009b).

> **CONCEPT 7.6**
>
> The State Children's Health Insurance Program (S-CHIP) has enrolled nearly 5 million children. Despite this success, the number of uninsured children nationally has been reduced only slightly. More than 60 percent of uninsured children are eligible for either Medicaid or S-CHIP, but they are not enrolled.

In February 2010, on the one-year anniversary of the CHIRPA, Health and Human Services Secretary Kathleen Sebelius issued the following challenge (Sebelius 2010):

> I am asking leaders from government and the private sector to step up their efforts to cover more children. We know there are about five million uninsured children in the U.S. who are currently eligible for Medicaid or CHIP coverage, but who are not enrolled. *The Secretary's Challenge: Connecting Kids to Coverage* is a five-year campaign that will challenge federal officials, states, governors, mayors, community organizations, faith leaders, and concerned individuals to build on our success and take the next step by finding and enrolling those five million children in Medicaid and CHIP.

Congress's goal was to add an additional 4 million children to the program by 2013.

## THE FUTURE OF MEDICAID AND S-CHIP WITH CONTINUING BUDGET PROBLEMS

While S-CHIP offers states an average federal reimbursement rate of 70 percent of all costs, many states continue to have difficulty funding their share of the program.

Similarly, as described above, the emergency increase to an average of 66 percent in the federal reimbursement rate to states for the Medicaid program was scheduled to revert to the previous rate of 57 percent at the end of June 2011. Responding to the budgetary constraints resulting from the 2009 recession, by 2010, 39 states had enacted further reductions in Medicaid payment to providers, and 15 states had reduced the level of benefits available to Medicaid recipients. In 2010, 44 states indicated that additional cuts to Medicaid were likely for 2011 (Kaiser Family Foundation 2010g). The rapidly rising costs faced by the states were in the context of the rapidly rising enrollment triggered by the recession that began in 2007. With unemployment jumping from 5 to 10 percent between December 2007 and December 2009, millions of workers lost their health insurance along with their job. After having been fairly stable between 2004 and 2007, the number of people enrolled in Medicaid jumped from 42.8 million in December 2007 to 48.5 million in December 2009. Between December 2008 and December 2009 alone, 3.7 million new beneficiaries enrolled in Medicaid—the largest 12-month increase since the program was enacted in the 1960s (Kaiser Family Foundation 2010c).

The experience over the past two decades, with repeated reductions in payment to providers and level of benefits in response to cyclical downturns in the economy, has underscored a potential weakness of the Medicaid and S-CHIP programs. The willingness and ability of many of the states to maintain these joint federal-state programs modeled after the previous Kerr-Mills program is coming into question. Especially with the expansion of Medicaid coverage under ACA, described below, the ability of Medicaid to meet its expected role of assuring access to health care for the nation's poor will come under increasing scrutiny.

## SUMMARY

At the same time that it passed Medicare, Congress also enacted the Medicaid program to provide health insurance for Americans living in poverty. Medicaid differs from Medicare in a number of important ways:

- Medicaid is administered by the states, whereas Medicare is administered by the federal government.
- Medicaid is financed from a combination of federal and state tax revenues, whereas Medicare is financed 100 percent from federal tax revenues.
- Medicaid is available only to certain categories of poor people, whereas Medicare is available essentially to all seniors.

In a manner similar to Medicare, Medicaid has a highly skewed pattern of paying for care. Poor people who are elderly or disabled make up 25 percent of covered beneficiaries but account for nearly 70 percent of costs. By comparison, poor children and their parents make up 75 percent of beneficiaries but use only about 30 percent of available funds.

As with Medicare, Medicaid continues to experience rapidly increasing costs. With states responsible for roughly 40 percent of the program's costs, many states are having substantial difficulty in continuing to fund the program. States have made repeated efforts to reduce their Medicaid expenditures by shifting beneficiaries to managed care while also reducing eligibility and benefits. During times of recession, these problems become more acute.

Realizing that Medicaid covered only children from poor or near-poor families, in 1997 Congress enacted S-CHIP to extend health insurance coverage to children in low-income working families. After initial success in enrolling these children, S-CHIP enrollment has since plateaued, leaving millions of children without health insurance. Ironically, nearly two-thirds of these uninsured children are eligible for either S-CHIP or Medicaid, but for one reason or another, they are not enrolled.

## THE AFFORDABLE CARE ACT AND ITS IMPACT ON MEDICAID AND S-CHIP

Among the policy changes resulting from the Affordable Care Act (ACA), one of the most profound is in the Medicaid program. As described above, Medicaid was initially designed as a program to provide health insurance only to some groups of those living in poverty. In contrast to Medicare, which provides insurance to all those age 65 or over who qualify for Social Security benefits, Medicaid has traditionally provided coverage only to poor families with children, the elderly poor, and the disabled poor. In most states, childless adults who were neither elderly nor disabled were not eligible for Medicaid benefits.

Beginning in 2014, ACA fundamentally changes the structure of Medicaid by making benefits available to *all* people who are poor, regardless of health status or family status. In addition, under ACA Medicaid will provide coverage to all those with incomes below 133 percent of the FPL, rather than the previous level of 100 percent. In essence, ACA makes Medicaid analogous to Medicare, in that it will provide the same level of benefits to all those in poverty. Both Medicare and Medicaid will provide universal coverage to eligible populations.

It is estimated that approximately 16 million uninsured individuals will obtain coverage through Medicaid as a result of ACA. In light of the financial burden the states have faced in paying their matching share of the cost of Medicaid, ACA defines a new level of federal support for those who become newly eligible for benefits under ACA. When the expanded Medicaid coverage becomes available in 2014, the federal government will initially pay 100 percent of the cost of the care provided to newly eligible enrollees. Over a period of six years the federal reimbursement rate for these enrollees will gradually drop to 90 percent, with the states ultimately responsible for 10 percent of the cost of their care.

For those who were already eligible for Medicaid at the time ACA was enacted, the federal government will maintain the previous reimbursement rate. Thus after 2014, states will receive a substantially higher federal reimbursement rate for those who become newly eligible for Medicaid than they will receive for the traditional Medicaid coverage groups. This split level of reimbursement, especially in light of the financial strains many states have been experiencing, may create a new area of disagreement and political tension. Many of the states may argue that the federal government should provide a 90 percent reimbursement rate for *all* Medicaid enrollees, not just new enrollees. Others may argue that such an expansion in federal responsibility for Medicaid will constitute an unwarranted federal takeover of health care. It will be important to watch the Medicaid program in coming years to see how these issues are resolved in the long term.

In addition to the expansion of Medicaid, ACA strengthens and extends S-CHIP.* ACA extends the authorization for S-CHIP through 2019, and provides funding through 2015. If a family with children eligible for S-CHIP are unable to enroll the children because the state in which they live has reached its enrollment cap, the family would become eligible for a federal tax credit that would allow the family to enroll the children in coverage through the newly established health benefit exchanges, described in Chapter 5.

Recognizing that low reimbursement rates for providers caring for Medicaid patients have resulted in many physicians not accepting Medicaid patients, ACA changes the way primary care physicians will be paid. Beginning in 2013, any primary care physician (defined as a physician in family medicine, general internal medicine, or general pediatrics) providing care to a patient on Medicaid will be paid at the same rate as would be paid under the Medicare system. Medicare reimbursement rates for primary care services are typically 30 to 40 percent higher than Medicaid rates. The federal government will reimburse states for 100 percent of the difference between the Medicare rate and the previous Medicaid rate.

A fundamental policy question that will only be resolved over time is whether there will be enough physicians willing to treat Medicaid patients once there are an additional 16 million such patients. ACA relies heavily on an expansion of nonprofit, community-based clinics to provide much of this needed care. Whether access to insurance through the newly expanded Medicaid program will be synonymous with access to high-quality health care is central to the ultimate success of the expansion of coverage to the poor under ACA.

---

* In 2009, it was renamed simply the Children's Health Insurance Program, or CHIP.

# The Increasing Role of For-Profit Health Care

## HISTORICAL CHANGES IN PERCEPTIONS ABOUT HMOs

As described in Chapter 5, in the 1980s health maintenance organizations (HMOs) such as Kaiser Permanente and the Group Health Cooperative of Puget Sound were shown to be extremely successful in providing high-quality health care at a cost that was about one-third less than the traditional, fee-for-service model. They developed broad support among both the public and politicians. In the discussions surrounding the HMO Act of 1973, they enjoyed strong, bipartisan support, as evidenced by the following two quotes:

> The Health Maintenance Organization concept is a central feature of my national health strategy . . . The HMO is a method . . . for providing health care that has won great respect. (President Richard Nixon 1972, p. 6)

> Health maintenance organizations have been proven to work . . . the HMO concept will result in the creation of organized health care delivery systems. (Senator Ted Kennedy 1973, p. 15497)

Then, in 1997, actress Helen Hunt, playing a beleaguered waitress in the movie *As Good As It Gets*, learns that her HMO has been shortchanging her in the care they provided for her asthmatic son. She blurts out, "Fucking HMO bastard pieces of shit!"

The crowd in the movie theater I was in burst out in loud cheers. Apparently, I was not alone. As Ellen Goodman (1998) wrote in the *Boston Globe*, "At this outburst—with none of the expletives deleted—audiences all over America spontaneously burst out in applause. It was one of those moments when you know the tide has turned . . . Managed-care companies are rapidly replacing tobacco companies as corporate demons . . . the HMOs are taking the place of the Russkies as the bad guys."

This single burst of cinematic obscenity captured the American mood and became a cultural icon of the growing disgust with HMOs. Matthew Rees (1998), offering the Canadian perspective, wrote in the *Ottawa Citizen* that "the story of how movie audiences erupt in cheers when HMOs are berated by Helen Hunt in the film *As Good As It Gets* has become the stuff of legend in Washington political circles."

What happened? How, in twenty-five years, did HMOs change from being widely popular to being widely reviled? The answer lies in a broad change in the health care market engendered by legislative changes adopted during the Reagan administration.

After passage of the HMO Act, HMOs became much more widespread, thanks to federal protections and subsidies contained in the act. To be eligible for federal support, an HMO had to meet three basic requirements.

1. The HMO had to offer a specified list of benefits to all members.
2. The HMO had to charge all members the same monthly premium, regardless of their health status (referred to as "community rating").
3. The HMO had to be structured as a nonprofit organization.

For the first several years of the expansion of HMOs, nearly the entire industry met these requirements, including the requirement that they operate on a nonprofit basis. In 1981, nearly 90 percent of HMO patients were members of nonprofit plans.

Throughout most of the twentieth century, there was little room in our health care delivery system for for-profit organizations. While a number of for-profit insurance companies offered health insurance as one of their products, the predominant model for health insurance was the Blue Cross/Blue Shield system, organized on a nonprofit basis. Physicians often practiced as professional corporations, but few worked for organizations that operated on a for-profit basis. Writing in 1951, Harvard sociologist Talcott Parsons described the view of medical care that predominated at that time: "The 'ideology' of the profession lays great emphasis on the obligation of the physician to put the 'welfare of the patient' above his personal interests, and regards 'commercialism' as the most serious and insidious evil with which it has to contend . . . The 'profit motive' is supposed to be drastically excluded from the medical world. This attitude . . . is perhaps more pronounced in the medical case than in any single [profession] except perhaps the clergy" (Parsons 1951, p. 435).

The 1980s brought a fundamental change to the American political landscape, however. Ronald Reagan was elected president and a Republican majority was elected to the Senate. Fundamental to President Reagan's free-market philosophy, legislation was introduced to end the government's ability to regulate HMOs. By 1988, the end of President Reagan's term in office, Congress had eliminated all federal funding for new

HMOs and had relaxed considerably the criteria for HMOs to obtain federal certification, including the elimination of any requirement that HMOs operate on a nonprofit basis. As a harbinger of things to come, by 1989, nearly half of all HMOs operated on a for-profit basis. By 1998, 79 million people were enrolled in HMOs (American Association of Health Plans 1999); nearly two-thirds of this enrollment was in for-profit plans. For-profit enrollment has continued at this level. Preferred provider organizations (PPOs), the principal managed care alternative to HMOs, are organized predominantly as for-profit entities. In 2009, 60 percent of workers covered by an employment-based health insurance were enrolled in a PPO (Kaiser Family Foundation and Health Research and Educational Trust 2009).

Many people were concerned that this shift to a for-profit orientation in the provision of health insurance created potential problems, including

- problems for the autonomy of physicians and other professionals (Would business managers end up telling physicians what they could and could not do?)
- problems for patients in obtaining needed care (Would for-profit corporations try to cut down on the level of care provided to increase profits?)
- ethical problems for physicians revolving around conflict of interest (Would physicians have to choose between making money for the corporation and doing what is best for the patient?)

The debate for and against for-profit plans was echoed in two articles published in 1996 in the *New England Journal of Medicine*. Malik Hasan, representing a for-profit health plan, referred to nonprofit plans as "a byproduct of the past." His principal concern was that nonprofit plans lack the accountability inherent in a for-profit corporation, and as a result develop inefficient operations that lead to higher costs. For-profit plans, on the other hand, lead to increased efficiency in the provision of health care, and as a result "more affordable health care." "This direct accountability in the marketplace sets the standard for both nonprofit and investor-owned plans . . . Nonprofit plans are organizationally less well suited to a competitive environment and are therefore less able, over the long haul, to ensure sufficient resources to meet patients' needs" (Hasan 1996, p. 1056).

Countering Hasan's view were Phillip Nudelman and Linda Andrews, representing the nonprofit Group Health Cooperative of Puget Sound. They argued that more important than the tax status of a health care organization were its purpose, values, and behavior. Nonprofit plans, they reasoned, would invest more of the health care dollar in care for covered patients, while for-profit plans would necessarily divert a substantial portion of the health care dollar to shareholder profit, thus reducing the amount and quality of the available care. "The need to show a profit focuses the for-profit plans on cost structure rather than the structure of care . . . Group Health Cooperative and similar not-for-profit health plans have the inherent values that the patient rather than the profit is the most important part of the health equation" (Nudelman and Andrews 1996, p. 1059).

This debate has not let up. Supporters of for-profit and nonprofit approaches to health care argue as vehemently today as these authors did a decade ago. I will consider below the data about which side is more accurate. It was this debate, and the shift to a health care system built largely on a for-profit organizational structure, however, that led to the public view of HMOs reflected by the cheers that erupted in response to Helen Hunt's obscene comments.

## THE EFFECTS OF FOR-PROFIT MANAGED CARE ON PUBLIC PERCEPTIONS OF THE QUALITY OF CARE

As discussed in Chapter 3, one of the key policy issues in health care, and one that differs substantially between the United States and Canada, is striking the proper balance between the marginal cost of health care services and their marginal benefit. In the RAND health insurance experiment (described in Chapter 5), the way that the HMO saved money compared to the fee-for-service system was by providing less hospital care that had a poor marginal benefit/marginal cost ratio. By doing a better job with this ratio, the HMO was able to eliminate unneeded hospital care and thus reduce costs.

The managers of the new for-profit HMOs realized that a great deal of inefficient care (that is, care with low marginal benefit and high marginal cost) was being provided. To reduce costs while maintaining overall quality, they would need to establish mechanisms to control the use of care. In the 1990s, HMOs and other managed care organizations developed a variety of utilization-control mechanisms. Some of the more common mechanisms are described below.

### Gatekeepers

A number of managed care organizations established a policy that patients must first see their primary care physician before being permitted to consult a specialist, have a test, or be admitted to the hospital. Patients could choose their primary care physician only from among those belonging to the medical group or plan they selected. Patients were referred to a specialist by the primary care physician; they were not free to select their own specialist. They usually could go to only the specialist chosen by the primary care physician. Thus, the primary care physician became the "gatekeeper" for other care the patient might need.

The gatekeeper approach was used in two general ways:

1. The primary care physician had no direct financial stake in whether a patient was referred to a specialist or for a test. The physician's only financial interest was in maintaining the economic health of the medical group.

2. The primary care physician received a fixed amount of money to provide all outpatient care and tests for each patient in his or her practice for a given period of time. Every time the physician referred a patient to a specialist or ordered a test, the money to pay for it came from this pool of money. Whatever was left in the pool was the physician's salary for that period of time. (While common during the early days of managed care, linking the gatekeeper function directly to the physician's income created an obvious ethical conflict and so this type of arrangement became much less common.)

## Utilization Review

Many managed care organizations maintained a staff of physicians and nurses who reviewed the care provided by physicians. Before a physician was permitted to hospitalize a patient or order an expensive test such as an MRI, he or she had to obtain permission from the utilization review department. Failure to obtain this prior authorization for nonemergency treatments and procedures might lead to the managed care company refusing to pay for the service. Once a patient had been hospitalized, the utilization review staff followed the patient's progress and made sure the physician did not keep the patient in the hospital too long.

## Physician Practice Profiles

Many managed care companies gathered statistics on how often each physician used expensive resources such as MRIs, drugs, hospitals, operations, and the like. The company then penalized physicians whose profile exceeded what the reviewers thought was appropriate. In a number of cases, managed care companies terminated the contract of physicians who continually exceeded expectations in the services they provided.

## Financial Incentives

Managed care companies developed a variety of financial incentives intended to encourage physicians to reduce the amount of care they provided. These incentives included the following:

• *Holdbacks*

Managed care companies that paid physicians on a fee-for-service basis (for example, independent practice association [IPA] HMOs) would often hold back a portion of the payment due to the physician, typically 10 to 15 percent. This money was held in a reserve account for each physician. If the medical group the physician belonged to provided more care, in aggregate, than the managed care company had budgeted, the money to cover the cost over-runs came from the pool of physicians' held-back pay. Physicians received only their portion of the pool that was left over at the end of the year.

• *Direct bonus*

Under many managed care contracts, each physician was eligible to receive a cash bonus at the end of the year, typically several thousand dollars. The amount of the bonus was determined by how well the physician had kept down costs during the year. Each physician's bonus was tied directly to the cost of the care that the physician had ordered during the year.

• *Indirect bonus*

In many medical groups that treated patients on a capitation basis, any surplus funds left over at the end of the year were placed in a bonus pool. Each physician in the group received a share of the pool in the form of a yearly bonus. Contrary to the direct bonus, in which the amount is tied directly to the individual physician's treatment decisions, the indirect bonus is tied to the ability of the medical group as a whole to hold down costs. (A consensus appears to have developed that the indirect bonus provides a more ethical type of financial incentive to physicians. It gives each physician a stake in the financial health of the overall medical group without tying bonuses directly to the physicians' specific treatment decisions during the year.)

## Education and Feedback

A number of medical groups that have assumed capitated risk for their patients have initiated structured programs of education and feedback to remind physicians which types of care are most appropriate and which types may be inappropriate. These programs do not directly involve any type of utilization control or financial incentive.

From the perspective of the health care manager in a for-profit plan, steps such as those described above may seem reasonable and rational. The manager's job is to reduce inefficient care and to curb physicians' historic tendency to use care that has small marginal benefit—that is, to "manage" care. In the words of Malik Hasan, such utilization-control activities "are in the best interests of consumers, patients, physicians, and payers and are imperative for a healthy economy" (Hasan 1996, p. 1056).

Utilization-control mechanisms raised serious public concern about the quality of care provided under for-profit managed care—but "quality" had a different meaning for the general public than for health plan managers. Both physicians and patients often approach quality in health care as reflecting both the process of care and the outcomes from care. Care that does not meet expectations regarding process can easily be perceived as low-quality care, even if health outcomes are maintained and economic efficiency is increased. Take, for example, the treatment of ankle injuries. There is ample scientific evidence that certain specific types of ankle injuries have an extremely low likelihood of involving injury to the bone. Taking X-rays of these patients will add substantial cost with little or no change in the eventual healing of the injury. Nonetheless, many patients who seek treatment for an injured ankle believe that unless the physician orders an X-ray, the quality of care has been substandard.

This focus on process over outcomes in defining quality became increasingly common as more and more patients experienced managed care. News reports included numerous instances of patients being denied care that on the surface seemed appropriate. Whether it was CAT scans for headaches, MRIs for knee injuries, hospitalization, referral to a specialist, use of the latest antibiotic, or access to surgery, many patients came away from their interaction with managed care systems believing that they had been denied appropriate care simply to save money. In the minds of many people (including the waitress played by Helen Hunt and the movie audiences who watched her), for-profit HMOs and other forms of managed care meant by definition low-quality care. Perhaps the public mood was best captured by a *New Yorker* cartoon that appeared in the 1990s. It showed Humpty Dumpty, having fallen off his wall, lying cracked on the ground. A passerby looks down and remarks, "He's in an H.M.O. Get some of the King's horses and a few of the King's men."

The rising public outcry over the limitations inherent in for-profit managed care led to increasing scrutiny of managed care organizations. Many employers and other large purchasers of care began to insist that managed care providers produce comprehensive data about the quality of the care they provide. The most prevalent data tool used to assess quality is the Healthcare Effectiveness Data and Information Set (HEDIS), a detailed reporting of adherence to certain process standards in care. (As with other monitoring tools, HEDIS does little to assess health outcomes.) In addition, the federal government and many state governments began to take steps to monitor and control the quality of care provided by HMOs and other managed care organizations. A growing list of actual or proposed legislation began to define what have come to be called "patients' rights" regarding health care, including a right to see a specialist, a right to have emergency room care paid for, and a right to appeal a denial of care. As a result of what came to be called the "managed care backlash," many, if not most, HMOs began in the late 1990s to reduce the stridency of their efforts at utilization control. As a result, costs began to rise, and the HMOs had little choice but to raise their rates to employers and individual subscribers. As shown in Figure 5.9, in the late 1990s, when for-profit HMOs and other managed care plans began to relax their control mechanisms, the steep rise in the cost of health care resumed.

(It is especially ironic that both government and the public began to refer to "patients' rights" to care in the context of managed care. As discussed in Chapter 2, the United States historically has failed to acknowledge a right to health care, a policy position that is unique among developed countries. As a society, we apparently acknowledge a right to expensive, often high-tech care for those with health insurance, while denying a right to basic care for those without health insurance. See Chapter 11 for further discussion of this issue.)

I should note that few of the more onerous methods of controlling the use of care were ever used by the large, nonprofit HMOs that formed the basis for federal policy in 1973. Kaiser Permanente, for example, included for many years an indirect bonus for physicians. The bonus pool was budgeted prospectively, however, and was always planned to be part of physician compensation. If the cost of care exceeded the amount budgeted, the bonus pool was used as a reserve cushion to make up the shortfall, and the remainder was distributed to physicians as part of their regular compensation. If, on the other hand, the cost of care was less than the amount budgeted, the surplus was not added to the bonus pool but rather was reinvested in the Kaiser Permanente system. Kaiser Permanente also relied heavily on physician education and feedback, and on gatekeeper systems that were not linked to physician compensation.

Outside of the Kaiser Permanente system, the conflict that developed between patients' expectations of care and the need of managed care organizations to constrain the amount of care provided in order to control costs often placed the physician directly in the middle. Physicians often found themselves in the role of wanting to provide a certain service or type of care but having the managed care company refusing to authorize or pay for care. Medical meetings and newsletters frequently bemoaned the added burden that had been placed on physicians by managed care. Physicians described spending hours on the phone with managed care reviewers (most of them with no medical training) debating the necessity of a certain type of care. Many physicians complained that clinical decision making had been taken out of their hands and placed in the hands of bureaucrats. (One orthopedic surgeon from a somewhat conservative medical community, whose son was in my health policy class at Stanford, shared his experiences with me by waving his hand under his chin and exclaiming, "I've had it up to here with HMOs!")

> **CONCEPT 8.1**
>
> The public has come to perceive many of the reductions in care initiated by managed care companies in an effort to control costs as unwarranted reductions in quality.

Many of these complaints and concerns about the effect of managed care on quality were in response to actions that were taken by the HMOs and that had substantial scientific support. When a physician asks for approval to undertake a procedure that has been shown to have little benefit in carefully controlled, scientific studies, it is both understandable and defensible to deny coverage for that care. This is precisely how HMOs and other managed care organizations save money. (See, for example, an article in the *New England Journal of Medicine* from 1994 titled, "I Had a Tough Day Today, Hillary," by Dr. Stephen D. Boren, the assistant medical director of a large insurance company.) Nonetheless, the public response to denials of this type is often one of criticism and complaint about low-quality care.

## PUBLICITY ABOUT THE "MEDICAL LOSS RATIO" AND PUBLIC REACTION TO IT

The insurance industry coined the term "loss ratio." For an insurance company, any claim that must be paid is viewed as a loss—that is, it decreases the company's profit for that year. The "loss ratio" is simply the percentage of premiums received from customers that are paid out in claims in a given period of time. The percentage obtained by subtracting the loss ratio from 100 percent measures the amount available to the company to cover administrative costs and provide a profit to shareholders. The lower the loss ratio, the more money is available as profit.

In the health insurance industry, analysts refer instead to the "medical loss ratio" (MLR). The MLR is the percentage of every dollar taken in as premiums that goes to pay for the provision of medical care. An MLR of 90 percent would mean that 90 percent of every premium dollar goes to pay for medical care, with the remaining 10 percent available to cover activities not involved directly in patient care such as marketing, administrative overhead, and shareholder profit. To many, MLR is an odd term, because it implies that health insurance companies consider any funds spent providing care to patients to be a loss and that they seek to keep this ratio as low as possible.

Historically, the MLR of nonprofit HMOs such as Kaiser Permanente has been in the range of 95 percent. The MLR for the Medicaid program is also typically about 95 percent, and for Medicare about 98 percent. Nearly all of the money in these traditional programs goes to pay for care. In the world of for-profit managed care, MLRs typically range from 70 to 85 percent. Any for-profit company that maintains an MLR above 80 to 85 percent is at a potentially serious competitive disadvantage. Their disadvantage, though, is not in competing for patients but rather in competing for stock market investment. In the face of rising cost pressures in health care, companies that are unable to maintain low MLRs will have difficulty giving shareholders an adequate return on their investment.

In the 1990s, newspapers began publishing the MLRs of various HMOs and other managed care plans. The MLR provided the public with a readily understandable measure of the extent to which for-profit health care organizations balance providing care to patients with the need to make a profit. Negative perceptions of the for-profit motive, coupled with public awareness of the pressure to maintain a low MLR, added to public concern and compounded the

> **CONCEPT 8.2**
>
> Negative perceptions of the expansion of for-profit care and growing awareness of efforts to reduce the medical loss ratio compounded the public's negative reaction to managed care, creating the "managed care backlash."

negative public reaction to the managed care industry, contributing to the "managed care backlash."

Neither the public nor legislators seem to be able to distinguish between problems in quality that stem from the profit motive and perceived problems that stem from otherwise justifiable efforts to control unnecessary care. The negative reaction to the managed care industry has been remarkably uniform and widespread, and seems to have lumped these two issues together. In this increasingly critical and competitive climate, investors began to lose interest in for-profit health care companies, sometimes with negative results for the companies. A number of large, for-profit managed care companies faced substantial financial losses starting in the late 1990s, leading to a series of mergers and acquisitions that resulted in considerable consolidation in the managed care industry. By 2001, the ten largest HMOs accounted for two-thirds of all HMO enrollment nationally. In 2009, a study by the AMA found that in twenty-four states, two managed care companies controlled 70 percent or more of the health insurance market within the state. In 54 percent of large metropolitan areas, a single health insurance company had a market share of 50 percent or more (American Medical Association 2010).

## THE QUALITY OF CARE IN FOR-PROFIT AND NONPROFIT MANAGED CARE PLANS

Much of the public debate about for-profit managed care plans centered on the issue of quality of care. The public perception was that for-profit plans offered lower-quality care as a result of efforts to maintain a low MLR. In response, supporters argued that for-profit plans were more responsive to competitive pressures in the market and were able to provide better care at a lower cost.

A series of studies have now been published in major journals, addressing this issue. I will describe three of them, covering the following questions:

1. How do for-profit and nonprofit plans compare on the quality-of-care measures included in the HEDIS scale?
2. Do for-profit plans provide the same quality care to poor children on Medicaid as they do to children with private insurance?
3. Do for-profit plans respond to financial incentives by restricting access to higher-cost procedures?

### Quality of Care on the HEDIS Scale

In 1991, a private consortium of large employers, health care corporations, and private foundations established the National Committee for Quality Assurance (NCQA). The NCQA's job was to create a reliable measure of the quality of care that could be used to compare health plans and medical groups. The NCQA developed and disseminated the Health Plan Employer Data and Information Set, commonly referred to by its acronym, HEDIS. Subsequently renamed as the Healthcare Effectiveness Data and Information Set, HEDIS does not measure health outcomes, such as death rates or complication rates. Rather, it measures how often health plans follow well-established guidelines for the prevention or treatment of certain conditions. Examples of items included in HEDIS are rates of immunization for children, frequency of Pap smears and mammograms as cancer screening in women, and the extent that the recommended treatment schedule is followed for patients with diabetes. These quality measures all pertain to the process with which care is provided. While process measures such as these reflect the quality of health care, they measure only one aspect of quality and may need to be combined with other aspects (for example, health outcomes, patient satisfaction) to give a full picture of quality. Nevertheless, HEDIS has come to be seen as an important means of comparing health plan quality. Accordingly, the NCQA gathers HEDIS scores from a variety of health plans and managed care organizations nationally.

In 1999, Himmelstein et al. published a major study that compared average HEDIS scores for 248 for-profit and 81 nonprofit HMOs. Combined, these 329 HMOs represented 56 percent of the total HMO enrollment in the country. Using data from 1996, they compared the plans on fourteen quality-of-care measures included in HEDIS. They found statistically significant differences in thirteen of the fourteen measures; in each case, for-profit HMOs scored lower than nonprofit HMOs.

## Quality of Care for Poor Children in For-Profit Managed Care Organizations

Thompson et al. (2003) also used HEDIS indicators to compare the quality of care provided to poor children enrolled in one of eighty-one private, for-profit managed health plans. Each of these plans covered both poor children enrolled through a Medicaid managed care contract and nonpoor children covered by their parents' private health insurance. The question the authors asked was, Do poor children receive the same quality of care as nonpoor children enrolled in the same plan? They found that poor children, despite being in the same health plan, had lower HEDIS scores for the following indicators: immunization rates, frequency of visits for well children and adolescents, and frequency of prenatal care for mothers. They also found significantly lower rates of tonsillectomy and myringotomy (inserting tubes into the ear drums for chronic fluid in the middle ear) for the poor children, although subsequent research has questioned the effectiveness of these procedures. The authors noted that a few of the plans maintained the same quality for their poor and nonpoor children, and they acknowledged that socioeconomic forces affecting poor children (for example, problems with transportation to scheduled visits) may be out of the health plan's control.

Nevertheless, the authors were able to conclude that "most commercial plans do not deliver high-quality care on a number of performance indicators for children enrolled in Medicaid."

## ACCESS TO HIGHER-COST PROCEDURES FOR MEDICARE BENEFICIARIES

Recall from Chapter 6 that several million Medicare beneficiaries have voluntarily enrolled in HMOs or other managed care plans as an alternative to traditional Medicare. These plans receive a yearly capitation payment from Medicare and must provide all necessary care to enrolled patients. The question arises as to whether for-profit managed care plans will define "necessary" in a more restrictive way than nonprofit plans, especially when it comes to using high-cost procedures such as cardiac catheterization or the insertion of artificial knee or hip joints. Schneider, Zaslavsky, and Epstein (2004) compared the rates at which twelve high-cost procedures were used for enrolled Medicare beneficiaries. Using data from 1997 on more than 3.7 million beneficiaries enrolled in one of 254 health plans, they compared procedure rates in for-profit and nonprofit plans. They tested the common assertion that for-profit plans, in an effort to hold down costs, will be more restrictive in the access they provide to these procedures.

After taking into account factors such as patients' age, income, education, and geographic region, they found that the for-profit plans had higher utilization rates for two of the twelve procedures measured; for the remaining ten, there were no differences between the for-profit and the nonprofit plans. The authors concluded that "contrary to our expectations about the likely effects of financial incentives, the rates of use of high-cost operative procedures were not lower among beneficiaries enrolled in for-profit health plans than among those enrolled in not-for-profit health plans" (p. 143).

> **CONCEPT 8.3**
>
> There is evidence that for-profit managed care organizations provide lower-quality care than nonprofit organizations, although the evidence is not consistent across all studies.

## THE MOVEMENT TOWARD FOR-PROFIT HOSPITAL OWNERSHIP

A move to for-profit ownership of hospitals has also taken place in the United States, in parallel with the movement to for-profit managed care, but it has not been nearly as extensive as in the case of HMOs. Hospitals have traditionally been run on a nonprofit basis in the United States. After the enactment of Medicare and Medicaid, many investors saw the potential of operating hospitals as money-making businesses. Beginning in the 1970s, investor-owned, for-profit corporations began to purchase hospitals and other types of institutional care facilities. Using capital obtained through the sale of stock, corporations took over formerly nonprofit hospitals and began to run them on a for-profit basis. Firms such as American Medical International and National Medical Enterprises developed chains of hospitals throughout the country, all operated as for-profit entities.

This trend continued into the 1990s, supported by the stock market boom. In the 1990s, newer firms such as the Hospital Corporation of America (later Columbia HCA) rapidly expanded their network of for-profit hospitals by using sales of new stock in the booming stock market to acquire community hospitals that were struggling with the problems of high costs and low occupancy described in Chapter 4. For-profit hospital chains, however, never developed the market penetration that for-profit HMOs did. In 1992, only 11 percent of community hospital beds were in for-profit hospitals; in 2003, that number was 14 percent (data from Kaiser Family Foundation website).

A number of eyebrows were raised in the medical community over the increasing role of for-profit corporations in hospital ownership and operation. In addition to the general concerns about for-profit care, cited above, there were also concerns about

- the goals and policies that for-profit hospitals would adopt (Would for-profit hospitals ignore local community needs and exploit employees?)
- the effects on medical research and education (Would for-profit hospitals benefit from publicly financed research and educational programs without contributing to them?)

In 1986, the Institute of Medicine, a branch of the federal National Academy of Sciences, looked into the effect of for-profit care in hospitals and issued a report (Gray 1986). The report found that, when compared to traditional nonprofit hospitals, for-profit hospitals

- are slightly *less* efficient in producing a given service or procedure
- charge somewhat more for comparable services
- provide less uncompensated care to low-income patients
- have been able to raise capital for expansion more easily than nonprofit hospitals (for-profit hospitals raise capital through issuing stock; nonprofit hospitals raise capital by borrowing it)

The report found no data available at that time to compare the quality of the care at for-profit and nonprofit hospitals. It did raise the question of whether for-profit hospitals "skim" the patient population (that is, treat only those patients with good insurance who can pay for their care, thus leaving the unprofitable patients for the nonprofit hospitals).

The report identified some arguments in favor of for-profit hospitals:

- For-profit hospital systems had the potential to provide care more efficiently if managed well; financial incentives could be structured to support efficient care.

- Competition among for-profit and nonprofit hospitals would, in theory, weed out inefficient systems of care, thus reducing overall costs.

Another study comparing for-profit with nonprofit hospitals was published in 1999 (Silverman, Skinner, and Fisher 1999). Rather than looking at quality per se, the study looked at the effect of for-profit hospitals on the rate of increase in spending to provide hospital care to Medicare beneficiaries. Also, rather than comparing individual hospitals, the study compared spending among more than three thousand "hospital service areas," which reflect local markets for hospital services. The study compared Medicare's average per capita spending on hospital care in 1989 with spending in 1995. After controlling for a number of possibly confounding characteristics, the study found that the lowest increase in per capita spending for hospital care was in those markets that remained predominantly nonprofit over the six-year study period. The largest increase in spending was found in those regions that had converted (through corporate acquisition) from predominantly nonprofit to predominantly for-profit. Regions that had remained consistently for-profit saw increases in spending that were slightly lower than those of the regions that converted to for-profit status, but substantially higher than those of the nonprofit regions. Coupled with the findings from the Institute of Medicine's study, these results suggest that, rather than reducing hospital costs, for-profit hospitals increase costs compared to nonprofit hospitals, without corresponding increases in quality or improvements in outcome. As stated by the authors of the 1999 study, "Our findings are consistent with the possibility that for-profit hospital ownership itself contributes to higher per capita costs for the Medicare populations served by these hospitals" (p. 425).

> **CONCEPT 8.4**
>
> The rise in for-profit ownership of hospitals in the United States has been associated with increases in hospital costs without evidence of concomitant increases in the quality of care or improvements in health outcomes.

## Physicians and For-Profit Care

Until now, this chapter has addressed the implications of the increasing prevalence of for-profit medical care in hospitals, HMOs, and managed care organizations. Physicians have been some of the loudest critics of the intrusion of these for-profit entities into what had previously been a system of health care centered on nonprofit organizations. What, though, has been the record of physicians themselves during the era of the expansion of for-profit care? Have they been immune from the financial incentives and opportunities available in this new world of medical care?

Sociologist Talcott Parsons was quite explicit regarding his views of how physicians should behave in the context of the profit motive: "The medical man is expected to place the welfare of the patient above his own self-interest, financial or otherwise . . . Thus the physician is both debarred from a variety of immediate opportunities for financial gain which are open to the businessman, and is positively enjoined to promote the welfare of his patients" (Parsons 1951, p. 472).

Parsons has been criticized for being overly idealistic in his view of how physicians are expected to behave. After all, the fee-for-service system of paying for medical care has built into it a financial incentive to provide more care than may be necessary. Recall also from Chapter 5 that even in the Kaiser Permanente system, the health plan and hospitals are organized on a nonprofit basis, but the Permanente Medical Group, representing the physicians within the system, is a for-profit corporation. Nonetheless, Parsons echoes the common perception that physicians, as part of their privileged position in society, face higher ethical standards regarding financial self-interest than those outside the profession who are engaged in business.

In considering this issue, I will not look at physicians who have chosen to enter directly into business related to health care. A number of physicians have become entrepreneurs and have been involved in the creation or management of HMOs, physician practice management companies, or biotech firms. These business activities do not relate concurrently to the practice of medicine, and so they should be judged by the ethical standards of business rather than medicine. There are a number of contexts, however, in which practicing physicians have become involved in the ownership or management of for-profit enterprises that offer care to the physicians' own patients. These physicians are in the somewhat tenuous dual role of self-interested businessperson and (presumably) disinterested physician. I will examine two such for-profit practice entities that have become quite common: kidney dialysis centers and specialty hospitals.

## For-Profit Kidney Dialysis Centers

As described in Chapter 6, the federal Medicare program covers patients who experience kidney failure, regardless of age. The treatment of kidney failure involves regular kidney dialysis, using a machine to do the work of cleansing the blood otherwise done by the kidneys. To survive, patients with kidney failure must undergo dialysis several times per week. Eventually, some of these patients will receive a kidney transplant, which, if successful, means that the patient no longer needs dialysis.

Patients with kidney failure come under the regular care of nephrologists—physicians specially trained in the treatment of kidney diseases. The nephrologist will refer the patient to a dialysis treatment center and will manage the patient's condition on an ongoing basis. Medicare will pay both for the care provided by the nephrologist and for the care provided by the dialysis center. Some dialysis centers are operated on a nonprofit basis by hospitals or other organizations, and some are operated on a for-profit basis with private ownership. This situation has created the opportunity for some nephrologists to become involved both in the care of the patient and in the ownership or management of the dialysis center. Some have questioned the ethics of such dual roles for physicians (see, for example, Bennett 2004) and also have suggested that for-profit centers may not provide high-quality care for their patients. Two major studies have addressed this issue.

Garg et al. (1999) followed more than 3,500 kidney patients for between 3 and 6 years, comparing the results of care received in for-profit dialysis centers with that received in nonprofit centers. After adjusting for patients' socioeconomic, demographic, and clinical circumstances, they were able to conclude two things:

1. Patients treated at for-profit dialysis centers had a higher death rate than patients treated at nonprofit centers.
2. Patients treated at for-profit dialysis centers were referred less often than patients treated at nonprofit centers for kidney transplantation as an alternative to dialysis.

In an editorial accompanying this study, Norman Levinsky concluded that "the increased mortality among patients treated at for-profit facilities, reported by Garg et al., and the lower quality of care in such facilities, reported by other investigators, suggest that, faced with the same financial pressures, for-profit facilities respond differently from not-for-profit facilities—to the detriment of patient care" (1999, p. 1692).

---

**CONCEPT 8.5**

Compared to treatment in nonprofit kidney dialysis centers, the treatment of patients with kidney failure in for-profit dialysis centers is associated with higher death rates and lower rates of referral for kidney transplantation. These for-profit centers also present potential ethical conflicts for physicians involved in their ownership or management.

---

Devereaux et al. (2002) reviewed the available literature comparing death rates in for-profit and nonprofit dialysis centers. They were able to identify eight separate studies, using data spanning the period 1973–97 and involving more than 500,000 patients. These authors concluded that "hemodialysis care in private not-for-profit centers is associated with a lower risk of mortality compared with care in private for-profit centers" (p. 2449).

## Private, For-Profit Specialty Hospitals

An editorial in the journal *Circulation* stated, "There is a suggestion in health care today that the nonprofit acute-care hospital has outlived its usefulness—that its days are numbered. Such hospitals are, in fact, anachronisms—a relic of another era. Their replacement? New, single-specialty, investor-owned hospitals or surgery centers, many of which are at least in part owned by physicians who can refer their own patients to these facilities" (Hupfeld 2004, p. 2379). These comments speak to a relatively new phenomenon in U.S. health care. Historically, the general hospital was the source of most medical care that could not be provided in physicians' offices. As surgical equipment and patient monitoring became more advanced, a number of surgical procedures previously performed only in a hospital could safely be done in outpatient "surgicenters"—free-standing operating rooms and recovery rooms, often affiliated with local physicians' groups.

In the early 1990s, as part of the general expansion of for-profit organizations, a number of investors—physicians among them—realized that certain aspects of hospital care were generally more profitable than others. While it might be relatively unprofitable to operate a labor and delivery ward or an emergency room, certain surgical procedures had relatively high rates of payment. For the general hospital, the low-profit centers and the high-profit centers balance each other out. What, though, if a hospital could focus on only those types of care with high reimbursement rates, and simply not offer the less profitable types of care? These types of specialized hospitals had the potential of generating substantial profit for the owners.

Physicians in several areas of the country began to invest in these "specialty hospitals." Principal among them were orthopedic hospitals and cardiac care hospitals. Typically, physicians whose practice included the type of specialized care offered in the hospital would team up with private investors to build the specialty hospital. Physicians would maintain their position on the staff of the general hospital, but they could now choose to refer patients to either the general hospital (in which they had no financial interest) or the specialty hospital (in which they maintained a financial interest). It should be apparent that such arrangements were disadvantageous from the perspective of the general hospital, and so general hospitals usually opposed them.

Specialty hospitals were advantageous to their physician owners in a number of ways. As licensed hospitals, they often received higher reimbursement rates from Medicare and other payers than surgicenters did for comparable care. In addition, the physician could select which patients to refer to the general hospital and which to refer to the specialty hospital, creating the opportunity to have the sicker (and thus more costly) patients treated in the general hospital and the less sick (and thus less costly) patients treated in the specialty hospital. A study by Horwitz (2005) confirmed that for-profit hospitals such as specialty hospitals are more likely than nonprofit or government hospitals to provide relatively profitable types of services.

Between 1997 and 2003, the number of specialty hospitals in the country went from 31 to 113. (During this same period, the number of surgicenters went from 2,462 to 3,735.) By 2003, 14 percent of general hospitals were operated on a for-profit basis, while more than 90 percent of specialty hospitals were operated on a for-profit basis (Iglehart 2005).

Cram, Rosenthal, and Vaughan-Sarrazin (2005) reported a study of nearly 70,000 patients who received cardiac revascularization surgery (unblocking clogged arteries to the heart) between 2000 and 2001 at either a general hospital or a cardiac specialty hospital. They were able to identify several differences between the two types of hospital:

- Specialty hospitals treated patients who tended to be less severely ill than patients in general hospitals.
- Specialty hospitals treated patients who tended to come from higher-income neighborhoods than patients in general hospitals.
- Specialty hospitals tended to have a higher volume of treatment than general hospitals. (It could not be determined from this study if the higher volume of treatment was because of a larger patient population served by the specialty hospitals, or a higher rate of treatment within the same patient population compared with that served by general hospitals.)
- Specialty hospitals reported lower unadjusted mortality rates than general hospitals; however, after adjusting for patients' severity of illness and the procedural volume at the hospital, the mortality rates did not differ.

Concerns such as these led Congress in 2003 to clamp a moratorium on new specialty hospitals until the issue could be studied in more depth. After hearing the reports from these preliminary studies, the Centers for Medicare and Medicaid Services acted in June 2005 to extend that moratorium.

> **CONCEPT 8.6**
>
> The number of specialty hospitals in the United States increased from 31 in 1997 to 113 in 2003; more than 90 percent of these hospitals are operated on a for-profit basis. Concerns about selective referral of patients and potential physician conflict of interest led Congress in 2003 to impose a moratorium on the opening of new specialty hospitals.

## THE "NEW" TYPE OF MEDICAL PRACTICE: THE PHYSICIAN CONCIERGE

In July 2005, an article appeared in the *New York Times* describing a physician who offered patients an exemplary level of service—longer appointments, no waiting, access to the doctor's cell phone number. Rather than reporting a resurgence in patient-centered medical care and the resurrection of Marcus Welby, M.D., this story was about a *new* type of medical practice that was taking root in many parts of the country—concierge medicine (Zipkin 2005). The physicians in these types of stories are entrepreneurs who believe that well-to-do patients will pay a cash premium for a superior level of service. Frustrated with the low reimbursement and high level of hassle offered by managed care companies, an increasing number of physicians are offering care only to patients willing to pay an enrollment fee, typically several thousand dollars, to be included in their practice. For this fee, the patient will be assured of increased personal service. The enrollment fee does not pay for that service, however—it simply provides the patient access to it. The patient must still pay the physician's full charge for treatment and must

"My fees are quite high, and yet you say you have little money.
I think I'm seeing a conflict of interest here."

FIGURE 8.1. The Downside of Concierge Medical Practice. *Source:* © The New Yorker Collection 1989 Leo Cullum from cartoonbank.com. All Rights Reserved.

not expect the physician to accept the patient's health insurance. While the physician's staff will assist the patient in filing a claim for reimbursement from the insurance company, payment of the physician's charge is solely the patient's responsibility.

There are two opposing views of this new level of service provided by physicians. (A 2005 editorial by Anthony DeMaria, editor-in-chief of the *Journal of the American College of Cardiology,* describes these two sides very well.) Some argue that concierge medicine is the only way to guarantee the level of quality patients deserve. In a local newspaper story, a concierge doctor in my community touted concierge practice as creating freedom for her and her patients from time constraints and regulations imposed by HMOs. (She also drives a Jaguar convertible.)

Others point to the obvious inequity inherent to concierge practice, as shown in a cartoon from the *New Yorker* (Figure 8.1). Only those patients who can afford the enrollment fee and the physician's charges for care—often substantially higher than charges approved by insurance companies—will receive the level of care offered by the physician concierge. Those without that level of income or wealth must continue to cope with the time constraints and regulations cited by concierge physicians as the reason they got out of mainstream medicine.

## THE RETAIL CLINIC: MEDICAL CARE AT A "BIG BOX" STORE

In about 2000, a new type of medical care resource began to become available—the retail clinic. These clinics are typically located within a "big box" retail store, such as a Wal-Mart or a large commercial pharmacy such as Walgreens or CVS. Typically operated by a for-profit enterprise that contracts with the larger store for clinic space, the clinics are typically available during the hours the store is open, usually including evenings and weekends. The clinic will usually be staffed by a nurse practitioner, and will provide care only for a specified list of conditions. About 90 percent of the care at these clinics is for ten common problems, such as upper respiratory infections, ear infections, urinary tract infections, or immunizations and other preventive care services (Mehrotra et al. 2010). Most of these clinics accept Medicare or other private insurance. When a patient presents to a retail clinic with a more serious problem, the nurse practitioner will refer the patient either to a physician's office or to an emergency room.

The concept behind retail clinics is making medical care for routine problems rapidly and conveniently available, at a lower cost than usually charged by a physician's office. By 2008, there were nearly one thousand retail clinics in operation. A study of the care provided by these clinics for three common problems (ear infection, sore throat, or urinary tract infection) found the quality of the care provided by the clinics to be comparable to care provided in a physician's office, but at a lower cost (Mehrotra et al. 2009). It remains to be seen to what extent these clinics will become a permanent part of our health care delivery system.

### SUMMARY

For better or for worse, health care in the United States has undergone a substantial shift over the past thirty years, from a system based primarily on provision of care in a nonprofit context to a system with a major role played by for-profit hospitals, clinics, HMOs, and managed care plans. Proponents of this shift argue that for-profit organizations are better able to react to the competitive environment of the health care market and are able to improve the efficiency and quality of care. Opponents argue that for-profit organizations reduce the quality of care by constraining access to care in an effort to maximize profits. There is evidence that these concerns may be justified.

Physicians have played a substantial role in the expansion of for-profit care. Whether in the creation of specialty hospitals, the expansion of specialized treatment centers, or the founding of concierge practices, a number of physicians have felt both comfortable and justified in combining the role of physician and entrepreneur.

Perceptions from the 1950s of the medical profession and the health care system always placing the interests of the patient first, immune from financial self-interest or the profit motive, have proven to be outdated in many cases. Instead, as described by Arnold Relman, former editor of the *New England Journal of Medicine*, health care in America has been "largely shaped by the entry and growth of innumerable private investor-owned businesses that sell health insurance and deliver medical care with a primary concern for the maximization of their income" (Relman 2007, p. 2668). Relman goes on to caution that "the continued privatization of health care and the continued prevalence and intrusion of market forces in the practice of medicine will not only bankrupt the health care system, but also will inevitably undermine the ethical foundations of medical practice and dissolve the moral precepts that have historically defined the medical profession" (p. 2669).

As health care in the United States enters an age of increasing scarcity of resources, and as our society re-examines its fundamental assumptions about the appropriate role and limits of health care, serious consideration must be given to defining the core ethical principles governing the role of the profit motive in the provision of care.

## THE AFFORDABLE CARE ACT AND FOR-PROFIT HEALTH CARE

Within the Affordable Care Act (ACA) are several provisions specifically targeting for-profit aspects of health care delivery. Many of these target managed care companies and insurance companies that operate on a for-profit basis. One of the most important of these provisions establishes new federal regulation of the MLR.

As described above, the MLR is the percentage of funds received by a managed care company in premiums that is paid out for the provision of health care to covered patients. Historically it has been typical for managed care companies to maintain MLRs in the range of 75 to 85 percent. This would imply that 15 to 25 percent of the premium income received by the company would go for administrative costs unrelated to the provision of care and for shareholder profit. ACA divides for-profit insurers into two groups: those providing coverage in the market for large employee groups, and those providing coverage for individuals and small employee groups. (New regulations will have to be adopted to provide a consistent dividing line between small group and large group markets.) ACA establishes a minimum MLR of 80 percent for plans in the small group market and 85 percent for plans in the market for large groups. Any plan with an MLR that falls below this mandated level will be required to provide a rebate to its enrollees covering the difference.

In the past, the issue of which administrative expenses were directly related to patient care and which were not received relatively little attention. Under ACA this will no longer be the case. Will administrative expenses incurred by gathering quality data about providers be considered an expense directly related to the provision of care? Will the costs of utilization review, described above, be within the acceptable MLR? Already there are early indications that for-profit care organizations are mounting lobbying efforts to have as many administrative expenses as possible counted as part of the acceptable MLR, thus leaving more of the revenue obtained from member premiums available for shareholder profit and management salaries.

In addition to regulating MLRs, ACA imposes a new fee that large health insurance companies will be required to pay, beginning in 2014, based on the size of their market share. Nonprofit managed care or insurance plans will pay a reduced fee. In 2014, these fees are expected to bring in approximately $8 billion in new revenue, rising to more than $14 billion in 2018.

In addition to the regulation of MLRs and the assessment of new fees, ACA also establishes a series of regulations on how health plans are administered. Historically, when an individual patient applied for health insurance coverage, a managed care plan or insurance company would have the applicant submit detailed information about his or her medical history. If the carrier determined that the applicant had a pre-existing medical condition that increased the likelihood of needing medical care, the plan would deny the application. Under ACA, companies are prohibited from considering pre-existing conditions to deny coverage to an applicant. Similarly, all applicants must be charged the same premium regardless of pre-existing conditions, with a few important exceptions. Different rates may be charged based on a patient's age, family composition, tobacco use, participation in a health promotion program, and geographic region of residence. Similarly, caps on the amount an insurance plan will pay for care, either per year or for a patient's lifetime, will be prohibited.

In addition to the above limitations, ACA requires health plans to report a range of new data, and will require health plans to be certified by the federal government in order to be eligible to participate in the health insurance exchanges established by ACA. As a response to public outcry over extraordinarily large increases in annual premiums reported by some insurers in the weeks leading up to its passage, ACA establishes a process by which annual increases in health plan premiums will be subject to federal review, with plans required to provide data justifying the increases.

One additional aspect of ACA is important to mention at this point. Under ACA, new physician-owned hospitals, discussed above, will not be permitted, and existing physician-owned hospitals will not be allowed to expand, except under strict conditions. It remains to be seen how and to what extent these new regulations will affect the future role of for-profit, physician-owned hospitals and similar care facilities in our health care system.

# Pharmaceutical Policy and the Rising Cost of Prescription Drugs

The way we organize, pay for, and deliver pharmaceutical products to patients has become one of the central issues of U.S. health policy. It is now a core issue for Medicare, with the initiation in 2006 of the Medicare prescription drug benefit. It remains a contentious issue for Medicaid, as state governments make difficult decisions about tradeoffs between rising costs and maintaining access to newer pharmaceutical products. Managed care organizations, both for-profit and nonprofit, struggle to stay within their budgets as a continuing stream of newer and very expensive products becomes available. In addition, discussions about pharmaceutical policy go directly to the heart of the debate over the role of for-profit corporations in U.S. health care. Understanding the history, structure, and problems of the pharmaceutical sector of our health care system will increasingly be a fundamental part of the knowledge base required of physicians, health care administrators, and health policy makers.

## THE ORIGINS OF THE PHARMACEUTICAL INDUSTRY

The modern pharmaceutical industry in the United States has its origins in the Pure Food and Drug Act, passed by Congress in 1906. Before that time, there was little regulation of the manufacturing or marketing of drugs and other remedies. There was, however, widespread popular concern about the safety of many of the remedies offered to doctors and patients—so-called patent medicines. As mandated by the act, the federal government established a mechanism to test pharmaceutical products through its Bureau of Chemistry. In close collaboration with the bureau, the American Medical Association (AMA) established its own Council on Pharmacy and Chemistry. At that time, the AMA had extensive influence with the editors and publishers of medical journals, which acted as the chief source of information about new drugs for practicing physicians. The AMA enforced a policy that permitted only those drugs that had been submitted for analysis and subsequently approved by the council to be advertised to physicians in medical journals. As a key part of its policy, the AMA's council would not approve any drug that was advertised by its manufacturer directly to the public. (This policy prohibiting the advertisement of prescription drugs directly to consumers was to have a continuing effect until it was altered by the federal government in 1997.)

Federal regulation of the pharmaceutical industry was strengthened in 1938, following a national scandal in which more than one hundred people died from taking a drug that was marketed for use in children and contained toxic materials. After Franklin Roosevelt signed the Food, Drug, and Cosmetic Act, the federal government required all new drugs coming to the market to be tested for safety before being made available for prescription by physicians. The act also strengthened the role of the Bureau of Chemistry, which had changed its name to the U.S. Food and Drug Administration (FDA). The FDA was charged with conducting the premarket testing for drug safety required by the act.

The FDA's role was expanded again in 1962 by the Kefauver-Harris Amendments, passed by Congress following a series of widely publicized hearings conducted by Senator Estes Kefauver (D-Tennessee). Manufacturers of new pharmaceutical products were required by the new law to provide the FDA with scientific proof of a new product's safety *and efficacy*. Before 1962, there was no requirement for scientific evidence that a drug worked—only that it did not cause harm.

At the time of the Kefauver hearings in 1962, relatively few pharmaceutical products were on the market, compared to the vast pharmacopoeia available to physicians today. Penicillin had been discovered only twenty years earlier, and many of the drugs used now for the treatment of common conditions such as diabetes, high blood pressure, and heart disease had yet to be identified. To encourage the development of new pharmaceutical products, Congress provided extensive patent protection to the developer of a new drug. Once a pharmaceutical company identified a new drug and a patent was granted, no other company was allowed to manufacture or sell that drug for a period of seventeen years. (The period of patent protection was extended to twenty years in 1995.) This does not mean that a manufacturer will be able to sell the drug exclusively for that long, as the time required to obtain FDA approval (often several years) is part of this period. It was typical for a manufacturer who developed and received approval for a new drug, however, to be able

---

**CONCEPT 9.1**

The federal government requires manufacturers of new pharmaceutical products to provide evidence of their safety and efficacy. It also grants the manufacturer patent protection for successful new products that allows for substantial economic gain in return for the manufacturer's investment in developing the products.

to sell the drug for ten years or more without any competition from other manufacturers. This period of patent protection created a government-sanctioned monopoly on the sale of that drug. As one might imagine, holding a protected monopoly on an important new drug conveys a tremendous economic advantage to the manufacturer, in that the manufacturer is permitted to charge whatever the market will bear for that new drug. A company that is able to bring a new drug to market under patent protection stands to make a tremendous profit. The reasoning behind this protection is that the economic gains to be realized from successful new drugs will provide a powerful incentive for manufacturers to invest the years of work and millions of dollars required to obtain marketing approval.

## THE RISING COST OF PRESCRIPTION DRUGS

Most of the new pharmaceutical products approved by the FDA are available only by prescription from a licensed physician or other health care provider. Some new products are available for sale "over the counter" (OTC)—directly to patients without a prescription—but these play a lesser role in pharmaceutical policy. At the time of the Kefauver hearings in the 1960s, the relatively small number of drugs available and their relatively modest cost meant that the cost of prescription drugs was not a major national policy concern. When Medicare was passed in 1965, Congress did not feel it was necessary to include coverage for prescription drugs in the program.

As the health care system began to experience rapidly increasing costs in the 1970s, the cost of prescription drugs also began to rise. Improved scientific and technical capabilities contributed to an increasing supply of new drugs coming to market. By 1980, prescription drugs accounted for 4.9 percent of all health care expenditures nationally (data from U.S. Centers for Medicare and Medicaid Services website). By 1990, their share of national health expenditures had risen slightly to 5.8 percent and remained there through 1994. Then, as shown in Figure 9.1, the cost of prescription drugs began to grow rapidly. By 2003, they had risen to 10.7 percent of all health expenditures. Between 1993 and 2003, while national health expenditures increased 89 percent, *expenditures for prescription drugs*

> **CONCEPT 9.2**
>
> Between 1993 and 2003, the overall cost of prescription drugs increased 249 percent, while the cost of health care in general increased 89 percent. The cost of prescription drugs is projected to remain at approximately 10 percent of national health expenditures through 2019.

*increased 249 percent!* Between 2003 and 2008, the cost of prescription drugs either remained flat or declined slightly, accounting for 10 percent of national health expenditures in 2008. The federal government has predicted that for the next decade, prescription drug costs will maintain a fairly constant share of overall health expenditures, reaching 10.2 percent of those expenditures in 2019.

The Kaiser Family Foundation (2004) analyzed federal data for the period 1997–

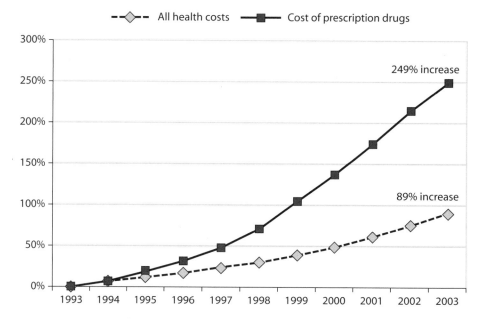

FIGURE 9.1. Increase in All Health Care Costs and Costs of Prescription Drugs, 1993–2003 (as a percentage of 1993 costs). *Source:* Data from U.S. Centers for Medicare and Medicaid Services

2002 on the factors that contributed to this rapid increase in expenditures for prescription drugs, and concluded that

- 42 percent of the increase in expenditures was due to increases in the number of prescriptions issued
- 25 percent of the increase was due to manufacturers' price increases for existing drugs
- 34 percent of the increase was due to shifting from a less expensive drug to a more expensive drug for the same illness

It should not be surprising that this rapid increase in spending, much of it on newer drugs still under patent protection, was beneficial to pharmaceutical manufacturers. For every year in the period studied by the Kaiser Family Foundation, pharmaceutical manufacturers enjoyed the highest profit margin of any industry in the United States.

As might be expected, the increase in the cost of prescription drugs is not experienced equally by all population groups. For example, a federal study of outpatient prescription drug use found that, for those patients who filled at least one prescription in 2000, the average number of prescriptions filled by a person younger than 65 was 10.1, at an average cost per year of $485. For those 65 and older, the average number of prescriptions filled was 23.5, at an average cost of $1,102. If, instead of looking at the cost of the drugs irrespective of who paid for them, we look instead at how much the patient paid out of pocket, we find an average expenditure of $199 for those younger than 65 and of $623 for those 65 and over (Stagnitti 2004). This wide difference in out-of-pocket expenditures was due largely to the lack of coverage for prescription drugs under Medicare before 2006. The disparate impact on seniors of rising drug costs is discussed later in this chapter, as part of the discussion of the Medicare prescription drug benefit.

## THE CONTROVERSY SURROUNDING PRESCRIPTION DRUG COSTS AND PHARMACEUTICAL MANUFACTURERS

Dr. Marcia Angell is a former editor-in-chief of the *New England Journal of Medicine,* one of the most respected medical journals in the country. The journal has a history of publishing only the most significant and scientifically accurate articles. In her tenure as editor, Dr. Angell upheld this tradition.

Dr. Angell left her position at the journal, and in 2004 published a book titled *The Truth about Drug Companies: How They Deceive Us and What to Do About It.* In this book, she characterized the U.S. pharmaceutical industry as "primarily a marketing machine to sell drugs of dubious benefit, [that] uses its wealth and power to co-opt every institution that might stand in its way, including the U.S. Congress, the Food and Drug Administration, academic medical centers, and the medical profession itself" (Angell 2004, p. xviii).

By any standard, Dr. Angell's remarks offer a scathing indictment of the pharmaceutical industry. Yet Dr. Angell was not alone in her criticisms—a number of scholars and analysts have leveled harsh criticism at the pharmaceutical industry. The appropriate role of the pharmaceutical industry and the issue of controlling or reducing the price of drugs are hotly debated topics, in the press as well as in scholarly books and journals.

The debate over pharmaceutical policy seems to revolve around one fundamental issue: how valuable are the new drugs developed and marketed by pharmaceutical companies? The differing positions on this issue can be summarized as follows.

• *Position in support of pharmaceutical companies*

One of the principal advances in medical care in the last twenty-five years has been the availability of a wide array of new pharmaceutical products. From drugs for heart disease and cancer to vaccines and drugs for HIV, medical care today has advanced substantially from where it was before. The policies that support patent protection for new drugs have been crucial in providing the economic incentive to invest the vast sums required (some say as high as $1 billion for each new drug that comes to market). If the government weakened that patent protection or adopted policies that reduce the price of drugs, pharmaceutical manufacturers could no longer afford to take the risk involved in developing new drugs, and our supply of new drugs would dry up in the future.

• *Position critical of pharmaceutical companies*

The research done by pharmaceutical companies does not really result in new drugs. Most of their research is dedicated to finding a way to develop a drug that is similar in effect to a drug patented by a competing manufacturer, but that is sufficiently different in chemical structure to qualify for a new patent under federal law. To boost the sales of their drug over a competing drug that does essentially the same thing, pharmaceutical companies spend billions of dollars for marketing and advertising. Many of these promotional activities—especially those targeting physicians—raise serious ethical concerns. In these times of health care scarcity, patients would be better served by selecting drugs based on value rather than on marketing glitz.

Resolving these competing claims is essential for any effort to establish a coherent national policy regarding pharmaceuticals. While there may be objectively derived data that speak to either side, it may not be possible to settle the argument based on data alone. For example, Keyhani and colleagues published a study in 2010 questioning the claim that higher prices and extended patent protection are necessary in the United States to maintain the incentive for pharmaceutical companies to develop new products through research. They found that the United States did not contribute disproportionately to innovation in the development of new types of drugs when compared to countries that had adopted price regulation for pharmaceuticals (Keyhani et al. 2010).

The debate over pharmaceutical policy also involves issues of cultural values and institutional structure. As discussed in Chapter 3, the U.S. health care system reflects the values and institutions that are unique to the United States. One of the principal differences between the United States and Canada is the approach we adopt to balancing marginal cost and marginal benefit in the allocation of health care resources. A system that values principally the right of patients to have available the most advanced treatment, regardless of its cost/benefit ratio, will accept treatments that are very costly but only marginally better than the alternatives. A system that values balancing the needs of all individuals in society, however, will not always consider the more costly option as the best choice.

## PHARMACEUTICAL RESEARCH AND THE ISSUE OF "ME-TOO" DRUGS

New pharmaceutical products fall into one of two general categories:

1. Drugs that are in an entirely new class of therapeutic agent
2. Drugs that are within an established class of therapeutic agents but have certain characteristics that distinguish them from other drugs within that category

The description in Chapter 3 of successive new classes of drugs to treat high blood pressure provides an excellent example of this distinction. Historically, diuretics were a mainstay of the treatment for high blood pressure. Among the diuretics, there were several products produced by several manufacturers. Then, scientists discovered calcium channel blockers, a new class of drug for high blood pressure. Within several years of their discovery, several alternative calcium channel blockers were available for physicians to use, each from a different manufacturer. Then came ACE-inhibitors as the newest class of drug, and again within several years of their introduction, several manufacturers offered drugs within this class.

It should be apparent that the manufacturer able to bring to market the first alternative within a new class of drugs has a tremendous economic advantage over its competitors. It may also be apparent that, for competing manufacturers, the sooner they can get their own drug approved within a new class, the sooner they will be able to tap into the economic advantage and share in the profits realized from newer, advanced treatments. (It should not be surprising that, in most cases, newer drugs are substantially more expensive than older alternatives.) The problem, of course, is that the manufacturer of the first drug enjoys patent protection, and it is against the law for a competing manufacturer to produce the same drug without permission.

This is where the research process known as "molecular manipulation" begins. It becomes the job of the scientists at the competing manufacturers to take the new drug into the lab and analyze the details of its chemical structure. If a new drug can be produced that has a different chemical structure ("different" according to federal guidelines) but maintains the beneficial therapeutic effect of the original

> **CONCEPT 9.3**
>
> Less than 10 percent of new drug applications approved by the U.S. Food and Drug Administration are for new compounds that represent a significant improvement in therapy. Most new drugs are chemical modifications of existing drugs.

drug, the second manufacturer can apply for a new patent, and if approved, market the second drug within the new class of drugs. Thus, a substantial part of the research of scientists within pharmaceutical companies is involved with the production of new chemical compounds that are patentable and still clinically effective—"me-too" drugs.

As an excellent example of this phenomenon, let us look at a category of drugs called the macrolides. These are antibiotics that have a well-defined spectrum of effectiveness in fighting infection and provide an alternative for patients who need a penicillin-type antibiotic but who are allergic to penicillin. The original member of the macrolide category is erythromycin. This drug has been available for several decades, originally under a few patented forms (most of them me-too reformulations of the original compound), but for several years erythromycin has been available as an inexpensive generic formulation no longer under patent protection. In 1996, two pharmaceutical manufacturers received approval for new macrolide antibiotics, clarithromycin and azithromy-

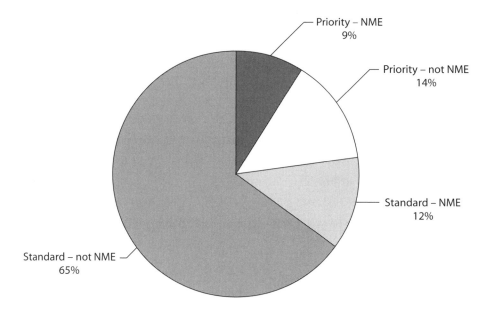

FIGURE 9.2. Types of New Drugs Approved by the U.S. Food and Drug Administration, 1990–2004 (NME = new medical entity. A total of 2,004 drugs were approved in this period.) *Source:* Data from U.S. Food and Drug Administration

cin, each chemically related to erythromycin. According to a commonly used on-line pharmacy, the retail price in 2005 for treatment with each of these drugs was slightly less than $10 for erythromycin, $96 for clarithromycin, and $121 for azithromycin. The manufacturer of each of the newer macrolide antibiotics heavily promoted its drug as superior to the others, usually based on factors such as ease of administration and fewer unpleasant side effects. We need not settle here which alternative is best; rather, we should simply note the phenomenon.

How many new drugs represent new classes of treatment rather than me-too reformulations of existing drugs? When the FDA receives an application for approval of a new drug, its scientists study the drug and assign it to one of two categories (U.S. Food and Drug Administration website):

1. Those drugs appropriate for "priority review" because they constitute a "significant improvement compared to marketed products in the treatment, diagnosis, or prevention of a disease"
2. Those drugs appropriate for "standard review" because they "appear to have therapeutic qualities similar to those of one or more already marketed drugs"

Beyond categorizing new drugs within this priority/standard framework, the FDA also determines whether a drug is a "new molecular entity" (NME) or a chemical derivative of an existing drug. Figure 9.2 shows the proportion of new drugs falling into these categories from among the 2,004 new drug applications that were approved by the FDA between 1990 and 2004. Of these new drugs, 23 percent were categorized as appropriate for priority review; about 4 in 10 of these "priority" drugs represented an NME. Thus, 9 percent of all new drug applications were for new compounds offering a significant improvement in therapy.

## THE MARKETING OF NEW DRUGS TO PHYSICIANS

Once a pharmaceutical manufacturer receives approval for a new drug that represents a chemical modification of an existing drug, it becomes incumbent on the manufacturer's marketing department to convince physicians that the new drug is superior to the original drug. Only a prescription by a physician will make the drug available to a patient. The issue becomes one of providing the physician with information about the drug in a format that the physician will pay attention to. There are three principal ways pharmaceutical companies do this:

1. Through advertisements in medical journals
2. Through educational meetings and conferences sponsored by the pharmaceutical company
3. Through direct marketing to the physician, using the mail and visits to the physician's office

### Marketing to Physicians through Medical Journal Advertisements

The link between pharmaceutical companies and medical journals was established more than one hundred years ago, and it continues today. Pick up nearly any journal intended for physicians and you will see colorful, expertly created ads—many of them occupying several successive pages—encouraging physicians to recognize the therapeutic advantage of the advertised drug over its competitors. These ads are expensive to produce and expensive to run, yet they are a mainstay of pharmaceutical marketing. The problem is that many journals rely on the income from drug ads to offset the costs of production and circulation. A number of the journals are free to physicians, because the entire cost of the journal is covered by revenue from drug ads. (My physician colleagues refer to these journals as "throw-away" journals.) Critics question whether the editor of the journal can exercise independent, scientific judgment in evaluating material related to the drugs advertised in the journal.

A second criticism regarding journal advertising relates to the accuracy of the research on which the claims in the ad are based. While a great deal of important research concerning new drugs is done in academic centers under strict rules about scientific methods, a substantial share of the research reported in journal advertising is done by the pharmaceutical company itself, free of academic oversight. Frequently, pharmaceutical companies will ask community-based physicians to use a new drug on a trial basis with a few of their patients. These studies are usually done according to an approved scientific protocol and in a manner that provides patient protections. The drug company, however, typically pays the physician a substantial fee for enrolling patients in the trial. Critics have questioned the ethics and accuracy of this type of research, although manufacturers respond that they are following the same ethical and scientific standards as academic researchers.

### Marketing to Physicians through Educational Meetings and Conferences

Most practicing physicians are required to participate in formal programs of continuing medical education (CME) to maintain their medical license. A substantial portion of CME takes place in meetings and conferences, often held in resort settings. While many of these meetings are organized by hospitals and medical schools with no direct financial interest in the drugs discussed, a substantial number of CME conferences are put on by for-profit companies referred to as medical education and communication companies (MECCs). About 90 percent of the revenues to MECCs come from pharmaceutical companies. The amount spent on CME by MECCs and other commercial sources went from $302 million in 1998 to $971 million in 2003 (Steinbrook 2005a).

The educational content of these types of CME events is often provided by speakers who are paid consultants of pharmaceutical companies. These relationships have led many to criticize the objectivity of the educational content of CME meetings supported by pharmaceutical companies. The Accreditation Council for Continuing Medical Education is an independent national body that certifies CME events. It established new standards that took effect in 2005–6 to address the issue of possible conflict of interest in commercially sponsored CME events. These standards apply equally to CME provided by private companies and that provided by hospitals and medical schools. It will be important to follow the changes resulting from these standards to determine if CME events are principally marketing events or are more accurately seen as educational events.

Dr. Arnold Relman, like Dr. Marcia Angell a former editor-in-chief of the *New England Journal of Medicine*, published an article in 2003 in the *New York Times* titled "Your Doctor's Drug Problem," describing the relationship that has evolved between pharmaceutical companies that put on CME events for doctors and the doctors who attend them. He describes this relationship in the following way: "As for the doctors attending these industry-sponsored educational programs, they like the slick presentations . . . They also like the low or nonexistent fees, the free food, and the numerous small gifts . . . And naturally they are confident that their own independence is wholly unaffected by all of this . . . But the companies providing the support wouldn't pour money into education unless they were confident of a return on their investment. And there is evidence that industry-sponsored programs increase the writing of prescriptions for the sponsor's products."

## Marketing Directly to Physicians

From their first days in the profession, young physicians are courted by the marketing representatives of pharmaceutical companies. When I was in medical school in the 1970s, we referred to these representatives as "detail men"—to "detail" was to provide physicians with the details about a new drug, and they were nearly all men. With substantial numbers of women now working as representatives of pharmaceutical companies, they are now more commonly referred to as "drug reps." Whether it is the 1970s or the 2010s, the issue is the same. Drug reps try hard to create a favorable impression with young physicians, and they do this to a substantial degree by providing them with gifts. When I was training, medical students routinely were offered gifts of textbooks, medical equipment such as stethoscopes, or simply free meals. Dr. David Blumenthal (2004a) described in some detail the types of financial inducements made available to physicians, both those in training and those in practice, by drug reps. It is not necessary to repeat the details of Dr. Blumenthal's analysis here. It is sufficient to say that pharmaceutical companies provide a physician with a wide array of incentives in exchange for one commodity: access to the physician.

Most physicians will receive regular calls from drug reps requesting the opportunity to meet with the physician to provide him or her with information about the new products available from that manufacturer. In addition to marketing brochures, the reps offer the physicians free starter-samples of the drug in question. These are packets containing a small supply of the drug being marketed—usually not enough for a full treatment—that the physician can give to patients free of charge. The physician is encouraged to try the drug, and if it proves effective, to use it with his or her patients. In all the marketing efforts, the drug rep emphasizes the benefit this drug has over its competitors—that is, its marginal benefit, as seen through the eyes of the pharmaceutical company's marketing department.

## OVERSIGHT OF PHYSICIANS' RELATIONSHIPS WITH THE PHARMACEUTICAL INDUSTRY

The recent awareness in the press and in the profession of potential problems in the ways pharmaceutical companies and physicians relate to each other has led to a number of changes in the standards governing professional conflict of interest. In an article published in 2004 in the *New England Journal of Medicine*, Studdert, Mello, and Brennan (2004a) summarized these changes. According to these authors, the changes were triggered by "a growing realization, inside and outside medical circles, of the troubling influence that pharmaceutical marketing can have on patient care" (p. 1891). In response, the Pharmaceutical Research and Manufacturers of America adopted its own standards for affiliated pharmaceutical companies to follow. The standards address in detail allowable conduct surrounding CME activities, and other issues with economic relationships that may place the physician in a position of conflict of interest. The authors conclude that this new attention and oversight may reflect "the same kind of sea change in business practices and industry oversight that other segments of corporate America faced in the wake of Enron and other corporate scandals" (Studdert, Mello, and Brennan 2004a, p. 1899).

The issue of the relationship between the medical profession and the pharmaceutical industry received added attention in 2009, with the publication of a report by the Institute of Medicine of the National Academies of Science, titled *Conflict of Interest in Medical Research, Education, and Practice* (Institute of Medicine of the National Academies of Science 2009). The report concluded that "there is growing concern among lawmakers, government agencies, and the public that extensive conflicts of interest in medicine require stronger measures. Responsible and reasonable conflict of interest policies and procedures will reduce the risk of bias and the loss of trust while avoiding undue burdens or harms and without damaging constructive collaborations with industry" (p. 3).

---

**CONCEPT 9.4**

Pharmaceutical manufacturers invest substantial resources in marketing to physicians through ads in medical journals, continuing medical education events, and visits to physicians' offices. Some of the practices of this marketing effort have raised questions about conflict of interest for physicians and have received increased regulatory scrutiny.

---

In a similar vein, in 2008 the Association of American Medical Colleges issued a report on the funding of medical education by pharmaceutical companies (Association of American Medical Colleges 2008). Among the recommendations of the report was the following: "Academic medical centers should establish and implement policies that prohibit the acceptance of any gifts from industry by physicians and other faculty, staff, students, and trainees of academic medical centers" (p. vii). The report went on to recommend that "academic medical centers should strongly discourage participation by their faculty in industry-sponsored speakers' bureaus" (p. viii).

## A NEW AREA FOR THE MARKETING OF PHARMACEUTICALS: DIRECT-TO-CONSUMERS

As described in the opening section of this chapter, in the early parts of the twentieth century the AMA prohibited manufacturers of prescription drugs from marketing their drugs directly to the public. Because only physicians and other practitioners had the necessary knowledge to select the most appropriate drug for a patient, it was seen as wholly inappropriate for manufacturers to target patients with their marketing efforts. Beginning in the 1980s, some manufacturers began to explore ways to include the general public in their marketing. They had some early success but also some problems related to unexpected side effects from the drugs they were marketing. At this point, the FDA stepped in and issued regulatory guidelines about the marketing of pharmaceutical products directly to consumers. In response to continually increasing marketing activity, in 1997 the FDA revisited the issue and published new guidelines that made it both easier and more attractive for manufacturers to sponsor direct-to-consumer ads, now commonly referred to as "DTC" ads.

In 1994, pharmaceutical manufacturers spent $266 million on DTC drug ads. By 1997, the year the new FDA guidelines were published, that amount had tripled, to $791 million. By 2000, it had tripled again, to $2.5 billion. Of this amount, $1.6 billion, or nearly two-thirds, was spent on television ads, with the remainder on print and other types of ads (Kreling et al. 2001). By 2007, the amount spent on DTC ads had grown to $4.9 billion.

Anyone in the United States who watched television during this time could not help but notice the extensive new presence of drug ads on television. A study done in the summer and fall of 2000 recorded 90 hours of network primetime television and 90 hours of network daytime television and found 319 ads for prescription drugs during the 180 hours of programming, for an average of 1.8 drug ads per hour (Lipton 2001).

This onslaught of DTC ads has been characterized in two ways. The manufacturers support them as providing valuable educational material to patients, encouraging them to discuss with their physicians new treatments that the patients may not have been aware of. Others criticize the ads as a purely profit-oriented attempt to get patients to request from their physicians the newest (and often most expensive) drug available.

A national survey of 643 physicians found that, when patients came to them requesting a medication they had seen in a DTC ad, 39 percent prescribed the requested drug. The five most common conditions for which patients requested drugs seen in a DTC ad were impotence, anxiety, arthritis, menopausal symptoms, and allergies. Physicians who did prescribe the requested DTC drug were about evenly split on whether that drug was the best alternative for the patient: 46 percent said that the drug was the most effective one for their patient, while 48 percent said that there were other, equally effective drugs that they might have used. While 74 percent of the physicians agreed that the DTC ads had positive educational aspects for their patients, 79 percent also concurred that DTC ads encouraged patients to seek treatment that they did not need (Weissman et al. 2004).

To evaluate the economic effect of the increase in DTC ads, the Kaiser Family Foundation commissioned an economic analysis by several leading scholars at Harvard University and MIT (Rosenthal et al. 2003). These researchers looked at changes in spending from 1999 to 2000 for the twenty-five classes of drugs with the highest retail sales. Combined, the drugs in these classes accounted for 75 percent of all pharmaceutical sales and 60 percent of DTC advertising expenditures. They estimated that 12 percent of the increase in pharmaceutical spending nationally was due to DTC ads, and that manufacturers realized approximately $4.20 in increased sales for every $1 they spent on DTC ads. A 2010 review of research on the effects of DTC advertising concluded that "the limited body of evidence suggests that DTCA-prompted prescription requests increase both appropriate and inappropriate prescribing" (Frosch et al. 2010, p. 27).

---

**CONCEPT 9.5**

Since 1997, pharmaceutical manufacturers have marketed their products directly to consumers, principally using TV ads.

---

It seems clear that, from a policy perspective, there are two sides to DTC ads (Berndt 2005). In a number of cases, they have affected the doctor-patient relationship in a positive way, contributing to patients' education about various health conditions. Many of these conditions, however, while doubtless important, are not the types of conditions in which increased investment in new, expensive pharmaceutical products is likely to yield substantial marginal returns in health status. The impact of DTC ads has been considerable, explaining a large portion of the recent increase in pharmaceutical spending and yielding high profits for pharmaceutical manufacturers.

## MARGINAL BENEFIT AS THE BASIS OF PHARMACEUTICAL MARKETING

In all three types of marketing to physicians, and especially in marketing directly to consumers, a pharmaceutical company emphasizes the marginal benefit of its drug over competitors in the same class of drugs or over those in different drug classes. Rarely does the marketing material address marginal cost, and almost never does it contain an unbiased evaluation of the marginal cost/marginal benefit relationship. This approach to marketing should not be surprising. It represents what has been proven over time to be the most successful way to increase sales and maximize profits of commodities distributed through the market. As health care in the United States has for more than a century been principally a market commodity, there seems to be little inconsistency in approaching pharmaceutical products in the same way.

---

**CONCEPT 9.6**

The marketing of pharmaceutical products to physicians and to consumers emphasizes the marginal benefits of one product over another. Issues of marginal costs rarely are considered.

---

While marketing based on perceived marginal benefit irrespective of added marginal cost seems wholly appropriate for consumer goods such as cars or sneakers, it raises disturbing issues when applied to pharmaceuticals and other core aspects of our increasingly troubled health care system. Our discussion in the previous chapters has identified this issue as central to many of the differences between health care in the United States and health care in Canada and other developed countries. In times of scarcity such as we are now confronting, when tradeoffs are inevitable among cost, quality, and access and between the absolute good of an individual patient and the aggregate good of all patients, serious reform of our system of health care will of necessity include a re-evaluation of our approach to this issue.

New drugs usually come under the influence of the "technologic imperative" and the "technologic benefit of the doubt," described in Chapter 3. Because they are new, they are commonly perceived to be better. How much better they are (that is, the magnitude of their marginal benefit) has typically been of substantially less importance. If we must allocate pharmaceutical resources under constrained budgets, however, it will mean that an extra dollar spent on a newer drug for one patient will mean one dollar less spent on providing drugs to another patient. As described below, we have entered an era of budgetary constraints in selecting pharmaceutical products. This is true for private-sector managed care plans, and it is true for Medicaid and Medicare.

## MANAGED CARE PLANS' EFFORTS TO CONTROL PHARMACEUTICAL COSTS

The rapid increases in pharmaceutical costs have had a substantial effect on private-sector managed care companies. Unless they are able to constrain increases in drug costs, managed care plans will have to raise their rates to employers and other purchasers by even more than they already have. Not surprisingly, they have focused on precisely the same issue as pharmaceutical manufacturers—marginal benefits versus marginal costs—but from the opposite perspective. Managed care plans have not focused their efforts on getting physicians to write fewer prescriptions, but rather on getting them to select the most cost-effective alternative within the class of medications needed to treat their patients. They have done this using a number of tools.

### Tiered Formularies

A formulary is a published list of medications approved for the treatment of certain conditions. Typically, a formulary will first divide drugs by the disease or medical problem treated, then by the classes of drugs available to treat those problems, and lastly by the name of specific drugs within each class. Using either its own experts or private consultants, the managed care company will then assess the relative cost and effectiveness of each drug. When multiple drugs with comparable effects are available, the formulary will typically identify one or more of them as the preferred choice for a given condition. The preferred drug is often one that is available in generic form. These are usually referred to as the "first-tier" alternative. It will then identify other drugs that are alternatives to the preferred drugs, but for reasons of either cost or effectiveness have some disadvantage. These are the "second-tier" drugs. The managed care company may further subdivide these second-tier drugs into those it is willing to provide partial coverage for, and those it will provide no coverage for. Drugs that receive no coverage under the plan are "third-tier" drugs. A study by the Kaiser Family Foundation (2004) found that 68 percent of workers who received their health insurance through their employment have at least three tiers of cost sharing in the drugs available to them.

Having defined the first-, second-, and third-tier drugs for each condition on the list, the managed care plan will leave it up to the physician and the patient to select the best option. While the plan will cover the cost of the first-tier drugs (less a small patient co-payment, typically $10 to $20), however, it will usually cover second-tier drugs at a lower level, requiring a higher co-payment from the patient, typically $25 to $35. If it covers third-tier drugs at all, the formulary will require the patient to make a much higher co-payment, in the range of $50 per prescription. Often, it will require the patient to pay the full cost of the third-tier option.

Some insurance plans have established a fourth tier of coverage. Instead of having the patient pay a fixed-dollar co-payment for second- or third-tier drugs, fourth-tier plans have started asking the patient to pay a fixed percentage of the cost of a drug, typically in the range of 20 to 33%. The drugs in the fourth tier are typically high-priced drugs for which there are few lower-priced alternatives. As reported in the *New York Times* in 2008, this shift has meant that some patients, despite having prescription drug coverage, can still end up paying thousands of dollars a month out of pocket (Kolata 2008).

## Pharmaceutical Benefit Managers

As one might imagine, the administrative work involved in creating and managing a drug formulary can be substantial. A number of private firms have been created to address this issue. These firms focus their business on managing the use of pharmaceuticals, and frequently on providing mail-order options for filling prescriptions as well. Many large managed care companies have subcontracted their capitated pharmaceutical coverage to these pharmaceutical benefit managers (PBMs). Patients who have health coverage that includes a PBM can often reduce their out-of-pocket costs by obtaining their prescriptions by mail directly from the PBM. While patients may need to make a separate co-payment for each thirty-day supply of medication obtained through a private pharmacy, they can typically get a ninety-day supply from the PBM's mail-order pharmacy for a single co-payment. This also allows the PBM to obtain large quantities of medications from manufacturers at more competitive prices than some smaller pharmacies.

A study from 2003 (Huskamp et al. 2003) looked at the effect of using a PBM to switch employees and their

---

**CONCEPT 9.7**

Managed care companies have used a number of methods to constrain rising pharmaceutical costs, including tiered formularies and pharmaceutical benefit managers.

families in two large firms to a three-tier formulary. The switch to the three-tier plan resulted in lower overall costs and increased use of medications from lower tiers for three classes of medication. It also resulted in some patients discontinuing therapy, however, which raises important questions about the effects of increasing co-payments on health care quality and access.

### Educational Efforts and Financial Incentives for Prescribing Physicians

A study of several large health plans in California (Wallack, Weinberg, and Thomas 2004) found that health plan managers were also increasing their efforts to educate their physicians about the relative cost and therapeutic advantages of alternative pharmaceutical products. Some of the plans also expanded financial incentives such as cash bonuses to encourage physicians to prescribe the least expensive available drug whenever appropriate.

## STATES' EFFORTS TO LIMIT MEDICAID PHARMACEUTICAL COSTS

As described in Chapter 7, Medicaid's overall costs have been going up sharply in recent years, leading a number of states to cut back on the benefits they provide under the program. Rising pharmaceutical costs have been a principal contributor to these problems. Recall that prescription drugs are not one of the benefits required by the federal government for states to participate in Medicaid; it is one of the optional benefits states are permitted to include in their program for which they can receive partial federal reimbursement.

Between 1996 and 2000, Medicaid expenditures for outpatient prescription drugs nearly doubled, from $10.6 billion to $21.0 billion (Iglehart 2003). Faced with worsening budget problems, states had to rethink their provision of prescription drugs to their Medicaid beneficiaries. A number of states initiated various programs to reduce their pharmaceutical costs. These programs have included

- requiring physicians to obtain prior authorization from Medicaid administrators before certain pharmaceuticals are prescribed
- requiring physicians to use the least expensive medication available within a class of medications
- requiring patients to make a co-payment for each prescription filled
- limiting the number of prescriptions patients may have filled each month

Cunningham (2005) used an existing national survey that included 1,600 adults on Medicaid to assess the effect of these policy changes on patients' access to medications. Depending on the type of program limitation, between 56 and 79 percent of respondents reported encountering limits on their access to prescription drugs.

Another way states have attempted to reduce pharmaceutical costs has been to conduct their own evaluations of the relative costs and benefits of various drugs within a treatment class. If they are unable to find scientific support for using a newer, more expensive drug rather than an older, generic drug no longer under patent protection, states have often required the use of the generic option. In 2001, Oregon began an effort to gather scientific evidence about the comparable benefits of alternatives in several drug classes. Working with researchers at the state's Health and Science University, they identified several classes of medication and began an extensive review of the available scientific evidence. After reviewing fifteen different drug classes, the medical director for the project reported that, "to date, we found no evidence that one drug was more effective than others intended to treat the same illness" (quoted in Pear and Dao 2004).

Finding no evidence that one drug is better than another does not prove that the drugs are equivalent. In most cases, it was impossible for the reviewers to identify a clearly preferable option, because few controlled studies had been done comparing drugs with each other. Most published research compared drugs to a placebo, not with each other (Padrez et al. 2005). Nonetheless, the findings represented the best available information about drug effectiveness and permitted the Oregon Medicaid program to develop a list of preferred drugs within a drug class, based on a combination of scientific evidence and relative costs. Several other states have teamed with Oregon to create a Drug Effectiveness Review Project (DERP), and to expand this research to include twenty-five of the most commonly used classes of medications. In addition to making the reports of the scientific reviews available to the participating state Medicaid programs, DERP is also making them available to the public on its website.

## MAKING PRESCRIPTION DRUGS MORE AFFORDABLE TO SENIORS: THE MEDICARE MODERNIZATION ACT

Until now, we have been looking at the efforts of managed care companies and state Medicaid programs to reduce pharmaceutical costs while maintaining the quality of available drugs. The federal Medicare program, described in Chapter 6, has had to deal with a different problem: expanding coverage to include pharmaceuticals. Since its creation in 1965, Medicare had excluded outpatient prescription drugs as a covered benefit. (Congress did add prescription drug coverage to Medicare for a few months as part of the Catastrophic Coverage Act of 1988, but when seniors found out they were going to have to pay the cost of coverage themselves, they lobbied fiercely and effectively to have the act repealed.) As the price of pharmaceuticals rose steeply in the years following 1988, seniors felt the brunt of the change. By 2003, the average per capita cost of pharmaceuticals for Medicare beneficiaries was $2,318. As with Medicare expenditures in general, this spending was highly skewed, with 28 percent of seniors using less than $500 in pharmaceuticals, while 16 percent used more than $4,000 (Kaiser Family Foundation 2004).

In 1999, 62 percent of seniors had some form of pharmaceutical coverage, leaving 38 percent of seniors with no coverage. Coverage for the 62 percent was partitioned as employer-sponsored coverage (28%), private Medigap coverage (7%), Medicare HMO (15%), Medicaid (10%), and other public programs (2%). Despite this coverage, seniors face substantial out-of-pocket expenses for pharmaceuticals. In 2000, the average Medicare beneficiary spent $644 on outpatient drugs; by 2004, that figure had reached $1,147. Recalling from Chapter 6 that in 2004 half of all elderly households in the United States had a total annual income under $24,500, it is easy to see that drug expenditures at this level can create a severe financial strain. Because of the cost of their medications, 30 percent of seniors with chronic medical problems such as heart failure, diabetes, or high blood pressure but without pharmaceutical coverage were found either to skip doses of medication or to fail to fill a prescription altogether (Kaiser Family Foundation 2004).

With the rising cost of prescription drugs having such a severe impact on seniors, President George W. Bush made a commitment when he was elected in 2000 to add coverage for prescription drugs to Medicare. While he was ultimately able to keep this commitment, finding a way to do so proved very difficult. The reason it was important to expand Medicare coverage, of course, was the rising cost of prescription drugs—but Medicare was already placing a severe strain on the federal budget, a strain projected only to get worse in coming years. President Bush needed to add prescription drug coverage in a way that was not perceived to increase the federal deficit unreasonably. That deficit had already ballooned in the early years of the Bush presidency as a result of the extensive tax cuts he had worked with Congress to pass. What he decided to do was to establish a budget cap for a prescription drug program, and then to leave it largely to Congress to design a program that stayed within that cap. He did indicate to Congress, though, that he could only support a program that provided prescription drug benefits through private carriers analogous to Medicare + Choice health plans. He did not want the federal government to become involved in the administration of the drug benefit in the same manner it administers the Part A hospital plan and Part B outpatient coverage.

The budget cap established by President Bush was $400 billion to cover the first ten years of the prescription drug plan. Congress spent several months debating the proposal and, in the end, passed the plan by a single vote—a vote obtained only at the last minute through the use of some heavy-duty arm twisting, in what John Iglehart referred to in the *New England Journal of Medicine* as "a pure power play" (see Iglehart 2004—an excellent account of the history and politics of the new law).

The Medicare Prescription Drug, Improvement, and Modernization Act, commonly referred to as the Medicare Modernization Act (MMA), was finally passed in November 2003. As the details of the plan became more widely known, it became clear that it was more than simply a new prescription drug plan. It also contained a provision to increase substantially the capitation rates paid to private Medicare + Choice health plans to attract more plans back into the program following their earlier exodus. The MMA also changed the way Part B premiums are calculated, expanded the role of medical savings accounts for the general public, increased payments to many rural hospitals, reduced payments to home health agencies, and blocked scheduled cuts in Part B payments to physicians triggered by the sustainable growth rate (SGR) formula discussed in Chapter 6.

Shortly after the MMA was approved by Congress and signed by President Bush, a controversy arose over the financial projections used during the congressional review process. As described, the MMA was passed in the House of Representatives by a single vote after contentious discussions in the House-Senate Conference Committee. The last votes in favor of the legislation came forward only after receiving assurance that the $400 billion cost of the program was accurate and would not be exceeded. Within a few months of final passage, news stories around the country reported that the chief actuary within Medicare had estimated the true ten-year cost to be closer to $530 billion. The stories also reported that the actuary's superiors within the executive branch had threatened to fire him if he made these estimates public. It is uncertain at best whether Congress would have passed the MMA had the financial projections from the Medicare actuary been shared with them.

To stay within the $400 billion target, congressional negotiators created a complex plan for covering prescription drugs for Medicare beneficiaries. The structure of the coverage is illustrated in Figure 9.3.

There are four tiers of coverage under the MMA:

Tier 1: The patient is responsible for the first $250 per year in pharmaceutical costs—this is referred to as the "deductible."

Tier 2: For yearly pharmaceutical costs between $250 and $2,250, Medicare will pay 75 percent and the patient will pay 25 percent.

Tier 3: Once a patient has incurred $2,250 in costs per year, the patient is responsible for 100 percent of additional costs, up to a total cost of $5,100.

Tier 4: After a patient incurs $5,100 in costs per year, Medicare will pay 95 percent of all additional costs for that year.*

This coverage plan has come to be called the "doughnut hole" plan, in that it provides coverage initially, then has nothing, then resumes coverage after the patient has

---

*The figures cited above were for the first year of the new pharmaceutical benefit. Each year they are adjusted for inflation.

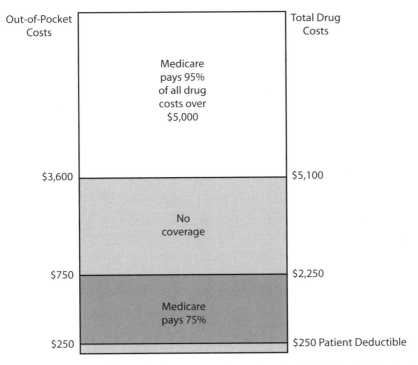

FIGURE 9.3. The Tiered Structure of the Pharmaceutical Benefit under the Medicare Modernization Act

spent $3,600 out of pocket. The gap in coverage between $2,250 in total costs and $5,100 in total costs is the "doughnut hole." The reason given for this plan was the need to accommodate the $400 billion budget cap established by President Bush. Congressional negotiators agreed on the need for the 95 percent catastrophic coverage for those few beneficiaries with extremely high costs. They also agreed on $250 as an appropriate level for the deductible. Once the high and low ends of the coverage were established, they began adding 75 percent coverage until they used up the budgeted funds. This occurred at $2,250 of total drug costs, so that was where they began the "doughnut hole." (It is worth noting what happens when one expands coverage for health care, but does so under a defined budget cap—one finds that one "can't treat all of the people all of the time," and instead must allocate resources based on relative need. Congress, it seems, followed Barr's Law, which is described in Chapter 13.)

Coverage under the MMA began on January 1, 2006. Consistent with the limitations President Bush established, all coverage under the MMA is provided by private, market-based companies. The enrollment period for coverage began on October 1, 2005. On that day, dozens of private companies offering pharmaceutical coverage began marketing their plans to Medicare beneficiaries. Because pharmaceutical coverage is optional rather than universal, it is up to the individual beneficiary to sign up with a plan. The large number of companies offering coverage and the intensity of their marketing efforts raised concerns that seniors would become confused, and they either would not sign up due to the confusion or may select a plan that did not best meet their needs. In Oregon, where seniors had twenty plans to choose from, the state Medicare coordinator was quoted in the *New York Times* as saying, "It's mind boggling. If you try to explain the whole program at one time, people will be shellshocked" (Pear 2005). In the same article, the director of the American Association of Retired Persons was quoted as saying, "The jury is out in terms of enrollment and public acceptance. Half of Medicare beneficiaries have no clue that the new program is on its way."

After this initial period of confusion, enrollment in the new prescription drug coverage progressed fairly smoothly. By January 2007, 23.3 million Medicare beneficiaries were enrolled in a drug plan—either a stand-alone plan (10.3 million), a plan that was part of a Medicare Advantage plan (6.7 million), or as part of Medicare-Medicaid dual coverage (6.3 million). By 2010, 27.7 million beneficiaries were covered, representing about 60 percent of all Medicare beneficiaries (Kaiser Family Foundation n.d.-b). An additional 14.1 million beneficiaries (about one-third of beneficiaries) had drug coverage through a private plan or a retirement health plan, leaving only about 4.5 million beneficiaries (approximately 10%) without any coverage. In 2010, approximately $55 billion was spent as part of Medicare Part D (Kaiser Family Foundation 2010f).

As is the case with Part B of Medicare, beneficiaries who choose to enroll in one of the available plans have to pay a monthly premium to cover 25 percent of the cost of the plan. The premium, typically in the range of $20 to $30 per month, is in addition to any out-of-pocket costs incurred under the plan. Once beneficiaries have signed up with a plan, Medicare will reimburse the plan for 75 percent of its costs. For a plan to be eligible, it must meet minimum federal standards for things such as numbers of drugs available in a class and expected costs for program coverage. Coincident with the relative slowing in the overall rise in the cost of prescription drugs nationally, the average premium paid by beneficiaries for coverage under Part D has remained fairly stable, averaging about $30 per month in 2011.

There are provisions to make the plans and the drugs they cover more affordable to poor and low-income seniors. Those beneficiaries below 135 percent of the federal poverty line (FPL) will not pay either a premium or a deductible, and their coverage will continue after they have reached their "doughnut hole." They will be required to pay a $2 co-payment for each prescription for a generic drug (those no longer under patent) and $5 for other prescriptions, with limits on yearly out-of-pocket expenditures. Those between 135 and 150 percent of the FPL will have slightly higher out-of-pocket costs, with small monthly premiums, a small deductible, and small required co-payments. In 2010, nearly 10 million Medicare beneficiaries benefited from these low-income subsidies, either through joint Medicare-Medicaid coverage or through the reduced pricing provisions.

It should be noted that Medicare will now offer prescription drug coverage to a number of poor seniors who previously had drugs covered by Medicaid. Medicaid will no longer cover prescriptions for seniors, and states will be required to reimburse the federal government for the state's share of prescription drug costs under the MMA for poor seniors, using the usual federal-state matching formula.

Actuarial projections of the benefits of the MMA suggest that they will help most Medicare beneficiaries somewhat and a few beneficiaries quite a lot. Overall, the 8.7 million beneficiaries who qualify for the low-income support in the program were expected to have their out-of-pocket drug expenditures reduced by 83 percent. The 20.3 million beneficiaries projected to enroll in the program who do not qualify for low-income support were expected to see a reduction in their out-of-pocket expenditures of 28 percent. Altogether, 3.8 million beneficiaries were expected to reach the "doughnut hole" in coverage without qualifying for catastrophic coverage, thus paying for all extra prescriptions themselves (Mays et al. 2004).

> **CONCEPT 9.8**
>
> The Medicare Modernization Act extended pharmaceutical coverage to Medicare beneficiaries, beginning in 2006. It includes four tiers of coverage, based on the amount of pharmaceuticals used during the year. It was estimated that it will reduce out-of-pocket expenditures for pharmaceuticals by 83 percent for low-income seniors and by 28 percent for other seniors.

Follow-up studies have largely confirmed these initial projections, although the savings in out-of-pocket costs have been somewhat lower than expected. A study published in 2008 found that, once enrollment in Part D plans had stabilized in mid-2006, average out-of-pocket costs decreased by 13.1 percent, with monthly drug utilization increasing by 5.9 percent (Yin et al. 2008). A second study found a "small but significant overall decrease" in the rate of Medicare patients not adhering to their prescribed drug regimen because of cost, although this decrease was not seen in the sickest beneficiaries (Madden et al. 2008). In 2007, 3.4 million beneficiaries had reached the "doughnut hole" in their coverage (Hoadley et al. 2008).

The MMA represents the best efforts of the federal government to deal with the pressing problem of rising pharmaceutical expenditures for seniors, many of whom have been unable to get the medications they need because of their high cost. Medicare will rely completely on private, market-based companies to administer the plans in a way that will remain within the ten-year budget cap established for the program. (Whether that cap is the $400 billion used by Congress or the $530 billion projected by the executive branch is still under analysis and debate.) As such, it is a major effort to deal with the rapidly rising cost of pharmaceutical products confronting the entire health care system. It remains to be seen whether the program will work as planned, or whether it will run into the same problems and frustrations as have other market-based efforts to constrain health care costs for publicly funded programs. Whatever the lessons learned from the MMA, they will provide valuable guidance in addressing the broader questions of health care reform.

## ADDITIONAL QUESTIONS OF PHARMACEUTICAL POLICY

Two other questions pertaining to pharmaceutical policy have been raised in the last few years that deserve our attention. The first is the issue of obtaining prescription drugs from Canada, something a growing number of Americans without pharmaceutical coverage have sought ways to do. The second is the question of the ability of the FDA to adequately identify potential side effects and risks of new drugs as part of the current review process.

### Reimporting Drugs from Canada

While the United States leaves the pricing of prescription drugs to the market, Canada has a federal policy of controlling drug prices. As a result, the price of prescription drugs is often substantially less in Canada. In many cases, the drugs in Canada are the same as those in the United States—same name, same manufacturer, sometimes even manufactured in the same plant. Canada has both a government review agency and drug review guidelines that are similar to those administered by the U.S. FDA.

A growing number of people in the United States have become aware of the availability of cheaper prices in Canada for the same (or substantially similar) drugs in the United States. Because Canadian law permits pharmacists in Canada to fill a prescription written by a physician in the United States, it has become common for people in the United States to turn to Canadian pharmacies to fill their prescriptions. This can be done in person by crossing the border into Canada, by mail order, or over the Internet. Under the Bush administration, the FDA declared this process to be illegal. The reason given is the threat to the patient's safety. Because the drugs have not been reviewed by the FDA, their safety cannot be assured, and they therefore should be banned from the U.S. market. Pharmaceutical manufacturers have voiced loud and enthusiastic support for this position. (Several high executive branch officers in the Bush administration were formerly executives of pharmaceutical companies.) Other observers have questioned this reason for prohibiting drug reimportation from Canada, suggesting instead that the threat to pharmaceutical company profits is the real reason behind the ban. (See Zuger 2003b and Choudry and Detsky 2005 for a further discussion of these issues.)

### Drug Safety and the FDA

In the mid- and late 1990s, a new class of drug came on the market. Named after the enzyme whose action they blocked, COX-2 inhibitors seemed to be an important new class of drug. They were used for the pain associated with inflammatory conditions such as arthritis. While no more potent at relieving pain than common, OTC alternatives, they seemed to have an important advantage: they caused less bleeding from the stomach and intestinal tract in older patients. Intestinal bleeding is a significant and dangerous complication for patients who require medication to relieve the pain of arthritis. Based on this perceived advantage, these drugs became what are known as "blockbuster" drugs—they rapidly took over a substantial share of the market for these types of pain relief drugs, and they accounted for billions of dollars in sales and profits. (The drugs were also heavily marketed in direct-to-consumer ads.)

In 2000, research evidence began to suggest that these drugs may have an unexpected side effect: they may cause or contribute to heart attacks. When a study designed to test specifically for this risk confirmed its existence, the manufacturer of one of the three main drugs in this class abruptly removed it from the market. A second drug in the class was later removed by its manufacturer.

As part of the inquiry into why a risk as serious as a heart attack was not identified in the initial drug review process, two concerns emerged:

1. The manufacturer of one of the drugs may have had prior knowledge of the risk of heart attacks from its own research, but did not fully disclose that risk. A series of lawsuits soon ensued addressing this issue.

2. Because of their close working relationship with pharmaceutical manufacturers, officials within the FDA may not have been as vigilant as they should have been in reviewing these drugs. While the courts are addressing the first issue, a number of experts have called for a reassessment of the FDA's policies and have raised the question of further separating FDA officials from any relationship with manufacturers that may present a conflict of interest.

(For further discussion of problems with the COX-2 inhibitors, see Psaty and Furberg 2005, Waxman 2005, and Drazen 2005. For further discussion of possible problems at the FDA, see Fontanarosa, Rennie, and DeAngelis 2004 and Steinbrook 2005b.)

## SUMMARY

Prescription drugs have become an increasingly important component of U.S. health care. While advances in the types of drug available have made substantial contributions to the treatment of many diseases, the cost of prescription drugs has been rising recently even faster than the cost of health care more generally. Between 1993 and 2003, expenditures for prescription drugs increased 249 percent.

There is a continuing debate over the implications of the rising cost of prescription drugs. Manufacturers justify the high price of newer drugs as necessary to support continuing research. Critics of the pharmaceutical industry suggest that manufacturers are more concerned with maximizing profits than with providing genuine advances in treatment.

A key aspect of pharmaceutical policy is the role of marketing new drugs. Manufacturers spend substantial sums marketing their newer products to physicians through journal ads, conferences, and directly in the physician's office. These physician-oriented marketing practices have come under new scrutiny, as questions have been raised about ethical issues. Manufacturers also spend substantial sums advertising products directly to consumers, principally through television and print ads.

In an effort to constrain the rising cost of pharmaceutical products, managed care companies have initiated a number of policies and procedures. Principal among these are the use of tiered formularies and PBMs. The Medicaid program has adopted similar approaches, although these vary from state to state.

In 2003, Congress added coverage for prescription drugs to the Medicare program. In a hotly debated and fiercely contested decision, the federal government adopted a market-based approach to making prescription drugs more affordable to seniors. With program costs expected to substantially exceed initial projections, the Medicare drug plan will be a key test of the extent to which private, market forces can succeed in constraining costs while also maintaining the quality and availability of health care.

## THE AFFORDABLE CARE ACT AND PHARMACEUTICAL POLICY

The principal impact of the Affordable Care Act (ACA) on pharmaceutical policy is on the "doughnut hole" gap in coverage under Medicare Part D plans. Effective in 2010, all beneficiaries who reached the "doughnut hole" gap in their coverage were eligible for a $250 rebate directly from Medicare. Beginning in 2011, any beneficiary reaching the gap and having a prescription for a brand-name drug (that is, a drug not yet available in generic form) will receive a 50 percent discount in the price of the drug, provided by the drug's manufacturer.

Also beginning in 2011, there will be a gradual increase in coverage provided in the gap. This added coverage will initially be only for generic drugs, but will expand in 2013 to include brand-name drugs. The amount the beneficiary who reaches the gap will have to pay will gradually decline from the original level of 100 percent of the cost of the drug, to 25 percent of the cost in 2020.

As a means of financing this increased level of coverage, ACA imposes a new fee on pharmaceutical manufacturers. These fees are expected to raise $2.8 billion in new revenue in 2012, rising to $4.1 billion in 2018, and then falling again to $2.8 billion in 2019 and beyond.

# 10

# Long-Term Care

Up to this point, this book has talked mostly about the system of acute care in the United States. Most of the money spent on health care and most of the attention given to recent changes in health policy have focused on the care we provide to people with specific conditions that need treatment from a physician or at a hospital.

What happens, though, when elderly or disabled people are not sick enough to require hospitalization but, due to chronic illness or general frailty, are not able to take care of themselves? These types of people are provided assistance through our system of long-term care. As the name implies, this type of care is ongoing and has less to do with the treatment of a specific disease until it is cured than with care for chronic conditions for which there is no cure.

There are many reasons why people need long-term care. Most often, an elderly person will simply have physical difficulty undertaking normal daily activities such as dressing, bathing, eating, and going to the toilet. (Activities such as these are referred to as activities of daily living, or ADLs.) Alternatively, a person may have a serious mental impairment such as Alzheimer disease that necessitates continuous supervision. Some people may have both physical difficulty with ADLs and mental impairment.

Traditionally, the need for long-term care was met principally by the family. As people became frail and in need of assistance, younger family members often teamed together to provide care. Because the dynamics of the American family has changed over the years, however, more and more frail elderly patients need organized institutions or services to help them. For example, between 1982 and 1994, the proportion of people in need of long-term care who were cared for in their home by family members or friends dropped from 74 percent to 64 percent (Liu, Manton, and Aragon 2000).

## THE GROWING NEED FOR LONG-TERM CARE AMONG FRAIL ELDERLY PEOPLE

Most people over 65 years old are able to care for themselves without any need for long-term care services. The problem of long-term care is mainly a problem of frail elderly individuals. It is very old people—those over 85—who typically need long-term care. Half of all people in nursing homes and one-fourth of all people with long-term care needs living in the community are over 85. Of the 39.6 million people age 65 or over in the United States in 2009, about 14 percent were age 85 or older (data from U.S. Census Bureau website). As Figure 10.1 shows, the number of people over 85 is growing much more rapidly than the number of elderly overall.

In 2009, 5.6 million people in this country were 85 years old or older. By 2020, this number is projected to increase to 7.3 million; by 2040, the number will be 15.4 million. As a result of the baby boom generation moving into their elder years, those over 85 will grow from 12.2 percent of the elderly population in 2000 to 19.2 percent by 2040. Whatever problems our health care system has in providing and financing long-term care will be multiplied within a few decades. As stated in a 1998 report submitted to Congress by the U.S. General Accounting Office, "Increased demand for long-term care, which will be driven in part by the aging baby boom generation, will contribute further to federal and state budget burdens" (p. 2). The report went on to

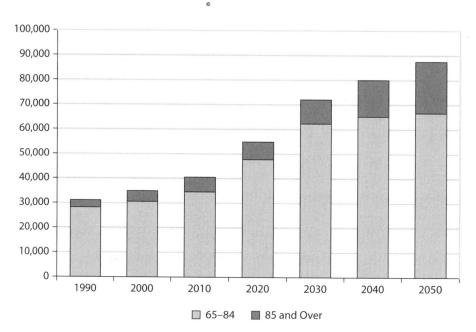

FIGURE 10.1. Projected Growth (in 1,000s) in the Elderly Population of the United States, 1990–2050.
*Source:* Data from U.S. Census Bureau

say that the increasing needs of the baby boom generation for long-term care "will lead to a sharp growth in federal entitlement spending that, absent meaningful reforms, will represent an unsustainable burden on future generations" (p. 3).

**CONCEPT 10.1**

The population group that is most in need of long-term care—those over 85 years old—is also the fastest-growing population group in the United States.

## NURSING HOME CARE

If an elderly or disabled person is in need of long-term care that, for whatever reason, cannot be provided in the home, that person can receive care in a nursing home or other type of residential care facility. At any one time, about 5 percent of elderly Americans, or about 1.7 million people, are receiving long-term care in some sort of nursing facility.

The average age of people in nursing homes is about 84. Seventy-two percent are women. Three-fourths of these residents needed assistance with at least three ADLs. Seventy percent had severe memory loss (data from Kaiser Family Foundation 1999 and National Center for Health Statistics website).

Not all people in nursing homes, however, are there for chronic long-term care. Many people will spend time in a nursing home following an acute illness or injury, and then will return home after a short stay. As many as 1 in 5 elderly people will spend at least some time in a nursing home at some point. In 1999, the average length of stay for residents in nursing homes was about 29 months; however, 68 percent of residents discharged from nursing homes had stays of less than 3 months. About 20 percent of nursing home residents stay there for 2 years or more.

Many people have the impression that Medicare pays for most of the nursing home care needed by elderly people, but this is usually not the case. Medicare pays for about 12 percent of nursing home care. To qualify for Medicare payment, a patient must have an acute medical problem that requires skilled nursing care as part of the treatment program. Examples of skilled nursing care would be the administration of intravenous antibiotics or assistance with rehabilitation following surgery or a stroke. In each case, a physician must certify that skilled care of this type is medically indicated. In most cases, the patient must have been in an acute care hospital just before entering the nursing home to qualify for Medicare payment. Even when a patient qualifies for skilled nursing care of this type, Medicare will pay the full cost only for the first 20 days. For skilled nursing care required beyond 20 days, the patient must pay $137.50 per day co-payment up to a maximum of 100 days of care. Any care required after 100 days is totally the responsibility of the patient, with no further coverage from Medicare.

Medicare distinguishes between *skilled nursing care* and *custodial nursing care*. Once a patient's medical condition has plateaued—that is, once he or she has attained the maximum level of healing or rehabilitation that can be expected in the short term—the patient no longer qualifies for Medicare's skilled nursing benefit. If the patient has to remain in the nursing home due to a need for assistance with ADLs, he or she is now considered to be receiving custodial care rather than skilled nursing care. Medicare does not pay for custodial care in nursing homes. Patients who need this type of care must find another way to pay for that care.

> **CONCEPT 10.2**
>
> Medicare pays very little of the cost of nursing home care. Patients who need long-term, custodial nursing home care are not eligible for Medicare payment.

One of the advantages of Medicare's health maintenance organization (HMO) option has been a relaxation in Medicare policies pertaining to the use of skilled nursing facilities. A physician in a Medicare HMO is allowed to treat a patient in a skilled nursing facility at his or her discretion. It is not necessary that a patient be in a hospital first. The cost of skilled nursing care comes out of the overall yearly capitation received by the HMO, so there typically will be some type of control on the use of long-term care. The type of utilization control depends on the type of HMO, but it often involves a case manager—a nurse or social worker who supervises the overall process of care a frail elderly patient will receive. The patient still must require skilled nursing care to be eligible for nursing home payment under Medicare HMOs, however. If the patient needs ongoing custodial care, Medicare HMOs, like traditional Medicare, provide no coverage.

What does the person do, then, who no longer requires skilled nursing care but still needs constant assistance with ADLs? Consider the case, for example, of an elderly widow who has been living alone in her own home, but who has had a stroke and is partially paralyzed. Medicare will pay the costs of a short-term rehabilitation program, but after a few weeks the patient is no longer eligible for coverage. Returning home is not a realistic option, so the patient finds herself in a nursing home. The cost of that nursing home will typically be between $60,000 and $80,000 per year—often more. Who pays for the ongoing care this patient needs? There are three principal sources to pay for this care: out of pocket, Medicaid, and private insurance.

### 1. Payment out of pocket for nursing home care

Many patients find themselves with no way to pay for nursing home care other than to pay out of pocket. In 2002, patients and their families paid 25 percent of the overall cost of nursing home care from personal resources. About one in four patients pays for nursing home care out of pocket when she or he is admitted. At $60,000 a year or more, it does not take long to exhaust the patient's resources. Few seniors have sufficient assets to be able to generate an income of $60,000 a year on an ongoing basis. Nonetheless, in many cases there is no alternative for the patient but to exhaust her personal assets in paying for care.

## 2. Medicaid payment for nursing home care

Unlike Medicare, the Medicaid program will pay the costs of ongoing, custodial care in nursing homes for poor seniors. Recall from Chapter 7 that nearly 70 percent of Medicaid funds goes to pay for the care of elderly and disabled people who are also poor. Elderly, poor people who need long-term care in a nursing home or other type of custodial care facility are eligible to have Medicaid pay the full cost of their care. This is our country's final safety net to assure that no elderly or disabled person who needs custodial nursing care will be denied that care because he or she is unable to pay for it. About 60 percent of nursing home residents nationwide are covered by Medicaid.

An irony of our system of paying for nursing home care is the extent to which it causes people who were not originally poor to become poor. As described above, about one nursing home resident in four who needs ongoing custodial care will pay for that care out of pocket. For many of these people, it takes little time to completely exhaust one's life savings paying for nursing home care. Once a person, such as the elderly widow who is partially paralyzed, spends all (or nearly all) of her money paying for nursing home care, she then becomes eligible for Medicaid payment for any further care. She is allowed to keep up to $2,000 in a personal savings account, but otherwise she must sell all her assets and use all her funds before Medicaid will pay for her care. Of those patients who initially pay for their nursing home care out of pocket and end up staying in the nursing home for two to three years or more, half will become impoverished and become eligible for Medicaid payment for their care.

> **CONCEPT 10.3**
>
> Medicaid will pay the cost of long-term, custodial nursing care for those seniors who need it. However, before becoming eligible for Medicaid payment, seniors must exhaust nearly all their own resources by paying for care out of pocket.

What happens in the case of an elderly couple who have been living in their own home for years and one spouse sustains an illness or injury that requires long-term, custodial care in a nursing home? The spouse in the nursing home requires ongoing care, yet the healthy spouse is still able to stay at home and live independently. Historically, both spouses were required to spend all their money, including exhausting their combined savings *and* selling their house, and use the proceeds to pay for the nursing home care of the ill spouse. It was necessary for both spouses to become impoverished for the care of the ill spouse to be covered by Medicaid. The spouse remaining in the couple's home faced a heart-wrenching choice: either spend all the money, lose the home, and become poor, or divorce the spouse and sever legal responsibility for the cost of the nursing home care. For a number of years, the need to protect the financial independence of the healthy spouse was a major contributor to the divorce rate among elderly couples, many of whom had been married for decades.

Fortunately, Congress changed the rules on what has come to be called "Medicaid spend-down." Now, if a couple faces the need to have one spouse cared for in a nursing home, the other spouse is allowed to maintain assets sufficient to remain in the couple's home and live independently.

What if an elderly person—again, let's consider the partially paralyzed widow—has substantial personal assets and finds that she needs to be in a nursing home? Why not simply give all her money to her children, thus becoming poor and qualifying for Medicaid? When Congress changed the law to protect the remaining spouse from Medicaid spend-down, it also changed the law regarding giving away one's assets. There is now a "look-back" period, typically about three to five years, in which Medicaid can look to see if the patient gave away significant assets to children or other family members. If it is found that she did give away assets that she otherwise would have been required to spend before qualifying for Medicaid, the family members who received the gifts must first use those funds to pay for the needed nursing home care. Only after the gifted funds have been used will the patient qualify for Medicaid coverage for her long-term care needs.

### 3. Private long-term care insurance

A number of private insurance companies offer insurance specifically to cover the cost of long-term care. These types of policies are usually made available to large employee groups. Only those not currently in need of long-term care are eligible to obtain the policies. The cost of these policies can be prohibitive—more than $2,500 per year for someone who is 65 years old and more than $7,500 per year for someone 75 years old. As a result, few individuals can afford such coverage. About 7 percent of the elderly population is covered by private long-term care insurance, and about 7 percent of the cost of nursing home care is paid by these policies.

### HOME HEALTH CARE

A substantial number of elderly or disabled people in this country need help with ADLs on an ongoing basis but are not so ill that they need to be in a nursing home. If they are provided with a limited amount of assistance, these people are capable of remaining in their home. Many of them qualify for in-home, long-term care under either Medicare or Medicaid.

Typically, people who qualify for home care assistance will have a nurse visit them on a regular basis, checking on their situation and assuring that their basic needs are met. These nurses can provide services such as monitoring the patient's medications, assessing the patient's nutrition, and evaluating ongoing home safety. In addition, some of these patients may be eligible to have the assistance of a home health aide. An aide of this type is not a nurse but rather someone trained specifically in providing assistance with ADLs. The aide will visit the patient on a regular basis and help with such activities as bathing and meal preparation. (See Levine, Boal, and Boling 2003 for further discussion of the clinical aspects of home health care.)

In 2010, Medicare spent $20 billion on home health care (data from U.S. Centers for Medicare and Medicaid Services website). By comparison, in 2008 the Medicaid program, covering both elderly and nonelderly people in need of home health care, spent $47.8 billion (data from the Kaiser Family Foundation website).

The Medicare home health benefit was originally intended to be similar to the nursing home benefit: it would cover only a short period of care and only after hospitalization for an acute medical problem. In the 1980s, Congress modified the eligibility rules in two important ways:

1. They removed the requirement that the patient must be in the hospital before being eligible for home care services.
2. They removed the cap on the number of services an eligible patient may receive per year.

Now, any Medicare beneficiary who meets the following criteria is eligible for payment of home health services on an ongoing basis. If the patient meets these criteria, he or she is eligible to have Medicare pay for both the skilled care services and the custodial care services provided in the home. The criteria are that

- the patient is homebound
- the patient is under the care of a physician, who periodically reviews the plan for home care services
- the patient has an intermittent need for skilled care services from either a nurse or other care provider (for example, physical therapist)
- the patient's care is provided by a home health agency that is a certified provider of services under the Medicare program

The costs associated with Medicare's home care program began to increase around 1980 when some of the initial program restrictions were relaxed. In 1989, there was a further loosening of eligibility requirements, and the costs of the program began to soar. In the nine years from 1980 to 1989, the cost of the program nearly tripled, from $662 million to $1.95 billion. A large part of the increase in the cost of the program was due to the increased frequency with which home care services were used over this time period. For most of the period from 1974 to 1989, those beneficiaries who qualified for Medicare home health services received about twenty-five visits per year. With the relaxation of eligibility requirements in the late 1980s, the average number of visits per home health care beneficiary jumped to nearly seventy-five per year.

The Medicare home health program was initially intended as a low-cost supplement to hospital care. In 1967, it accounted for less than 1 percent of all Medicare expenditures. Over the next thirty years, it became a major service program, accounting for nearly 5 percent of Medicare expenditures by 1997. In 2002, home health care accounted for 4.5 percent of overall Medicare expenditures.

As discussed in Chapter 6, the cost of home health care originally came out of the Part A Medicare trust fund. As Part A costs rose and the trust fund was facing potential insolvency, Congress modified Medicare's home health program in 1997 as part of the Balanced Budget Act. It reallocated most of the costs of the program to Medicare Part B and instituted new limitations on the use of home health services. These changes in eligibility and payment were successful in reducing costs, with a 12.9 percent decline in expenditures between 1997 and 1998.

## HOSPICE CARE

Consider the case of an elderly patient who discovers that he has cancer or some other terminal illness and is told by his doctor that he will most likely die within the next six months. Often this type of patient is not sick enough to be in the hospital, or alternatively, simply does not want to be in the hospital due to the futility of future attempts at treatment. It can be difficult for the family by itself to provide adequate care to a dying person, yet neither the patient nor the family wants placement in a nursing home. For this patient, a hospice may provide the best care available.

A hospice can be either a place for a person with a terminal disease to go for treatment or a team of professionals who assist the family to provide care to the terminally ill at home, or both. The hospice program focuses on relieving suffering rather than prolonging life. Hospice care involves a shift in the emphasis of care away from further attempts at cure to controlling the symptoms of the illness and providing emotional support during the dying process. Emotional support is offered both to the patient and to family members. Hospice care begins at the point that the inevitability of death is recognized and carries beyond the patient's death to help family members adjust to the loss.

The modern hospice movement, with an emphasis on symptom control and on dying as a process, began in England in the 1960s. The first modern hospice was named St. Christopher's and is described in the following quotation: "Several factors differentiate St. Christopher's from hospitals: allowing children to visit and play, personalized care, little patient-staff protocol, an informal social life, a continuum of care including home care, freedom to issue drugs and liquor as requested for symptom control, and follow-up with the family members after the patient's death" (Plumb and Ogle 1992, p. 812).

As it has developed in the United States over the past thirty years, a hospice program usually involves a health care team, often including a physician, a nurse, a social worker, a member of the clergy, trained home health aides, and community volunteers. The team will come to the patient's home and provide as much care as is feasible. Team members often will provide respite care for the family, relieving them for periods of time so they can take a break from the intense responsibilities of caring for a dying person. Some hospice programs will also have a care center, similar to that described for St. Christopher's. The patient who needs intensive assistance can stay in the facility, with family members visiting freely. Alternatively, the patient can split his or her time, spending part of the week in the hospice facility and part of the week at home with family members. As one might expect, hospice patients are three times as likely to die at home than in a hospital or nursing home when compared to patients who do not use hospice services.

Congress amended the Medicare program in 1982 to allow payment of hospice services for beneficiaries. To be eligible for hospice care, the beneficiary

- must be certified by a physician to have an incurable disease and be expected to live six months or less
- must agree to waive Medicare coverage for treatment of the illness provided outside the hospice program

Thus, a hospice patient under Medicare agrees to forgo further surgery or other types of therapy that are not intended for palliation and symptom relief. In return, the beneficiary is eligible for a substantially wider range of services than is available under traditional Medicare, such as drugs required for symptom relief, respite care at an inpatient facility, and bereavement counseling for the family.

An important study from 2010 evaluated the effect of receiving palliative care, such as that provided by hospice services, for patients with metastatic lung cancer—a condition that carries with it a grave prognosis. The patients in the study were not actually enrolled in hospice programs. They thus maintained the option of aggressive care, even as they neared the end of their life. Nonetheless, those patients receiving palliative care were less likely to choose aggressive care (33% as compared to 54% for those not receiving palliative care). Despite reduced use of aggressive care, the palliative care patients actually survived longer than patients not receiving palliative care (11.6 months as compared to 8.9 months) and reported a significantly better quality of life (Temel et al. 2010). An editorial accompanying the report of the study concluded "that life-threatening illness, whether it can be cured or controlled, carries with it significant burdens of suffering for patients and their families and that this suffering can be effectively addressed by modern palliative care teams. Perhaps unsurprisingly, reducing patients' misery may help them live longer" (Kelley and Meier 2010, p. 782).

The number of Medicare beneficiaries choosing to use hospice programs increased substantially during the 1990s, from 143,000 in 1992 to nearly 488,000 in 2000. During this same time period, the number of hospice programs providing care grew from 1,208 in 1992 to 2,244 in 2001 (data from U.S. Centers for Medicare and Medicaid Services website).

As the use of hospice programs and facilities expanded, the type of patient using hospice care changed somewhat. In 1992, 76 percent of all hospice patients were eligible for services because of a diagnosis of cancer. In 2008, this number had decreased to 31 percent. An increasing number of patients with diseases such as heart disease, lung disease, stroke, and Alzheimer disease had entered hospice programs. Despite this relative decline, nearly half of all Medicare patients who died of cancer were enrolled in a hospice program at the time of their death.

---

**CONCEPT 10.5**

Hospice care has become an increasingly important source of care for people with terminal illness. Hospice care involves treating symptoms rather than prolonging life, as well as providing emotional support for the dying person and his or her family.

---

Although Medicare beneficiaries are eligible for a full six months of hospice care, the actual length of time in a hospice program before death is usually considerably shorter. In 1992, the median length of hospice service was twenty-six days. In 2000, the median had decreased to seventeen days. This means that half of all hospice patients in 2000 received fewer than three weeks of service.

Looking instead at the average length of stay, we find that it has risen somewhat, from forty-eight days in 2000 to seventy-one days in 2008. These data suggest that it is often difficult for physicians, patients, and family members to face the inevitability of death that confronts many patients, and to begin to plan for death in advance of the final stages of illness.

## LIFE-CARE COMMUNITIES AS AN ALTERNATIVE TO LONG-TERM CARE

The options for long-term care have expanded recently by the addition of a relatively new type of senior care facility—the life-care community. A life-care community offers a permanent place for seniors to live, in which their needs for assistance with living will be taken care of no matter how long they need them. Whatever level of services a resident needs will be provided for one fixed cost.

In a life-care community, different levels of care typically are available:

### 1. Independent living

The life-care community provides individual apartments or condominiums for those residents capable of living alone. Residents in this level of care are fully independent, providing their own meals, and do not rely on assistance for any activities of daily living. They may, however, obtain meals from a central dining facility when desired, have assistance with transportation, and have someone always available for assistance in case of an emergency.

### 2. Assisted living

Some residents are not fully capable of living independently but are not frail enough to require constant assistance. Typically, the life-care facility provides these residents with an apartment in a central facility that has staff immediately available. These residents can make the apartment their own home. They usually require little if any help with ADLs, although they may eat in a central dining room and may have assistance managing their medications and bathing. The apartments usually have call buttons and other surveillance devices, so if a resident ever needs assistance, it is immediately available. These facilities are staffed around the clock, usually with aides rather than nurses.

### 3. Custodial care

Some residents in life-care communities have an illness or injury that necessitates round-the-clock assistance with ADLs or medical needs. This is the level of care that is usually provided in a nursing home. The life-care facility has a fully staffed nursing center available for these residents. They may need this level of care for only a short period of time, after which they can move back to their own home or apartment, or they may need this care for the rest of their life, in which case they will remain in the nursing center.

The unique aspect of life-care communities is that all these services are available for one fixed fee. The fee usually includes both a cash buy-in when the resident first enters the community and a monthly maintenance fee. In return for the buy-in and the monthly fee, residents are guaranteed whatever level of care they need, for the rest of their life. The only requirements are that the residents demonstrate sufficient income to assure lifetime payment of the maintenance fees, and that they enter the community at level 1 (that is, they are healthy enough initially to live independently).

Life-care communities offer an attractive alternative to many seniors who face the prospect of growing old alone at home and possibly ending their life in a nursing home. For a life-care community to work, however, seniors must plan for their remaining years when they are still relatively healthy. If they wait until they need extensive assistance, they are no longer eligible to enter these communities.

As one might imagine, it can often be very expensive to enter a life-care community, making them realistic alternatives for only the wealthiest seniors. A number of religious and other nonprofit institutions have established life-care communities, however, making them available to people without a large number of assets.

## FUTURE POLICY ISSUES IN LONG-TERM CARE

A number of policy questions remain to be answered regarding the future of long-term care in the United States. As difficult as the problems of the health care system are in general, the problems confronting our long-term care system are often even more vexing and are complicated by the relative lack of attention long-term care receives in the public health policy arena.

### How Will We Provide Long-Term Care for the Growing Number of Frail Elderly People?

As discussed above, the number of people in this country over 85, the population most in need of long-term care services, is expected to more than triple in the next forty years, growing to 19 percent of the population. Many of these people will need nursing home care. Many states placed limits on the construction of new nursing home beds, leading to an 18 percent nationwide decline between 1974 and 1994 in the number of beds per 1,000 people over 85. How will we build the nursing home facilities to meet the growing future need?

An alternative to building more nursing home beds is to develop more community-based services. In many cases a well-designed program of home health services can allow patients in need of substantial assistance to remain in the home with their families. For those without families to help them, smaller, community-based residential facilities that provide more of a homelike atmosphere can be an attractive alternative to traditional nursing homes.

### How Will We Pay for Long-Term Care in the Future?

More challenging than simply building the facilities needed for care is the question of how we will pay for that care. Few will argue that the current system of financing long-term care is optimal. Many question whether the impoverishment of elderly, middle-class nursing home residents is a wise choice. Is the best option to ask people to pay for nursing home care out of pocket? Similarly, is the way we split responsibility between Medicaid and Medicare wise, with Medicaid paying for nursing home care and Medicare paying for home health care?

Long-term care can be seen as a broad social need that must be addressed through broad social policy. A system of social insurance, similar to the Medicare system of paying for acute care, could potentially meet the financing needs for long-term care. To do so, however, the system will need to be broadly financed by all taxpayers, not just those who need care. The American taxpayer has been especially reluctant in recent years to take on new social programs. Yet, a substantial portion of the financing burden of long-term care falls on middle-class families and individuals. Will the American taxpayer be willing to invest in long-term care now so that needed care is available in the coming decades?

## How Will We Maintain the Quality of the Long-Term Care System?

For years there has been concern over the quality of long-term care services, especially care in nursing homes. As many as one nursing home in four has been found to have ongoing problems with quality (Feder, Comisar, and Niefeld 2000). Issues such as the appropriate level of staffing, the use of physical and chemical restraints, and the quality of the nursing services provided have led to continued federal and state oversight.

One of the issues contributing to these problems has been the relatively low level of Medicaid payment for nursing home care. As with acute medical care, Medicaid pays providers substantially less than private sources pay. With the large number of Medicaid beneficiaries in nursing homes, it has often been difficult for providers both to meet quality requirements and to maintain financial viability. The tradeoff between cost and quality will remain an important issue in long-term care.

## Who Will Provide Medical Care for Frail Elderly People?

Good-quality long-term care requires the continuous participation and oversight of medical personnel. A number of physicians, however, are either unwilling or unable to provide active supervision of long-term care. Recent years have seen a reduction in interest in primary care among physicians. If the growing needs of the elderly are to be met, interest in primary care will have to expand and will need to include additional emphasis on geriatric care. This can be done either by including more involvement in geriatric care in the training of general internists and family physicians, or by increasing the number of physicians who focus their practice on geriatric care. As an alternative, nurse practitioners and other types of mid-level health care practitioners can assume a greater role in monitoring and supervising long-term care.

## What Are the Ethical Issues Surrounding Care of Frail Elderly People?

In recent years, increased attention has focused on important ethical aspects of long-term care. The increasing role of advanced directives, such as living wills and durable power of attorney, has provided the opportunity for many elderly people to consider the appropriate level of care they wish to receive in the event that they become seriously ill. Issues of the autonomy and privacy of nursing home residents, especially those with cognitive impairment, are only beginning to be examined. The question of physician-assisted suicide has begun to receive increased attention as an option for patients facing inevitable death combined with intractable suffering. Future policy discussions will need to include consideration of these and other ethical issues that surround long-term care.

## SUMMARY

Policy issues pertaining to long-term care tend to receive less attention than those pertaining to health care more generally. Nonetheless, as the baby boom generation ages—especially as they move into their eighties—long-term care will become more of a central policy concern.

Care in nursing homes is one of the largest components of the long-term care system. Medicare provides only limited coverage and only for the cost of skilled nursing care. When frail elderly people or younger people with disabilities need assistance with basic ADLs such as dressing and bathing, they must either pay for it themselves or (after having exhausted most of their savings) go on Medicaid. A small but growing sector of the private market for health insurance provides some protection for the costs incurred when one must enter a nursing home.

Providing nursing and other support services in a person's home is another core component of the long-term care system. Medicare's coverage of home health care is substantially more extensive than its coverage of care in a nursing home. Other options for long-term care include life-care communities and, for those with a terminal illness, hospice care.

Finding ways to pay for the expected increase in the need for long-term care services will be one of the key policy challenges facing our country in coming years. Additional policy issues involve maintaining the quality of long-term care services and ensuring adequate personnel to provide these services.

## THE AFFORDABLE CARE ACT AND LONG-TERM CARE

There are relatively few changes to long-term care as a result of the Affordable Care Act (ACA). ACA establishes a "community living and assistance services and supports" (CLASS) program that will offer a new type of long-term care insurance to those who wish to purchase it. The benefits of the program may be used to purchase support services that allow individuals in need of assistance to maintain a residence in the community. It is expected that some employers will enroll in the plan and make it available to their employees on a voluntary basis.

ACA also establishes a series of new reporting requirements for skilled nursing facilities, covering issues such as ownership, accountability, expenditures, and quality data. This information will be posted to a website so Medicare enrollees can review it in order to compare facilities.

# The Uninsured

To gain access to most types of health service in this country, an individual or family needs to be covered by some sort of health insurance plan. The high cost of care, even relatively simple care, is often more than most people can afford to pay out of pocket. Fortunately, the vast majority of Americans are covered by some type of plan that will pay for their care when needed. In 2009, 83.3 percent of Americans had some form of health insurance coverage.

The remaining 16.7 percent of Americans—50.7 million people—faced the prospect of illness or injury with no health insurance, however, and thus no way to pay for their health care. One in six Americans remained uninsured throughout the entire year and as a result was often unable to obtain needed care due to the cost of that care. An even higher percentage went without health insurance for at least part of the year. Compared to people with insurance, the uninsured seldom obtain the type of preventive health services that can substantially reduce rates of illness and death (Ayanian et al. 2000). Providing health care to these people has for years been one of the most difficult policy issues facing the United States.

## THE CREATION AND EXPANSION OF HEALTH INSURANCE IN THE TWENTIETH CENTURY

Our focus on the issue of the uninsured developed relatively recently in U.S. political history. For much of the twentieth century, being uninsured was the norm and was not thought to pose a serious national policy issue. Before the Great Depression of the 1930s, few Americans were covered by any type of health insurance plan. Most insurance companies shied away from providing health insurance because of the difficulties in predicting or controlling the cost of care. It was the national economic crisis of the 1930s that stimulated the first widespread interest in health insurance.

Many hospitals were facing severe financial difficulties during the Depression, due largely to patients' inability to pay their hospital bills. The survival of the U.S. system of voluntary, nonprofit hospitals required some type of prepaid hospital insurance. If enough people were willing to pay a small amount each month to insure against the possible costs of a hospitalization, these funds could then be pooled to pay for the care of those who did become sick. Rather than relying on private insurance companies to offer this type of insurance, hospitals in most parts of the country banded together to form their own, nonprofit hospital insurance program. This was the birth of the national Blue Cross movement.

The Blue Cross insurance plans were principally intended to pay the costs of hospitalization. They did not pay for the cost of physician care. Shortly after the creation of the Blue Cross system, physicians in many areas of the country created a parallel system of nonprofit insurance for the cost of physician care: the Blue Shield program. The American Hospital Association (AHA) and the American Medical Association (AMA) worked together to assure that "the Blues" (as the combined Blue Cross/Blue Shield programs were often called) remained under the local control of hospital and physician associations and out of the hands of commercial insurers (a situation that changed dramatically in the 1990s, as discussed in Chapter 8).

These new insurance plans had a potential problem that could threaten their financial stability: adverse selection. Because health insurance was a relatively new option for most Americans, there was a risk that only those individuals who were facing illness would choose to have coverage. The success of the programs depended on spreading the cost of care over as many people as possible. If only sick people signed up for the plans, the cost of care would be more than the premiums paid by patients could support.

The solution to this problem lay in focusing on large groups of relatively healthy people as the principal market for the new health insurance. The best way to enroll large numbers of healthy people was to offer the insurance through employee groups. The concept of health insurance as an employee benefit was established through the marketing of the Blues to employee groups.

---

**CONCEPT 11.1**

At the beginning of World War II in 1941, fewer than 10 million Americans were covered by health insurance. The vast majority of the population was uninsured, paying for needed health care out of pocket.

---

By the beginning of World War II, the idea of health insurance had caught on. Seeing the initial success of the Blues in enrolling large numbers of subscribers, private, for-profit insurance companies began to follow suit and offer plans of their own. By 1940, more than 6 million people had enrolled in the Blues, with more than 3 million people covered by some type of private health insurance. The vast majority of Americans, however, were still uninsured and paid for health care out of pocket.

Chapter 5 describes the two major policy decisions enacted by the federal government that led over time to employer-provided health insurance becoming the norm.

1. The federal government exempted employer-paid fringe benefits from the national wage/price controls that were imposed during World War II.
2. The federal government decided that fringe benefits obtained through work would not be taxable as income to the worker.

These two policy decisions created powerful economic incentives for the expansion of employer-sponsored health plans. As labor unions bargained for improved wages and benefits for workers, one of the first benefits sought after was health insurance. By the 1960s, most large companies routinely offered health insurance to their full-time workers. Health insurance became the norm for most Americans.

The 1960s saw two major shifts in health care policy: (1) the expansion of health insurance to the poor and elderly through the Medicaid and Medicare programs and (2) the beginning of the rapid escalation in health care costs. By 1970, the cost of health care began to rise more rapidly than the national economy and continued to do so for the next forty years. In 1970, the average per capita cost of health care for all Americans was $297. By 1993, the year of the debate over President Bill Clinton's proposed health care reforms, this figure had increased by a factor of 10 to $2,937 per capita.* As the cost of health care rose relentlessly throughout the 1970s and 1980s, more and more people at the economic margins of American society found it difficult if not impossible to find or maintain health insurance for themselves and their families. By 1980, more than 31 million people lacked health insurance.

## THE ISSUE OF THE UNINSURED FINDS THE AMERICAN MAINSTREAM: WOFFORD VERSUS THORNBURGH, 1991

Until 1991, there was relatively little emphasis in either the public policy arena or the national media on how many Americans did or did not have health insurance. This situation changed dramatically following the upset victory of Harris Wofford over Richard Thornburgh in the 1991 Pennsylvania election for U.S. senator. Wofford had been appointed on an interim basis to fill an empty Senate seat. A special election had been called for November 5, 1991, to fill the seat on a permanent basis. Wofford, a Democrat, had been a co-founder of the Peace Corps and former state labor secretary, but he was relatively unknown in either Pennsylvania or national politics. His Republican opponent was Richard Thornburgh, who had been governor of Pennsylvania from 1979

---

*These data are from the federal government and are not adjusted for inflation.

to 1987 and attorney general in the George H. W. Bush administration. Wofford had been given little chance of beating Thornburgh. At one point, he trailed Thornburgh by 40 points in pre-election polls.

Wofford made a strategic decision that was to have far-reaching national implications. He began to focus his campaign on the plight of the uninsured and the need for national health insurance. This message struck a chord with Pennsylvanian voters, and Wofford rapidly gained ground on Thornburgh. On election day, Wofford defeated Thornburgh by a margin of 10 percent. By focusing the public spotlight on the uninsured, Wofford had not only beaten one of the strongest contenders in the Republican Party but also set the stage for Clinton's proposal for national health care reform and the changes that followed it, as discussed in Chapter 5.

## WHO ARE THE UNINSURED, AND WHY ARE THEY UNINSURED?

The successive victories by Harris Wofford and Bill Clinton placed the problem of the uninsured squarely before the American public. The defeat of the Clinton health reform proposals meant that the problem remained in front of us as we entered the 2008 election cycle. As shown in Figure 11.1, the proportion of uninsured Americans has grown nearly continuously since the Wofford and Clinton elections.*

When Wofford campaigned in 1991 on the issue of national health insurance, 13 percent of Americans were uninsured. When the Clinton health reform proposals were defeated in 1994, 14 percent were uninsured. By 1998, the number had grown to 14.6 percent of people without insurance. Dipping in 2000 to 13.7 percent after years of economic expansion and strikingly low rates of unemployment, by 2001 the number of uninsured began to rise again, reaching 15.8 percent of the population in 2007, the year before the economy went into recession. As a consequence of the recession and the high rate of unemployment that went along with it, the number of uninsured jumped to 16.8 percent in 2009 (U.S. Census Bureau 2010).

> **CONCEPT 11.2**
>
> The problem of the uninsured is not principally a problem affecting low-income families. Two-thirds of uninsured Americans are in families with annual household income above $25,000.

In addition to the 50.7 million people who fell into the category of "uninsured" in 2009, millions of others were without insurance for some period of time during the year but were not uninsured for the entire year. Many people will change jobs and be without coverage in the interim. Many college students go without health insurance coverage for short periods between graduation and beginning employment. People who are self-employed may cancel

---

*It should be noted that, in 2000, the Census Bureau changed the way it defined "uninsured," leading to an approximate 8 percent decrease in the number of uninsured calculated using the previous method. In reporting the number of uninsured in years before 2000, I have applied this adjustment factor, so that data before and after 1999 use the same measurement instrument.

their coverage for a period of time and enroll with a new insurance carrier. These are not the people we are talking about when we discussed the uninsured. The data below apply only to those who are without health insurance for the full year.

Figure 11.2 shows the breakdown of the population of uninsured Americans in 2009 by household income. The first thing to note is that only 30.5 percent of the unin-

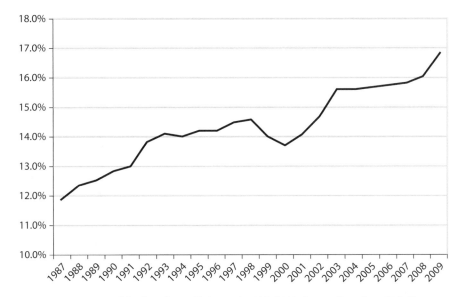

FIGURE 11.1. Percentage of the Population Uninsured, 1987–2009. *Source:* Data from U.S. Census Bureau; data previous to 2000 adjusted for change in methodology

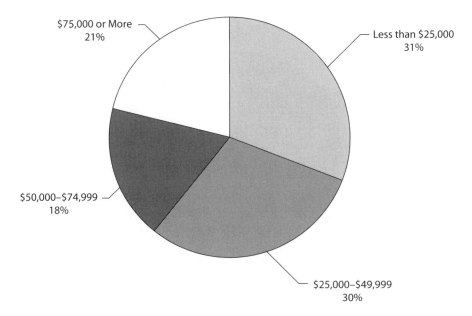

FIGURE 11.2. The Uninsured, by Household Income, 2009. *Source:* Data from U.S. Census Bureau

sured come from low-income families (families with income less than $25,000). Nearly half of the uninsured are from families with a household income between $25,000 and $75,000 per year.

Figure 11.3 looks at the uninsured by age. As would be expected, only 1 percent of the uninsured are elderly. Medicare has been effective in maintaining nearly univer-sal coverage for elderly Americans. Forty-one percent of the uninsured are young adults between 18 and 34. Fifteen percent of the uninsured are children. This high rate of uninsured children persists despite expansions in Medi-caid eligibility for children and creation of the State Chil-dren's Health Insurance Program (S-CHIP).

> **CONCEPT 11.3**
>
> The uninsured are made up mostly of young Americans—in 2009, 15 percent were children and 41 per-cent were young adults.

By looking at Figure 11.4, we see that the uninsured are not distributed equally among the principal ethnic groups in the United States. In 2009, about 65 percent of the U.S. population was white (non-Hispanic), while only 47 percent of the uninsured were white (non-Hispanic). The overall population was about 13 percent black, while the uninsured were 16 percent black. The population was 16 percent Hispanic, while the uninsured were 32 percent Hispanic. Asian/Pacific Islanders made up about 5 percent of the population and 5 percent of the uninsured.

> **CONCEPT 11.4**
>
> Minority ethnic groups are over-represented among the uninsured. This is especially true for Hispanics.

As shown in Figure 11.5, the problem of the uninsured is principally a problem of working families. During 2009, only 31 percent of uninsured adults did not work. Thirty-

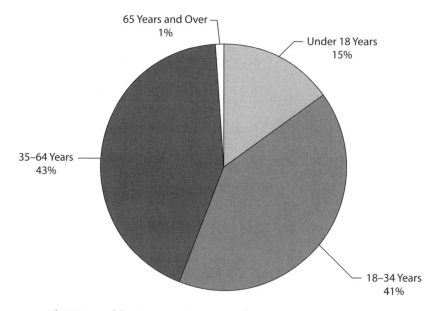

FIGURE 11.3. The Uninsured, by Age, 2009. *Source:* Data from U.S. Census Bureau

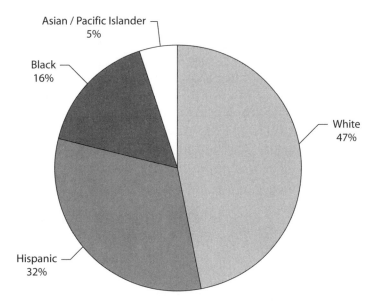

FIGURE 11.4. The Uninsured, by Ethnic Group, 2009. *Source:* Data from U.S. Census Bureau

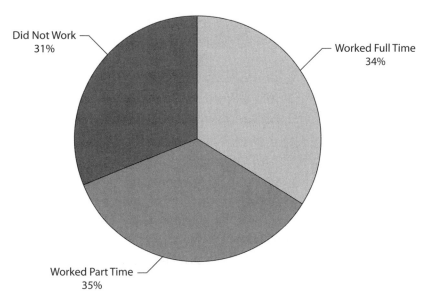

FIGURE 11.5. Uninsured Adults, by Work Status, 2009. *Source:* Data from U.S. Census Bureau

four percent of uninsured workers were employed full-time during the year, with the remaining 35 percent working part-time.

From the above data, it is possible to draw the following conclusions. Those Americans who are uninsured are principally

- young (56% under 35 years of age)
- from middle-income, working families (34% of adults work full-time, 70% of families have incomes above $25,000 per year)
- more likely to be from minority ethnic groups (32% Hispanic and 16% black)

The problem of the uninsured is not primarily a problem of the poor and the unemployed. It is a problem of middle-class, working families. How is it that, with most people obtaining health insurance through their work, so many working Americans remain without coverage? To answer this question, I will look in detail at the employment characteristics of the uninsured.

## THE SOURCE OF THE UNINSURED: LOW-WAGE WORKERS AND SMALL EMPLOYERS

Not all workers have equal access to health insurance through their work. In addition, not all workers take advantage of the availability of health insurance at their work. The likelihood a worker will have coverage available and the likelihood the worker will accept coverage when offered seems to be closely associated with the worker's hourly wage. Figure 11.6 shows data from 2001 that illustrate this point. At that time, only 53.3 percent of workers who earned $7.00 per hour or less were offered the chance to participate in employer-sponsored health insurance. Either their employer did not sponsor a plan, or the worker was not eligible for the employer's plan. For workers earning between $7.01 and $10.00 per hour, the figure rose to 72.2 percent. Ninety-two percent of workers earning more than $15.00 per hour had health insurance offered to them through their work.

Even if an employer offered health insurance coverage to workers, not all workers accepted this coverage. Typically, the employer will pay only part of the cost of coverage, with the employee responsible for paying the balance. It is possible to arrange to have the employee's share of the insurance premium exempt from income tax. For lower-wage workers, however, the advantage of tax exemption holds less benefit, because these workers typically pay taxes at a lower rate (if at all). In addition, the impact of the reduction in take-home pay resulting from enrolling in the employer's health insurance plan will be greater for low-wage workers than for higher-wage workers. As a result, even when offered coverage through their work, low-wage workers choose to accept that coverage less often than their higher-wage counterparts. Of those earning $7.00 per hour or less in 2001 who were offered health insurance, only 71.4 percent accepted the offer and enrolled

---

**CONCEPT 11.5**

Low-wage workers are offered employer-sponsored health insurance less often and accept enrollment less often than higher-wage workers. As a result of the combination of these two forces, the rate of health insurance coverage is substantially lower among low-wage workers than higher-wage workers, even though many employers make coverage available.

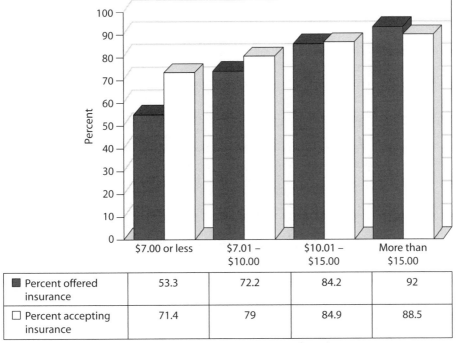

| | $7.00 or less | $7.01 – $10.00 | $10.01 – $15.00 | More than $15.00 |
|---|---|---|---|---|
| ■ Percent offered insurance | 53.3 | 72.2 | 84.2 | 92 |
| ☐ Percent accepting insurance | 71.4 | 79 | 84.9 | 88.5 |

Hourly wage of employee

FIGURE 11.6. The Availability and Acceptance of Employer-Sponsored Health Insurance for Workers at Different Income Levels, 2001. *Source:* Data from Kaiser Family Foundation

in the employer's health plan. The comparable number for higher-wage workers was 85 to 89 percent.

The rate of health insurance coverage depends not only on the wage of the employee but also on the size of the firm in which the worker is employed. In 2010, only 44 percent of workers employed in firms with fewer than twenty-five employees were covered by their employer's health insurance. This compares to 60 percent of employees in firms with 25 to 199 employees, and 63 percent of employees in firms with 200 or more employees (Kaiser Family Foundation and Health Research Educational Trust 2010).

There may well be substantial overlap between the effect of hourly wage and the effect of the size of the firm on the likelihood of coverage. Many small firms such as restaurants and independent retail stores rely on lower-wage workers to maintain their business. The cost of providing health insurance to these workers can be prohibi-

CONCEPT 11.6

Workers in small firms (fewer than twenty-five employees) are substantially less likely to be covered by health insurance than workers in large firms (one hundred employees or more).

tive. When Congress discussed requiring all employers to provide health insurance to their workers as part of the debate over the Clinton health reform proposals, small businesses spoke with a clear voice that such a mandate would be a severe hardship for them.

Our system of employer-based health insurance has evolved over several decades since the federal government made the two policy decisions described above. These decisions were intended to address specific issues of wage stabilization and taxation, however, and not to create national health policy. The employment-based system we have now was neither consciously designed nor explicitly adopted. It simply developed as a result of market forces and the unintended consequences of federal tax and wage policies. While the system works well for most Americans, it has failed a growing segment of our population and has contributed substantially to the national policy dilemma of finding a way to extend coverage to the uninsured.

A number of people have argued that if we are going to have a system that provides health insurance through one's work, all employers should be required to provide that insurance. Employers provide other types of mandatory benefits—coverage for unemployment or on-the-job injuries, for example—so it would be straightforward to mandate that employers also provide health insurance. Opponents to this "employer mandate" approach have argued in response that it would place an unreasonable burden on employers, especially smaller businesses, to pay for health insurance for their workers. While a number of states have considered adopting a statewide employer mandate for health insurance, only one has actually adopted such a policy.

## EXPANDING HEALTH INSURANCE COVERAGE IN HAWAII: THE EMPLOYER MANDATE

In 2009, only 8.2 percent of the population of the state of Hawaii was without health insurance coverage. Of all fifty states, only Massachusetts had fewer uninsured. By comparison, in 2009 California had 20.0 percent of its population uninsured and Texas had 26.1 percent (U.S. Census Bureau 2010). Much of the credit for Hawaii's high rate of health insurance coverage for its population rests with the Prepaid Health Care Act (PPHCA), the country's only statewide employer-mandate system of health insurance.

In the 1970s, the number of uninsured in Hawaii was typical of the rest of the United States, with 12 percent of the population without hospital insurance and 17 percent without insurance for physician care (Lewin and Sybinsky 1993). Seeing the rising cost of health care as a threat to the local population and the local economy, the Hawaii state legislature enacted PPHCA in 1974. Virtually all employers were required to provide health insurance for employees working at least half-time. The cost of the insurance was to be paid by a payroll tax on employees (not to exceed 1.5% of wages), with the balance paid by the employer. With these funds, the employer would purchase a basic health insurance policy, covering at least a specified list of services, from one of the private health insurance providers in the state. The mandated coverage would be for the employee only, but employers and employees would have the option of covering other family members. (Most employers extended coverage to family members.)

The law was successful, with between 4 and 5 percent of the population remaining without insurance by the mid-1980s. A serious economic downturn in Hawaii following the Asian currency crisis of the early 1990s led to higher rates of unemployment in the state. For example, the unemployment rate in Hawaii was 2.6 percent in January 1991 and rose to 6.4 percent in January 1997. In the same period, the overall U.S. unemployment rate fell from 6.4 to 5.3 percent (data from U.S. Bureau of Labor Statistics website). Even with this rise in unemployment relative to the rest of the country, Hawaii had one of the lowest uninsured rates of all fifty states. Those who remain without health insurance in Hawaii are part-time workers, the unemployed, and dependents of low-income workers.

Whenever an employer mandate to provide health insurance to workers is proposed, whether at the national or state level, the business community raises serious objections. The principal concern has been that such a mandate would place an unreasonable burden on businesses, especially small businesses. The concern is that adding the cost of health insurance to the other costs of doing business would drive some firms out of business and lead others to scale back the number of people they are willing to employ. The result is predicted to be higher unemployment and reduced business activity. Similar predictions were made when PPHCA was first proposed in 1974.

In Hawaii, these predictions did not prove to be accurate. A study by the federal government showed that PPHCA did not adversely affect businesses in Hawaii (Lewin and Sybinsky 1993). More than 90 percent of businesses in Hawaii employ fewer than fifty people. In a state with one of the highest proportions of small businesses in the country, the creation of an employer mandate for the provision of health insurance did not appreciably harm small business owners or employees.

> **CONCEPT 11.7**
>
> Requiring all employers to provide health insurance to their regular employees and their families has been demonstrated to reduce the number of uninsured substantially without imposing undue hardship on small businesses.

One aspect of the PPHCA that was especially important, and which holds particular significance for consideration of the general policy issue of the employer mandate, was the experience with the premium supplementation fund. As part of PPHCA, employers that have eight or fewer employees and that are not able to afford the added costs of health insurance for workers are eligible to apply for state assistance in paying these premiums. In the first seventeen years of the program, only $85,000 was expended from this fund. Even the smallest businesses in Hawaii seem to have been able to comply with the employer mandate without undue hardship.

Hawaii's experience with an employer mandate for health insurance suggests that this method of extending health insurance to all workers and their families holds substantial promise. The year after PPHCA was enacted, however, the federal government passed the Employee Retirement Income Security Act (ERISA), which forbids other states from establishing new employer mandates. As a result, for many years the success of the Hawaii experiment was not duplicated elsewhere in the country.

## EXPANDING HEALTH INSURANCE COVERAGE IN MASSACHUSETTS: THE INDIVIDUAL MANDATE

Largely as a consequence of the restrictions imposed on state governments by ERISA, no other state followed Hawaii's lead in attempting to reduce the number of uninsured through the imposition of an employer mandate. In 2006, however, Massachusetts addressed the issue of the rising number of uninsured through another mechanism: the individual mandate.

In 1997, Massachusetts was granted a Section 1115 Medicaid waiver by the federal government, which provided added federal funding to allow Massachusetts to expand access to care to the uninsured. The extra funds provided by the waiver—more than $300 million per year—were scheduled to expire in 2006. With the help of Senator Ted Kennedy, Massachusetts was able to negotiate an agreement with the federal government. If, by July 1, 2006, Massachusetts was able to enact a statewide program of a near-universal coverage, the state could keep the extra federal funding to assist in paying for the expanded coverage. After a series of intense negotiations involving not only the governor and the legislature but private interests as well, in April 2006 the legislature approved and the governor signed the Massachusetts Health Care Reform Plan.

The central element of the law was a new requirement that, by July 1, 2007, all adults in Massachusetts must acquire health insurance. Those who did not meet this requirement would be assessed a penalty on their yearly tax return. In the first year of the program the penalty for individual noncompliance was fairly small: $219. In subsequent years the penalty was to increase to approximately half the price of the lowest-price health plan available, up to a maximum of $912 per year in 2008. In certain circumstances, individuals who could provide documentation that they could not afford to purchase coverage were exempted from this penalty.

In addition to establishing a mandate that individuals who can afford to must acquire health insurance, the new law gave employers with eleven or more employees a choice: either provide health insurance to employees, or contribute what was referred to as a "fair share" contribution to the state (initially $295 per employee per year). The state would use these funds as part of a pool to provide subsidized health insurance to those unable to obtain coverage through their work. Thus, the state did not technically mandate that employers provide health insurance to their workers. Rather, it gave employers a choice of paying a new fee to the government or providing coverage to workers in lieu of the fee.

Some in Massachusetts were concerned that the state's imposition of an individual mandate and "fair share" obligation for employers would be seen as violating ERISA. Most analysts concur, however, that the approach adopted by Massachusetts does not violate ERISA. During the early years of the plan no serious legal challenge was brought against it based on ERISA violations.

Realizing that most of the uninsured were in low-income families or worked for employers who did not offer coverage, Massachusetts established two new programs to make coverage available to these groups. The first was referred to as Commonwealth Care. Under this plan, individuals and families with incomes below 300 percent of the federal poverty level (FPL) were eligible to enroll in one of a series of managed care plans that had previously contracted to provide care to those eligible for MassHealth, Massachusetts's Medicaid program. Those in Commonwealth Care would not technically be enrolled in Medicaid. Instead, they were provided a sliding-scale subsidy to enroll in the plan directly. For those with incomes below 150 percent of the FPL, the state provided a full subsidy to cover the price of health coverage in one of the plans. Those with incomes between 150 and 300 percent of the FPL paid an increasing share of the premium.

For those residents with incomes greater than 300 percent of the FPL but without health insurance coverage from their work, Massachusetts established the Commonwealth Health Connector. The Health Connector was modeled after the Health Insurance Purchasing Cooperative, described in Chapter 5. Managed by a Connector Board, the Connector arranged for several insurance companies in the state to make their plans available for purchase by individuals or small businesses. Each plan offered through the Connector first had to be reviewed and approved by the Connector Board. Beginning in May 2007, the approved plans were available for purchase by the public. Thus, everyone in Massachusetts who lacked health insurance yet had an income above 300 percent of the FPL had a single place to go to review and select among available health insurance options, thereby satisfying the requirements of the state's individual mandate.

By January 2008, 6 months after the imposition of the individual mandate and the "fair share" requirement for employers, 316,000 formerly uninsured residents had acquired coverage. This number represented nearly half of the estimated 650,000 uninsured residents in 2006, the year before the law went into effect (The Commonwealth Fund 2008). More than half of these newly insured residents were enrolled in Commonwealth Care. By 2009, 97.3 percent of Massachusetts residents were covered by some form of health insurance that met minimum state standards of coverage, giving Massachusetts by far the lowest rate of uninsured residents of any state (Weissman and Bigby 2009).

While the Massachusetts Health Care Reform Plan was largely successful in its principal goal of bringing near-universal health insurance coverage to residents of the state, there was another problem the plan was not able to address successfully: the rising cost of health care. While access to health insurance in Massachusetts expanded markedly between 2006 and 2009, the cost of health care continued to increase rapidly. To study the issue, Massachusetts created a Special Commission on the Health Care Payment System. In July 2009, the commission reported its findings (Massachusetts Department of Health and Human Services 2009). The commission's report underscored that per capita health care costs in Massachusetts, already among the highest in the country, would continue to grow substantially faster than per capita gross domestic product (GDP). With the ongoing obligation to subsidize the cost of health insurance for large numbers of state residents, the government of Massachusetts would face growing budgetary pressures. The impact on state revenues of the recession of 2008–9 only exacerbated those pressures.

Realizing that Massachusetts's commitment to near-universal coverage for its residents would be seriously threatened by continuing escalation in the cost of care, the Massachusetts legislature charged the Special Commission with recommending alternative means of constraining rising health care costs. In its report, the commission was explicit about what it saw as the root cause of rising health care costs, and what it saw as the best means of constraining those costs.

> It is widely recognized that the current fee-for-service health care payment system is a primary contributor to the problem of escalating costs and pervasive problems of uneven quality . . . To promote safe, timely, efficient, effective, equitable, patient-centered care, and thereby reduce growth and levels of per capita health care spending, the Special Commission recommends that global payments with adjustments to reward provision of accessible and high quality care become the predominant form of payment to providers in Massachusetts. (pp. 4, 10)

As described by Robert Steinbrook in the *New England Journal of Medicine*, Massachusetts's Special Commission "proposed that Massachusetts effectively end fee-for-service medicine . . . and replace it with a system of global payments" (Steinbrook 2009, p. 1026).

The commission recommended that the state encourage health care providers to create accountable care organizations (ACOs) that are "composed of hospitals, physicians and/or other clinician and non-clinician providers working as a team to manage both the provision and coordination of care for the full range of services that patients are expected to need" (Massachusetts Department of Health and Human Services 2009, p. 53). An ACO would then receive a risk-adjusted payment that would "prospectively compensate providers for all or most of the care that their patients may require over a contract period, such as a month or year" (p. 8). The commission was careful to distinguish its concept of global payments from the concept of capitation payment adopted in the 1990s as part of the managed care revolution. (See Chapter 5.) To prevent some of the abuses that developed as part of the earlier capitation system, global payments would be coupled with a requirement of electronic health records that would permit ongoing monitoring of the quality of care provided and of patients' access to care.

The Massachusetts legislature has not yet followed through with the commission's recommendations, so Massachusetts continues to struggle to find a way to pay for its expansion of health insurance. As discussed below, many aspects of ACA may relieve Massachusetts of some of its responsibility for subsidizing the acquisition of health insurance by lower-income residents.

There is an additional aspect of the impact of Massachusetts's health insurance reform that warrants acknowledgment. While overall access to care has been substantially increased by the expansion of health insurance coverage, a growing segment of Massachusetts residents is finding it difficult to find a physician who will accept them into their practice. Data from surveys of Massachusetts residents from 2008 and 2009 found growing numbers of people "who reported difficulties obtaining care because a provider was not accepting patients—either not accepting new patients, or not accepting patients with the respondent's type of insurance" (Long and Stockley 2010, p. 1238). As discussed in more detail in the following chapter, access to health insurance is not synonymous with access to health care. In order to provide access to care for those with newly acquired insurance coverage, Massachusetts is focusing continued attention on expanding the availability of primary care services in the state.

## PREDICTING THE FUTURE NUMBERS OF UNINSURED PEOPLE

The Office of the Actuary at the federal Centers for Medicare and Medicaid Services reported that in 2009 national health care expenditures grew by 5.8 percent, to a total of $2.5 trillion (Sisko et al. 2010). This translated into 17.3 percent of GDP. While the rise to 17.3 percent of GDP was worrisome, it was not wholly unexpected. In addition to reporting historical data about health care costs, the federal government also publishes yearly predictions about the direction health care expenditures will take in the next ten years.

Whereas the U.S. Department of Health and Human Services (HHS) reports data on health care costs, the U.S. Census Bureau reports data on the number of Americans who are uninsured. In August 2010, the Census Bureau reported that the proportion of the U.S. population that was uninsured grew from 15.4 percent in 2008 to 16.7 percent in 2009. While the Census Bureau does not report future projections of the number of uninsured, it does report historical data going back to 1987—when the uninsured made up 12.9 percent of the population.

While the two rates—the percentage of GDP going to health care and the percentage of the population that is uninsured—are reported by different federal agencies at different times of the year, it is useful to compare historical trends in these two indicators. Figure 11.7 combines data about the rising numbers of uninsured from Figure 11.1 with data about rising health care costs for the same time period. These two percentages seem to follow nearly identical trajectories. Except for the period 1995–2000, when the number of uninsured remained high despite a temporary flattening in the health care costs curve associated with the shift to managed care, the two rates seem to follow similar patterns. It should not be surprising that they do, as the economic forces that affect one also affect the other. Health care costs as a percent of GDP will rise or fall based on changes in either the numerator (aggregate health care costs) or the denominator (GDP) of the fraction. When aggregate health care costs go up, many at the margins of the health insurance market lose coverage, independent of what is happening to GDP. Correspondingly, a falling GDP indicates a shrinking economy, with falling levels of employment and concomitant losses in employment-based insurance coverage. It makes sense that health insurance rates and health insurance costs should be closely related. (See Chernew, Cutler, and Keenan 2005 and Gilmer and Kronick 2005 for a more mathematical discussion of this fundamental principle of U.S. health policy.)

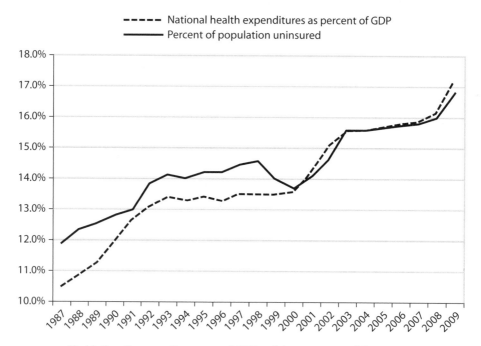

FIGURE 11.7. Health Care Costs as a Percentage of GDP and the Percentage of the Population that Is Uninsured, 1987–2009. *Sources:* Data from U.S. Centers for Medicare and Medicaid Services; U.S. Census Bureau

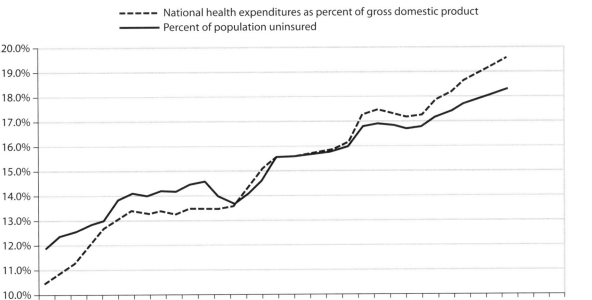

National health expenditures as percent of gross domestic product
Percent of population uninsured

FIGURE 11.8. Predicting Future Uninsured Rates Using Current Projections of Future Health Care Costs. *Sources*: Data from U.S. Department of Health and Human Services, historical (1987–2009) and projected (2010–19) costs; U.S. Census Bureau, historical rates of the uninsured through 2009

If health insurance costs and uninsured rates are so highly correlated, it might make sense to use the federal government's existing predictions about the change in health care costs over the next decade to estimate the percentage of the population that will be uninsured a decade from now. Figure 11.8 does this.

Between 1987 and 2009, the average ratio of the yearly rise in the percentage of the population without health insurance to the rise in the percentage of GDP going to health care was 0.69. Based on the assumption that this ratio will be about the same, on average, over the next ten years as it has been over the previous twenty years, we are able to gain a rough idea of the proportion of the U.S. population that would be without health insurance in 2019 if the Affordable Care Act (ACA) had not been passed: 18.5 percent. Using Census Bureau projections of future population growth, we find that, if ACA had not been enacted, 62 million Americans would have been uninsured in 2019.

## SUMMARY

While nearly 84 percent of the U.S. population had some form of health insurance in 2009, 16.7 percent—more than 50 million people—went without health insurance throughout the year. This number has been growing steadily for more than a decade and is projected to continue to grow for the next decade.

The problem of the uninsured has historically been a problem principally among young, working families. With Medicare providing near-universal coverage for seniors and Medicaid and S-CHIP covering many of the poorest people in our country, relatively few of the uninsured have an income below the FPL. In a substantial majority of uninsured families, there is at least one adult who is working on a regular basis.

While we have adopted an employment-based system for providing health insurance for most Americans, that system tends to break down for low-wage workers, especially those working in small firms. Whereas most high-wage workers in larger firms have health insurance provided as a fringe benefit from work, small employers find it economically unfeasible to extend that coverage to their lower-wage workers. As low-wage workers are disproportionately drawn from minority racial and ethnic groups, it is not surprising that these groups are disproportionately uninsured as well.

One approach to reducing the number of the uninsured has been to require employers to provide health insurance to all their workers. While federal law constrains the ability of individual states to adopt this approach, Hawaii's law requiring employers to provide health insurance predates the federal policy. Hawaii's "employer mandate" policy has worked very well in reducing the number of uninsured without placing an undue economic burden on employers.

In contrast to Hawaii's experience, Massachusetts has relied on creating an individual mandate that requires nearly all residents of the state either to obtain health insurance or to pay a penalty. To support this expansion among low-income families, Massachusetts provides a range of subsidies to pay for health insurance, with full subsidies for those under 150 percent of the FPL and a sliding-scale subsidy for those with incomes between 150 and 300 percent of the FPL. For those with incomes over 300 percent of the FPL who do not receive health insurance from their employer, Massachusetts has organized a Health Connector—an organized exchange where individuals can select coverage from a range of alternatives made available by health insurers. In response to continuing increases in the cost of care, Massachusetts is encouraging providers to organize ACOs to take responsibility for providing comprehensive, high-quality care on a prepaid basis.

## COVERING THE UNINSURED UNDER THE AFFORDABLE CARE ACT

Throughout the development and the enactment of ACA, its supporters had one principal goal in mind: expanding health insurance coverage to the uninsured. While the debate over how this expansion would be accomplished was often intense, most of those opposing the final version of ACA had earlier supported at least some form of expansion of coverage to reduce the number of uninsured. Accordingly, the core elements of ACA focus on this issue.

In order to reduce the number of uninsured Americans, ACA does the following.

1. As described in Chapter 7, ACA extends Medicaid coverage to all citizens and permanent residents with incomes below 133 percent of the FPL.

2. ACA requires that, beginning in 2014, all citizens and permanent residents with incomes at or above 133 percent of the FPL either obtain private health insurance coverage or pay a tax penalty not to exceed 2.5 percent of taxable income.

3. For those with incomes between 133 and 400 percent of the FPL who do not receive health insurance from their employer, ACA provides a tax credit to subsidize the purchase of private coverage. The credit will cap the amount an individual or family must pay for coverage, starting with a cap of 2 percent of income for those at 133 percent of the FPL and increasing to a cap of 9.5 percent of income for those at 400 percent of the FPL.

4. In order to assure that affordable, private health insurance coverage is available to all those who wish to purchase it, ACA requires states to establish health benefit exchanges (HBEs), operated either by the state government or by a nonprofit organization. Each exchange will offer at least two options for health insurance coverage, one of which must be offered by a nonprofit insurer. Insurers will be able to offer different predefined levels of care for different premiums. For those enrollees with incomes below 400 percent of the FPL, the plans must cap out-of-pocket expenses according to a predefined schedule. States are permitted to collaborate to form regional exchanges. In states failing to establish an exchange before 2014, the federal government will create and manage the exchange.

5. ACA requires employers with more than fifty employees either to provide coverage for employees or to pay a penalty of $2,000 for each employee without coverage from work who instead acquires coverage from the state insurance exchange. ACA exempts employers with fifty or fewer employees from this requirement, and also exempts larger employers from paying the penalty on the first thirty employees who obtain coverage from an exchange.

It should not be difficult to notice the similarity between the steps ACA takes to expand health insurance coverage and the steps the Massachusetts Health Care Reform Plan took to expand coverage. Both rely on an individual mandate coupled with penalties for employers not offering coverage, with subsidized coverage for those below certain incomes who purchase care privately and a publicly organized exchange for the acquisition of coverage. It was the intent of those developing ACA to use the Massachusetts plan as a model.

Some policies adopted by ACA differ from the Massachusetts plan. For example, ACA places a complex set of restrictions on the coverage of abortion under plans offered through the state exchanges. In addition, ACA relies on existing Medicaid programs for coverage for those with incomes below 133 percent of the FPL who previously were uninsured, while Massachusetts provides private coverage for those below 150 percent of the FPL without previous coverage. ACA also imposes additional restrictions on how insurers can set premiums.

Based on estimates developed by the Congressional Budget Office at the time of the enactment of ACA, there is general agreement that the steps outlined above will extend health insurance coverage to an additional 32 million Americans by the time it is fully implemented in 2019. Approximately half of these newly insured will be covered through the expansion of Medicaid, with the other half covered either through expansion of employer-provided coverage or through the newly established health insurance exchanges.

It is important to recall, however, that Massachusetts was successful in expanding coverage to most of the uninsured in the state, but that many of those with newly acquired coverage had difficulty finding a doctor or other provider willing to take them as patients. I explore this issue in more depth in the following chapter.

We must also recall that Massachusetts continues to experience continued increases in the cost of health care that make the expansion of coverage unsustainable without fundamental reform in the way providers are paid. While ACA addresses the issue of expanding coverage to the uninsured, there is little in ACA that will slow the continued rise in the cost of health care in the foreseeable future. As described above, the Office of the Actuary at the federal Centers for Medicare and Medicaid Services has estimated that, as a result of ACA, national health spending will grow from 17.3 percent of GDP in 2009 to 19.6 percent of GDP in 2019. Previous estimates that did not include the effects of ACA had projected a spending level of 19.3 percent of GDP in 2019. ACA will have a relatively small impact on the long-term growth in health care spending, leaving the sustainability of the current health care system and its underlying financing structure open to serious question. I discuss this issue in more depth in the final chapter of this book.

# 12

# Factors Other Than Health Insurance That Impede Access to Health Care

As discussed in Chapter 11, the growing number of Americans with no health insurance has for years been a major national problem. The principal focus of the Affordable Care Act (ACA) is to reduce the number of Americans without health insurance. It is important, however, to note that simply having health insurance does not always assure full access to care. As complex as the issue of universal health insurance is, the issue of universal access is even more so.

A number of barriers to gaining access to high-quality care have little to do with whether or not a person has health insurance. These barriers generally stem from forces within the organizational environment of the health care delivery system or within the broader social system itself. In this chapter, I examine a number of these forces and describe how they create barriers to full access to health care.

## TYPE OF HEALTH INSURANCE COVERAGE AND ACCESS TO CARE FOR URGENT PROBLEMS

Certain types of urgent medical problems, once diagnosed, have a well-defined treatment. Acute appendicitis is one such problem. While it is not always easy to diagnosis appendicitis, once diagnosed the treatment is clear: appendectomy (the surgical removal of the appendix). In addition, it is well known that delays in the diagnosis and treatment of appendicitis will increase the chances of developing a potentially serious complication: rupture of the appendix.

A study reported by Braveman et al. in 1994 asked, Will the type of insurance a patient has affect the chances of developing a ruptured appendix for those patients with acute appendicitis? Appendicitis was studied because

- it is an illnesses that is apparently not affected by social or lifestyle factors, and thus it can be expected to occur with approximately equal frequency in different socioeconomic groups
- once diagnosed, it is promptly treated in almost all cases, regardless of insurance status

The key variable in whether a patient will have his or her appendix removed before it ruptures is how easily the patient is able to obtain access to care. The study looked at this question in four groups, three of which had health insurance coverage:

1. Patients with traditional fee-for-service insurance
2. Patients with insurance through a health maintenance organization (HMO)
3. Patients on Medicaid
4. Patients with no health insurance

The study had two important findings:

1. Patients with either Medicaid or no insurance had approximately a 50 percent greater risk of developing a ruptured appendix than patients with HMO coverage.
2. Patients with fee-for-service insurance were at a 20 percent greater risk of developing a ruptured appendix than those with HMO coverage.

For patients with Medicaid, it appears that the barriers to obtaining care for acute appendicitis are similar to the barriers faced by patients with no insurance at all. Lacking a regular source of care, both populations frequently have to rely on the emergency room of large, often crowded hospitals to obtain care for urgent problems. The study by Tang and colleagues (2010), described in Chapter 7, confirmed the continuing pressure on emergency rooms from patients covered by Medicaid, but nonetheless still having to rely on busy hospital emergency rooms to obtain access to care, even routine care. Between 1999 and 2007, the rate at which Medicaid patients sought care from emergency rooms increased by 37 percent. In many areas of the country, for those on Medicaid simply having health insurance does little to assure prompt access to health care.

It is interesting, though, that in the Braveman study the patients with traditional, fee-for-service insurance also faced an increased chance of developing a ruptured appendix when compared to HMO patients. Though the difference between fee-for-service and HMO patients was smaller than that between Medicaid patients and HMO patients, it was nonetheless substantial. Why would patients with full insurance have problems obtaining prompt diagnosis and treatment for acute appendicitis? Although the study did not definitively answer this question, there are two possible explanations:

1. Patients with fee-for-service insurance do not automatically have a physician available to them as part of their insurance. They still have to seek out a physician on their own. Patients with full insurance but no established physician can face delays in obtaining care and may end up finding care in the emergency room. By comparison, patients with HMO insurance are given a list of providers from which to choose, and they are often required to select a primary care physician at the time of their enrollment. Having a previously identified provider can facilitate obtaining care in an urgent situation.

2. Fee-for-service insurance often involves deductibles and co-payments that the patient must pay. These out-of-pocket expenses are typically higher for fee-for-service patients than for patients with HMO coverage and, as a result, may lead to patients delaying necessary care.

> **CONCEPT 12.1**
>
> For patients with health insurance coverage, the type of insurance may affect the accessibility of care, with potential adverse health consequences.

In the following sections, I will look more closely at the way out-of-pocket expenses for health care can affect access to care, and the effect of Medicaid coverage on access to care.

## THE EFFECT OF OUT-OF-POCKET EXPENSES ON THE RATE AT WHICH PATIENTS ACCESS CARE

The RAND health insurance experiment, conducted in the 1970s and 1980s, looked closely at the question of how the amount a patient has to pay out of pocket to obtain care will affect the frequency with which the patient seeks care. This study demonstrated an association between the amount a patient must pay and the frequency with which the patient will obtain care (Newhouse et al. 1981). The study looked at people who were randomly assigned to one of four different insurance plans, each with a different level of payment required from the patient:

1. The patient pays nothing out of pocket.
2. The patient pays 25 percent of the first $4,000.
3. The patient pays 50 percent of the first $2,000.
4. The patient pays 95 percent of the first $1,053.

The percentage of the cost that the patient must pay is called the "co-insurance rate." In plans 2–4, the patient had a yearly cap of $1,000 in out-of-pocket expenditures. After that amount, all additional care was 100 percent covered. Table 12.1 shows the results of this study, comparing the frequency with which the patient visited the doctor and the overall cost of care for different co-insurance rates.

It can be seen that the amount of co-insurance a patient faces will affect both the fre-

Table 12.1. Results from the Rand Health Insurance Experiment Showing the Effect of Co-insurance on the Use of Services and the Average Annual Cost of Health Care

| Level of Insurance | Doctor's Office Visits per Year | Average Annual Cost of Care |
|---|---|---|
| Free care | 5.4 | $401 |
| 25 percent co-insurance | 4.4 | $346 |
| 50 percent co-insurance | 3.2 | $328 |
| 95 percent co-insurance | 3.7 | $254 |

quency with which the patient visits the doctor and the overall cost of care (including both doctor care and hospital care) for that patient. Patients with free care visited the doctor 23 percent more often than those with 25 percent co-insurance and 69 percent more than patients with 50 percent co-insurance.

These findings raise the question, Will co-insurance prevent patients from seeking out needed care? The researchers looked at the types of outpatient visits and hospitalizations the different groups made, using a panel of experts to categorize the care received (or forgone) as necessary or unnecessary. They found that those with higher co-insurance had fewer visits and hospitalizations characterized as "necessary" as well as those characterized as "unnecessary." From this study, we can conclude that when a patient is responsible for paying for part of the cost of care, he or she is less likely to use that care. This association applies to necessary care as well as to unnecessary care.

> **CONCEPT 12.2**
>
> When a patient is responsible for paying for part of the cost of care, he or she is less likely to use that care. A 25 percent co-insurance rate was associated with a 14 percent reduction in the overall cost of care. Having a 25 percent co-insurance rate was associated with a decrease in necessary care as well as a decrease in unnecessary care.

Based on the conclusion from the RAND health insurance experiment that people who are required to pay a substantial share of their initial health care costs end up using less health care, the George W. Bush administration adopted a policy of encouraging more individuals and families to shift to health insurance policies that included high deductibles, that is, that required patients to pay out-of-pocket all health care costs up to a certain limit. In order to encourage this model of health insurance, President Bush included in the Medicare Modernization Act (MMA) of 2003 two provisions that did two things: (1) a provision removing the cap on the number of Medicare beneficiaries who could establish medical savings accounts to supplement their Medicare coverage (see Chapter 6); and (2) a provision that granted those not on Medicare a tax exemption for funds set aside in a special savings account, either by an employee or his or her employer, to pay the employee's out-of-pocket medical expenses. The tax exemption was conditioned on the employee also enrolling in a health insurance plan with a high deductible amount. The minimum annual deductible required to qualify for this tax exemption was $1,000 for individuals and $2,000 for families. The accounts into which these funds are paid were referred to as "health savings accounts" (HSAs), while those intended for Medicare beneficiaries were referred to as "medical savings accounts" (MSAs).

The intent of this new policy was to encourage more employees to shift out of HMOs or other plans that had higher coverage and lower deductibles (and thus, it was believed, contributed to the rising cost of health care) and to enroll instead in a high-deductible health plan (HDHP). As reported in Chapter 5, by 2009, approximately 8 percent of employees who receive their health insurance through their work had opted for the HDHP/HSA option.

## THE EFFECT OF MEDICAID COVERAGE ON ACCESS TO PRIMARY CARE

In Chapter 7, we learned that people with Medicaid insurance may still have problems accessing care.

- Due to low reimbursement rates, only a minority of physicians have been will-ing to accept new Medicaid patients in their practice.
- In many communities, so few physicians are willing to see Medicaid patients that the only regular source of care is the hospital emergency room

In the Braveman et al. (1994) study discussed above, we also learned that

- Medicaid patients have difficulty accessing care for acute appendicitis, leading to a rate of ruptured appendix that is 50 percent greater than the rate in HMO patients

A 1994 study took a detailed look at the experience Medicaid patients face in trying to obtain medical care for common problems (Medicaid Access Study Group 1994). Researchers called a wide variety of private doctors' offices, hospital-based clinics, and community clinics in several locales. The callers posed as a Medicaid patient and asked to obtain care for a common, relatively minor type of complaint (low back pain, blad-der infection, sore throat). They asked if they could be seen for this problem, and if so, how quickly. The researchers let a few weeks go by, and then they called back many of these same offices and clinics, this time posing as someone with full private insurance. They asked for an appointment for the same problem as the Medicaid caller. They recorded how many of the physicians or clinics were willing to see them, and how soon they could be seen. The results are shown in Table 12.2.

Since 1994, when this study was done, a majority of Medicaid patients have been enrolled in managed care plans, reducing somewhat this barrier to access. A more re-cent study, conducted in a manner similar to the 1994 study, however, suggests that the problem of access to care for Medicaid recipients persists. Asplin et al. (2005) trained

Table 12.2. Percentage of Offices and Clinics That Offered Appointments
for Callers during the Study of Medicaid Access to Care

| | |
|---|---|
| Medicaid recipients | |
| Appointment available at any time | 44 |
| Appointment available within two days | 35 |
| Patient with private insurance | |
| Appointment available within two days | 60 |

*Source:* Data from Medicaid Access Study Group 1994.

graduate students to call clinics and doctors' offices, stating that they had recently been discharged from an emergency room and had been told by the ER doctor that they had a potentially serious medical problem that required medical attention within one week. The problems included pneumonia, severe high blood pressure, and possible ectopic pregnancy. The callers asked for an appointment to see a doctor within this recommended time frame. On a randomized basis, the callers would state that they had private health insurance, Medicaid, or no health insurance. The trained callers would then wait two weeks and call back the same clinic or office, this time stating that they had the opposite type of insurance (for example, if they had previously stated they had Medicaid or were uninsured, they would state on the second call that they had full private insurance).

For medical problems that had potentially serious consequences if not treated promptly, patients with private insurance were able to get an appointment for follow-up care within one week 64 percent of the time, whereas patients with Medicaid were able to get such an appointment 34 percent of the time. Callers who stated they were uninsured and could afford to pay only $20 on the day of the visit were able to get an appointment 25 percent of the time; uninsured callers who stated they would bring full payment in cash on the day of the visit were able to get an appointment 63 percent of the time.

It is important to appreciate that, even in the era of managed care, having Medicaid insurance still does not guarantee access to care. Any state or national policy proposal—for example, ACA—that seeks to extend health insurance coverage to those currently uninsured by expanding the Medicaid program will have to cope with this problem of access.

## RACIAL BARRIERS TO ACCESS TO CARE

Throughout much of the twentieth century, the United States maintained a health care system that, in many parts of the country, divided access to care along racial lines: the race of the patient as well as the race of the physician. There were separate hospitals for black patients and white patients. Even those physicians and clinics that agreed to treat both groups of patients often maintained separate waiting rooms for black and white patients. Separate medical schools were created to train black physicians. With the official sanctioning of national and local medical societies, fully qualified black physicians were prevented from joining the medical staff of white hospitals.

In the 1960s, as part of the civil rights movement and following landmark civil rights legislation, the federal government took action against this segregated system of care. Hospitals that maintained segregated treatment and medical staff policies were ineligible to obtain federal payment through the Medicare and Medicaid programs. Over the period of a few years, the segregated system of care was largely dismantled. Black patients and black doctors finally obtained access to previously all-white institutions.

The hope was that by desegregating the health care system our country could attain a level of care that, while still depending on a patient's ability to pay, otherwise treated all patients equally. Unfortunately, we have seen a continuing litany of evidence that we have not yet met this goal. One of the first studies that pointed to continuing racial barriers in access to care looked at the way in which patients receive care for heart attacks in the federal Veterans Affairs (VA) health system.

The VA health system operates a series of hospitals throughout the United States. Many of these hospitals are affiliated with academic medical centers. Eligibility for care depends on a patient having served in the U.S. armed forces and meeting certain income requirements. Once deemed eligible, any veteran may receive free medical care.

A study looked closely at the experience of male patients, all eligible for VA care, who came to a VA hospital in the years 1988–90 with a heart attack (Peterson et al. 1994). At that time, it was common practice at most hospitals, including VA hospitals, to consider all patients with an acute heart attack for a procedure called cardiac revascularization. Because a heart attack is caused by a blocked artery in the heart, using a surgical procedure to reopen the blocked artery can improve the patient's outcome. There are two principal types of revascularization procedure:

1. Angioplasty, in which a thin balloon is inserted into the blocked vessel, and by inflating the balloon, the vessel is reopened
2. Coronary artery bypass graft surgery (referred to as CABG), in which a section of blood vessel is taken from the patient's leg and is surgically implanted into the blocked vessel in a way that bypasses the blockage

Before either procedure is done, the patient undergoes cardiac catheterization, in which dye is injected directly into the arteries of the heart and X-rays are taken, showing the exact location and size of the blockage. The VA study examined whether black patients and white patients, all coming to a VA hospital with a heart attack, received different levels of treatment. After controlling for individual characteristics of the patients (age, other illness, etc.), the study came to the following conclusions:

- Blacks were 33 percent less likely than whites to undergo cardiac catheterization.
- Blacks were 42 percent less likely than whites to undergo angioplasty.
- Blacks were 54 percent less likely than whites to undergo CABG surgery.
- Blacks were 54 percent less likely than whites to undergo any type of revascularization procedure.

The study then went on to look at the likelihood a patient would survive his heart attack, examining whether the demonstrated differences in access to revascularization procedures were associated with differences in survival. It came to some interesting conclusions:

> **CONCEPT 12.3**
>
> Among male patients who came to a VA hospital for treatment of a heart attack, blacks were significantly less likely than whites to receive aggressive care involving revascularization. While the lower rate of revascularization did not affect long-term survival, it did result in a lower quality of life for black patients.

- In the first thirty days after the heart attack, survival among black patients was significantly *higher* than among white patients.
- At one year and two years after the heart attack, there was no difference in survival among whites and blacks.
- When one looked at the quality of life for patients who did survive the heart attack, surviving black patients had more chest pain and a lower overall quality of life than white patients.

Since the VA heart study was published, a number of additional studies have been reported about racial differences in access to care. These papers paint a disturbing picture of continuing racial differences in access. Among the findings are the following:

- Black patients with heart disease and other serious health problems receive less aggressive and lower-quality care, even after taking into account the type of insurance the patient has (Kahn et al. 1994; Ayanian et al. 1999b).
- Black patients with early-stage lung cancer (a stage at which patients have a higher chance of cure if treated appropriately) are treated less aggressively, with lower rates of surgery than comparable white patients (Bach et al. 1999).
- Black patients with kidney failure who are receiving regular kidney dialysis (thus being automatically eligible for Medicare insurance coverage) are referred less often than white patients for consideration of kidney transplantation (Ayanian et al. 1999a).
- Despite a higher incidence among the black population of a form of bone marrow cancer called multiple myeloma, blacks with the disease receive bone marrow transplantation less often than whites, even though the evidence shows that this treatment substantially prolongs survival (Boyce 2000).

- Both black patients (Todd et al. 2000) and Hispanic patients (Todd, Samaroo, and Hoffman 1993) who receive emergency treatment for broken bones receive less pain medication while in the emergency room than white patients with similarly broken bones.

The question arises as to whether other racial and ethnic minorities face the same disadvantages as blacks in obtaining full and equal access to care. Fewer studies have been done looking at Hispanics, Native Americans, Asians, and other groups, so we do not fully know the answer to this question. Future research will need to be done to understand whether racially based differences in access to care also exist for other ethnic groups.

Decades after the federally mandated integration of health care facilities in this country, the issue of racial disparities in our medical care system persists. Why do black patients receive less access to medical care than white patients, even after taking into account economic differences and differences in insurance coverage? The Institute of Medicine of the National Academy of Sciences—one of the most respected and prestigious scientific groups in the country—attempted to answer this question. They convened a national panel of experts from a variety of disciplines, and they asked this panel to review the scientific evidence pertaining to racial disparities in access to medical care that are not based on economic or insurance differences. The panel reviewed several hundred published research reports and, in its published report in 2003 (Smedley, Sith, and Nelson 2003), concluded that three basic factors contribute to these ongoing disparities:

> **CONCEPT 12.4**
>
> For a variety of serious medical conditions and in a variety of settings and geographic locations, black patients receive less aggressive and lower-quality medical care than white patients with the same disease, even after taking into account the type of insurance the patient has.

1. Factors pertaining to the patient's approach to medical care, including issues such as personal preferences, mistrust of the system, and refusal of recommended treatment
2. Factors pertaining to the health care system, such as language barriers, cultural barriers, or a lack of coordination of care
3. Factors pertaining to the physician, such as the application of racial stereotypes and the effects of racial bias, either conscious or unconscious

The Institute of Medicine report generated quite a controversy. Could it be that physicians in this country are biased in the way they approach patients from differing racial groups? Some were incensed at the accusation that physicians in the United States continued to exhibit racial bias, pointing instead to decades of efforts to strip bias from the health care system. Others responded that bias continues to pervade U.S. health care, only in ways that are less obvious than historical forms of explicit racial discrimination.

The question of racial bias raises important ethical issues yet often triggers powerful emotional responses. This dilemma is not unique to medical care. Whether in housing, employment, education, or health care, the history of racial discrimination in the United States evokes memories of reprehensible behavior on the part of individuals and governments, often involving hatred and open hostility toward blacks and other minorities. The available evidence suggests, however, that intentional, explicit racism of this type is probably not the most likely explanation of the widespread racial differences we continue to see in treatment and outcomes. Approaching racial bias as a single, uniform phenomenon inappropriately simplifies what is a complex, multifaceted set of psychological mechanisms.

Racial bias can exist and exert its effects on many levels and in many ways, even in people who would honestly be horrified to have racist beliefs attributed to them. Hatred and overt bigotry represent only one type of bias, although this form of bias is what most people think of when the issue is discussed. We can identify other mechanisms that do not involve conscious racism but that nonetheless can lead to differences in the treatment of members of differing racial groups.

## Statistical Bias

Statistical bias involves an individual making a seemingly rational decision based on data about differences in behavior among racial groups. The example of the inner-city taxi driver illustrates statistical bias. In deciding whether to pick up a potential customer, is it justifiable to consider the race of the customer? Though the likelihood of robbery with any customer is exceedingly small, in many inner-city contexts the incidence of robbery is higher among black taxi customers than among white customers. Can we blame the driver who passes a black man hailing the cab and picks up a white man instead?

In choosing to pick up the white customer, the cab driver is assigning a stereotyped group characteristic to an individual perceived to be a member of that group. In this case, the perceived group is all blacks living in the area where the driver works; the pertinent group characteristic is the probability the customer will attempt to rob the driver. The driver has no information pertaining specifically to the potential customer other than racial appearance. Nonetheless, an argument can be made that, in the absence of other information, it is "rational" to assign the group characteristic to the individual.

A decision of this type, purportedly based on principles of rationality, can lead to unequal outcomes for racial groups. The unequal outcomes do not necessarily invalidate the decision. In some contexts, for certain public purposes, however, we can preclude the application of statistical inference based on racial groupings. In New York City, for example, cab drivers are enjoined from racial differentiation among customers based on the over-riding public need to have transportation by cab equally available to all.

In the medical care setting, statistical bias can exist in many ways. For example, many physicians will consider the potential for patient compliance in deciding whether to recommend certain types of procedures. Kidney specialists, for example, may believe that black patients are more likely than white patients to have difficulty in following the stringent medication schedule required to prevent rejection after a kidney transplant, and they may in response hesitate in referring those patients for transplantation. In attributing the likelihood of noncompliance to a patient based on racial grouping, the kidney specialist creates the same fundamental situation as the cab driver. The public value of treating people as individuals in matters as crucial as the availability of organ transplantation (or cardiac revascularization, or cancer treatment) over-rides the validity of assigning clinical characteristics to individual patients based on group inference.

## Unconscious Bias

There is considerable empirical evidence that even self-described color-blind individuals can manifest racially discriminatory attitudes of which they are unaware (Dovidio and Gaertner 1998). While these people openly endorse fair and equal treatment of all racial groups and disavow overt racism, they harbor some type of negative feelings or association toward blacks or other minorities. When interacting with someone of a different race, they may feel discomfort on an unconscious level. They may express this discomfort in subtle ways that can have the effect of disadvantaging minority groups. Despite their biased actions, people acting on this unconscious level are not racists, but rather they are acting based on cultural preferences learned long ago. (See Calman 2000 for a description of how this type of bias affected one patient in particular.)

A study in the medical literature concluded that physicians, without necessarily being conscious of personal bias, react differently to patients of different races (Van Ryn and Burke 2000). The study's authors evaluated the care given to 618 patients who had recently undergone cardiac catheterization, the procedure to test for blocked arteries in the heart. Of the patients in the study, 265 were black and 353 were white. All had recently completed a visit to their physician to discuss the results of their test. The researchers first surveyed the patients about their personal circumstances and about their perceptions of the visit with the physician. They then surveyed the physicians about their perceptions of the patients they had just seen. In comparing them to their white patients, the physicians responded that they perceived their black patients to be

- less likely to comply with medical advice
- less likely to participate in cardiac rehabilitation
- less likely to want a physically active lifestyle
- more likely to abuse drugs

The physicians also responded that, compared to their white patients, their black patients appeared less intelligent and less well educated—even when the patients' levels of education and income were the same. Studies such as this one led the Institute of Medicine researchers to conclude that "bias, stereotyping, prejudice, and clinical uncertainty on the part of healthcare providers may contribute to racial and ethnic disparities in healthcare . . . Stereotyping and biases may be conscious or unconscious, even among the well intentioned" (Smedley, Sith, and Nelson 2003, p. 178).

> **CONCEPT 12.5**
>
> Based on stereotypes and subtle, often unconscious bias, physicians may treat patients from certain minority ethnic groups differently from comparable white patients. While this bias may not necessarily constitute racism in the classical sense, it nonetheless can result in lower-quality care for black and other minority patients.

Another study looked at the attitudes of first- and second-year medical students toward patients seen on a video. It demonstrated that these students adopted a more aggressive approach to diagnosing a white, male patient with heart disease than a black, female patient, even though each was an actor reading the same script (Rathore et al. 2000). The unconscious bias that may lead to racially based differences in treatment appears to exist even before physicians receive their clinical training.

A series of articles was published in 2005, looking at changes over time in patterns of racial disparities in care. Each examined a different aspect of historical disparities. The authors found that

- for the period 1992–2001, there was "no evidence, either nationally or locally, that efforts to eliminate racial disparities in the use of high-cost surgical procedures were successful" (Jha et al. 2005a, p. 683)
- for the period 1994–2002, racial differences in access to therapy for clogged arteries in the heart (referred to as "reperfusion therapy") did not narrow (Vaccarino et al. 2005, p. 671)
- for the period 1997–2003, "racial disparities declined for most, but not all, HEDIS [Health Plan Employer Data and Information Set] measures we studied" (Trivedi et al. 2005, p. 692)

While the last study did find some reduction in racial disparities, the other two studies carried the disturbing message that, in the words of an accompanying editorial, "disparities between white patients and black patients have not substantially improved during the past decade or so" (Lurie 2005, p. 727).

In 2007, Blendon and colleagues reported results of a national survey administered to more than four thousand randomly selected adults, representing fourteen different racial or ethnic groups (Blendon et al. 2007).They found that two groups in particular reported continuing problems in accessing high-quality care. African Americans born in the United States and Native Americans were significantly more likely than other racial or ethnic groups (including African Americans born in Africa or the Caribbean) to report that they had received poor quality medical care because of their race or ethnicity. The same two groups were also more likely than other groups to report having experienced racial discrimination when they tried to obtain medical care.

The U.S. Agency for Healthcare Research and Quality (AHRQ) is charged by Congress with monitoring on an ongoing basis racial and ethnic disparities in access to and quality of health care. In their report for 2009, AHRQ found that "disparities related to race, ethnicity, and socioeconomic status still pervade the American health care system. Although varying in magnitude by condition and population, disparities are observed in almost all aspects of health care" (U.S. Agency for Healthcare Research and Quality 2009). The report went on to consider the extent to which differences in socioeconomic status, and associated differences in access to health insurance, might explain these continuing disparities. After using multivariate analysis to control for these factors, the report concluded that "uninsurance did not explain all differences in care related to race, ethnicity, and socioeconomic status, suggesting that mitigating uninsurance would greatly reduce but not completely eliminate disparities in care."

## LIVING CONDITIONS AND ACCESS TO CARE

It is well recognized that certain types of economic and living conditions can affect the health of individuals and social groups. Can living conditions also affect the way in which patients access care? This question can be answered, at least in part, by considering two separate studies looking at poor children with asthma.

The first study looked at differences in the way black children and white children with asthma use health services (Lozano, Connell, and Koepsell 1995). The study considered only children who were covered by Medicaid. All children in the study lived in the same city, had the same insurance coverage, and had access to the same hospitals and clinics. It found that black children went to the doctor's office less frequently yet had higher use of the emergency room and the hospital. Something other than insurance led to black children with asthma being sicker than their white counterparts, and to the parents of black children relying more on the emergency room for care than the doctor's office.

The second study (Rosenstreich et al. 1997) was ingenious. The researchers thought that there might be something in poor children's home environment, especially in the child's bedroom, that could cause an allergic reaction in some children, triggering an asthma attack. They took a group of poor children with asthma and tested them for allergy to the following three typical components of house dust:

- Cat dander
- Dust mites
- Cockroach droppings or body parts

The researchers then went into the bedroom of each of the children in the study and vacuumed up all the dust they could find. They took the dust to the laboratory and analyzed it for these same three components. The study found that those children who were both allergic to cockroaches and had cockroaches in their bedroom were significantly sicker from their asthma than other children. Neither children with bedroom cockroaches but no allergy to cockroaches nor children who were allergic to cockroaches but had no cockroaches in their bedroom had as much problem with their asthma as those children with both conditions. The combination of cat or dust mite allergy and cat dander or dust mites in the bedroom did not seem to affect children nearly as much.

It appears that cockroaches in the home may have a lot to do with the pattern asthma takes in poor children. While there were no data about the presence or absence of cockroaches in the bedrooms of the children in the first study, one has to wonder whether the differences in the pattern of illness and medical care for poor black and white children with asthma may have to do, at least in part, with differences in the living conditions of black and white families within the same city.

## OTHER FACTORS THAT MAY AFFECT ACCESS TO CARE
### Location

Regardless of their type of insurance, many patients in rural areas simply are not as close to health care facilities and thus face greater problems with access compared to patients in urban areas. The growing difficulty of rural hospitals to survive financially may lead to increased differences in access to care for urban and rural populations. Similarly, the relative scarcity of health care services and facilities in many inner-city areas and other low-income neighborhoods makes access difficult even for those with insurance. Problems with transportation, arranging child care, and taking take time off work to seek care may all contribute to geographic differences in access to care.

### Culture

Language frequently presents a barrier to obtaining care. Patients who do not have facility in speaking English may find it difficult to find a source of care. Realizing just how serious a barrier to access language could be, in 2000 the U.S. Department of Health and Human Services (HHS) published its National Standards on Culturally and

Table 12.3. National Standards on Culturally and Linguistically Appropriate Services in Health Care

| | |
|---|---|
| Standard 4 | Health care organizations must offer and provide language assistance services, including bilingual staff and interpreter services, at no cost to each patient/consumer with limited English proficiency at all points of contact, in a timely manner during all hours of operation. |
| Standard 5 | Health care organizations must provide to patients/consumers in their preferred language both verbal offers and written notices informing them of their right to receive language assistance services. |
| Standard 6 | Health care organizations must ensure the competence of language assistance provided to limited English-proficient patients/consumers by interpreters and bilingual staff. Family and friends should not be used to provide interpretation services (except on request by the patient/consumer). |
| Standard 7 | Health care organizations must make available easily understood patient-related materials and post signage in the language of the commonly encountered groups and/or groups represented in the service area. |

Source: U.S. Department of Health and Human Services, www.omhrc.gov/inetpub/wwwroot/clas/index.htm.
 Note: Standards 4, 5, 6, and 7 are currently mandated for all recipients of federal funds.

Linguistically Appropriate Services in Health Care, referred to as the CLAS standards (U.S. Department of Health and Human Services website). While ten of the fourteen standards are voluntary, all health care providers who receive federal funds are required to adhere to four of them pertaining to language access. These four are shown in Table 12.3.

Despite these efforts to improve language access, a study by Blendon and colleagues described above found persistent problems in communication between patients and physicians or other providers of care. The authors found that about 20 percent of Mexican, Puerto Rican, and Central/South Americans as well as Vietnamese Americans "felt that they received poor care because of their inability to speak English" (Blendon et al. 2007, p. 1446).

In addition to language barriers, cultural belief systems about the nature of illness may delay obtaining care. The book *The Spirit Catches You and You Fall Down* (Fadiman 1997) tells the story of an immigrant family from Asia whose child had a seizure disorder. The strikingly different perceptions about the nature of seizure disorders and how the disorder should be treated led to a serious schism between the family and the health care system, with unfortunate results.

Concerns about language and cultural barriers to health care access have led medical educators and government officials alike to call for better training of physicians and other health care providers in what has come to be called "cultural competence." A joint committee sponsored by the American Medical Association (AMA) and the Association of American Medical Colleges published a standard describing the level of cultural competence expected of physicians and students in U.S. medical schools: "The faculty and students must demonstrate an understanding of the manner in which people of diverse cultures and belief systems perceive health and illness and respond to various symptoms, diseases, and treatments. Medical students should learn to recognize and appropriately address gender and cultural biases in health care delivery, while considering first the health of the patient" (Association of American Medical Colleges 2005, p. 1).

## Diagnosis

Many physicians and other health care providers are hesitant to treat patients with AIDS. Similarly, many providers may feel uncomfortable treating people with chronic mental illness for their physical problems. Drug and alcohol abusers have numerous physical problems, yet many providers do not want to treat these patients, even if they are fully insured.

## ORGANIZATIONAL COMPLEXITY OF HEALTH CARE AS A BARRIER TO CARE

Our system of health care has moved from one based on fee-for-service care provided mostly by independent physicians in relatively small offices and groups to one in which care is provided, often on a capitation basis, by complex systems of care increasingly involving large groups of physicians. In many cases, physicians have shifted from being independent health care professionals to being employees of large systems of care. Unfortunately, these changes have contributed to a sense of breakdown in the relationship between the physician and the patient. Nowhere is this truer than at the primary care level.

Maintaining high quality in the delivery of primary care depends primarily on maintaining a strong relationship between the doctor and the patient. From a variety of research, it has been possible to identify factors that create a satisfying doctor-patient relationship from the perspective of the patient.

- *Humanistic behavior by physicians*
Patients need to have a sense that the doctor cares about them as a person and will take the time to listen to and understand their concerns.
- *Caring interpersonal interaction with other employees*
Patients need to be treated in a sensitive and courteous manner by the other employees who work with the doctor.
- *Continuity of care*
Patients need to develop an ongoing relationship with a physician they can count on seeing over a period of time.
- *Accessibility of care*
Patients need to be able to arrange to see their physician in a timely manner when the need arises and to be able to get through to the doctor's office easily by phone or e-mail.
- *Physician satisfaction with work conditions*
To be fully satisfied with their relationship with their physician, patients need to have a

sense that their physician is also satisfied in the work he or she does. There appears to be a strong correlation between patient satisfaction with the quality of their relationship with their physician and physician satisfaction with work conditions.

When you ask patients to describe what constitutes high quality in primary care, they will usually describe the factors listed above. The technical competence of the physician seems to be less important than the humanistic competence, at least at the level of primary care. Thus, patient satisfaction has emerged as a principal measure of primary care quality. While health care regulators and health care managers who measure quality may look at the technical competence of the physician and the extent to which the physician follows standard procedures, patients tend to look more at the strength of their personal relationship with their doctor.

Unfortunately, throughout the history of HMOs and other types of managed care delivery systems, reductions in the cost of care have often been at the expense of the quality of primary care as measured by patient satisfaction. Recall from Chapter 5 that, in both the RAND health insurance experiment (Table 5.2) and the Medical Outcomes Study (Table 5.3), HMOs score significantly lower than traditional fee-for-service systems on issues of the interpersonal nature of care, access to care, and continuity of care. As managed care delivery systems have become the rule rather than the exception, problems in patient satisfaction similar to those identified in these research studies have become more widespread. Looking at the changes in U.S. health care that have accompanied the managed care revolution, one group of authors concluded, "Our patients want high quality service and do not believe they receive it" (Kenagy, Berwick, and Shore 1999, p. 661).

Why would a change in the way health care is organized and financed lead to a decrease in the quality of the relationship between the patient and the physician? To answer this question, we need to understand some general principles of organizations theory (Barr 1995). Two characteristics of managed care are especially pertinent in this regard: (1) the increasing size of medical practice groups that typically comes with a shift to managed care and (2) the strengthening of management controls over certain aspects of medical practice.

In general, as an organization such as a medical practice group increases in size, it tends to become more complex internally. This complexity involves increasing task specialization, with individual workers performing a narrower range of duties. For example, while in a smaller medical practice one person may answer the phones, greet patients, and make appointments, in a larger group each task is done by a separate person. Task specialization often leads to increasingly complex paths of communication and to a more complex process for the customer (in this case, the patient) to interact with the organization.

Added to the increased organizational complexity associated with increased organizational size is the effect on the medical care process of strengthened management systems. The capitation method of payment for health care requires that someone manage the provision of care to stay within the established budget. No individual practitioner has a sufficiently broad perspective to keep track of how available resources are being spent and how the demand for care is being met. Managed care as it is often constructed requires a set of managers and management tools that are sufficiently removed from the care process to maintain direction and control of organizational activities.

A problem arises out of the potential conflict such a management structure creates when the purpose of the organization is to provide a human service such as health care. As with other human services, health care, particularly at the primary care level, is based on high-quality interaction between the provider and the patient. While cognizant of the need for strong provider-patient interaction, managers of a human service organization nonetheless tend to emphasize efficiency in the work of the organization. Efficiency in this context is often measured in units of production per unit of time (for example, patients seen per hour). It is difficult to provide high-quality human service while under pressure to be efficient.

This type of role conflict, however, often extends beyond the physician to encompass all types of employees who interact directly with patients. In general, these workers want to be able to provide good service to patients, having chosen a service occupation over other alternatives. They, too, often face pressure to work more quickly and efficiently, based on management's need to maintain the efficiency of overall organizational processes. This situation has the potential to lead to what is described as role conflict: the conflict faced by a worker caught between the patient's desire for good service and management's emphasis on efficient work. Role conflict often leads to decreased worker satisfaction and a tendency to become less sensitive to the needs of patients.

The sum of these effects, associated with the larger organizations that are increasingly typical of managed care, is the potential for a less satisfactory experience for patients. In the managed care setting, patients often encounter systems that tend to be more complex and impersonal than the smaller types of medical groups that predominated under the historical fee-for-service system. It is these characteristics of primary care in a managed care setting that have resulted in the spread of "concierge medicine," described in Chapter 8. The problems in patient satisfaction associated with large, complex managed care systems such as those studied in the RAND health insurance experiment and the Medical Outcomes Study may have been caused by these types of characteristics associated with large organizational systems.

> **CONCEPT 12.6**
>
> The large organizational systems that are typical of managed care tend to be more complex and more impersonal, and to have problems with patient satisfaction with care.

In my own research, I have looked at the extent to which factors within the organizational environment of a large primary care delivery system can affect patients' perceptions of the quality of their direct interaction with the physician (Barr, Vergun, and Barley 2000). Using a survey questionnaire that has been widely used in medical practice, we asked 291 patients who visited a primary care physician the following questions about their visit.

In terms of your satisfaction, how would you rate each of the following?

- The time spent with the doctor you saw
- The explanation of what was done for you
- The technical skills of the doctor you saw
- The personal manner of the doctor you saw

Each question was answered on a 5-point scale, ranging from excellent to poor. We also asked patients to rate the quality of their interaction with the nurses and receptionists they encountered during their visit, using the same 5-point scale. When we analyzed the data, we found that 20 percent of the variation in the way patients rated their satisfaction with their direct interaction with the physician could be explained by two main factors:

> **CONCEPT 12.7**
>
> Factors external to the doctor-patient interaction can exert a strong influence on patients' perceptions of the quality of the care they receive from their doctor.

1. How courteously they were treated by the nurses and receptionists
2. How long they had to wait at the doctor's office to see the doctor

Chang and colleagues published a study confirming that patients' perceptions of the quality of care they receive from their physician are powerfully affected by the quality of the communication between doctor and patient (Chang et al. 2006). In a study of 245 elderly patients receiving care from a managed care organization, using the same measure of patient satisfaction we used in our research, the authors measured patients' reported satisfaction with:

1. the technical quality of the care they received from their doctor
2. the quality of their communication with their doctor
3. the overall quality of the care they received

They found that patients' perceptions of the quality of the doctor-patient communication was significantly associated with their overall rating of the quality of care, while patients' perceptions of the technical quality of the physician's care were not associated with overall satisfaction with care.

> **CONCEPT 12.8**
>
> "Unfortunately, the track record of American health care, especially in recent times, does not support the belief that coverage is equivalent to access." (Friedman 1994, p. 1535)

## SUMMARY

This chapter has identified a variety of factors that can impede access to medical care. These factors have little to do with whether a patient does or does not have health insurance. Issues as divergent as geographic location, cultural norms, racial bias, and organizational complexity can get in the way of patients having full access to medical care.

Barriers in access to care can be as simple as how much the patient is expected to pay for care. Some insurance policies require patients to pay a substantial part of the cost of visits to a doctor. Research has shown that, in the face of these "co-payments," patients will sometimes avoid needed care.

The Medicaid program offers another example of impeded access to care for those with insurance. In many states, the Medicaid program pays physicians an amount that is substantially lower than their usual fee, with the result that many doctors refuse to treat Medicaid patients. Without an available source of primary care, many Medicaid patients have no choice but to go to hospital emergency rooms to obtain treatment for problems that would be more appropriately treated in a medical office or clinic.

Racial and ethnic factors also impair access to care, even for those with insurance. When language barriers exist or when providers have difficulty understanding or accepting a patient's cultural beliefs, access to care is often reduced. In addition, numerous research studies and government advisory reports have identified lingering racial bias on the part of physicians and other providers. While this bias is most likely unintended and often unconscious, it nonetheless creates one of the most important challenges to the medical profession and the health care system.

Finally, a growing emphasis on the provision of care by large health care organizations has created an added barrier to access. These organizations, by their very nature, are often more complex and less personal than smaller types of health care organization. Because access to care is one of the key components of quality of care, any discussion of new policies for the organization, financing, and delivery of care should include this important principle.

## THE AFFORDABLE CARE ACT AND ACCESS TO HEALTH CARE

As described in the previous chapter, one of the largest changes ACA will effect is an expansion of health insurance to an estimated 32 million people who previously were uninsured. Of these, approximately half, or 16 million, will gain coverage through an expansion of Medicaid. As described above, however, patients on Medicaid historically have had difficulty finding a physician or other source of regular care. Adding 16 million new enrollees to Medicaid will inevitably confront the issue of identifying providers willing to accept these new enrollees as regular patients. As described by Pitts and colleagues, "Today's primary care physicians are hard pressed to meet existing levels of demand, much less the pent-up needs of the estimated thirty-two million Americans who will soon acquire health insurance" (Pitts et al. 2010, p. 1626).

ACA has a number of new and expanded programs to address the issue of access to care for the newly insured. A first step ACA takes in this regard is to provide for an increase in reimbursement for primary care physicians who treat Medicaid patients. (In this context, "primary care" means care provided by a physician in family medicine, general internal medicine, or general pediatrics.) Effective January 1, 2013, these physicians will be paid at 100 percent of the rate paid by the Medicare program, with the incremental cost of the increased reimbursement paid by the federal government. The hope is that by equalizing the payment rate for Medicare patients and Medicaid patients, those primary care physicians who include Medicare patients in their practice will also be willing to include Medicaid patients.

Realizing that simply paying physicians more to treat Medicaid patients will not assure access to care, ACA also invests heavily in the expansions of nonprofit community health centers. Often referred to as federally qualified health centers (FQHCs), these clinics receive extra federal funding to treat Medicaid patients. ACA expands this funding, allowing FQHCs to hire additional personnel. In an effort to expand the number of physicians selecting a primary care specialty, ACA allocates additional funding to allow primary care residency programs to expand their training sites to include FQHCs and other community-based resources. ACA also expands support for the National Health Service Corps, the federal program that provides medical students with either scholarship support during medical school or educational loan repayment after medical school in return for spending a period of years in primary care practice in a rural or urban community that has a documented shortage of health manpower.

ACA also provides additional support for FQHCs to strengthen their organizational capacity to act as the "patient-centered medical home" (PCMH) (American Academy of Family Physicians, American Academy of Pediatrics, American College of Physicians, and American Osteopathic Association 2007) for their patients by developing a team-based approach to the management of chronic disease. Through expansion of electronic health records and the strengthening of connections with referral sources of specialty care, organizations adopting the PCMH model are expected to be able to increase the comprehensiveness of care, the continuity of care, and ultimately the quality of care for their patients.

While ACA does not address directly the issue of disparities in access to care based on a patient's race or ethnicity, it does impose on providers the responsibility for collecting data on the race, ethnicity, primary language, disability status, and similar demographic characteristics of the patients cared for. The federal government will then analyze this data to monitor racial and ethnic disparities in access to care.

# 13

# Key Policy Issues for Deciding the Direction of Health Care Reform

Three principles, each addressed earlier in this book, largely define the problem facing policy makers, health care managers, health care providers, and patients alike:

1. The cost of health care is higher in the United States than anywhere else in the world. After a period of relative stability in the 1990s, these costs are once again on the rise.

2. The American public has largely come to expect the highest-quality care available, regardless of the cost. Recent data have highlighted shortcomings in the quality of health care in the United States. Attempts to hold down the cost of care by constraining the availability of care have been met with resistance on many fronts.

3. The United States is the only industrialized country that does not guarantee access to health care for all its citizens. In the years leading up to the passage of the Affordable Care Act (ACA), an increasing segment of the U.S. population has lived without even basic health insurance, with negative consequences for access to care, quality of care, and health outcomes.

Each of these issues is pressing in its own right. Each deserves our attention. The conundrum of U.S. health care is that all three exist simultaneously and that attempting to remedy one will inevitably affect the others.

The problem of U.S. health care can be represented by an equilateral triangle. As illustrated in Figure 13.1, each point of the triangle represents one of these fundamental policy issues: cost, quality, or access. Imagine that the triangle is made of cardboard and that it is situated horizontally. It is possible to find a single point of balance for this

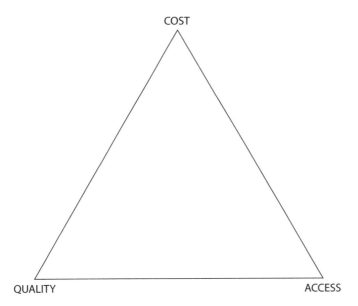

COST

QUALITY                         ACCESS

FIGURE 13.1. The Dilemma of U.S. Health Care

cardboard triangle. Once you find this point, it is possible to balance the triangle on the tip of your finger. So long as you leave the triangle alone, it will remain balanced. Now try to move one of the points of the triangle either up or down. Moving any one point in this manner will inevitably cause the other points to move.

The same is true for our health care system. As soon as we try to address one of the fundamental problems facing the system, we find that our proposed solution will affect the other parts of the system, often adversely. Consider the following:

- If we try to control the cost of care, we either will reduce the quality of the care by making fewer services available or will further decrease access to care by providing health insurance coverage to fewer people.
- If we increase access by expanding insurance coverage to those who are currently uninsured, as ACA is expected to do, we will further increase the overall cost of care. Attempts to improve access while also reducing cost will often be perceived as impairing quality.
- Attempts to improve the quality of care by introducing new treatments, technologies, or medications will add to the cost of the health care system, with the risk of driving more people into the ranks of the uninsured.

For decades, the U.S. health care system was like the triangle, perched on its balance point, albeit somewhat unsteadily. While serious problems remained in our system, we had achieved a rough equilibrium between the competing needs of cost, quality, and access. The extension of health insurance to the elderly and the poor through the

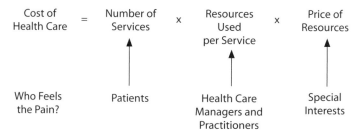

FIGURE 13.2. Health Care Costs Too Much: So, How Can You Reduce Costs? *Source:* Based on Fuchs 1993c

federal Medicare and Medicaid programs of the 1960s coincided with the beginnings of the explosion in medical technology. Attempts in the 1990s to hold down the cost of care through the expansion of HMOs led to the perception that quality was being impaired in ways that were unacceptable. Each point of our triangle had the forces of social and political change tugging at it. As a result, our health care system was thrown out of balance and today continues to wobble precariously.

How are we to gain control of our health care system in a way that adequately addresses and balances competing problems and needs? This is the dilemma of U.S. health care.

Victor Fuchs, one of the founders of the discipline of health economics, described our dilemma accurately and succinctly: "No pain, no gain" (Fuchs 1993a). He pointed out that the issue of health care costs can be seen as simple arithmetic, represented by the equation illustrated in Figure 13.2.

To calculate overall health care costs, one simply has to multiply the following three numbers:

*1. The number of services provided to patients*
This includes the number of office visits, the number of hospitalizations, the number of operations and other procedures, the number of tests, and the number of medications.

*2. The number of resources used in producing each service*
Here is where the issue of technology enters in so clearly. Does the doctor's office include all types of new, high-tech apparatus? Does the hospital include all the latest monitoring and diagnostic equipment? Will an operation incorporate laser scalpels and fiber optics? Will we rely on newer, high-priced medications over less expensive standbys?

*3. The price of the various resources used in providing services*
How much will we pay doctors for their care? How much will we pay hospitals? Will we allow the producers of medical equipment and pharmaceutical products to charge whatever the market will bear?

It is a simple fact of arithmetic that, to reduce the cost of health care, we will have to reduce at least one of the numbers appearing on the right side of the equation. The problem is, whenever we reduce one of these numbers, someone feels pain. When someone feels pain, he or she generally complains.

- If you try to reduce the number of services provided to patients, patients will perceive the reduction as a decrease in quality. Recent history has shown that, in response to constraints on the availability of services inherent to many types of health maintenance organizations (HMOs), patients turned both to legislators and to the courts to prevent the reduction in their perceived access to the care they wanted.

- If you try to reduce the intensity of the resources used in providing services, patients, providers, and producers alike will oppose the reductions. Patients often view the latest, high-tech treatment as the only acceptable alternative. Physicians frequently oppose constraints on the use of technology in providing service. Producers such as pharmaceutical companies and device manufacturers are often adamantly opposed to formal limitations on the way physicians use medications or devices.

- There have been numerous attempts to reduce the cost of care by reducing the amount we pay for specific services. Most recently, attempts at cost control have often been through limitations in the amount physicians and hospitals are paid for providing care. Both HMOs in the private market for care and government programs such as Medicare and Medicaid have reduced or restricted the amount they are willing to pay health care providers. These reductions have begun to have serious effects on many of these providers. In addition, a number of physician groups have responded to further reductions in reimbursement by refusing to see patients covered by these insurance plans.

A powerful social force acting against health care reform is the tremendous heterogeneity of American society. Often, gains by one segment of society are perceived as losses by another segment, and thus they are resisted. As the above equation illustrates, however, our need both to expand health care access and to contain costs will necessitate some form of limitations on the amount of health care we make available. Unfortunately, for those who currently have few limits on the amount of care available, any imposition of new limits will be seen as an unwarranted rationing of care. The very concept of rationing in health care seems somehow to be fundamentally un-American. Thus, in creating as part of ACA the Medicare Independent Payment Advisory Board and charging it with restraining Medicare spending in the future, Congress nonetheless mandated that any proposals for reducing future Medicare spending "shall not include any recommendation to ration health care" (ACA Section 2403).

## RATIONING HEALTH CARE: IS IT INEVITABLE?
## CAN IT BE ACCEPTABLE?

To understand the concept of rationing as it applies to health care, I will look first at the rationing of consumer goods that took place during World War II, and then at recent experiences the United States has had with explicit, federally sanctioned health care rationing: the rationing of flu shots and the rationing of health care to the poor as part of the Oregon Health Plan, discussed in Chapter 7.

### Rationing Consumer Goods during World War II

During World War II, certain foods and industrial raw materials were in scarce supply. These scarce resources were not enough both to supply the war effort and to meet the needs of the civilian population. Under government direction, these scarce resources were allocated on a prioritized basis. The military often had first priority. Those in the civilian population who were most in need came next (babies got milk; ambulances got tires). Finally, those resources still available were allocated on an even basis to those remaining. The system of rationing of scarce consumer goods was widely perceived to be both generally fair and in support of a crucial national goal. As such, the rationing received wide support.

> **CONCEPT 13.1**
>
> Rationing involves the prioritized allocation of scarce resources.

### Rationing Flu Shots

Each year, the federal government collaborates with private manufacturers to identify the strains of influenza most likely to strike the American public during the coming flu season. Flu shots have proven to be effective in reducing serious illness and death from the flu, especially in vulnerable populations such as frail elderly people. In 2004, the United States projected that 100 million doses of flu vaccine would be needed to provide adequate protection to the public. Unfortunately, one of the principal manufacturers of flu vaccine discovered serious problems with possible bacterial contamination of its vaccine, and the manufacturer was unable to supply the approximately 50 million doses that providers in the United States had ordered. It was too late in the season for other manufacturers to produce more vaccine. The country suddenly faced the prospect of going through a flu season with only half the number of flu shots it needed.

The shortage of flu shots received broad coverage in the press. A public consensus rapidly developed around how the available doses of vaccine would be distributed: to those who needed it most (DesRoches, Blendon, and Benson 2005). Few argued that flu shots should go to those willing to pay the most. For a commodity as necessary to the public's health as flu vaccine, it would be unethical to distribute that commodity on the basis of ability to pay rather than the basis of relative need. After extensive consul-

Table 13.1. Priority Groups Established by the Federal Government for
Influenza Vaccination at Times of Vaccine Shortage

| Priority Group | |
| --- | --- |
| 1A | Persons aged > 65 years with comorbid conditions<br>Residents of long-term care facilities |
| 1B | Persons aged 2–64 years with comorbid conditions<br>Persons aged > 65 years without comorbid conditions<br>Children aged 6–23 months<br>Pregnant women |
| 1C | Health care personnel<br>Household contacts and out-of-home caregivers of children<br>    aged < 6 months |
| 2 | Household contacts of children and adults at increased risk<br>    for influenza-related complications<br>Healthy persons aged 50–64 years |
| 3 | Persons aged 2–49 years without high-risk conditions |

*Source:* U.S. Centers for Disease Control and Prevention 2005.

tation, the federal government published the list shown in Table 13.1 that prioritized population subgroups by relative need.

The supply of flu vaccine in the United States remained both stable and adequate until a new flu strain showed up unexpectedly: H1N1 flu. In April 2009, two boys in California, one 10 years old and one 8 years old, were diagnosed with a new strain of the influenza virus that had never been identified before. Based on its unique genetic markings, the virus was named Influenza H1N1. As the two boys lived 150 miles apart and had never met, the federal Centers for Disease Control and Prevention (CDC) became quite concerned about the early signs of a more widespread outbreak of the new flu strain (Centers for Disease Control and Prevention 2010). Within two weeks of the initial identification of the new flu strain in these two boys, the CDC had identified the H1N1 virus in blood samples from several patients in Mexico who had become ill with influenza. Concerned that a new and potentially dangerous strain of the flu was spreading rapidly in North America, the CDC notified the World Health Organization (WHO), and on April 25 the director-general of WHO declared the 2009 H1N1 outbreak a "Public Health Emergency of International Concern." By June 2009, the WHO had relabeled the H1N1 outbreak as a "Global Pandemic."

The CDC immediately began working with vaccine manufacturers to produce enough vaccine to vaccinate a majority of Americans. It was clear, though, that it would take months to produce sufficient vaccine for all those who needed it. Accordingly, the CDC developed a prioritized list of those most at risk for serious outcomes from H1N1. This listing included pregnant women; household contacts and caregivers for children younger than 6 months of age; health care and emergency medical services personnel; children from 6 months through 18 years of age; young adults 19 through 24 years of age; and persons aged 25 through 64 years who had health conditions associated with higher risk of medical complications from influenza (Centers for Disease

CONCEPT 13.2

In the case of the 2004 shortage of flu vaccine and the 2009 shortage of H1N1 flu vaccine, the federal government and the American public agreed on the following fundamental ethical principle: in a situation of scarcity of a crucially important health care resource, that resource should be allocated on the basis of need rather than ability to pay.

Control and Prevention 2009). By October, the H1N1 vaccine began to become available, and was administered on a prioritized basis to those in these high-risk groups. Those at lesser risk were able to receive the vaccine only after the high-risk groups had been vaccinated. Supplies were carefully rationed, based upon relative need. There was widespread public support for this approach. The concept of making the vaccine preferentially available to those in a low-risk group who nonetheless were willing to pay a high price for it was never seriously considered.

Our experience with the 2004 vaccine shortage and the sudden need for H1N1 vaccine underscores a fundamental ethical principle, one the federal government and the American public have agreed on (at least in the case of flu vaccine). In a situation of scarcity of a crucially important health care resource, the scarce resource should be allocated on a prioritized basis based on relative need rather than ability to pay.

## Rationing Health Care for Poor People as Part of the Oregon Health Plan

The reasons behind and structure of the original Oregon Health Plan (OHP) are described in Chapter 7. In allocating health care services for poor adults in Oregon, the broadly representative Oregon Health Services Commission applied the same ethical principle as that used in distributing scarce flu shots. Figure 13.3 illustrates again the fundamental concept behind the plan.

Oregon decided that it was better both for its low-income adults and for the state overall to reallocate some health care funds. By explicitly withholding some services from previous Medicaid beneficiaries, the funds thus saved were redirected to provide broader coverage (albeit limited in number of services) to all those under the federal poverty line (FPL). Health services were rationed so that more could benefit from basic coverage. The rationing was based on the relative need for services.

When Oregon first proposed rationing health care in this manner, a number of sources voiced opposition. Rationing of health care, it was argued, was simply not acceptable. It somehow ran contrary to fundamental American principles to ration something so important.

How should we respond to such arguments? How should we view plans for rationing health care in general? The OHP involved the prioritized allocation of a scarce resource: health care for the poor. It allocated that resource on the basis of need. Those services that provided the highest benefit were provided to all. Those services that provided the lowest benefit were provided to none. Some people had to forgo services that had a low level of expected benefit so that all people could receive those services with

Medicaid Population

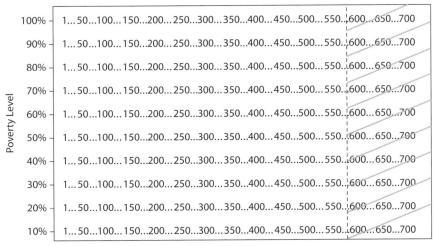

FIGURE 13.3. The Oregon Health Plan: Rationing Health Care Based on Need

Medicaid Population

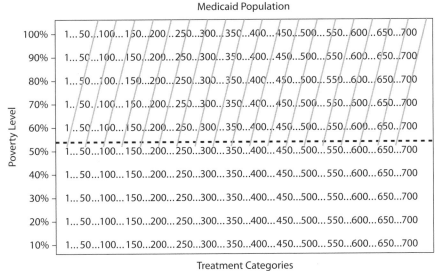

FIGURE 13.4. Before the Oregon Health Plan: Rationing Health Care Based on Income

a high level of expected benefit. It appears that the OHP was fully consistent with the ethical principle identified above in our discussion of flu vaccines.

It is important to appreciate, however, that the OHP did not create rationing where rationing did not previously exist. It simply shifted public policy from one form of rationing to another form. To understand this, let us look again at the situation that existed in Oregon before the establishment of the OHP, as illustrated in Figure 13.4.

Even before the establishment of the OHP, the Oregon state government approached health care for poor adults as a scarce commodity. It prioritized the allocation of Medicaid coverage; it did so based on the income of the poor adult. Only the poorest Oregonians—those with an income below 60 percent of the FPL—were covered. So that the poorest could receive full coverage, those among the poor with an income above this level received no coverage at all.

> **CONCEPT 13.3**
>
> The Oregon Health Plan did not create rationing where none previously existed. It instead shifted state policy from rationing health care based on income to rationing care based on need.

Before the OHP, Oregon rationed health care to poor people based on income. After the plan was established, Oregon rationed care to the poor based on relative need. It simply switched from one form of rationing to another. The previous rationing of care was done implicitly, without a formal public decision to do so. The new rationing was done explicitly, after a thorough process of public discussion and debate.

The above discussion is about how health care was made available to poor people in Oregon. If, instead, we look at how health care has been made available to people throughout this country, we find the situation described below. Figure 13.5 illustrates the distribution of health care in the United States at the time of the passage of ACA, in a format similar to the one used to look at health care in Oregon. The horizontal axis again lists all the services potentially available to people, from the most necessary to the least necessary. (There is, of course, no mechanism to establish such a list for the United States as a whole. For the purposes of discussion, I use the ranking of services created for the OHP as if it were to apply to the entire country.) In this case, the vertical axis is not the percentage of the poverty line a person falls into but rather the income percentile at which a person is located. A person who earns the median income would be at 50 percent. Low-income people are at low percentiles and high-income people are at high percentiles.

Given the complexity of our insurance system and the inequity between the very poor who are covered by Medicaid and the somewhat poor who are mostly without health insurance, the diagonal line representing the division between those who are covered and those who are not is not actually straight. A truly accurate line would be somewhat zigzagged at the bottom income percentiles. The principle, though, is the same: health care in the United States is distributed largely along income lines. The lower your income, the less care you have available to you. In the United States, as in Oregon before the OHP, we have for many years rationed health care according to income.

> **CONCEPT 13.4**
>
> The health care system in the United States involves rationing health care according to income. In contrast to the Oregon Health Plan, this rationing is implicit, with no explicit decision to ration care ever having been agreed to.

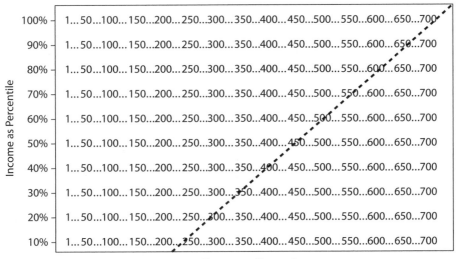

FIGURE 13.5. The Way We Ration Health Care in the United States

We have done so, however, implicitly, never having engaged in a public debate about whether we should ration health care and on what basis we should do so.

In the case of Oregon, why didn't the state government simply provide enough money to cover all its poor residents with comprehensive health insurance? In the case of the U.S. health care system, why doesn't the federal government simply adopt a pro-gram of full, comprehensive health care, providing all ser-vices to all people? The answer in both cases is fairly simple. Oregon could not afford to provide all care to all poor peo-ple in the state. Similarly, the U.S. government cannot af-ford to pay for health care for all American people without limitation. Health care has become so expensive that it sim-ply is not feasible for government, whether state or federal, to assure full access to all services for all people. This inev-itable conclusion leads us to the central conundrum of U.S. health care, stated below, which my students refer to as "Barr's Law." I offer it with apologies to Abraham Lincoln.

> **CONCEPT 13.5**
>
> You can treat some of the people all of the time, or you can treat all of the people some of the time, but you can't treat all of the people all of the time (Barr's Law).

> You can treat some of the people all of the time, or you can treat all of the people
> some of the time, but you can't treat all of the people all of the time.

This is the conundrum for politicians. Their constituents will not accept the rationing of their medical treatment. People do not want to be told that good health has a price. On the other hand, neither the politicians nor their constituents want to pay the higher taxes or higher insurance premiums required for unlimited health care.

To date, the United States has been unable to find a solution to this conundrum. Some would say that the problem is not one of being unable to find a solution, but rather of being unwilling. As a consequence, we have failed to arrive at a consensus about a uniform national policy concerning access to health insurance. As the cost of providing high-tech, high-quality care has gone up, it has historically been our national policy largely to look the other way as more and more people found themselves without health insurance. There have been incremental attempts to address the issue of the uninsured, but until the passage of ACA, we were unable to agree on a consistent national policy approach. The continuing controversy over the full implementation of ACA suggests that we still may not have been able to reach such a consensus.

Even if ACA is fully implemented, finding a solution to the three-pointed dilemma of U.S. health care will still be extremely difficult. If we are ever to constrain costs, assure increased access, while also maintaining quality, we are going to need to lessen our expectations somewhat about what type health care we should receive. As a society, we are going to need collectively to agree that in some cases, for some people, we will need to forgo certain care that might still hold out the possibility of some benefit.

Recall from our discussion of marginal cost and marginal benefit in Chapter 3 that we often make decisions in health care that we would not make for other types of goods or services. Victor Fuchs has underscored our differing perceptions of economic efficiency and medical efficiency. In economic theory, allocation of marginal resources that result in marginal benefits that are of lesser value constitutes what Fuchs refers to as "economic waste." By contrast, Fuchs suggests that, as a society, we have come to view "medical waste" only in the case of an "intervention that has no possible benefit for the patient or in which the potential risk to the patient is greater than potential benefit" (Fuchs 2009, p. 2481). For many people, as long as a procedure has any measureable marginal benefit, any effort to prevent access to that procedure constitutes unwarranted rationing. An illustration of this principle is provided by the public reaction to updated recommendations issued in 2009 regarding mammography screening.

## NEW RECOMMENDATIONS FOR MAMMOGRAPHY SCREENING: RATIONING, OR RATIONAL?

The U.S. Preventive Services Task Force (USPSTF) is an independent advisory body, made up of medical experts with a range of backgrounds and charged with the task of reviewing scientific evidence regarding preventive health services. In November 2009, USPSTF published the results of its review of the best available scientific evidence regarding mammography screening for breast cancer in women (U.S. Preventive Services Task Force 2009; Nelson et al. 2009). In 2002, USPSTF had issued a recommendation that all women age 40 or over get mammography screening every 1 to 2 years. Based on more recent research, USPSTF changed its recommendation to suggest that only women between ages 50 and 74 get routine screening, and that they do so every 2 years. The report then recommended that women aged 40 to 49 years not be routinely screened; instead, women in this age group should consult with their doctor to discuss the pros and cons of screening, and make an individual decision based a woman's individual risk profile and preferences.

As soon as the new guidelines were issued, there was a loud public outcry from many quarters regarding the recommendation that women aged 40 to 49 not be routinely screened. As summarized in a story in the *New York Times* by Kevin Sack, "the science of medicine bumped up against the foundations of American medical consumerism: that more is better, that saving a life is worth any sacrifice, and that health care is a birthright" (Sack 2009).

The USPSTF did conclude that routine, annual screening for women aged 40 to 49 would save lives. In order to save one woman's life through early detection of breast cancer, however, 1,900 women would need to get mammograms every year for 10 years. It was not the cost of these 19,000 mammograms that gave the task force pause; it was the toll these extra screening examinations would take on the women undergoing them (Mandelblatt et al. 2009). The task force found that for every 1,000 screening mammograms there would be an average of 99 false positive results—examinations that identified suspicious lesions that, after further testing and, for many of the women after surgical biopsy of the breast, turned out not to be cancer. Thus, for any individual woman, the risk was substantially higher that she would experience the stress and the anxiety of a false positive result and the additional procedures necessary to confirm that the lesion was not actually cancer. As stated in an editorial published concurrently with the USPSTF recommendations, the results of scientific studies "provide consistent results and suggest that the number of additional breast cancer deaths averted by starting screening mammography at age 40 is small and the earlier screening involves important harms" (Kerlikowske 2009, p. 750).

With the USPSTF's explicit acknowledgment that following the new guidelines would result in more women dying (albeit few women), did the updated recommendations constitute a recommendation that we ration care? One commentator writing in the *New England Journal of Medicine* suggested that they did. In a commentary titled "Screening Mammography and the 'R' Word," Truog (2009, p. 2502) concluded that "critics of the Task Force recommendations and of health care reform in general are offering a false choice. The choice is not about health care rationing and some undefined alternative, since there is no alternative. Rather, the choice concerns what principles we will use to ration health care . . . If the debate about health care reform is to progress with clarity, transparency, and honesty, we must lose our fear of the 'R' word and discuss how, not whether, we should ration health care."

In commenting on what they referred to as the "Mammography Wars," Quanstrum and Hayward emphasize an important principle underlying the USPSTF recommendations. "Behind the panel's conclusions regarding mammography lurks an unwelcome reality that our profession has often failed to acknowledge. Every medical intervention—no matter how beneficial for some patients—will provide continuously diminishing returns as the threshold for intervention is lowered. Mammography is just one case in point" (Quanstrum and Hayward 2010, p. 1076).

As a society, we commonly elect to receive (and have come to expect) many types of care that have a small marginal benefit relative to marginal cost—either the cost in dollars or the cost in added risk or discomfort. Because the marginal benefit of that care is small, this also implies that forgoing that care would lead to only a small decrement in our health. Once we as a society come to appreciate that health care is truly a scarce commodity, one for which resources are limited, it will become easier for us to accept the form of health care rationing that will be necessary if we are to solve our dilemma. If health care is seen as a zero-sum commodity, it will mean that any extra care provided to one person will necessarily lead to a reduction in care for someone else. (This clearly was the case in the flu vaccine shortages discussed above.) If we are able to accept this conclusion as a principle of our social policy, we will be able to develop mechanisms that ensure that we attain a rough level of justice in health care, under which no one is denied care so that someone else may receive care of lesser benefit.

Consistent with our comparison in Chapter 3 of the U.S. and Canadian health care systems, a system of fully equal access for all is probably not compatible with our national emphasis on the needs of the individual over the needs of the group. Whatever system we adopt will doubtless need to include the option for those with enough money to be able to purchase whatever level of care they wish. If there is a level of care that has small marginal benefit but large marginal cost, and an individual still wants to purchase it with his or her own money, our system need not prevent that. Rather than adopting the one-class system found in Canada, we will probably need to adopt a form of the two-class system found in Great Britain, where those wishing to buy care outside the National Health Service are free to do so.

Whatever system we adopt, it will need to incorporate some limits on care, and it will need to be seen as fair. Without widely held perceptions of fairness, few will be willing to forgo care so that someone else may be treated instead. Changes in our system of care occurring over the last two decades, however, may have made this goal of fairness substantially more difficult to attain.

## PROFIT AS A COMPETITOR TO COST, QUALITY, AND ACCESS

As discussed in Chapter 8, U.S. health care has undergone a major change over the last twenty years. Once organized largely on a nonprofit basis, our health care system now includes an increasing number of for-profit corporations: for-profit HMOs and

COST            PROFIT

QUALITY            ACCESS

FIGURE 13.6. The New Dilemma of U.S. Health Care

other insurers, for-profit hospitals, and for-profit medical care providers. This shift to for-profit health care has added a fourth factor to our national health care dilemma: the need to maintain shareholder profits. This new health care dilemma is illustrated in Figure 13.6.

Once represented by the triangle of cost, quality, and access, we now have a system stretched among four points: cost, quality, access, and profit. At nearly every level, the issue of profit plays some role in deciding who will receive what care. For-profit hospitals have to factor in the need to maintain shareholder return in decisions about which patients to admit, what equipment to buy, and how to measure quality. For-profit insurers must factor shareholder profit into their decisions about how much of the premiums they receive from employers is available to be paid as payments to physicians and other providers, and about what types of services and medications will be included under the coverage they offer.

As difficult as it may be to somehow find a new equilibrium between cost, quality, and access, the added presence of the profit motive makes finding a comprehensive solution to the problems of U.S. health care even more difficult to attain.

To understand why this is, consider a patient in the position of having to forgo care so that someone else can receive care of greater marginal benefit. If we are able to create a system of care in which the medical needs of all patients are fairly balanced, patients can have some assurance that by giving up certain care, some other patient will benefit directly, and the marginal benefit for that patient is greater than the marginal decrement of forgoing care. It may be possible to move to this type of system so long as this assurance can be maintained.

In the new, four-cornered American system of care, this assurance cannot be maintained. In a system in which profit competes with quality and access for scarce health care dollars, it is impossible to be certain that money saved by forgoing care of small marginal benefit but large marginal cost will go to providing care to other patients who need it more. It may well be the case that money saved in this way would also go to provide added profit to shareholders. It is simply not reasonable to expect any patient at any level of income to willingly forgo care, regardless of the cost/benefit profile of that care, if the money saved by doing so will end up going to corporate profit.

I once had as a patient a professor of economics. That professor was upset because his for-profit health insurance company had established a medication formulary, with payment available only for those specific drugs on the list. A medication the professor had previously taken was excluded from the list, and in its place was another, less expensive medication that was equally effective in treating the professor's problem. The second medication, however, had some unpleasant (but not dangerous) side effects. I suggested to the professor that a rational economic argument could be made to have only the less expensive medication covered. The marginal benefit of the more expensive drug (fewer side effects) did not justify its substantial marginal cost over the less expensive yet equally effective alternative. The professor, however, contended that issues of marginal cost and marginal benefit were not appropriate when it was his health that was involved. The insurance company had no right, he argued, to withhold the more expensive drug simply to make a profit.

I could offer little in response. Were I in his situation, I would probably feel the same way. The presence of the profit motive throughout our health care system makes it unreasonable to expect either individual patients or society as a whole to be willing to move toward an accommodation of the competing needs of cost, quality, and access. So long as we have a system that includes a major role for for-profit corporations, we will be unlikely to find a national health policy that can guarantee access to basic, high-quality health care to all people at a cost our society can afford.

## PHYSICIAN, HEAL THYSELF: PHYSICIANS AND THE PROFIT MOTIVE

Physicians, both individually and collectively, are not strangers to the profit motive. A review of the history of medical practice throughout much of the twentieth century (Starr 1982) reveals that medical practice in this country was historically based on the profit motive: profit for the individual physician. Individual physicians practicing medicine under the fee-for-service system of payment were acting as for-profit entrepreneurs. A physician was not only allowed but also encouraged to do everything he could for the patient, so long as he did not harm the patient directly. The more the physician did, the more the physician was paid. For decades there were essentially no limits on how much income a physician could earn, and no one was looking over the physician's shoulder to ask how necessary or appropriate the care being provided was. At that time, however, the incentive to make more profit by providing more care coincided closely with the patient's desire to receive all possible care.

As it turns out, the appropriateness of much of the care provided in the fee-for-service system was questionable. It appears that in many instances physicians were offering if not actually encouraging unnecessary tests and procedures, with a resulting increase in their income. This history of mixing the economic self-interest of the physician with the medical needs of the patient led Dr. George Lundberg, at that time editor of *JAMA,* to offer the following warning: *"Caveat aeger*—let the patient beware" (Lundberg 1995). Dr. Lundberg suggested that few physicians are in medicine just for the money (those he labels "money grubbers") and few exhibit pure altruism (those he labels "altruistic missionaries"). Most physicians are somewhere in between, and include at least some level of economic self-interest in their medical decisions. Each physician strikes his or her own balance between the needs of the patient and economic self-interest.

Dr. Lundberg suggested that physicians are approximately evenly distributed across a wide spectrum in the way they balance these competing needs. According to Dr. Lundberg's model, this distribution of physicians approximates the shape of the bell-shaped curve, which statisticians refer to as the "standard normal distribution." This curve is illustrated in Figure 13.7.

Students of statistics will recall that the standard normal distribution has certain characteristics. The mean, median, and mode of the curve are all the same. Ninety-five percent of all points under the curve will lie within 2 standard deviations of the mean.

If Dr. Lundberg's model is correct (and I suspect it is), this would suggest that the medical profession in the United States is about equally divided between those situated

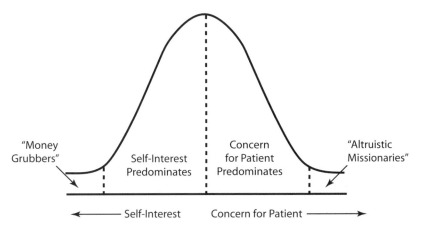

FIGURE 13.7. The Distribution of Physicians in the United States along a Scale of Self-Interest versus Concern for the Patient. *Source:* Adapted from Lundberg 1995

to the left of the median and those situated to the right of the median. This would mean that, while most physicians attain some type of balance between their own economic needs and the needs of their patients, half of all physicians are more self-interested than they are interested in the benefit of their patients. While few physicians are in it just for the money (those in the left tail of the curve), few physicians are purely altruistic in their approach to care (those in the right tail of the curve). All the rest of us are situated somewhere between the missionaries and the money grubbers.

This conclusion presents an ethical dilemma for physicians. What steps should we take to assure that neither physicians' self-interest nor the financial interests of for-profit corporations take precedence over the genuine medical need of patients? In discussing this dilemma, Leon Eisenberg suggests that medicine as a profession needs to strengthen and reinforce the culture of professionalism, and in doing so strengthen the commitment of physicians to the needs of their patients. To those of us in the role of teachers and mentors he suggests, "It can only promote cynicism among our students if we preach humanism and ignore the realities of the contemporary scene . . . The words 'physician' and 'patient' are embedded in a proud ethical tradition. Have we always lived up to the ideal we profess? It is obvious that the answer is no . . . No physician could proclaim that the business of medicine is business without losing the respect of her peers. Physicians ought to be advocates for their patients. The best always have been" (Eisenberg 1995, p. 333).

I suggest that it is up to the U.S. health care professionals, including physicians, nurses, public health analysts, and others, to lead the way toward a system and an ethic that addresses this issue of economic interests and the needs of the patient. Our professional practice should embrace simultaneously the tremendous advances medicine has made in the last fifty years and a genuine commitment to justice in the allocation of health care resources. Part of this concept of justice in health care must be a clear commitment that the needs of the patient come before the financial needs either of individual physicians or of health care corporations.

Many of you who are reading this book will be faced with these issues and these challenges. I suggest that each of you currently working or planning to work either as a physician or in some other capacity in the health care system consider fully the issues raised here. Many forces in society are pushing individual professionals toward the left side of the diagram. These forces include the high cost of a professional education, the need to put children through college, and simply the desire to live comfortably. The forces strengthening the right side of the diagram are the ethical tradition of medicine and a commitment to service on behalf of the patient. Every health care professional needs to be aware of this choice.

I propose that each of you in the health professions, from time to time throughout your career, ask the following three questions:

1. In my current professional work, where on this diagram am I situated?
2. Where on this diagram do I want to be situated?
3. Am I willing to do what is necessary to move from where I am now to where I want to be?

## SUMMARY

In Chapter 2 of this book, I identified the three problems that lie at the center of U.S. health policy: (1) constraining the cost of care, (2) maintaining and improving the quality of care, and (3) increasing access to care. As we have gone through this book, we have learned that these are not three separate problems. Instead, they are the three faces of a single problem. Policies that address only one of these issues will inevitably affect the other two.

To be successful in restructuring the U.S. system of health care, we will need to deal with all three problems simultaneously. Despite our technological sophistication and the substantial resources we invest in our health care system, we are confronted by the reality of "Barr's Law": we cannot provide all imaginable care to all of the people all of the time. We can optimize our system of health care only if we establish and maintain a policy of making care available according to a system of prioritization and only if that system has popular support.

Accepting the inevitability of limits on the amount of care we can provide and the need for prioritizing the care we do provide implies the need to ration health care. Often considered to be antithetical to the core values of American society, a closer examination reveals that approaching health care as a market commodity, available preferentially to those with the economic means to pay for it, is in itself a form of rationing. The challenge facing the American public as well as the American medical profession is finding a way to distribute our scarce health care resources that optimizes outcomes and reduces the role of providers' economic self-interest.

## THE AFFORDABLE CARE ACT AND THE ALLOCATION OF HEALTH CARE RESOURCES

In the debate over ACA, one of the central aspects under scrutiny was its impact on the cost of health care and on the federal deficit. The Congressional Budget Office thoroughly evaluated the final legislation and concluded that the combination of increased federal spending and increased revenues under ACA would result in a net reduction in the federal deficit of $124 billion over ten years. While ACA is expected to result in a net reduction in federal outlays for health care, it will also result in a net increase in overall health care expenditures. As described in Chapter 11, the actuary at the federal Centers for Medicare and Medicaid Services has concluded that, as a result of ACA, overall national expenditures for health care will rise faster than they would have had

ACA not been adopted. By 2019, national health expenditures under the provisions of ACA are predicted to rise to 19.6 percent of GDP, as compared to 19.3 percent had ACA not been enacted.

Thus, ACA has addressed the issue of access to care through its expansion of health insurance to include an estimated 32 million people who otherwise would have been uninsured. Yet it appears to have left unaddressed the issue of cost. As described in Chapter 6, ACA establishes a new mechanism for addressing the specific issue of the rising cost of the Medicare program. ACA establishes a new Independent Payment Advisory Board (IPAB) and delegates to it responsibility for monitoring the rate at which Medicare's spending increases over time. If Medicare spending rises faster than new targets established under ACA, IPAB has the responsibility of coming up with a plan to rein in spending to meet the target amount. ACA ties the hands of IPAB somewhat, however, by requiring that steps taken by the board "shall not include any recommendation to ration health care, raise revenues [that is, taxes] or Medicare beneficiary premiums . . . or otherwise restrict benefits or modify eligibility criteria" (ACA Section 3403).

Embodying what Kevin Sack above referred to as "the foundations of American medical consumerism: that more is better, that saving a life is worth any sacrifice, and that health care is a birthright," by explicitly prohibiting any form of rationing or other reduction in benefits (at least to Medicare beneficiaries), ACA seems to have left the issue of cost containment for another day. Can we afford to pay 19.6 percent of GDP on health care in 2019? This is a question that deserves, but to date has been without, a clear answer.

# 14

# Epilogue/Prologue to Health Care Reform in America

From the discussion in the previous chapters it should now be apparent that our current system of health care in the United States is not sustainable in the long term. There are simply too many areas of potential financial instability to expect our system to survive much longer without additional reform. While enactment of the Affordable Care Act (ACA) will substantially reduce the number of Americans who are uninsured, it will not change the underlying cost structure of American health care. At some point in the future, we will either run out of the money or lose the political will to maintain our current system of care.

As a society, we have never openly and explicitly confronted the fundamental questions of social norms and public policy on which a system of health care is founded. We identified these questions as part of discussion in Chapter 3 of the fundamental differences between the U.S. and Canadian systems of health care. We were able to identify four questions, the answers to which form the core of our social policy regarding health care:

1. Should we acknowledge a right to a basic level of health care for all Americans?
2. Should we establish explicit caps on the national health care budget?
3. Should the federal government take principal responsibility for the organization and financing of the health care system?
4. Should we establish a uniform standard of care for all people?

We know what the system looks like if we answer "no" to all four questions. We have the system that was in place before the passage of ACA, with all its inherent problems. We have never explicitly established "no" as our answer to these questions in a national forum—our system has simply evolved to these answers over a period of decades and through a series of incremental decisions, many of them dealing with health care only peripherally. (The decision to rely on an employment-based system, as described in Chapter 5, is an example of a decision not directly pertaining to health policy yet having profound effects on the structure of our system.)

If we were instead to answer "yes" to all four questions, as Canada has done, we would have a Canadian-style system. This option for reform has been before the American public since 1989, when Himmelstein and Woolhandler first suggested it as an alternative to Enthoven's proposal for managed competition, discussed in Chapter 5. This "single-payer" (SP) proposal, as a Canadian-style approach has come to be called, was published in 2003 in revised form by Physicians for a National Health Program (Physicians' Working Group 2003).

The SP system would establish a right to comprehensive health care and would use a budgeting and payment system modeled on the Canadian system. As in Canada, it would rely on tax revenues to pay for care, and it would sever the historical link between employment and health insurance. By relying on global budgets for hospitals and other capital equipment such as MRI scanners, it would create a fixed level of available care, relying on physicians to select those patients needing care the most. In doing so, it can be reasonably expected to result in waiting lists—queues—for certain types of tests or procedures, as is the case in Canada.

The Canadian system of care is based on and consistent with the fundamental organization of Canadian society. To successfully import an SP system based on the Canadian model requires that the United States shift the basic organizing principles underlying our social structure. Our outlook and our cultural norms would have to coincide with those of Canada. This change simply does not seem feasible. For this reason, a pure SP approach has garnered only narrow support, despite having been in the public forum for more than two decades.

How does ACA answer the four questions? It would seem that ACA offers two qualified "yes" answers and two "no" answers. As for a right to health care, perhaps President Barack Obama stated it most clearly. Upon signing ACA, Obama spoke to the American public regarding the implications of what he had just done: "We have now just enshrined the core principle that everybody should have some basic security when it comes to their health care" (Obama 2010).

Is a "core principle" the same as a "right"? Not exactly. ACA does not intend to cover everyone living in the United States by right. Rather, it proposes to offer *most* Americans the opportunity to purchase affordable health insurance if it is not otherwise available to them either through their work or as part of a government program. Those who work for firms with fewer than fifty employees may still face the prospect of being uninsured, as such small employers are exempt from the requirements of ACA. Individuals who provide evidence that they cannot afford even the subsidized premiums available through the newly established health exchanges will likewise be exempted from the requirement to maintain coverage. Finally, those immigrants who live in our country and participate in our society, yet who are undocumented, will not have access to heath insurance through ACA.

The second "yes" ACA applies to the series of four questions pertains to the appropriate role of government in organizing and financing the delivery system. For much of the twentieth century, the federal government played a relatively small role in how health care was organized and financed. That began to change in 1965, with the establishment of the Medicare and Medicaid programs. The federal government became further involved with enactment of the HMO Act of 1973, and with the various reforms of the manner in which Medicare pays doctors and hospitals. Even before ACA, the federal government had developed a major role in determining how health care in America would be delivered.

With passage of ACA, more than half of all health care expenditures will be from public sources, either federal, state, or local. As it is responsible for a majority of health expenditures, it should not be surprising that government is asserting substantial influence over the organization and financing of care. Several aspects of ACA will increase that influence. As the federal government invests increasingly in comparative effectiveness research (CER), both the medical profession and the public will gain increased understanding of which of the available alternative treatments seems optimal. Similarly, as ACA develops and enforces standards for private health insurance options, the market for these plans will come under tighter government scrutiny.

It is not clear if the increased government influence that will come as a consequence of ACA will constitute "principal responsibility" for the organization and financing of health care delivery. The private market will still play a substantially larger role in the United States than in Canada. It is clear, however, that the era of limited government involvement in health care in the United States is over.

While ACA provides a qualified "yes" in response to two of the four core questions of health policy listed above, it also leaves our response to the remaining two questions as "no." At no time during the debate leading up to enactment of ACA was there serious consideration of adopting a single, uniform standard of health care for all people in the United States. Such a uniform standard continues to be both the norm and the law in Canada, with some growing exceptions as discussed in Chapter 3. The idea that those with more wealth can purchase a different level of care than those without wealth continues to be anathema to most Canadians.

Quite the contrary, the concept that those with more wealth might be prevented by law from purchasing a different level of care than those without wealth remains anathema to many people in the United States (at least to those with the financial resources to purchase the higher level of care). President Obama committed to assuring all Americans "some basic security when it comes to their health care." This standard is consistent with the standard articulated by the Universal Declaration of Human Rights, as discussed in Chapter 2. That declaration asserts that all people have a right to a level of health care that is "adequate for the health and well-being of himself and of his family." The principle established both by the declaration and by President Obama's statement is that there is a basic level of health care that all people should have access to, and that level will be measured by its adequacy to maintain well-being. Nothing in this assurance, however, suggests that those with greater resources should be prevented from acquiring, with their own resources, a higher level of care.

In a similar vein, ACA is largely silent on the issue of establishing explicit caps on the national budget for health care—either a cap on federal expenditures or a cap on aggregate national expenditures. There are systems of care in the United States that function under a fixed global budget, and do so quite successfully. The Kaiser Permanente system, discussed in Chapter 5, has done so for several decades. The federal Veterans Affairs (VA) Health System also provides high-quality care to millions of veterans under a global budget. ACA, however, does not extend this model to the health care system more generally, thus leaving us open to the continued adverse impacts of rising health care costs.

## LONG-TERM IMPLICATIONS OF HEALTH CARE COSTS AFTER THE AFFORDABLE CARE ACT

The enactment of ACA did mark a major milestone in the history of health policy in the United States. It was the first time we came even close to acknowledging and supporting a right to a basic level of health care for all Americans. By 2019, an estimated 32 million people who previously were uninsured will benefit from health insurance coverage. Access to health insurance, however, is only part of the story, and part of the problem.

Recall from our discussion of Figure 13.1 that our health care system is multidimensional. We can evaluate that system from at least three perspectives: access, cost, and quality. No one of these dimensions defines the success of our system. We must simultaneously evaluate that success from those three perspectives. ACA will substantially improve access to health insurance, and we hope access to health care (although, as discussed in Chapter 12, providing people with health insurance does not guarantee that there will be a provider willing to accept that insurance). As projected by the Office of the Actuary of the Centers for Medicare and Medicaid Services, however, ACA will not reduce the continuing escalation in the cost of our health care system, measured as percent of gross domestic product (GDP). In fact, ACA is predicted to *increase* the percent of GDP going to health care, albeit by a small amount.

For more than two decades we have seen a strikingly consistent rise in national health care expenditures measured as percent of GDP. Between 1987 and 2009, that percentage increased from 10.5 to 17.3 percent. Over this time period the average annual increase measured as a percent of GDP was 0.31 percent. At this rate of increase, the percent of GDP going to health care increases 3.1 percent every decade. This rate of increase is unsustainable. At some point the health care system will put such a drain on the rest of the U.S. economy that overall economic stability will be threatened. Whether that point will be at 19.6 percent of GDP, or 22.7 percent of GDP, or whether we have already reached that point, is unclear.

In an Op-Ed published in 2010 in the *New York Times*, Peter Orszag, director of the White House Office of Management and Budget under President Obama, suggested that we may already have topped out in our ability to fund the health care system (Orszag 2010). He cited data that, in order to pay the continually rising costs of the Medicaid program, many states had substantially reduced funding to public higher education, including flagship public universities such as the University of California, Berkeley. As a consequence, the ability of these universities to attract and retain top faculty and to maintain academic programs has been seriously compromised. Orszag also argued that constraining health care costs is "central to raising workers' take-home pay, because increasing costs for health care are holding down wages."

Our central problem is that we have no mechanism, either political or economic, to define a national cap in health care spending. There have been proposals to establish mechanisms to cap national health care spending, but they have never received the political support necessary for passage. In 2005, Ezekiel Emanuel, a medical ethicist at the National Institutes of Health and subsequently a health policy advisor to President Obama, and Victor Fuchs, a health economist at Stanford University, proposed a health care system that would have established near universal coverage under a national cap in spending by relying on health care vouchers (Emanuel and Fuchs 2005). They proposed to fund their system with a new value-added tax (VAT) dedicated solely to paying for health insurance. That health care tax would have been separate and distinct from general income tax revenues and thus would not have added to the federal deficit. National spending for health care would have been capped at the amount collected under the VAT. That amount would have been distributed in a way that assured all Americans basic health insurance coverage. While individuals would have been free to spend additional funds over and above the basic coverage, they believed that relying on a fixed source of funding under the VAT would have stabilized the share of GDP going to health care.

The health reform proposals under President Bill Clinton would also have created a mechanism to cap national health expenditures through the establishment of a national board with the power to cap premiums charged by health insurance companies participating in the health insurance exchanges the Clinton proposal would have created. The specter of bureaucrats arbitrarily capping health insurance premiums and in so doing denying Americans necessary medical care was one of the images used by opponents of the Clinton proposal to defeat it.

As early as 1970, Senator Ted Kennedy had proposed a national plan that would have provided universal coverage while also capping national health expenditures. He proposed a nationally regulated system that combined capitated payments to nonprofit managed care plans (or for-profit plans, if the patient prefers), combined with the option for direct hospital and physician payment under regional global budgets. Kennedy's proposal, titled the Health Security Act of 1970, called for a system of universal coverage in which consumers could either enroll in a capitated plan or select care from physicians not affiliated with a plan. If they chose the unaffiliated option, it would be up to the physicians as a group to establish local or regional policies to stay within the regional budget for care. That budget was to be determined according to the number of consumers who selected this option. If the physicians were unsuccessful in remaining within the budget, their reimbursement rates would be reduced accordingly, as has been the case in Canada for more than two decades.

It is interesting to note the striking similarity between the plan Senator Kennedy proposed in 1970 and the recommendations issued in 2009 by the Massachusetts Special Commission on the Health Care Payment System (discussed in Chapter 11). The commission recommended that, in order to sustain the state's new health plan, Massachusetts will need to shift away from an open-ended, fee-for-service system of paying for care, to a global payment system of care, relying on accountable care organizations (ACOs) to administer and provide care under the fixed budget inherent to such capitated systems.

ACA has essentially avoided the issues addressed by the Massachusetts Special Commission. Absent a mechanism to cap expenditures, either through global payments, vouchers, or similar approaches, it is understandable that the slope of the curve measuring long-term health care cost escalation has hardly moved. What movement there is will be in the upward direction. Discussions about "bending the curve" of health care costs, a regular part of the debate over ACA before it was enacted, are not reflected in the final legislation.

## GOVERNMENT OR MARKET: WHICH IS BETTER TO GUIDE SPENDING ON HEALTH CARE?

In Chapters 5–6 we saw that capitation systems of health care are able to eliminate certain types of inefficiencies within a given institutional context, but on their own they seem powerless to change the surrounding context. Constraining the rapid escalation of technology, minimizing local variations in patterns of care, and coping with defensive medicine have proven to be no less a problem for well-run managed care plans than they were for their fee-for-service predecessors. Would a system that relies on market-based capitated care, such as that recommended by the Massachusetts commission, be able to achieve alone the balancing of costs and outcomes required for ACA or any other universal health care reform to succeed?

If the inefficiencies embedded in the health care system were all based on market factors, then market mechanisms alone might hold promise of success. As I have discussed throughout this book, however, the institutions in the United States that have led to increasing costs and resultant limited access for many stem from a range of social, political, and professional forces. Improving the market for health care can overcome problems created by the market, but it cannot change all of society. In the words of Victor Fuchs, "The market is a powerful and flexible instrument for allocating most goods and services, but it cannot create an equitable, universal system of insurance, cannot harness technologic change in medicine, and cannot cope with the potentially unlimited demand for health care by the elderly" (1993b, p. 1679).

Changing only market structures will not be sufficient to change the institutional structure of U.S. health care. Any additional movement toward a more optimal balancing of costs, quality, and access beyond what markets alone can achieve requires a shift in the surrounding social, political, and professional institutional context. Few forces affect all segments of society and are sufficiently powerful to alter the broad range of existing health care institutions so as to guide the system toward needed improvements. To be effective, such a force would have to exert its influence concurrently in the market for health care, in the system of professional knowledge and norms that govern the medical profession, in the political system, and in the expectations of society at large. Only by acting across all levels of our social and professional system can we change the beliefs of both patients and providers to redefine what constitutes appropriate care in a way that attains a more appropriate balance of cost, quality, and access.

The federal government is one of the few forces in our society with the potential to act across this broad range of institutions to shift the direction of health care. Historically in this country, as in Canada, it has been the federal government that has acted to shift our core health care institutions. Several of the most important changes in U.S. health care have been initiated by the federal government. Medicare and Medicaid are clear examples of the power of the federal government to change the direction of health care. The HMO Act of 1973, while not achieving all its intended goals, nonetheless replaced a historic hostility to health maintenance organizations (HMOs) with widespread acceptance and general success (at least initially). The prospective payment system (PPS) and the resource-based relative value scale (RBRVS) schedule of physician payment fundamentally altered how we pay for government-sponsored health care and have affected payment patterns in the broader market for health insurance. By guiding the market for health care while not controlling it, the U.S. federal government has shown that it has the ability to alter in a constructive way inefficient institutions that structure health care.

In order for us finally to constrain the ongoing increase in the cost of our health care system—in order to "bend the curve" of health care costs—I believe it will be necessary for the federal government to assume a considerably larger role in the market for health care, even larger than that called for in ACA, while stopping short of the monopsony control. The central element currently missing from that role is a mechanism to define and enforce a national cap on health care spending.

It seems inevitable that the American public and the American Congress will be discussing and debating this issue again. Not to do so would simply perpetuate the escalation of health care costs that is already starting to put both our economy and our system of care in jeopardy. When we do confront the cost issue, we will have to do so in the context of maintaining health care quality. If we continue to define "quality" in terms of getting the newest, most high-tech (and most expensive) care available, however, we are going to have trouble. As described by Daniel Callahan, achieving a new balance of cost and quality that will sustain the increased access provided by ACA "will require nothing less than changes in medical and professional values, patients' demands and expectations, industry profit seeking, research aims and aspirations, and the culture of American medicine, much of which has been dedicated to unlimited progress and technological innovation, cost be damned" (Callahan 2009).

What Callahan seems to be saying is that we as a society will have to make a fundamental choice. We will either have to reduce the expansion in access to care created by ACA, or we will have to accept that unlimited access to the most advanced technology without consideration of comparative costs or comparative effectiveness is no longer a viable basis for our system of care. In other words,

> We can treat some of the people all of the time, or we can treat all of the people some of the time, but we can't treat all of the people all of the time.

Debates about the "R" word, about whether such a system would invoke health care rationing, are essentially vacuous. We must come to grips with the reality that health care resources are not unlimited, and that under the condition of scarcity created by limits on key resources, a system of prioritized allocation of those resources is essential. The key question we have yet to answer is whether the allocation of our inevitably scarce health care resources will be based on concepts of justice and relative need, rather than on wealth and relative income.

## SUMMARY

Solving the conundrum of balancing health care cost, quality, and access in the face of powerful economic forces will, of necessity, invoke an examination of core American values. Is health care a right? Are health care resources limited? What role should the government play? Should we establish a uniform level of care for all people?

Answering these questions explicitly provides a means to identify future options for stabilizing and securing our system of health care. We have historically shied away from open public debate on these issues. Finding a path to the next step in health care reform may require that we address these issues head on, relying on the democratic process to balance the interests of all.

# APPENDIX
## Summary of the Changes Contained in the Affordable Care Act

### HOW THE AFFORDABLE CARE ACT ADDRESSES THE ISSUES OF HEALTH CARE COST, QUALITY, AND ACCESS

- Starting in 2014, health insurance will become available to an estimated 32 million people who previously were uninsured. This expansion of coverage will take place through a combination of reform of the private market for health insurance and a major expansion of the existing federal-state Medicaid program.
- These expansions will result in nearly 95 percent of all Americans having health insurance coverage. Those remaining uninsured will typically be those working for small companies not required under the new law to provide health insurance to their workers and those residents who are undocumented.
- The Affordable Care Act (ACA) addresses the issue of cost containment in two main ways: (1) changes to the Medicare program and (2) new sources of tax revenues.
- ACA addresses the issue of maintaining the quality of health care in two principal ways. The first is through an expansion of primary care services through a restructuring of the way primary care is delivered. The second is through a major expansion of comparative effectiveness research (CER).
- CER will bring a major new focus to the issue of comparing the clinical outcomes of alternative ways of approaching the diagnosis and treatment of illness. CER, if successful, will shift the definition of "quality" in medical care from one that focuses on whether a treatment is newer or more high-tech, to one focusing on how well the treatment actually works in the context of alternative approaches to care.

### PROVISIONS IN THE AFFORDABLE CARE ACT TO ADDRESS THE APPROPRIATE USES OF MEDICAL TECHNOLOGY AND OTHER HIGH-COST MEDICAL CARE

- In order to expand the reach and impact of CER, ACA established a national Patient-Centered Outcomes Research Institute (PCORI). PCORI is structured as an independent, nonprofit organization. It will have a nationally representative board of governors, a series of national advisory panels, and a staff of experienced researchers. With funding provided by ACA, PCORI will either carry out or arrange to have carried out a series of research studies that compare existing alternatives for diagnosis or treatment.
- ACA is explicit in requiring that CER provide recommendations for the optimal approach to care, but not create mandates as to how specific conditions should be approached. Similarly, CER results are not to be used to determine insurance coverage or payment for differing approaches to care. Thus CER, at least as carried out under ACA, is not intended to be cost-effectiveness research, in that it will not make recommendations as to which of the available alternatives provides the optimal balancing of costs and benefits.
- ACA leaves unanswered the question of when, if ever, it is appropriate to deny a patient care that has some small yet well documented marginal benefit, but an extremely high marginal cost.

## PROVISIONS IN THE AFFORDABLE CARE ACT TO EXPAND PRIMARY CARE DELIVERY

- ACA shifts funding for graduate medical education (GME) away from programs that train specialists and redirects it to programs that train primary care physicians. It also provides for new types of primary care training programs that are based in community settings rather than the traditional hospital setting. These "teaching health centers" will represent collaborations between academic training centers and nonprofit, federally certified community clinics.
- ACA provides for increased payment for primary care services. Beginning in 2011, the federal Medicare program will provide a 10 percent bonus payment to primary care physicians who treat Medicare beneficiaries. Beginning in 2013, primary care physicians who treat Medicaid patients will see their payment rate, historically substantially lower than Medicare rates, raised to the same rate as that paid by Medicare.
- ACA provides increased federal funding for the National Health Service Corps and other programs that provide repayment of educational loans for primary care physicians who practice in areas of the country, typically rural areas and inner cities, which have documented medical manpower shortages.
- ACA provides substantially increased support for a new model of organizing primary care: the patient-centered medical home (PCMH). The PCMH will involve a team of providers, including physicians, allied professionals such as nurse practitioners or physician's assistants, as well as support personnel with a range of professional skills. This team approach will be supported by an electronic health record system that will enable providers access to the records of a patient's care and facilitate ongoing quality assessments of the care provided to patients.
- By expanding the training of primary care physicians, increasing the payment for primary care services, and supporting high-quality PCMHs, ACA will expand access to primary care for those expected to obtain new health insurance coverage.

## THE AFFORDABLE CARE ACT AND THE MARKET FOR HEALTH INSURANCE

- In order to expand health insurance coverage to those currently uninsured, ACA requires every employer with more than fifty employees to offer health insurance coverage to their workers or else pay a tax to the federal government.
- ACA mandates that all U.S. citizens and permanent residents obtain health insurance coverage. If workers are unable to obtain that coverage through their employer, they will be guaranteed the option of obtaining coverage through a newly created entity: the health benefit exchange (HBE).
- The HBE is an organization that is to be created by each state with the purpose of making competing health insurance plans available to those individuals and families who do not obtain coverage through their work. States have the option of collaborating among themselves to create multi-state, regional exchanges. Large states can create multiple exchanges within the state, so long as each one serves an identified geographic area. In states that are unable or unwilling to create an exchange by 2014, the federal government will be authorized to establish and operate an exchange on behalf of the state.
- The purpose of the HBE is to match those seeking health insurance coverage with companies offering coverage. In order to have their plans made available through the HBE, health

insurance companies will have to obtain certification from the operator of the exchange that the plan meets certain requirements having to do with level of benefits, and that the company offering the plan has met licensure and regulatory requirements.

- Each exchange must arrange for at least two qualifying plans to be available, one of which must be offered by a nonprofit organization. Qualified plans will offer one of four predefined level of benefits, referred to as bronze, silver, gold, and platinum. Other than variations in price based on the subscriber's age, family composition, tobacco use, and geographic area of residence, each plan must be available at the same price to all subscribers without regard to the subscriber's past medical history.
- Beginning in 2014, individuals who do not receive coverage through their work will be eligible to contact the HBE, get information about competing plans and their comparative prices for a given level of coverage, and select a plan for himself or herself and their family. In addition, small businesses with up to one hundred employees will be eligible to obtain coverage for their employees through the HBE, with employees selecting from among the competing plans.
- For individuals and families earning between 133 and 400 percent of the federal poverty level (FPL), there will be a cap on the premium paid by the subscriber, with the balance paid through a federal subsidy. The cap ranges from 2 percent of income for those earning 133 percent of the FPL to 9.5 percent of income for those earning 400 percent of the FPL.

## CHANGES IN MEDICARE UNDER THE AFFORDABLE CARE ACT

- ACA revised the formula under which Medicare Advantage (MA) plans will be paid. Beginning in 2011, the rates paid to plans participating in MA will be gradually reduced, with the expectation that by 2014 they will be more nearly equivalent to the average cost of providing care for a beneficiary under traditional Medicare. Payments will also be risk-adjusted based on an enrollee's current and previous health status, so as to avoid favorable selection among MA enrollees. ACA also sets explicit quality targets for the care provided by plans under MA, paying a bonus to those plans that meet or exceed the target.
- ACA makes changes to the Medicare prescription drug benefit, described in more detail below.
- Beginning in 2011, Medicare beneficiaries will have no co-payment or deductible charged for certain types of preventive health services that have been recommended by the U.S. Preventive Services Task Force. In addition, beneficiaries may receive a yearly general preventive examination and consultation without charge.
- ACA does not directly address the issue of the sustainable growth rate (SGR) formula.
- ACA establishes a new mechanism for addressing the issue of the rising cost of Medicare over time. This issue will now be the responsibility of a newly established Independent Payment Advisory Board (IPAB), to be made up of fifteen members appointed by the president and confirmed by the Senate. It will be the explicit responsibility of IPAB to monitor the rate at which Medicare's per beneficiary spending increases over time. ACA sets a target rate of growth for Medicare spending, tied initially to the growth in the consumer price index and subsequently to the overall growth in GDP. Beginning in 2014, if it turns out that projected per beneficiary spending will exceed the target amount, IPAB is charged with the responsibility of coming up with a plan to rein in spending to meet the target amount. The secretary of health and human services must then carry out the IPAB's plan to control spending, unless Congress overrides the plan with one of its own.
- In granting IPAB responsibility for enforcing the limits on Medicare spending growth,

Congress has limited IPAB's effectiveness. Section 3403.d.2.A.ii of ACA specifically states that any proposal from IPAB "shall not include any recommendation to ration health care, raise revenues [that is, taxes] or Medicare beneficiary premiums . . . or increase Medicare beneficiary cost sharing (including deductibles, coinsurance, and copayments), or otherwise restrict benefits or modify eligibility criteria." ACA does not define what is meant by "rationing" care under Medicare.

- ACA provides new funding for demonstration projects intended to identify new ways to reduce costs while maintaining quality. ACA creates a new Center for Medicare and Medicaid Innovations (CMMI) to study these new arrangements for care.
- One focus of CMMI is on encouraging groups of physicians and hospitals to come together to form accountable care organizations (ACOs). An ACO would take full responsibility for the care of a group of Medicare beneficiaries, planning, coordinating, and providing their care. If the ACO is able to reduce the cost of caring for its patients as compared to Medicare's average per beneficiary cost, the ACO would receive a share of the cost savings as an incentive payment.
- Through demonstration projects, ACA extends the prospective payment system (PPS), used previously to pay for hospital care, to encompass physician care, hospital care, outpatient services such as laboratory or X-ray, and rehabilitative services.
- ACA changes the formula by which the Part A Medicare payroll tax is calculated, increasing the tax rate from 1.45 to 2.35 percent for high-income taxpayers. It also creates some new taxes to be imposed on pharmaceutical companies, medical device companies, and certain health insurance companies.
- ACA increases somewhat the Medicare Part B premiums on high-income beneficiaries.
- ACA reduces certain payments to hospitals. Among these are payments previously made to hospitals that provide a disproportionate amount of care to the poor and the uninsured.
- ACA changes the way yearly updates in payment rates to providers will be calculated. ACA assumes that, over time, providers of services under Medicare will be able to improve their efficiency and productivity, and thus their cost of providing service. Based on these assumed efficiency enhancements, Medicare's increases in payment to providers will be about 1.1 percent less each year than they would have been without the expected changes in provider efficiency.
- The Medicare trustees estimate that, as a result of ACA, the predicted exhaustion of the Part A trust fund will be postponed, from 2017 (before ACA) to 2029.
- Under ACA, annual increases in the cost of Part B are expected to fall from historical growth rates that were 4.2 percent greater than the growth in GDP, to rates approximately equal to the growth in GDP.

## THE AFFORDABLE CARE ACT AND ITS IMPACT ON MEDICAID AND S-CHIP

- Beginning in 2014, ACA fundamentally changes the structure of Medicaid by making benefits available to *all* people who are poor, regardless of health status or family status. In addition, under ACA Medicaid will provide coverage to all those with incomes below 133 percent of the FPL, rather than the previous level of 100 percent. It is estimated that approximately 16 million uninsured individuals will obtain coverage through Medicaid as a result of ACA.
- ACA makes Medicaid analogous to Medicare, in that it will provide the same level of benefits to all those in poverty. Both Medicare and Medicaid will provide universal coverage to eligible populations.

- ACA defines a new level of federal support for those who become newly eligible for benefits under ACA. When the expanded Medicaid coverage becomes available in 2014, the federal government will initially pay 100 percent of the cost of the care provided to newly eligible enrollees. Over a period of six years the federal reimbursement rate for these enrollees will gradually drop to 90 percent, with the states ultimately responsible for 10 percent of the cost of their care. For those who were already eligible for Medicaid at the time ACA was enacted, the federal government will maintain the previous reimbursement rate. Thus after 2014, states will receive a substantially higher federal reimbursement rate for those who become newly eligible for Medicaid than they will receive for the traditional Medicaid coverage groups.
- This split level of reimbursement, especially in light of the financial strains many states have been experiencing, may create a new area of disagreement and political tension. Many of the states may argue that the federal government should provide a 90 percent reimbursement rate for *all* Medicaid enrollees, not just new enrollees.
- ACA extends the authorization of the State Children's Health Insurance Program (S-CHIP) through 2019, and provides funding through 2015.
- If a family with a child eligible for S-CHIP is unable to enroll the child because the state in which they live has reached its enrollment cap, the family would become eligible for a federal tax credit that would allow the family to enroll the child in coverage through the newly established HBEs.
- Beginning in 2013, any primary care physician (defined as a physician in family medicine, general internal medicine, or general pediatrics) providing care to a patient on Medicaid will be paid at the same rate as would be paid under the Medicare system. The federal government will reimburse states for 100 percent of the difference between the Medicare rate and the previous Medicaid rate.

## THE AFFORDABLE CARE ACT AND FOR-PROFIT HEALTH CARE

- The medical loss ratio (MLR) is the percentage of funds received by a health insurance company in premiums that is paid out for the provision of health care to covered patients. ACA divides insurers into two groups: (1) those providing coverage in the market for large employee groups and (2) those providing coverage for individuals and small employee groups. ACA establishes a minimum MLR of 80 percent for plans in the small group market and 85 percent for plans in the market for large groups. Any plan with a MLR that falls below this mandated level will be required to provide a rebate to its enrollees covering the difference.
- ACA imposes a new fee that large health insurance companies will be required to pay, beginning in 2014, based on the size of their market share. Nonprofit managed care or insurance plans will pay a reduced fee. In 2014, these fees are expected to bring in approximately $8 billion in new revenue, rising to more than $14 billion in 2018.
- ACA establishes a series of regulations on how health plans are administered. Under ACA, companies are prohibited from considering pre-existing conditions to deny coverage to an applicant. Similarly, all applicants must be charged the same premium regardless of pre-existing conditions, with a few important exceptions. Different rates may be charged based on a patient's age, family composition, tobacco use, participation in a health promotion program, and geographic region of residence. Similarly, caps on the amount an insurance plan will pay for care, either per year or for a patient's lifetime, will be prohibited.
- ACA requires health plans to report a range of new data, and will require health plans to

be certified by the federal government in order to be eligible to participate in the health insurance exchanges established by ACA. ACA also establishes a process by which annual increases in health plan premiums will be subject to federal review, with plans required to provide data justifying the increases.

- Under ACA, new physician-owned hospitals will not be permitted, and existing physician-owned hospitals will not be permitted to expand, except under strict conditions.

## THE AFFORDABLE CARE ACT AND PHARMACEUTICAL POLICY

- The principal impact of ACA on pharmaceutical policy is on the "doughnut hole" gap in coverage under Medicare Part D plans. Effective in 2010, all beneficiaries who reached the "doughnut hole" gap in their coverage were eligible for a $250 rebate directly from Medicare. Beginning in 2011, any beneficiary reaching the gap and having a prescription for a brand-name drug (that is, a drug not yet available in generic form) will receive a 50 percent discount in the price of the drug, provided by the drug's manufacturer. Also beginning in 2011, there will be a gradual increase in coverage provided in the gap. This added coverage will initially be only for generic drugs, but will expand in 2013 to include brand-name drugs. The amount the beneficiary who reaches the gap will have to pay will gradually decline from the original level of 100 percent of the cost of the drug, to 25 percent of the cost in 2020.
- ACA imposes a new fee on pharmaceutical manufacturers. These fees are expected to raise $2.8 billion in new revenue in 2012, rising to $4.1 billion in 2018, and then falling again to $2.8 billion in 2019 and beyond.

## THE AFFORDABLE CARE ACT AND LONG-TERM CARE

- ACA establishes a "community living and assistance services and supports" (CLASS) program that will offer a new type of long-term care insurance to those who wish to purchase it. The benefits of the program may be used to purchase support services that allow individuals in need of assistance to maintain a residence in the community.
- ACA establishes a series of new reporting requirements for skilled nursing facilities, covering issues such as ownership, accountability, expenditures, and quality data. This information will be posted to a website so Medicare enrollees can review it in order to compare facilities.

## COVERING THE UNINSURED UNDER THE AFFORDABLE CARE ACT

- ACA extends Medicaid coverage to all citizens and permanent residents with incomes below 133 percent of the FPL.
- ACA requires that, beginning in 2014, all citizens and permanent residents with incomes at or above 133 percent of the FPL either obtain private health insurance coverage or pay a tax penalty not to exceed 2.5 percent of taxable income.
- For those with incomes between 133 and 400 percent of the FPL who do not receive health insurance from their employer, ACA provides a tax credit to subsidize the purchase of private coverage. The credit will cap the amount an individual or family must pay for coverage, starting with a cap of 2 percent of income for those at 133 percent of the FPL and increasing to a cap of 9.5 percent of income for those at 400 percent of the FPL.

- ACA requires states to establish HBEs, operated either by the state government or by a nonprofit organization. Each exchange will offer at least two options for health insurance coverage, one of which must be offered by a nonprofit insurer. Insurers will be able to offer different predefined levels of care for different premiums. For those enrollees with incomes below 400 percent of the FPL, the plans must cap out-of-pocket expenses according to a predefined schedule. States are permitted to collaborate to form regional exchanges. In states failing to establish an exchange before 2014, the federal government will create and manage the exchange.
- ACA requires employers with more than fifty employees either to provide coverage for employees or to pay a penalty of $2,000 for each employee without coverage from work who instead acquires coverage from the state insurance exchange. ACA exempts employers with fifty or fewer employees from this requirement, and also exempts larger employers from paying the penalty on the first thirty employees who obtain coverage from an exchange.
- ACA places restrictions on the coverage of abortion under plans offered through the state exchanges.
- There is general agreement that the steps outlined above will extend health insurance coverage to an additional 32 million Americans by the time it is fully implemented in 2019. Approximately half of these newly insured will be covered through the expansion of Medicaid, with the other half covered either through expansion of employer-provided coverage or through the newly established health insurance exchanges.

## THE AFFORDABLE CARE ACT AND ACCESS TO HEALTH CARE

- ACA provides for an increase in reimbursement for primary care physicians who treat Medicaid patients. In this context, "primary care" means care provided by a physician in family medicine, general internal medicine, or general pediatrics. Effective January 1, 2013, these physicians will be paid at 100 percent of the rate paid by the Medicare program, with the incremental cost of the increased reimbursement paid by the federal government.
- ACA invests in the expansions of nonprofit community health centers. Often referred to as federally qualified health centers (FQHCs), these clinics receive extra federal funding to treat Medicaid patients. ACA expands this funding, allowing FQHCs to hire additional personnel.
- ACA allocates additional funding to allow primary care residency programs to expand their training sites to include FQHCs and other community-based resources.
- ACA expands support for the National Health Service Corps, the federal program that provides medical students with either scholarship support during medical school or educational loan repayment after medical school in return for spending a period of years in primary care practice in a rural or urban community that has a documented shortage of health manpower.
- ACA provides additional support for FQHCs to strengthen their organizational capacity to act as the "patient-centered medical home" (PCMH) for their patients by developing a team-based approach to the management of chronic disease, expanding the use of electronic health records, and strengthening connections with referral sources of specialty care.
- ACA requires providers to collect data on the race, ethnicity, primary language, disability status, and similar demographic characteristics of the patients cared for. The federal government will then analyze these data to monitor racial and ethnic disparities in access to care.

## LONG-TERM IMPLICATIONS OF HEALTH CARE COSTS AFTER THE AFFORDABLE CARE ACT

- The Congressional Budget Office has projected that ACA will result in a net reduction in the federal deficit of $124 billion over ten years.
- ACA is expected to result in a net increase in overall health care expenditures. The actuary at the federal Centers for Medicare and Medicaid Services has concluded that, as a result of ACA, overall national expenditures for health care will rise faster than they would have had ACA not been adopted. By 2019, national health expenditures under the provisions of ACA are predicted to rise to 19.6 percent of GDP, as compared to 19.3 percent had ACA not been enacted.

## WEB RESOURCES TO LEARN MORE ABOUT THE AFFORDABLE CARE ACT

U.S. Department of Health & Human Services, HealthCare.Gov—Understanding the Affordable Care Act, www.healthcare.gov/law/introduction/index.html

The Commonwealth Fund - Health Reform Resource Center, www.commonwealthfund.org/Health-Reform/Health-Reform-Resource.aspx

Kaiser Family Foundation—Health Reform Source—The Basics, http://healthreform.kff.org/the-basics.aspx

# ON-LINE DATA SOURCES

### 1. THE AFFORDABLE CARE ACT AND THE POLITICS OF HEALTH CARE REFORM

U.S. Department of Health & Human Services, HealthCare.Gov website at www.healthcare.gov

The Commonwealth Fund—Health Reform Resource Center, available at www.commonwealth fund.org/Health-Reform/Health-Reform-Resource.aspx

Kaiser Family Foundation—Health Reform Source—The Basics, available at healthreform.kff .org/the-basics.aspx

### 2. HEALTH, HEALTH CARE, AND THE MARKET ECONOMY

Agency for Healthcare Research and Quality. www.ahrq.gov/.

Kaiser Family Foundation. Data about the number of uninsured are available at www.kff.org/.

Organisation for Economic Co-operation and Development (OECD). Data about comparative national health statistics are available at www.oecd.org/.

U.S. Census Bureau. Data about the number of uninsured are available at www.census.gov/.

U.S. Centers for Medicare and Medicaid Services. Data about national health care expenditures in the United States are available at www.cms.gov/NationalHealthExpendData/.

### 3. HEALTH CARE AS A REFLECTION OF UNDERLYING CULTURAL VALUES AND INSTITUTIONS

Organisation for Economic Co-operation and Development (OECD). Data about comparative national health statistics are available at www.oecd.org/.

### 4. THE HEALTH PROFESSIONS AND THE ORGANIZATION OF HEALTH CARE

American Medical Association. www.ama-assn.org/.

Association of American Medical Colleges. FACTS—Applicants, Matriculants, and Graduates, 1993–2004 is available at www.aamc.org/data/facts/.

U.S. Health Resources and Services Administration. www.hrsa.gov/.

### 5. HEALTH INSURANCE, HMOS, AND THE MANAGED CARE REVOLUTION

RAND Corporation. Information about the RAND Health Insurance Experiment is available at www.rand.org/health/projects/hie/.

U.S. Centers for Medicare and Medicaid Services. Data about national health care expenditures in the United States are available at www.cms.gov/NationalHealthExpendData/.

### 6. MEDICARE

Internal Revenue Service (IRS). Information about health savings accounts is available from Publication 969—Health Savings Accounts and Other Tax-Favored Health Plans. Available at www.irs.gov/publications/.

Kaiser Family Foundation. Extensive data and charts about Medicare are compiled and are available at www.kff.org/medicare/index.cfm.

Medicare Payment Advisory Commission (MedPAC). Detailed data about the Medicare program are available at www.medpac.gov/.

Medicare Trustees. The annual report of the Medicare trustees is available at www.ssa.gov/OACT/TR/.

RAND Corporation. Information about the RAND Health Insurance Experiment is available at www.rand.org/health/projects/hie/.

U.S. Centers for Medicare and Medicaid Services. Extensive information about Medicare and other federal programs is available at www.cms.hhs.gov/.

## 7. MEDICAID AND THE STATE CHILDREN'S HEALTH INSURANCE PROGRAM

Kaiser Family Foundation is a nonprofit organization that works extensively on health policy issues. It has created a major research effort, the Kaiser Commission on Medicaid and the Uninsured. As part of its ongoing study of Medicaid and SCHIP, it has prepared the following reports, all available on line:

- Managed Care and Low-Income Populations: A Case Study of Managed Care in California. May 2000. www.kff.org/medicaid/2169-index.cfm.
- Managed Care and Low-Income Populations: Four Years' Experience with the Oregon Health Plan. September 1999. www.kff.org/medicaid/2127-index.cfm.
- Managed Care and Low-Income Populations: Four Years' Experience with TennCare. September 1999. www.kff.org/medicaid/2129-index.cfm.
- The Medicaid Resource Book. January 2003. www.kff.org/medicaid/2236-index.cfm.

Kaiser Family Foundation. State Health Facts is a project run by the Kaiser Family Foundation and is available at www.statehealthfacts.org.

U.S. Census Bureau. Information about health insurance coverage is available at www.census.gov/hhes/www/hlthins/hlthins.html.

U.S. Centers for Medicare and Medicaid Services. Extensive information about Medicaid and SCHIP in the form of both narrative reports and data tables is available at www.cms.gov/home/medicaid.asp / or at www.cms.gov/home/chip.asp/.

## 8. THE INCREASING ROLE OF FOR-PROFIT HEALTH CARE

Kaiser Family Foundation. Trends in health care are charted as part of the Health Care Marketplace Project. A chartbook, Trends and Indicators in the Changing Health Care Marketplace, is updated regularly and is available at www.kff.org/insurance/7031/index.cfm.

RAND Corporation. Information about the RAND Health Insurance Experiment is available at www.rand.org/health/projects/hie/.

## 9. PHARMACEUTICAL POLICY AND THE RISING COST OF PRESCRIPTION DRUGS

U.S. Centers for Medicare and Medicaid Services. Data about prescription drug expenditures in the United States are available at www.cms.hhs.gov/.

U.S. Food and Drug Administration. The Center for Drug Evaluation and Research provides information on drug approvals at www.fda.gov/AboutFDA/CentersOffices/CDER/.

U.S. Food and Drug Administration reports the number of new drug applications approved, by year of approval, therapeutic potential, and chemical type. www.fda.gov/cder/rdmt/pstable .htm.

## 10. LONG-TERM CARE

National Center for Health Statistics. Information about nursing home care is available at www .cdc.gov/nchs/fastats/nursingh.htm. Data about home care and hospice care are available at www.cdc.gov/nchs/about/major/nhhcsd/nhhcshomecare3.htm.

U.S. Census Bureau. Current data and projections about future population statistics are available at www.census.gov/.

U.S. Centers for Medicare and Medicaid Services. Data on nursing home expenditures are available at www.cms.hhs.gov/.

U.S. General Accounting Office. Several reports about long-term care are available at www.gao .gov/, including:

- Long-Term Care Insurance: Better Information Critical to Prospective Purchasers. 2000. Report No. GAO/T-HEHS-00-196.
- Medicare: More Beneficiaries Use Hospice but for Fewer Days of Care. 2000. Report No. GAO/HEHS-00-182.
- Long-term Care Financing: Growing Demand and Cost of Services Are Straining Federal and State Budgets. 2005. Report No. GAO-05-564T.

## 11. THE UNINSURED

Kaiser Family Foundation. Numerous reports and data about the uninsured are published through the Kaiser Commission on Medicaid and the Uninsured available at www.kff.org.

U.S. Bureau of Labor Statistics. Unemployment data are available at http://stats.bls.gov.

U.S. Census Bureau. Extensive information about the uninsured is available at www.census .gov/.

U.S. Centers for Medicare and Medicaid Services. Data about national health care expenditures in the United States are available at www.cms.gov/NationalHealthExpendData/.

## 12. FACTORS OTHER THAN HEALTH INSURANCE THAT IMPEDE ACCESS TO CARE

RAND Corporation. Information about the RAND Health Insurance Experiment is available at www.rand.org/health/projects/hie/.

U.S. Department of Health and Human Services. Information about the National Standards on Culturally and Linguistically Appropriate Services in Health Care is available from the Office of Minority Health available at www.omhrc.gov/.

# REFERENCES

Abell I. 1938. Address to the special session of the House of Delegates of the American Medical Association. *JAMA* 111:1192–94.

Agency for Healthcare Research and Quality. 2009. National Healthcare Quality Report, www.ahrq.gov/qual/nhqr09/Key.htm.

Aiken LH, Cheung RB, and Olds DM. 2009. Education policy initiatives to address the nurse shortage in the United States. *Health Affairs* 28(4):w646-w656.

Aiken LH, Clarke SP, Sloane DM, Sochalski J, and Silber JH. 2002. Hospital nurse staffing and patient mortality, nurse burnout, and job dissatisfaction. *JAMA* 288:1987–93.

Alexander GC, and Stafford RS. 2009. Does comparative effectiveness have a comparative edge? *JAMA* 301:2488–90.

ALLHAT Collaborative Research Group. 2002. Major outcomes in high-risk hypertensive patients randomized to angiotensin-converting enzyme inhibitor or calcium channel blocker vs diuretic. *JAMA* 288:2981–97.

American Academy of Family Physicians, American Academy of Pediatrics, American College of Physicians, and American Osteopathic Association. 2007. Joint principles of the patient-centered medical home, March, www.medicalhomeinfo.org/downloads/pdfs/JointStatement.pdf.

American Academy of Nurse Practitioners. n.d. About nurse practitioners, www.aanp.org/AANPCMS2/AboutAANP/About+NPs.htm.

American Academy of Physician Assistants. 2009. National Physician Assistant Census Report, www.aapa.org/about-pas/data-and-statistics/aapa-cenus/2009-data.

American Association of Health Plans. 1999. Enrollment, Growth, Accreditation. www.aahp.org/.

American Medical Association. 1932. The committee on the costs of medical care (editorial). *JAMA* 99:1950.

American Medical Association. 1934a. Minutes of the eighty-fifth annual session. *JAMA* 102:2200.

American Medical Association. 1934b. Proceedings of the House of Delegates from June 12, 1934. *JAMA* 102:2199–2201.

American Medical Association. 1935. Minutes of the special session of the House of Delegates of the American Medical Association. *JAMA* 104:747–53.

American Medical Association. 1938. Minutes of the special session of the House of Delegates of the American Medical Association. *JAMA* 111:1191–1217.

American Medical Association. 1948. Report of the council on medical services. *JAMA* 138:683–86.

American Medical Association. 1965. AMA urges defeat of Medicare. *JAMA* 192:15–17.

American Medical Association. 2010. AMA study shows competition disappearing in the health insurance industry. *American Medical Association News,* February 23.

Anderson GF, Hussey PS, Frogner BK, and Waters HR. 2005. Health spending in the United States and the rest of the industrialized world. *Health Affairs* 24(4):903–14.

Andriole GL, Crawford ED, Grubb RL, et al. 2009. Mortality results from a randomized prostate-cancer screening trial. *New England Journal of Medicine* 60:1310–19.

Angell M. 2004. *The Truth about Drug Companies: How They Deceive Us and What to Do about It.* New York: Random House.

Arrow K. 1963. Uncertainty and the welfare economics of medical care. *American Economic Review* 53:941–69.

Asplin BR, Rhodes KV, Levy H, et al. 2005. Insurance status and access to urgent ambulatory care follow-up appointments. *JAMA* 294:1248–54.

Association of American Medical Colleges. 2005. Cultural Competence Education for Medical Students. www.aamc.org/meded/tacct/culturalcomped.pdf.

Association of American Medical Colleges. 2008. *Industry Funding of Medical Education: Report of an AAMC Task Force,* http://services.aamc.org/publications/index.cfm?fuseaction=Product.displayForm&prd_id=232&prv_id=281.

Ayanian JZ, Cleary PD, Weissman JS, and Epstein AM. 1999a. The effect of patients' preferences on racial differences in access to renal transplantation. *New England Journal of Medicine* 341:1661–69.

Ayanian JZ, Weissman JS, Chasen-Taber S, and Epstein AM. 1999b. Quality of care by race and gender for congestive heart failure. *Medical Care* 37:1260–69.

Ayanian JZ, Weissman JS, Schneider EC, et al. 2000. Unmet health needs of uninsured adults in the United States. *JAMA* 284:2061–69.

Bach PB, Cramer LD, Warren JL, and Begg CB. 1999. Racial differences in the treatment of early-stage lung cancer. *New England Journal of Medicine* 341:1198–1205.

Baker RB, Caplan AL, Emanuel LL, and Latham SR, eds. 1999. *The American Medical Ethics Revolution: How the AMA's Code of Ethics Has Transformed Physicians' Relationships to Patients, Professionals, and Society.* Baltimore: Johns Hopkins University Press.

Baker RB, Washington HA, Olkanmi O, et al. 2008. African American physicians and organized medicine, 1846–1968. *JAMA* 300:306–13.

Ball RM. 1995. What Medicare's architects had in mind. *Health Affairs* 14(4):62–72.

Bardy GH, Lee KL, Mark DB, et al. 2005. Amiodarone on an implantable cardioverter-debrillator for congestive heart failure. *New England Journal of Medicine* 352:225–37.

Baron RJ. 2010. What's keeping us so busy in primary care? A snapshot from one office. *New England Journal of Medicine* 362:1632–36.

Barr DA. 1995. The effect of organizational structure on primary care outcomes under managed care. *Annals of Internal Medicine* 122:353–59.

Barr DA, Vergun P, and Barley SA. 2000. Problems in using patient satisfaction data to assess the quality of care of primary care physicians. *Journal of Clinical Outcomes Management* 7(9):1–6.

Barry MJ. 2008. Screening for prostate cancer—the controversy that refused to die. *New England Journal of Medicine* 360:1351–54.

Bennett WM. 2004. Ethical conflicts for physicians treating ESRD patients. *Seminars in Dialysis* 17(1):1–3.

Berndt ER. 2005. To inform or persuade? Direct-to-consumer advertising of prescription drugs. *New England Journal of Medicine* 352:325–28.

Blendon RJ, Altman DE, Benson JM, et al. 2008a. Voters and health care reform in the 2008 presidential election. *New England Journal of Medicine* 359:2050–61.

Blendon RJ, Altman DE, Dean C, et al. 2008b. Health care reform in the 2008 presidential primaries. *New England Journal of Medicine* 358:414–22.

Blendon RJ, Buhr T, Cassify EF, et al. 2007. Disparities in health: Perspectives of a multi-ethnic, multi-racial America. *Health Affairs* 26(5):1437–47.

Blumenthal D. 2004. Doctors and drug companies. *New England Journal of Medicine* 351:1885–90.

Boards of Trustees of the Federal Hospital Insurance and Federal Supplementary Medical Insurance Trust Funds. 2009. 2009 Annual Report, www.cms.gov/ReportsTrustFunds/.

Boren SD. 1994. "I had a tough day today, Hillary." *New England Journal of Medicine* 330:500–502.

Bowman JG. 1918. Standard of efficiency. *Bulletin of the American College of Surgeons* III, no. 3:1.

Boyce EA. 2000. Access to Bone Marrow Transplants for Multiple Myeloma Patients: The Role of Race. Undergraduate thesis, Program in Human Biology, Stanford University.

Braveman P, Schaaf VM, Egerter S, Bennett T, and Schecter W. 1994. Insurance-related differences in the risk of ruptured appendix. *New England Journal of Medicine* 331:444–49.

Brennan TA, Leape LL, Laird NM, et al. 1991. Incidence of adverse events and negligence in hospitalized patients: Results of the Harvard Medical Practice Study I. *New England Journal of Medicine* 324:370–76.

Brennan TA, Sox CM, and Burstin HR. 1996. Relation between negligent adverse events and the outcomes of medical-malpractice litigation. *New England Journal of Medicine* 335: 1963–67.

Brenner DJ. 2010. Medical imaging in the 21st century—getting the best bang for the rad. *New England Journal of Medicine* 362:943–45.

Brotherton SE, and Etzel SI. 2009. Graduate medical education, 2008–2009. *JAMA* 302:1357–61.

Buerhaus PI. 2008. Current and future state of the US nursing workforce. *JAMA* 300:2422–24.

Burke GL, Sprafka JM, and Folsom AR. 1991. Trends in serum cholesterol levels from 1980 to 1987. *New England Journal of Medicine* 324:941–46.

Callahan D. 2009. Cost control—time to get serious. *New England Journal of Medicine* 361:e10.

Calman NS. 2000. Out of the shadow. *Health Affairs* 19(1):170–74.

*Canadian Journal of Cardiology.* 2005. Vol. 21:Supplement A contains a series of papers reporting on the guidelines for the use of ICDs and the policy considerations surrounding their use.

Centers for Disease Control and Prevention. 2009. H1N1 vaccination recommendations, www.cdc.gov/h1n1flu/vaccination/acip.htm.

Centers for Disease Control and Prevention. 2010. The 2009 H1N1 pandemic: Summary highlights, April 2009–April 2010, www.cdc.gov/h1n1flu/cdresponse.htm.

Chang JT, Hays RD, Shekelle PG, et al. 2006. Patients' global ratings of their health care are not associated with the technical quality of their care. *Annals of Internal Medicine* 144:665–72.

Chernew M, Cutler DM, and Keenan PS. 2005. Increasing health insurance costs and the decline in insurance coverage. *Health Services Research* 40:1021–39.

Chernew ME, Baicker K, and Hsu J. 2010. The specter of financial Armageddon—health care and federal debt in the United States. *New England Journal of Medicine* 362:1166–68.

Choudry NK, and Detsky AS. 2005. A perspective on US drug reimportation. *JAMA* 293:358–62.

Cleary BL, McBride AB, McClure ML, and Reinhard SC. 2009. Expanding the capacity of nursing education. *Health Affairs* 28(4):w634–w645.

The Commonwealth Fund. 2008. Massachusetts health care reform—on secondary anniversary of passage, what progress has been made? States in Action, April/May, www.commonwealthfund.org/Publications/Newsletters/States-in-Action.aspx.

Congressional Budget Office. 2006. The sustainable growth rate formula for setting Medicare's physician payment rates, September, www.cbo.gov/ftpdocs/75xx/doc7542/09-07-SGR-brief.pdf.

Conway PH, and Clancy C. 2009. Comparative-effectiveness research—implications of the Federal Coordinating Council's report. *New England Journal of Medicine* 361:328–30.

Cram P, Rosenthal GE, and Vaughan-Sarrazin MS. 2005. Cardiac revascularization in specialty and general hospitals. *New England Journal of Medicine* 352(14):1454–62.

Cunningham PJ. 2005. Medicaid cost containment and access to prescription drugs. *Health Affairs* 24:780–89.

Cunningham PJ, Hadley J, and Reschovsky J. 2002. The effects of SCHIP on children's health insurance coverage: Early evidence from the community tracking study. *Medical Care Research and Review* 59:359–83.

Cunningham PJ, and May JH. 2006. Medicaid patients increasingly concentrated among physicians. Center for Studying Health System Change, August, www.hschange.org/CONTENT/866/#ib1.

David PA. 1985. Clio and the economics of QWERTY. *AEA Papers and Proceedings* 75:332.

Davies AR, Ware JE, Brook RH, et al. 1986. Consumer acceptance of prepaid and fee-for-service medical care: Results from a randomized controlled trial. *Health Services Research* 21:429–49.

Davis K, Schoen C, Schoenbaum SC, et al. 2007. Mirror, mirror on the wall: An international update on the comparative performance of American health care. The Commonwealth Fund, May, available at www.commonwealthfund.org/Content/Publications/Fund-Reports/2007/May/Mirror-Mirror-on-the-Wall—An-International-Update-on-the-Comparative-Performance-of-American-Healt.aspx.

Davis RM. 2008. Achieving racial harmony for the benefit of patients and communities: Contrition, reconciliation, and collaboration. *JAMA* 300:323–25.

De Alteriis M, and Fanning T. 1991. A public health model of Medicaid emergency room use. *Health Care Financing Review* 12(3):15–20.

DeMaria AN. 2005. Concierge medicine: For better or for worse? *Journal of the American College of Cardiology* 46:377–78.

DesRoches CM, Blendon RJ, and Benson JM. 2005. Americans' responses to the 2004 influenza vaccine shortage. *Health Affairs* 24(3):822–31.

Devereaux PJ, Schunemann HJ, Ravindran N, et al. 2002. Comparison of mortality between private for-profit and private not-for-profit hemodialysis centers: A systematic review and meta-analysis. *JAMA* 288:2449–57.

DiMaggio PJ. 1988. Interest and agency in institutional theory. Pp. 3–21 in Zucker L., ed., *Institutional Patterns and Organizations*. Cambridge, Mass.: Ballinger.

Docteur E, and Berenson RA. 2009. How does the quality of U.S. health care compare internationally? The Urban Institute, August, www.urban.org/publications/411947.html.

Dovidio J, and Gaertner S. 1998. On the nature of contemporary prejudice: The causes, consequences, and challenges of aversive racism. In Eberhardt J, and Fiske S, eds., *Confronting Racism: The Problem and the Response*. Thousand Oaks, Calif.: Sage Publications.

Drazen JM. 2005. COX-2 inhibitors: A lesson in unexpected problems (editorial). *New England Journal of Medicine* 352:1131–32.

Eisenberg L. 1995. Medicine: Molecular, monetary, or more than both? *JAMA* 274:331–34.

Emanuel EJ, and Fuchs VR. 2005. Health care vouchers: A proposal for universal coverage. *New England Journal of Medicine* 352:1255–60.

Enthoven A. 1980. *Health Plan: The Only Practical Solution to the Soaring Cost of Medical Care*. Reading, Mass.: Addison-Wesley.

Enthoven AE, and Kronick R. 1989. A consumer-choice health plan for the 1990s. *New England Journal of Medicine* 320:29–37 (Part 1); 94–101 (Part 2).

Enthoven AE, and Kronick R. 1991. Universal health insurance through incentives reform. *JAMA* 265:2532–36.

Entman SS, Glass CA, Hickson GB, et al. 1994. The relation between malpractice claims history and subsequent obstetrical quality. *JAMA* 272:1588–91.

Fadiman A. 1997. *The Spirit Catches You and You Fall Down*. New York: Farrar, Straus and Giroux.

Feder J, Komisar HL, and Niefeld M. 2000. Long-term care in the United States: An overview. *Health Affairs* 19(3):40–56.

Fishbein M. 1948. Health and Social Security. *JAMA* 138:1254–56.

Flexner A. 1910. *Medical Education in the United States and Canada.* New York: Carnegie Foundation for the Advancement of Teaching.

Fontanarosa PB, Rennie D, and DeAngelis CD. 2004. Postmarketing surveillance: Lack of vigilance, lack of trust. *JAMA* 292:2647–50.

Freidson E. 1970. *Profession of Medicine: A Study of the Sociology of Applied Knowledge.* New York: Dodd, Mead.

Friedman E. 1994. Money isn't everything: Nonfinancial barriers to access. *JAMA* 271:1535–38.

Frosch DL, Grande D, Tam DM, and Kravitz RL. 2010. A decade of controversy: Balancing policy with evidence in the regulation of prescription drug advertising. *American Journal of Public Health* 100:24–32.

Fuchs VR. 1983. *Who Shall Live?* New York: Basic Books.

Fuchs VR. 1986. *The Health Economy.* Cambridge, Mass.: Harvard University Press.

Fuchs VR. 1993a. Cost containment: No pain, no gain. Chapter 10 in Fuchs VR, *The Future of Health Policy.* Cambridge, Mass.: Harvard University Press.

Fuchs VR. 1993b. Dear President Clinton. *JAMA* 269:1678–79.

Fuchs VR. 1993c. The "competition revolution" of the 1980s. Chapter 11 in Fuchs VR, *The Future of Health Policy.* Cambridge, Mass.: Harvard University Press.

Fuchs VR. 1993d. *The Future of Health Policy.* Cambridge, Mass.: Harvard University Press.

Fuchs VR. 2009. Eliminating "waste" in health care. *JAMA* 302:2481–82.

Fuchs VR. 2010. Health care is different—that's why expenditures matter. *JAMA* 303:1859–60.

Furman B. 1948. Truman gets report urging big 10-year health program. *New York Times,* September 3.

Garfield S, Cutting C, Feldman R, Taller SL, and Collen MF. 1987. Total health care project: Final report. Oakland, Calif.: Permanente Medical Group.

Garfield SR. 1974. The Permanente Medical Group—historical remarks. Presented to the Executive Committee on April 24.

Garg PP, Frick KD, Diener-West M, and Powe NR. 1999. Effect of the ownership of dialysis facilities on patients' survival and referral for transplantation. *New England Journal of Medicine* 341:1653–60.

Gawande A. 2009. The cost conundrum—what a Texas town can teach us about health care. *The New Yorker,* June 1, www.newyorker.com/reporting/2009/06/01/090601fa_fact_gawande?currentPage=1.

Gilmer T, and Kronick R. 2005. It's the premiums, stupid: Projections of the uninsured through 2013. *Health Affairs* (Web Exclusive) W5:143–51. http://content.healthaffairs.org/cgi/content/abstract/hlthaff.w5.143v1.

Gold M, Phelps D, Jacobson G, and Neuman T. 2010. Medicare Advantage 2010 data spotlight: Plan enrollment patterns and trends. Kaiser Family Foundation, June, www.kff.org/medicare/8080.cfm.

Goodman E. 1998. The HMO horror show. *Boston Globe,* March 29.

Grassley C. 2009. Health care reform—a Republican view. *New England Journal of Medicine* 361:2397–99.

Gray B. 1986. *For-Profit Enterprise in Health Care.* Washington, D.C.: National Academies Press.

Hall, MA. 2011. Clearing out the underbrush in constitutional challenges to health insurance reform. *New England Journal of Medicine.* 10.1056/nejmp1101252, published on-line February 2, at www.nejm.org.

Hamilton WH. 1932. Statement. Pp. 189–200 in *Medical Care for the American People: The Final*

*Report of the Committee on the Cost of Medical Care, Adopted October 31, 1932.* Chicago: University of Chicago Press.

Hasan MM. 1996. Let's end the nonprofit charade. *New England Journal of Medicine* 334:1055–57.

*Health Affairs.* 2008. The imaging boom. *Health Affairs* 27(6):1466.

Health Canada. 2009. Canada Health Act Annual Report 2008–2009, www.hc-sc.gc.ca/hcs-sss/pubs/cha-lcs/2009-cha-lcs-ar-ra/index-eng.php#intro.

Herszenhorn DM. 2009. An invitation to protestors. *New York Times,* November 5.

Herszenhorn DM. 2010. Budget reconciliation. *New York Times,* March 3.

Hibbard JH, Stockard J, and Tusler M. 2005. Hospital performance reports: Impact on quality, market share, and reputation. *Health Affairs* 24(4):1150–60.

Hickson GB, Clayton EW, Entman SS, et al. 1994. Obstetricians' prior malpractice experience and patients' satisfaction with care. *JAMA* 272:1583–87.

Hillman BJ, and Goldsmith JC. 2010. The uncritical use of high-tech medical imaging. *New England Journal of Medicine,* June 23, www.nejm.org.

Himmelstein DU, and Woolhandler S. 1989. A national health program for the United States: A physicians' proposal. *New England Journal of Medicine* 320:102–8.

Himmelstein DU, Woolhandler S, Hellander I, and Wolfe SM. 1999. Quality of care in investor-owned vs not-for-profit HMOs. *JAMA* 282:159–63.

Hoadley J, Hargrave E, Cubanski J, and Neuman T. 2008. The Medicare Part D coverage gap: Costs and consequences in 2007. Kaiser Family Foundation, www.kff.org/medicare/7811.cfm.

Horwitz JR. 2005. Making profits and providing care: Comparing nonprofit, for-profit, and government hospitals. *Health Affairs* 24(3):790–801.

Howlett K, Paperny AM, and Walton D. 2009. Private-clinic patients jump the line for flu shot. *The Globe and Mail,* November 2.

Hulse C. 2010. Another long march in the name of change. *New York Times,* March 21.

Hupfeld S. 2004. Evolution of the American hospital system: Subspecialization and physician ownership. *Circulation* 109(20):2379–80.

Huskamp HA, Deverka PA, Epstein AM, Epstein RS, McGuigan KA, and Frank RG. 2003. The effect of incentive-based formularies on prescription-drug utilization and spending. *New England Journal of Medicine* 349(23):2224–32.

Iglehart JK. 1993a. The American health care system: Community hospitals. *New England Journal of Medicine* 329:372–76.

Iglehart JK. 1993b. The American health care system: Medicaid. *New England Journal of Medicine* 328:896–900.

Iglehart JK. 2000. Revisiting the Canadian health care system. *New England Journal of Medicine* 342:2007–12.

Iglehart JK. 2002. Medicare's declining payments to physicians. *New England Journal of Medicine* 346:1924–30.

Iglehart JK. 2003. The dilemma of Medicaid. *New England Journal of Medicine* 348:2140–48.

Iglehart JK. 2004. The new Medicare prescription-drug benefit: A pure power play. *New England Journal of Medicine* 350:826–33.

Iglehart JK. 2005. The emergence of physician-owned specialty hospitals. *New England Journal of Medicine* 352:78–84.

Iglehart JK. 2007. The fate of SCHIP—surrogate marker for health care ideology? *New England Journal of Medicine* 357:2104–77.

Iglehart JK. 2008. Grassroots activism and the pursuit of an expanded primary care supply. *New England Journal of Medicine* 358:1741–49.

Iglehart JK. 2009a. Building momentum as Democrats forge health care reform. *New England Journal of Medicine* 360:2385–87.

Iglehart JK. 2009b. Expanding coverage for children—the Democrats' power and SCHIP reauthorization. *New England Journal of Medicine* 360:855–57.

Iglehart JK. 2009c. Prioritizing comparative effectiveness research—IOM recommendations. *New England Journal of Medicine* 361:325–28.

Iglehart JK. 2010a. The Democrats' last ditch—reconciliation or bust. *New England Journal of Medicine* 362:e39.

Iglehart JK. 2010b. Historic passage—reform at last. *New England Journal of Medicine* 362:e48, posted March 24, 2010, http://content.nejm.org/cgi/content/full/362/14/e48.

Ignagni K. 2009. Health insurers at the table—industry proposals for regulation and reform. *New England Journal of Medicine* 361:1133–34.

Institute of Medicine of the National Academies of Science. 2009. Conflict of interest in medical research, education, and practice. April, httm://iom.edu/Reports/2009/Conflict-of-Interest-in-Medical-Research-Education-and-Practice.aspx.

Interdepartmental Committee to Coordinate Health and Welfare Activities. 1938. *JAMA* 111: 432–54.

Jacobs LR. 2008. All over again? Public opinion and health care. *New England Journal of Medicine* 358:1881–83.

Jeffe DB, Whelan AJ, and Andriole DA. 2010. Primary care specialty choices of United States medical graduates, 1997–2006. *Academic Medicine* 85:947–58.

Jha AK, Fisher ES, Li Z, Orav EJ, and Epstein AM. 2005a. Racial trends in the use of major procedures among the elderly. *New England Journal of Medicine* 353:683–91.

Jha AK, Li Z, Orav EJ, and Epstein AM. 2005b. Care in U.S. hospitals: The Hospital Quality Alliance program. *New England Journal of Medicine* 353:265–74.

Johnson H, and Broder DS. 1996. *The System.* Boston: Little, Brown.

Kahn KL, Pearson ML, Harrison ER, et al. 1994. Health care for black and poor hospitalized Medicare patients. *JAMA* 271:1169–74.

Kaiser Family Foundation. 1999. Long-term care: Medicaid's role and challenges. Publication No. 2172. www.kff.org/medicaid/2172-index.cfm.

Kaiser Family Foundation. 2004. Prescription drug trends. Fact Sheet No. 3057. www.kff.org/rxdrugs/3057.cfm.

Kaiser Family Foundation. 2005. Medicaid: A primer. Publication No. 7334. www.kff.org/medicaid/7334.cfm.

Kaiser Family Foundation. n.d.-a. Medicaid/CHIP data, www.kff.org/Medicaid/index.cfm.

Kaiser Family Foundation. n.d.-b. Tracking Medicare health and prescription drug plans, www.kff.org/medicare/advantagetrackingreport_current.cfm.

Kaiser Family Foundation. 2009. Health coverage of children: The role of Medicaid and CHIP, October, www.kff.org/uninsured/7698.cfm.

Kaiser Family Foundation. 2010a. CHIP enrollment June 2009: An update on current enrollment and policy directions, April, www.kff.org/Medicaid/upload/7642–04.pdf.

Kaiser Family Foundation. 2010b. Kaiser health tracking poll, April, www.kff.org/kaiserpolls/upload/8067-F.pdf.

Kaiser Family Foundation. 2010c. Medicaid enrollment: December 2009 data snapshot. September, www.kff.org/Medicaid/upload/8050–02.pdf.

Kaiser Family Foundation. 2010d. Medicare, a primer. April, www.kff.org/medicare/7615.cfm.

Kaiser Family Foundation. 2010e. Medicare at a glance. January, www.kff.org/medicare/factsheets.cfm.

Kaiser Family Foundation. 2010f. Medicare spending and financing. August, www.kff.org/medicare/7305.cfm.

Kaiser Family Foundation. 2010g. State fiscal conditions and Medicaid. February, www.kff.org/Medicaid/7580.cfm.

Kaiser Family Foundation. 2010h. Summary of key changes to Medicare in 2010 health reform law, www.kff.org/healthreform/7948.cfm.

Kaiser Family Foundation and Health Research and Educational Trust. 2009. Employer Health Benefits 2009 Annual Survey, http://ehbs.kff.org/.

Kaiser Family Foundation and Health Research and Educational Trust. 2010. Employer Health Benefits 2010 Annual Survey, http://ehbs.kff.org/.

Katz SJ, Cardiff K, Pascali M, Barer ML, and Evans RG. 2002. Phantoms in the snow: Canadians' use of health care services in the United States. *Health Affairs* 21(3):20–31.

Kelley AS, and Meier DE. 2010. Palliative care—a shifting paradigm. *New England Journal of Medicine* 363:781–82.

Kenagy JW, Berwick DM, and Shore MF. 1999. Service quality in health care. *JAMA* 281:661–65.

Kennedy E. 1973. Senate speech regarding the Health Maintenance Organizations Act of 1973, May 14. *Congressional Record-Senate* 15497.

Kerlikowske K. 2009. Evidence-based breast cancer prevention: The importance of individual risk. *Annals of Internal Medicine* 151:750–52.

Keyhani S, Wang S, Hebert P, Carpenter D, and Anderson G. 2010. US pharmaceutical innovation in an international context. *American Journal of Public Health* 100:1075–80.

Kingdon JW. 1984. *Agendas, Alternatives, and Public Policies.* Boston: Little, Brown.

Kirby JB, Machlin SR, and Cohen JW. 2003. Has the increase in HMO enrollment within the Medicaid population changed the pattern of health service use and expenditures? *Medical Care* 41(7 Suppl.):III-24–III-34.

Kohn LT, Corrigan JM, and Donaldson MS, eds. 1999. *To Err Is Human: Building a Safer Health System.* Washington, D.C.: National Academies Press.

Kolata G. 1993. How demand surged for unapproved prostate test. *New York Times,* September 29.

Kolata G. 2008. Co-payments go way up for drugs with high prices. *New York Times,* April 14, p. 1.

Krahn MD, Mahoney JE, Eckman MH, et al. 1994. Screening for prostate cancer: A decision analytic view. *JAMA* 272:773–80.

Krasner SD. 1983. *International Regimes.* Ithaca, N.Y.: Cornell University Press.

Krauss C. 2005. Canadian court chips away at national health care. *New York Times,* June 9.

Kreling DH, Mott DA, Wiederholt JB, Lundy J, and Levitt L. 2001. Prescription drug trends: A chartbook update. Publication No. 3112. The Kaiser Family Foundation. www.kff.org/rxdrugs/3112-index.cfm.

Larson EB, and Reid R. 2010. The patient-centered medical home movement. *JAMA* 303:1644–45.

Leff B, Thomas E, and Finucane TE. 2008. Gizmo idolatry. *JAMA* 299:1830–32.

Lett D. 2008. Private health clinics remain unregulated in most of Canada. *Canadian Medical Association Journal* 178:986–87.

Levine SA, Boal J, and Boling PA. 2003. Home care. *JAMA* 290:1203–7.

Levinsky N. 1999. Quality and equity in dialysis and renal transplantation. *New England Journal of Medicine* 341:1691–93.

Levinson W. 1994. Physician-patient communication, a key to malpractice prevention. *JAMA* 272:1619–20.

Lewin JC, and Sybinsky PA. 1993. Hawaii's employer mandate and its contribution to universal access. *JAMA* 269:2538–43.

Lewis S. 1924. *Arrowsmith.* New York: Penguin-Putnam. Reprinted 1998.

Liebhaber A, and Grossman JM. 2007. Physicians moving to mid-sized, single-specialty practices, August, www.hschange.org/CONTENT/941/.

Lindeenaurt PK, Rothberg MB, Pekow PS, et al. 2007. Outcomes of care by hospitalists, general internists, and family physicians. *New England Journal of Medicine* 357:2589–2600.

Lipset SM. 1990. *Continental Divide.* New York: Routledge, Chapman, and Hall.

Lipton S. 2001. Comparison of Direct-to-Consumer Prescription Drug Advertising on Hispanic versus Mainstream Broadcast Media. Undergraduate thesis, Program in Human Biology, Stanford University.

Liu K, Manton KG, and Aragon C. 2000. Changes in home care use by older people with disabilities, 1982–1994: Executive summary. Washington, D.C.: AARP Public Policy Institute.

Localio AR, Lawthers AG, Brennan TA, et al. 1991. Relation between malpractice claims and adverse events due to negligence. Results of the Harvard Medical Practice Study III. *New England Journal of Medicine* 325:245–51.

Long SK, and Stockley K. 2010. Sustaining health reform in a recession: An update on Massachusetts as of fall 2009. *Health Affairs* 29(6):1234–41.

Lozano P, Connell FA, and Koepsell TD. 1995. Use of health services by African-American children with asthma on Medicaid. *JAMA* 274:469–73.

Lundberg GD. 1995. The failure of organized health system reform: Now what? (Caveat aeger—let the patient beware). *JAMA* 273:1539–41.

Lurie N. 2005. Health disparities: Less talk, more action. *New England Journal of Medicine* 353:727–29.

Mackey J. 2009. The whole foods alternative to ObamaCare—eight things we can do to improve health care without adding to the deficit. *Wall Street Journal,* August 11, Opinion page.

Madden JM, Graves AJ, Zhang F, et al. 2008. Cost-related medication nonadherence and spending on basic needs following implementation of Medicare Part D. *JAMA* 299:1922–28.

Mandelblatt JS, Cronin KA, Bailey S, et al. 2009. Effects of mammography screening under different screening schedules: Model estimates of potential benefits and harms. *Annals of Internal Medicine* 151:738–47.

Mann C, and Artiga S. 2004. The impact of recent changes in health care coverage for low-income people: A first look at the research following changes in Oregon's Medicaid program. Report #7100. Prepared for the Kaiser Commission on Medicaid and the Uninsured. www.kff.org/medicaid/7100a.cfm.

Mann C, and Artiga S. 2006. New developments in Medicaid coverage: Who bears financial risk and responsibility. Kaiser Family Foundation, June, www.kff.org/Medicaid/upload/7507 .pdf.

Manning WG, Leibowitz A, Goldberg GA, et al. 1984. A controlled trial of the effect of a prepaid group practice on use of services. *New England Journal of Medicine* 310:1505–10.

Marleau D. 1995. Letter RE: Canada Health Act, January 6, 1995, in Health Canada (2009), p. 229.

Marmot MG, and Theorell T. 1988. Social class and cardiovascular disease: The contribution of work. *International Journal of Health Services* 18:659–74.

Marron DB. 2006. Medicare's physician payment rates and the sustainable growth rate. Testimony before the Subcommittee on Health, Committee on Energy and Commerce, U.S. House of Representatives. July 25. www.cbo.gov/ftpdocs/74xx/doc7425/07-25-SGR.pdf.

Massachusetts Department of Health and Human Services. 2009. Recommendations Special

Commission on the health care payment system, July 16, p. 1, www.mass.gov/?pageID= eohhs2subtopic&L=4&L0=JP,e&L1=Government&L2=Special+Commissions+and+ Initiatives&L3=Special+Commission+on+the+Health+Care+Payment+System&sid= Eeohhs2.

Maule WF. 1994. Screening for colorectal cancer by nurse endoscopists. *New England Journal of Medicine* 330:183–87.

Mays J, Brenner M, Neuman T, Cubanski J, and Claxton G. 2004. Estimates of Medicare beneficiaries' out-of-pocket drug spending in 2006—modeling the impact of the MMA. Publication No. 7201. Actuarial Research Corporation and the Kaiser Family Foundation. www.kff.org/medicare/7201.cfm.

McClellan MB, and Tunis SR. 2005. Medicare coverage of ICDs. *New England Journal of Medicine* 352:222–24.

McNaughton-Collins M. 2009. Perspective roundtable: Screening for prostate cancer. *New England Journal of Medicine* 360:e18, http://content.nejm.org/cgi/reprint/360/13/e18.pdf.

Medicaid Access Study Group. 1994. Access of Medicaid recipients to outpatient care. *New England Journal of Medicine* 330:1426–30.

Medical Group Management Association. 2009. Physician Compensation and Production Survey, 2009, www.aafp.org/online/etc/mediallib/aafp_org/documents/press/charts-and-graphs/ median-income-by-specialty.Par.0001.File.tmp/MedianIncome2007.pdf.

Medicare Boards of Trustees. 2010. 2010 annual report, www.cms.gov/ReportsTrustFunds/.

Medicare Payment Advisory Commission. 2009. Report to the Congress: Medicare payment policy, March, www.medpac.gov/docuoment_TOC.cfm?id=563.

Mehrotra A, Adams JL, Armstrong K, et al. 2010. Health care on aisle 7—the growing phenomenon of retail clinics. RAND Health, www.rand.org/pubs/research_briefs/RB9491–1/.

Mehrotra A, Liu H, Adams JL, et al. 2009. Comparing costs and quality of care at retail clinics with that of other medical settings for 3 common illnesses. *Annals of Internal Medicine* 151:321–28.

Meilicke CA, and Storch JL, eds. 1980. *Perspectives on Canadian Health Services Policy: History and Emerging Trends.* Ann Arbor, Mich.: Health Administration Press.

Mello MM, Studdert DM, and Brennan TA. 2003. The new medical malpractice crisis. *New England Journal of Medicine* 348:2281–84.

Miller RS, Dunn MR, Richter TH, and Whitcomb ME. 1998. Employment-seeking experiences of resident physicians completing training during 1996. *JAMA* 280:777–83.

Mitka M. 2010. Recession helped put brakes on growth in US health care spending for 2008. *New England Journal of Medicine* 303:715.

Nash IS, and Pasternak RC. 1995. Physician, educate thyself. *JAMA* 273:1533–34.

Nelson HD, Tyne K, Naik A, et al. 2009. Screening for breast cancer: An update for the U.S. Preventive Services Task Force. *Annals of Internal Medicine* 151:727–37.

Newhouse JP, Manning WG, Morris CN, et al. 1981. Some interim results from a controlled trial of cost sharing in health insurance. *New England Journal of Medicine* 305:1501–7.

Nixon R. 1972. Message from the President of the United States relative to his health care program. House of Representatives Document No. 92-261, March 2.

North DC. 1986. *Institutions, Institutional Change and Economic Performance.* New York: Cambridge University Press.

Nudelman PM, and Andrews LM. 1996. The "value added" of not-for-profit health plans. *New England Journal of Medicine* 334:1057–59.

Obama B. 2009a. Remarks to a joint session of Congress on health care, September 9, www

.whitehouse.gov/the_press_office/remarks-by-the-president-to-a-joint-session-of-congress-on-health-care/.

Obama B. 2009b. Why we need health care reform. *New York Times,* August 16.

Obama B. 2010. Remarks at the health care bill signing. *New York Times,* March 23.

Oliver T. 2004. Policy entrepreneurship in the social transformation of American medicine: The rise of managed care and managed competition. *Journal of Health Politics, Policy and Law* 29:701–33.

Orszag, Peter. 2010. A health care plan for colleges. *New York Times,* September 19, Op-Ed Page.

Padrez R, Carino T, Blum J, and Mendelson D. 2005. The use of Oregon's evidence-based reviews for Medicaid pharmacy policies: Experiences in four states. Publication No. 7319. The Health Strategies Consultancy LLC, published by the Kaiser Family Foundation. www.kff.org/medicaid/7319.cfm.

Parsons T. 1951. *The Social System.* New York: Free Press.

Parsons T. 1975. The sick role and the role of the physician revisited. *Millbank Memorial Fund Quarterly* 53:257.

Patel MR, Peterson ED, Dai D, et al. 2010. Low diagnostic yield of coronary angiography. *New England Journal of Medicine* 362:886–95.

Pear R. 2000. Forty states forfeit health care funds for poor children. *New York Times,* September 24.

Pear R. 2005. Drug plans in Medicare start effort on marketing. *New York Times,* October 1.

Pear R, and Dao J. 2004. States' tactics aim to reduce drug spending. *New York Times,* November 21.

Peterson ED, Wright SM, Daley J, and Thibault GE. 1994. Racial variation in cardiac procedure use and survival following acute myocardial infarction in the Department of Veterans Affairs. *JAMA* 271:1175–80.

Pham HH, Grossman JM, Cohen G, and Bodenheimer T. 2008. Hospitalists and care transitions: The divorce of inpatient and outpatient care. *Health Affairs* 27(5):1315–27.

Phillips C. 1949. Bitter debate begins over health program. *New York Times,* February 27.

Physicians' Working Group for Single-Payer National Health Insurance. 2003. Proposal of the Physicians' Working Group for single-payer national health insurance. *JAMA* 290:798–805.

Picard A. 2006. Public wants Medicare changed, poll finds. *The Globe and Mail,* June 8.

Pilote L, Saynina O, Lavoie F, and McClellan M. 2003. Cardiac procedure use and outcomes in elderly patients with acute myocardial infarction in the United States and Quebec, Canada, 1988 to 1994. *Med Care* 41(7):813–22.

Pitts SR, Carrier ER, Rich EC, and Kellerman AL. 2010. Where Americans get acute care: Increasingly, it's not at their doctor's office. *Health Affairs* 29(9):1620–29.

Plumb JD, and Ogle KS. 1992. Hospice care. *Primary Care; Clinics in Office Practice* 19(4):807–20.

Pollack A. 2008. The minimal impact of a big hypertensive study. *New York Times,* November 28.

Pope GC, Kautter J, Ellis RP, et al. 2004. Risk adjustment of Medicare capitation payments using the CMS-HCC model. *Health Care Financing Review* 25(4):119–41.

Psaty BM, and Furberg CD. 2005. COX-2 inhibitors: Lessons in drug safety. *New England Journal of Medicine* 352:1133–35.

Quanstrum KH, and Hayward RA. 2010. Lessons from the mammography wars. *New England Journal of Medicine* 363:1076–79.

Rathore SS, Lenert LA, Weinfurt KP, et al. 2000. The effect of patient sex and race on medical students' ratings of quality of life. *American Journal of Medicine* 108:561–66.

Rees M. 1998. Will Helen Hunt save U.S. health care? *Ottawa Citizen,* July 2.

Reinhardt UE, and Relman AS. 1986. Debating for-profit health care and the ethics of physicians. *Health Affairs* 5(2):5–31.

Relman A. 2003. Your doctor's drug problem. *New York Times,* November 18.

Relman AS. 2007. Medical professionalism in a commercialized health care market. *JAMA* 298: 2668–70.

Romanow RJ. 2002. Building on values: The future of health care in Canada. Final Report of the Commission on the Future of Health Care in Canada. www.hc-sc.gc.ca/english/care/ romanow/index1.html.

Romanow RJ. 2005. Now's the time to stand up for Medicare. *The Globe and Mail,* June 10.

Rosenstreich DL, Eggleston P, Kattan M, et al. 1997. The role of cockroach allergy and exposure to cockroach allergen in causing morbidity among inner-city children with asthma. *New England Journal of Medicine* 336:1356–63.

Rosenthal MB, Berndt ER, Donohue JM, Epstein AM, and Frank RG. 2003. Demand effects of recent changes in prescription drug promotion. Publication No. 6085. Kaiser Family Foundation. www.kff.org/rxdrugs/6085-index.cfm.

Ross JS. 2002. The committee on the cost of medical care and the history of health insurance in the United States. *Einstein Quarterly Journal of Biology and Medicine* 19:129–34.

Royal Commission on Health Services. 1964. *Report.* Ottawa: Queen's Printers.

Sack K. 2009. Screening debate reveals culture clash in medicine. *New York Times,* November 20.

Sade RM. 1971. Medical care as a right: A refutation. *New England Journal of Medicine* 285: 1288–92.

Safran D, Tarlov AR, and Rogers WH. 1994. Primary care performance in fee-for-service and prepaid health systems. *JAMA* 271:1579–86.

Salkever DS, Skinner EA, Steinwachs DM, and Katz H. 1982. Episode-based efficiency comparisons for physicians and nurse practitioners. *Medical Care* 20(2):143–53.

Schemo DJ. 2000. Medical school applications dip sharply; minorities rise slightly. *New York Times,* October 27.

Schneider A. 2004. Tennessee's new "medically necessary" Standard: Uncovering the insured? Publication No. 7139. www.kff.org/medicaid/7139.cfm.

Schneider EC, Zaslavsky AM, and Epstein AM. 2004. Use of high-cost operative procedures by Medicare beneficiaries enrolled in for-profit and not-for-profit health plans. *New England Journal of Medicine* 350:143–50.

Schröder FH, Hugosson J. Roobol MJ, et al. 2009. Screening and prostate-cancer mortality in a randomized European study. *New England Journal of Medicine* 360:1320–28.

Scott WR. 1987. The adolescence of institutional theory. *Administrative Science Quarterly* 32: 493–511.

Sebelius, K. 2010. A message from Health and Human Services Secretary Kathleen Sebelius, February 4, www.insurekidsnow.gov/chip/report.html.

Silverman EM, Skinner JS, and Fisher ES. 1999. The association between for-profit hospital ownership and increased Medicare spending. *New England Journal of Medicine* 341:420–26.

Simpson J. 2005. The new face of medicare. *The Globe and Mail,* June 10.

Sisko AM, Truffer CJ, Keehan SP, et al. 2010. National health spending projections: The estimated impact of reform through 2019. *Health Affairs.* 10.377/hlthaff.2010.0788, published online September 9.

Skocpol T. 1997. *Boomerang: Health Care Reform and the Turn against Government.* New York: W. W. Norton.

Sloss EM, Keeler EB, Brook RH, et al. 1987. Effect of a health maintenance organization on physiologic health. *Annals of Internal Medicine* 106:130–38.

Smart DR. 2010. *Physician Characteristics and Distribution in the US.* Chicago: American Medical Association.

Smedley BD, Sith AY, and Nelson AR, eds. 2003. *Unequal Treatment: Confronting Racial and Ethnic Disparities in Health Care.* Washington, D.C.: National Academies Press.

Smillie JG. 1991. *Can Physicians Manage the Quality and Costs of Health Care? The Story of the Permanente Medical Group.* New York: McGraw-Hill.

Smith DB. 1999. *Health Care Divided: Race and Healing a Nation.* Ann Arbor: University of Michigan Press.

Stagnitti MM. 2004. Statistical Brief #21: Trends in outpatient prescription drug utilization and expenditures, 1997–2000. Agency for Health Care Research and Quality. www.meps.ahrq.gov/papers/st21/stat21.htm.

Stange KC, Nutting PA, Miller WL, et al. 2010. Defining and measuring the patient-centered medical home. *Journal of General Internal Medicine* 25:601–21.

Starr P. 1982. *The Social Transformation of American Medicine.* New York: Basic Books.

Steinbrook R. 2005a. Commercial support and continuing medical education. *New England Journal of Medicine* 352:534–35.

Steinbrook R. 2005b. Financial conflicts of interest and the Food and Drug Administration's Advisory Committees. *New England Journal of Medicine* 353:116–18.

Steinbrook R. 2009a. Easing the shortage in adult primary care—it's all about money. *New England Journal of Medicine* 360:2696–99.

Steinbrook R. 2009b. The end of fee-for-service medicine? Proposal for payment reform in Massachusetts. *New England Journal of Medicine* 361:1036–38.

Steinhauer J. 2000. Many not eligible in state program to insure children. *New York Times,* September 30.

Studdert DM, Mello MM, and Brennan TA. 2004a. Financial conflicts of interest in physicians' relationships with the pharmaceutical industry: Self-regulation in the shadow of federal prosecution. *New England Journal of Medicine* 351:1891–1900.

Studdert DM, Mello MM, and Brennan TA. 2004b. Medical malpractice. *New England Journal of Medicine* 350:283–92.

Tang N, Stein J, Hsia RY, Maselli JH, and Gonzales R. 2010. Trends and characteristics of US emergency department visits, 1997–2007. *JAMA* 304:664–70.

Taylor MG. 1987. *Health Insurance and Canadian Public Policy,* 2nd ed. Montreal: McGill-Queens University Press.

Temel JS, Greer JA, Muzikansky A, et al. 2010. Early palliative care for patients with metastatic non-small-cell lung cancer. *New England Journal of Medicine* 363:733–42.

Thompson JW, Ryan KW, Pinidiya SD, and Bost JE. 2003. Quality of care for children in commercial and Medicaid managed care. *JAMA* 290:1486–93.

Thorpe KE, Florence CS, and Joski P. 2004. Which medical conditions account for the rise in health care spending? *Health Affairs* (Web Exclusive) W4:437–45. http://content.healthaffairs.org/cgi/content/abstract/hlthaff.w4.437.

Todd KH, Deaton C, D'Adamo AP, and Goe L. 2000. Ethnicity and analgesic practice. *Annals of Emergency Medicine* 35:11–16.

Todd KH, Samaroo N, and Hoffman JR. 1993. Ethnicity as a risk factor for inadequate emergency department analgesia. *JAMA* 269:1537–39.

Tribe, LH. 1011. On health care, justice will prevail, *New York Times,* Op-Ed Column, February 7.

Trivedi AN, Zaslavsky AM, Schneider EC, and Ayanian JZ. 2005. Trends in the quality of care and racial disparities in Medicare managed care. *New England Journal of Medicine* 353:692–700.

Truffer CJ, Keehan S, Smith S, et al. 2010. Health spending projections through 2019: The recession's impact continues. *Health Affairs* 29(3):522–29.

Truog, RD. 2009. Screening mammography and the "R" word. *New England Journal of Medicine* 361:2501–3.

United Nations General Assembly. 1948. The Universal Declaration of Human Rights. Resolution 217 A (III). www.un.org/Overview/rights.html.

U.S. Agency for Healthcare Research and Quality. 2009. National Healthcare Disparities Report, 2009. Key themes and highlights From the National Healthcare Disparities Report, www.ahrq.gov/qual/nhdr09/Key.htm.

U.S. Census Bureau. 2005. Income, poverty, and health insurance coverage in the United States, 2004. Publication No. P60-229. www.census.gov/hhes/www/hlthins/hlthin04.html.

U.S. Census Bureau. 2010. Income, poverty, and health insurance coverage in the United States: 2009. September, www.census.gov/hhes/www/hlthins/hlthins.html.

U.S. Centers for Disease Control and Prevention. 2005. Tiered use of inactivated influenza vaccine in the event of a vaccine shortage. *MMWR* (*Morbidity and Mortality Weekly Report*) 54(30):749–50.

U.S. Congress, Office of Technology Assessment. 1986. *Nurse Practitioners, Physician Assistants, and Certified Nurse-Midwives: A Policy Analysis.* Washington, D.C.: U.S. Government Printing Office.

U.S. General Accounting Office. 1998. Long-term care: Baby boom generation presents financing challenges. Report No. GAO /T-HEHS-98-107. www.gao.gov/.

U.S. Preventive Services Task Force. 2008. Screening for prostate cancer: U.S. Preventive Services Task Force recommendation statement. *Annals of Internal Medicine* 149:185–91.

U.S. Preventive Services Task Force. 2009. Screening for breast cancer: U.S. Preventive Services Task Force recommendation statement. *Annals of Internal Medicine* 151:716–26.

Vaccarino V, Rathore SS, Wenger NK, et al. 2005. Sex and racial differences in the management of acute myocardial infarction, 1994 through 2002. *New England Journal of Medicine* 353:671–82.

Van Ryn M, and Burke J. 2000. The effect of patient race and socioeconomic status on physicians' perceptions of patients. *Social Science and Medicine* 50:813–28.

Vladeck BC. 2010. Fixing Medicare's physician payment system. *New England Journal of Medicine* 362:1955–57.

Wachter RM, and Goldman L. 1996. The emerging role of "hospitalists" in the American health care system. *New England Journal of Medicine* 335:514–17.

Wallack SS, Weinberg DB, and Thomas CP. 2004. Health plans' strategies to control prescription drug spending. *Health Affairs* 23:141–48.

Waxman HA. 2005. The lessons of Vioxx: Drug safety and sales. *New England Journal of Medicine* 352:2576–78.

Wehrwein AC. 1965. A.M.A. opens bid to kill Medicare. *New York Times,* January 27.

Weinstein MC, and Skinner JA. 2010. Comparative effectiveness and health care spending— implications for reform. *New England Journal of Medicine* 364:460–65.

Weissman JS, and Bigby JA. 2009. Massachusetts health care reform—near-universal coverage at what cost? *New England Journal of Medicine* 361:2012–15.

Weissman JS, Blumenthal D, Silk AJ, et al. 2004. Physicians report on patient encounters involving direct-to-consumer advertising. *Health Affairs* (Web Exclusive) W4:219–33. http://content.healthaffairs.org/cgi/content/abstract/hlthaff.w4.219v1.

Wennberg JE. 1993. Future directions for small area variations. *Medical Care* 31:YS75–YS80.

Wennberg JE, Barnes BA, and Zubkoff M. 1982. Professional uncertainty and the problem of supplier-induced demand. *Social Science and Medicine* 16:811–24.

Wennberg JE, and Cooper MM, eds. 1998. *The Dartmouth Atlas of Health Care, 1998.* Chicago: American Hospital Publishing.

Wennberg JE, and Gittelsohn A. 1973. Small area variations in health care delivery. *Science* 182: 1102–8.

Whitcomb ME, and Cohen JJ. 2004. The future of primary care medicine. *New England Journal of Medicine* 351:710–12.

Wijeysundera HC, Machado M, Farahatin F, et al. 2010. Association of temporal trends in risk factors and treatment uptake with coronary heart disease mortality, 1994–2005. *JAMA* 303:1841–47.

Williams SC, Schmaltz SP, Morton DJ, Koss RG, and Loeb JM. 2005. Quality of care in U.S. hospitals as reflected by standardized measures, 2002–2004. *New England Journal of Medicine* 353:255–64.

World Health Organization. 2000. Health systems: Improving performance. The World Health Report 2000. www.who.int/whr/en/.

Yin W, Basu A, Zhang JX, et al. 2008. The effect of Medicare Part D prescription benefit on drug utilization and expenditures. *Annals of Internal Medicine* 148:169–77.

Zarabozo C, and Harrison S. 2009. Payment policy and the growth of Medicare Advantage. *Health Affairs* 28(1):w55–w67.

Zipkin A. 2005. The concierge doctor is available (at a price). *New York Times,* July 31.

Zuger A. 2003a. In an age of specialists, one doctor is primary. *New York Times,* January 7.

Zuger A. 2003b. Rx: Canadian drugs. *New England Journal of Medicine* 349:2188–90.

# INDEX